Reading Our Lives

Reading Our Lives

THE POETICS OF GROWING OLD

WILLIAM L. RANDALL

A. ELIZABETH McKIM

OXFORD

UNIVERSITY PRESS

2008

OXFORD
UNIVERSITY PRESS

Oxford University Press, Inc., publishes works that further
Oxford University's objective of excellence
in research, scholarship, and education.

Oxford   New York
Auckland   Cape Town   Dar es Salaam   Hong Kong   Karachi
Kuala Lumpur   Madrid   Melbourne   Mexico City   Nairobi
New Delhi   Shanghai   Taipei   Toronto

With offices in
Argentina   Austria   Brazil   Chile   Czech Republic   France   Greece
Guatemala   Hungary   Italy   Japan   Poland   Portugal   Singapore
South Korea   Switzerland   Thailand   Turkey   Ukraine   Vietnam

Copyright © 2008 by Oxford University Press, Inc.

Published by Oxford University Press, Inc.
198 Madison Avenue, New York, New York 10016
www.oup.com

Oxford is a registered trademark of Oxford University Press

Library of Congress Cataloging-in-Publication Data
Randall, William Lowell, 1950–
Reading our lives : the poetics of growing old / William L. Randall & A. Elizabeth McKim.
p. cm.
Includes bibliographical references and index.
ISBN 978-0-19-530687-3
1. Memory in old age. 2. Autobiographical memory. 3. Aging. I. McKim, A. Elizabeth.
II. Title.
BF724.85.M45R36 2008
155.67—dc22   2007034719

Every person is born into life as a blank page—and every person leaves life as a full book.

—Christina Baldwin (2005, p. ix)

Preface

What is true of many books is true of this one, too. We have written it for ourselves. While our convictions about the poetics of growing old have definite academic roots—most notably, in the turn toward *narrative* that is affecting many fields—they have deeply personal ones as well. Like many of our generation, and the negatives of aging notwithstanding, we are keen to age as positively, as mindfully, indeed as creatively as we can. In fact, if there were one single message that runs through all that follows, it would be that such aging is possible—if not essential—for us all. To express the point in terms whose meaning will gradually become clearer, none of us is too young to grow old—not *get* old, but *grow* old. And a key way that we do so is by learning to read—specifically, to read our own lives.

Of course we have written the book for others as well, certainly those who study aging. Besides gerontologists, however, we have had in mind scholars in such disciplines as psychology and sociology, anthropology and history—wherever interest has been awakened about the storied complexity of lives-in-time. Even those who labor in fields like philosophy or theology may find our musings relevant, insofar as we inquire into the nature of spirituality and wisdom, themes that, possibly because so difficult to define, tend to fall through the cracks of scholarly debate. We have also written the book for practitioners, above all for those who offer counseling or mentoring to people who are navigating the often uncertain waters of mid- and later life. Those working in healthcare—including palliative care—may find its ideas pertinent, too, as should educators, in settings where memory-work, creative writing, or self-reflective activity of one sort or other is central to the learning, where personal development is a principal aim, and where respect for people's stories is a fundamental value.

We have also written the book for older adults themselves. However, we say this with a certain trepidation. Although, as children of the "baby boom,"

each of us has made a good start into the so-called second half of life, we
have yet to wrestle with the more dramatic sorts of challenges that later life
can bring. Aspects of our thesis have still to be tested, therefore, by the realities of our own existence. As an 80-something colleague, a fellow gerontologist, is fond of pointing out, one must really be a senior oneself before one
can know whereof one speaks.

In terms of the scope of the book, there are at least three key areas where,
admittedly, we have had to restrict our line of thinking to what can be managed in a single volume. First, some readers may prefer that we had said
more about gender as a variable in how we story our lives over time. As fellow narrativist Ruth Ray (1996) insists, "the study of aging, by sheer force of
demographics, is necessarily a women's issue" (p. 674). How women narrate
and interpret their experiences differently from men, and the effect of such
differences on their ways of knowing and being, is an issue that we certainly
acknowledge at several junctures. Yet, ultimately, it does not predominate to
the extent that the demographics might require. Our main agenda has simply been to sketch the broad contours of a *poetics* of aging—something that,
to the best of our knowledge, has yet to be attempted. If our attempts here
are viewed as valid, then the spelling-out of their implications in relation to
gender, as to other vital topics, can be explored more fully soon enough.

A second area is life-writing, a broad category that encompasses everything from biography to autobiography and memoirs to journals. Our reasons for saying less on this area than might be expected are comparatively
simple. Although the study of life-writing treats many of the topics we will
be delving into here—memory, self, consciousness, time—the focus of such
study, in the end, is actual texts, especially those of a markedly literary nature. Since most autobiographers tend to compose their works later in life
rather than sooner, gerontologists are understandably curious about how
the process of aging is experienced by the autobiographers themselves, and
about what imagery and metaphors they employ to articulate their memories, thoughts, and feelings. It is such questions, of course, that those working in the area of literary gerontology (see Wyatt-Brown, 2000) are actively
asking. Here, however, we take a rather different approach.

Instead of focusing on autobiographical *products,* so to speak, we look
more at autobiographical *processes*—in other words, the internal texts of our
lives more than the external ones, inasmuch as the two can be pried apart.
Our focus is on lives themselves—experienced and understood, and continually under construction—as quasi-literary works. Autobiography scholar
Paul John Eakin (1985) captures the sort of distinction we assume. "The autobiographical act," he says, "is revealed as a mode of self-invention that is

always practised first in living and only eventually—sometimes—formalized in writing" (pp. 8–9). "The impulse to write autobiography," he maintains, "is but a special heightened form of that reflexive consciousness which is the distinctive feature of human nature" (p. 9). For this reason, our own interests in the poetics of aging are reflected in the title of one of Eakin's (1999) more recent books: *How Our Lives Become Stories: Making Selves*. Given the phase of "the autobiographical act" we are most concerned with here, however, a slight reconstruing of such a title would reflect still better the aim of our inquiry: *How Our Selves Make Sense of the Stories That Our Lives Become*.

Third, a number of readers might wish that we had written more extensively about the implications of a poetics of aging for what no doubt constitutes one of the severest challenges to narrative development in the latter half of life: dementia. This troubling topic—although highly relevant in light of what we say in Chapter 2 about the neurological basis of autobiographical activity—is, in the final analysis, outside of our range. Instead, we have confined our gaze to so-called normal aging: to people whose capacities for remembering are neither physiologically nor pathologically impaired.

On this point, some readers may feel that we are outlining an approach to growing old that, even still, exceeds the abilities of the typical aging person, by assuming a level of introspection, of literacy, and of overall cognitive competence—not to mention a nurturing interpersonal environment—comparatively few of us are apt to have access to as we age. Our response to this objection would be that reading our lives is something that all of us are engaged in anyway, all the time, and it differs only in degree from what we do when engrossed in a novel or lost in a movie. Indeed, judging by the ever-burgeoning entertainment industry, we are probably far more immersed in narrative in the present age (at least as consumers) than at any other point in human history. What we are attempting to accomplish here, however, is to bring such narrative activity to the fore, especially the process of interpreting—or reading—stories, and to identify ways to experience that process more mindfully in relation to the stories of our own lives. To that extent, a prescriptive theme, and not simply a descriptive one, will be discernible throughout the book. While making sense of lived experience in the manner we will be considering has its complicated aspects and does indeed assume a certain intentionality, one can always read one's life more deeply than one is doing at the present. No matter who we are or what our talents, there is always room for growth.

The poetics of aging, we believe, is a process and an experience that, to some degree, can be realized in every person's life. However, the often terrifying features of our world—political, environmental, and the like—can seem to dwarf the ups and downs of daily life for the vast majority of humanity, rendering aging, let alone *poetic* aging, a far-off possibility. To this, three brief points need to be made.

First, if we envisage global tensions as essentially complex conflicts of stories, then we quickly realize that it has ever been thus. The poetics of growing old is not therefore some arcane topic, nor a self-indulgent exercise open only to the fortunate elite. It is as relevant now, for everyone, as at any point before us. Surely the challenge in every era is to find stories that we can live by, and grow by, without *de*-storying others. Second, the poetics of aging is about self-development, not self-obsession. It is not a matter of a solitary "I" endeavoring to perfect the particular work of art that is his or her life. For better or worse, lives-as-stories unfold within communities. Directly or otherwise, "the stories we are" (Randall, 1995) are coauthored through relationship with others. In a world where all systems and all creatures are ultimately interdependent, as one of us ages well, then, theoretically, others will be empowered to do the same. Third, the poetics of aging is not a synonym for "successful" aging, nor is it contingent on a stress-free, pain-free life. If anything, it might well thrive the most where challenges abound. Without some element of suffering or failure, there may be little by way of a story—of a *life*story—to be told or read at all.

Finally, the ideas that are central to this book have emerged out of projects we have been involved in before—individually, together, or with others—on the narrative dimensions of human life (e.g., Kenyon & Randall, 1997; Randall & Kenyon, 2001; Randall & McKim, 2004). The majority of those others are our colleagues at St. Thomas University, a small liberal arts institution in which collaborations across disciplinary lines are delightfully common. Not only that, but without its provision of sabbaticals at strategic junctures, the book might never have been completed. We are also grateful for the support and encouragement of particular friends, both in our respective departments (English for Beth and Gerontology for Bill) and beyond. First and foremost is Gary Kenyon, not just for being a valued companion in numerous intellectual ventures, but also for his persistence in bringing a narrative perspective to the attention of the wider gerontology community. Among the many others we wish to thank for their interest and support at various points along the path are Ella Allen, Ernst Bohlmeijer, Avis Booth, Alan Bourassa, Rosemary Clews, Timothy Diamond, Janet Fowler, Dolores Furlong, Stephen Griew, Maureen Hughes, Russ Hunt, Bill Joyce, Mary Lou Joyce, Pamela Kenna, Gordon Kenney, Khurram Khurshid, George Lang, Jane Ann Lang, Philip Lee, Patrick Malcolmson, Sylvia

Malcolmson, Kathleen McCombe, Kathleen McConnell, John McKendy, Ryan O'Shea, Lisa Parrott, Carol Randall, William Randall, Sr., Susan Reid, Anita Saunders, Andrea Schutz, Marianne Skarborn, Susanne Sutton, and Sharon Yale. We are especially grateful, however, to Margie Reed for assisting us on countless occasions, not to mention members of Bill's class on Narrative Gerontology and Beth's on Literature and Medicine for their feedback, frank or veiled, on the digestibility of our ideas.

Others to whom we are indebted are colleagues in the broader community of narrative studies whose work, as will soon become apparent, has been an inspiration to our own. Among these are Jerome Bruner, whose name, quite appropriately, appears in the acknowledgements of countless other authors who are exploring narrative themes; Mark Freeman, whose many subtly reasoned publications testify to the power of such themes in deciphering the dynamics of human development; Dan McAdams for his pioneering research on the narrative complexity of personality and identity; Ruth Ray for her insights into the transformative potential of life-writing work; and Antonio Damasio for his groundbreaking yet accessible writings on the neurology of human consciousness.

Finally, we wish to extend special thanks to Warren Dennis, who generously gave us permission to reproduce his painting, *Couple Reading,* on the cover of our book, and to Toni Carlton (www.carltonartgallery.com), who kindly facilitated the permission process. And, of course, we are deeply grateful to Oxford University Press—particularly Jennifer Rappaport, Lori Handelman, Jenna Hocut, and Lynda Crawford—for supporting this project from the outset and for shepherding it toward its final shape.

Contents

PART I READING OUR LIVES: POETICS EXPLORED

Chapter 1 Rethinking Aging: The Story of My Life 3

Chapter 2 Narrating Experience: The Autobiographical Self 22

Chapter 3 Storying Life: The Development of Identity 49

Chapter 4 Reading Literature: The Interpreting of Text 73

Chapter 5 Reading Life: The Interpreting of Texistence 95

PART II GROWING OLD: POETICS APPLIED

Chapter 6 Restorying Our Lives:
The Need for Narrative Development 117

Chapter 7 Expanding Our Stories: The Mystery of Memory 141

Chapter 8 Examining Our Stories: The Quest for Meaning 176

Chapter 9 Transforming Our Stories: The Unfolding of Wisdom 212

Chapter 10 Transcending Our Stories:
The Poetics of Spiritual Aging 247

References 285

Index 315

Part 1   Reading Our Lives: Poetics Explored

RETHINKING AGING:
THE STORY OF MY LIFE

> *When you truly possess all you have been and done, which may take some time, you are fierce with reality.*
> —Florida Scott-Maxwell (1968, p. 42)

> *There are both advantages and disadvantages in being very old. The disadvantages are obvious and uninteresting.... The advantages seem to me more interesting. A long retrospect gives weight and substance to experience.*
> —Bertrand Russell (1994, p. 367)

> *The unexamined life is not worth living.*
> —Socrates (Plato, 2002, p. 41)

COMPOSING OUR LIVES:
NARRATIVE AS ROOT METAPHOR

Perhaps we can begin with the obvious. From the instant of our birth, we start getting older. But in getting older are we *growing* older, too? To the extent that we are, or hope that we are; to the extent we would counter the decline that, physically at least, aging can entail, then what does growing older mean? Might it mean that, amid the decline and possibly *because* of the decline, we can become better in some sort of way: riper, wiser, more mature? To borrow from psychologist Florida Scott-Maxwell (1968) in her little book, *The Measure of My Days,* written in her eighties and regarded as "a canonical text in the literature on aging" (Waxman, 1997, p. 261), can we become more "fierce with reality" (p. 42)? Common sense says that we can, and for many this is certainly the case. But if so, then what does "maturity" mean? Or "wisdom"? Or "growth"? And how might such concepts connect with notions about "successful aging" (Rowe & Kahn, 1998) or "healthy aging" (Weil, 2005) that are regularly espoused?

In an era when rising life expectancies are fueling apocalyptic fears about the burden of an aging population on society's resources, these questions take on an urgency it is hard to sweep aside if we hope to look at later life as anything but "a problem to be solved" (Cole, 1992, p. 241). Yet they are scarcely peculiar to our present generation. Concern with "aging well" (Chapman, 2005) has figured in one form or another in every philosophy and faith, every culture and creed, that has framed the ways we think. With this concern as our motivation, our aim here is to investigate—or, as the case may be, to resurrect—an understanding of aging that the study of aging has all but overlooked.

In its brief but vigorous history, mainstream research in the discipline devoted to that study, gerontology, has tended to be carried out in terms of one or more of three broad approaches: an empiricist paradigm that is committed to delineating constructs and quantifying phenomena; a social policy perspective that is brought to bear on everything from healthcare, to homecare, and housing to pensions; or a biomedical model that essentially equates aging with what happens to our bodies. All of these approaches, though worthy in their own right and no doubt impelled by the most compassionate of intentions, have led to a concentration far more on the "outside" than the "inside" of aging (Ruth & Kenyon, 1996; Ruth, Birren, & Polkinghorne, 1996; Schroots & Birren, 2002). Downplaying the "deeper dimensions of aging" (Bianchi, 1991, p. 58) and portraying aging in terms that, in our estimation, are decidedly thin, gerontology has unwittingly defaulted to the bad news on aging far more than the good. It has been lured to the darker side of the aging story; to what cultural studies scholar Margaret Gullette (1997, 2004) calls the narrative of "decline." In terms of that narrative, aging is about passively *getting* old, not actively *growing* old. It is a tragedy of accumulating deficits, diminishing reserves, and deteriorating attractiveness and strength: nothing more than denouement. It is a "sickness unto death" (Kierkegaard, 1968/1849): a sad saga in which we inch our way to "mere oblivion," in Shakespeare's stark expression, "sans teeth, sans eyes, sans taste, sans everything" (1623/1974a, 2.7.166–167).

Encouraged by the emergence of a more *critical* gerontology and, in particular, the incorporation of themes from the humanities into treatments of aging (see Cole, Achenbaum, Jakobi, & Kastenbaum, 1993; Cole, Kastenbaum, & Ray, 2000), we hope to address this somewhat puzzling imbalance by contributing insights into the other half of the aging story, a more "progressive" (Gullette, 2004), more growth-focused, and, so to speak, thicker version of that story which has been left largely unexamined. A variation on the so-called art of living and an extension of the "poetics of selfhood" to which psychologists such as Mark Freeman (1999b) have been devoting increasing attention, we call it *the poetics of aging*.

To use the metaphor of cultural anthropologist Mary Catherine Bateson (1989), living a life is a matter of "composing a life." "A self," echoes cognitive psychologist Jerome Bruner (2002), whose thinking in recent decades encourages the sort of perspective we are putting forward here, "is probably the most impressive work of art we ever produce." And "surely," he adds, "the most intricate" (p. 14). Our goal in what follows is to explore the nature of those intricacies. Guiding our exploration, which will require traversing disciplines as divergent as developmental psychology, neuroscience, and literary theory, is the conviction that human beings are first and foremost meaning-making beings, and that their principal means of making it is narrative. From the standpoint of subjective experience, that is, lives are not simply assemblages of naked facts or strings of raw events. Rather, they are stories: thus the proverbial "story of my life" or "book of life"—phrases we may find ourselves employing more and more with age, as the impulse accelerates to talk about our lives, and to pass along our unique collection of learnings to whoever will listen—or at least to ponder it privately inside our own minds. In effect, our lives are essentially texts: inner texts that precede and make possible the outer text of an actual autobiography, should we feel led to compile one. Indeed, "it is only by textualization," says Bruner, with colleague Susan Weisser (1991, p. 136), "that one can 'know' one's life" at all.

These texts—the texts we are perpetually weaving in memory and imagination (Olney, 1998), the texts we (sometimes) transform into spoken or written form, the texts by which we live: in short, our *texistence*—are as intricate as any we can envision. And over time, they are not merely lengthening but continually thickening as well, their countless strands becoming ever more intertwined, not just with one another but with the texts of others' lives as well. What is more, they are woven through with countless larger texts in turn: the *contexts* of the families, relationships, and communities by which our personal worlds are shaped. Most important, they are texts whose potential for meaning intensifies with time. In effect, they are living works of literature—blends of fact and fiction that grow more imbued with depth, emotional and metaphorical, as the end draws nigh. They are narratives-in-the-making that (and this is key) we are composing and comprehending from within: narratives of which we are simultaneously author and narrator, character and reader. Unique to us in both content and form, our narrative-worlds are vast, quasi-literary compositions that, sooner or later, as Socrates insisted, it is essential to examine. They are *novels* it behooves us to read.

Happily, much has been written about the benefits of *telling* our stories in later life, among them "renewed self-confidence, elevated self-esteem, increased self-understanding" (de Vries & Lehman, 1996, p. 150; see also Birren & Deutchman, 1991). But up to now, little attention has been paid, explicitly at least, to *reading* our stories. While telling and reading are certainly linked, reading is its own distinct process. Whether the "text" in question be literary or lived, reading is a complex intellectual activity. It involves remembering, to be certain; but more than this, it involves reflecting and reviewing, analyzing and anticipating, interpreting and interrogating. It involves a continual shuffling back and forth in time, as we ponder what sort of story it is and what it might mean.

In relation to the stories that we live, however, reading (as we shall see) is in fact prior to telling, insofar as any telling is by definition a reading, elementary though that reading might be. It is an interpretation of, a "take" on, whatever we are reading. Overall, reading our lives is a dimension of thinking itself, a central and natural dynamic of autobiographical consciousness. On some level, we read our lives all of the time, all life long. Yet the deliberate cultivation of that activity, and thus the heightening of our self-awareness, stands before us as a pivotal developmental task for the second half of life. In effect, it means nurturing a richer relationship with our own unique selves. It means fostering a mindful, intentional presence to the internalized text of our interpreted experience—a form of "reflective meditation," as one source calls it, that "aims at *understanding, interpretation,* and *evaluation* of what we discover in ourselves" (Assagioli, 1974, p. 223). As such, reading our lives constitutes a variety of literary competence, which we call *literary self-literacy.* Reading our lives is the soulful consideration of the stories, past, present, and future, through which we have understood our identity across the years and enshrined our share of sorrows and joys, including the themes those stories embody and the larger narrative realities in which they are embedded. For this reason, reading our lives involves an ironic openness to the multiple interpretability of our stories, and to the *restorying* to which that openness can lead.

What happens all too often, however, is that as texts, the lives of many of us, perhaps most of us, go both under-told and under-read—as tragic a fate, no doubt, as that of a novel on which its author has labored long and hard languishing forgotten on the shelf. Just when the material that constitutes our inner lives is at its thickest and richest, we fail to tackle the "philosophic homework" it presents us with (Schachter-Shalomi & Miller, 1995, pp. 124–126), defaulting instead to a kind of "narrative foreclosure" (Freeman, 2000). In short, we shut our stories down, even as our lives themselves continue to unfold. We stop developing and, story-wise, give in to getting—as opposed to growing—old. As a consequence, we miss the chance for "aging in depth" (Bianchi, 1991, p. 60), thereby squandering a rich resource for meaning, for spirituality, and for wisdom, qualities by which both our own lives and others' lives could clearly be enriched.

As intellectual constructs, both the *poetics of aging* and *reading our lives* owe their energy to the idea of life as story, or to what psychologist Theodore Sarbin (1986) calls the "narrative root metaphor." But what is *narrative?* It is by no means a simple question. Narratologists Susana Onega and José Angel García Landa (1996) define it as the "representation of a series of events meaningfully connected in a temporal and causal way" (p. 3). Given that narratologists are literary theorists (narratology being the branch of literary theory that deals with the nature of narrative), it is not surprising that the definitions they put forward usually emphasize the *medium* of narrative: most often language, but also film, music, dance, or visual art. Paul Cobley (2001), for example, defines narrative as "the showing or telling of … events and the mode selected for that to take place" (p. 6). By emphasizing expression, however, narratologists' definitions restrict narrative quite narrowly. Arguably, narrative encompasses far more than simply the expression of a story. Rather, as psychologists and other social scientists are suggesting, it is a broad term that is not only not limited to fiction, but embraces a spectrum of phenomena: events recounted as they happened chronologically, or even events as they are perceived in the act of happening; events as they are arranged into a pattern of some sort, whether causal or symbolic; and finally, the mode by which those events are expressed.

The distinctions narratologists regularly make between *story* and *plot* on one hand, and *story* and *discourse* on the other, are valid, of course, for textual analysis. They reflect an effort to prevent confusion between the order in which events occurred and the order in which they are later expressed, or the order in which events are expressed and the language or medium in which the expression is crafted—not to mention, confusion as to who is creating the discourse, under what conditions, to what audience, and with what end in mind. However, all of these are aspects of the larger category of *narrative,* and in our exploration of the poetics of aging all must be taken into account. The perception of time passing, the memory of a particular event in one's life, the expression of that event to others, or the recollection of it that never goes beyond private reminiscence—all of these activities are narrative in nature, and our understanding of what narrative is and does must be broad enough to embrace them.

Given the range of implications that narrative thus possesses, it is not surprising that it has inspired something of a paradigm shift across the human sciences, as perhaps chaos has across the natural ones (Randall, 2007). Described in some circles as the "narrative turn" (Hinchman & Hinchman, 1997, p. xiii), it is transforming how we conceptualize subjects as disparate as memory and identity, emotion and ethics, culture and relationships, learning and cognition. Psychologists such as Bruner (1986), Donald Polkinghorne (1988), and David Olson (1990), as well as others (Mattingly, 1991; Charon, 2006), have written persuasively, for instance, about the centrality of "narrative thinking" or "knowing" or "reasoning"—of "narrative intelligence" (Randall, 1999) or "imagination" (Randall & McKim, 2004)—to the fabric of daily life. To comprehend that fabric fully, what must be factored into the mix is what we call the *narrative variable.*

As much as we are gendered creatures, and as profoundly as culture, class, and race can inform our lives, we are storied creatures too: *homo narrans,* in anthropologist Barbara Myerhoff's apt expression (1992). Given that, etymologically, "narrative" is rooted in the Sanskrit word *gna,* which has come down to us through the Latin words for both "knowing" (*gnarus*) and "telling" (*narro*), narrative is no mere optional adornment to ordinary life but "a universal tool" for "absorbing knowledge as well as expressing it" (Abbott, 2002, p. 11). To put the point more strongly, because we are inveterately interpretive beings—because we are hermeneutical beings (Freeman, 1997b)—narrative is the very medium of our existence. For this reason, seeing our lives *as* stories can, for many, be a perplexing conceptual leap. Narrative is much more than mere metaphor, and *the story of my life* far more than a figure of speech. It is not that a life is *like* a story. On some extremely basic level, it *is* a story—a *lifestory*—a story that is "telling itself in the living" (Bridges, 1980, p. 71); and a story, moreover, that may reach its fullest unfolding and attain its profoundest potential for meaning only in its latter chapters.

Life and story, existence and text, experience and narrative: these, we believe, are tightly entwined, and not just psychologically or philosophically but, as we shall see in Chapter 2, physiologically as well. We do not impose narrative *upon* experience so much as we experience *in* narrative. Experience itself, above all our experience of time, possesses a fundamentally narrative quality (Crites, 1971; Carr, 1986; Widdershoven, 1993). Narrativity and temporality are intrinsically linked (Ricoeur, 1980). "Narrative," writes literary scholar H. Porter Abbott (2002), "is the principal way in which our species organizes its understanding of time" (p. 3). When it comes to our experience of aging, which involves nothing if not the awareness of time's relentless passage and, as such, is "the *narrative* phase par excellence" (Freeman, 1997a, p. 394), narrative is not just a handy analogy for the way things are inside of us. It *is* the way things are.

Although aware that metaphors can be "notoriously seductive" (Rigney, 2001, p. 5), and also that story is but one of many metaphors for understanding life, we are guided by the conviction that what is needed in the study of aging is more serious attention to its narrative dimensions, its autobiographical component, its "biographicity" (Alheit, 1995, p. 65). What is needed is an understanding of "biographical aging" (Ruth & Kenyon, 1996) that is every bit as robust as the ongoing focus on biological aging. However much we may learn about the latter, it can never tell us the whole story of aging. Even at their frailest or most demented, for example, older persons can possess a measure of narrative agency; they can still be "biographically active" (Gubrium, 1993; see also Crisp, 1995; Basting, 2003). It is in the context, therefore, of a form of critical gerontology called "narrative gerontology" (Ruth & Kenyon, 1996) that we tackle the topics that concern us in this book.

Narrative gerontology needs to be distinguished, however, from other important approaches with which it overlaps. In keeping with Kenneth Burke's (1941) image of academic discourse as an ongoing conversation—which its participants enter and exit while the discussion continues (pp. 110–111)—one of the areas with which a discussion of "reading our lives" obviously intersects is the psychology of aging, or *geropsychology*. Among the themes such scholars are concerned with is the nature of development in later life, the dynamics of memory and reminiscence, the impact of aging on identity and personality, and the concept of wisdom as a potential end-point of our journey through time. With respect to *educational gerontology*, the notion of reading our lives links with interest in such topics as "biographical knowledge"(Alheit, 1995), "biographical self-reflection" (Mader, 1995), and "autobiographical learning" (Nelson, 1994). As for *religious gerontology*, a poetics of aging can contribute insights into the nature of spirituality in later life, not to mention the overall issue of existential meaning. *Social gerontology* is another broad area with which a narrative perspective on aging is clearly compatible, inasmuch as lives are never storied in isolation but in interaction with others' lives as well, within complex webs of larger stories still. An even closer cousin to narrative gerontology, though, is *qualitative gerontology*, which profiles the unique potential of qualitative research methods over quantitative ones to enrich our "insight into the meaning and significance of the aging experience" (Rowles & Schoenberg, 2002, p. xii).

At first glance, narrative gerontology in general and the poetics of aging in particular overlap most closely of all with an approach to understanding aging known as *literary gerontology* (see Woodward, 1991; Holstein, 1994; Wyatt-Brown, 2000). Literary gerontologists are interested in images of aging that can be discerned in works of literature, including autobiography, plus such media as film. They ponder what such images can tell us about subtleties of aging and attitudes to aging that otherwise cruise beneath the radar, thereby thickening our understanding of the aging experience. In particular, they attend to "the interplay of age, gender, race, class, and ethnicity" (Cole, Kastenbaum, & Ray, 2000, p. xv) that can be detected within the texts. In addition, they assess how authors' style and vision may change over their careers, and what such change can tell us about complexities and possibilities that are inherent in the experience of getting old.

What we are interested in here, however, is a whole set of corollary issues that surface once lives themselves are seen as literary entities, and aging is envisioned as a creative, indeed a literary, process (McKim & Randall, 2007). We will not be critiquing autobiographies written *by* particular older people, or novels written *about* them, valuable though this strategy surely is. Rather, we will be endeavoring to develop an overall framework for thinking about the "narrative fabric of the self" (Freeman, 1998) through time—for thinking about the autobiographical complexities of aging itself. "Aging" in this context, though, is defined, not in terms of later life alone, but as a process we become increasingly conscious of from midlife on (see Willis & Reid, 1999). Indeed, from the perspective we are advancing in this book, the middle years of life—in which biographical well-being is, arguably, as important as physical well-being—are absolutely critical to the poetics of growing old.

To return to our central thesis: just as the art of telling literary stories is rooted in our ability to tell stories about everyday events, so the process of reading our own "lived texts" precedes that of reading literary ones. Reading lives is the primary activity. Reading literature, although we engage in it more intentionally and more mindfully, is the secondary one. We are able to do the latter only insofar as we are already doing the former. As with narrative in general, then, reading our lives is not merely a metaphor for how we make sense of our lives. It *is* how we make sense of our lives.

And yet in what ways, really, is our life a text that can be read? What does such a notion even mean? To respond to such questions, we need to situate our interest in the poetics of aging within the framework of broader intellectual trends that have been shaping how we view our world. It is vital that we do this. Little in this book can be properly appreciated without a sense of the larger story that lies behind it, a story of the world itself as text.

THE WORLD AS TEXT: POSTMODERNISM, POIESIS, AND THE IRONIC STANCE

The world as text is hardly a new idea. In Christian theology, it goes back as far as time itself: "In the Beginning was the Word ..." (John 1:1, King James Version). Taken together with the account of creation in Genesis, the association of language, not only with a creative deity, but also with that which is created, provided a powerful metaphor comparing word and world, a metaphor that has regularly resurfaced in the history of Western thought. As the medium of expression became more complex—as speaking was recorded on stone and clay tablets, and as tablets gave way to papyrus, parchment, and books—so the metaphor developed, as well. Alberto Manguel (1996) records, for example, that near the end of his life, the Italian Renaissance poet Francesco Petrarch composed a series of imaginary dialogues between himself and St. Augustine. At one point, Augustine points out to Petrarch: "'Francesco's life is a book like those in the poet's library, but one that Francesco does not yet know how to read'" (p. 63). The same might be said of all of us, and indeed, that is the point of this book: to explore the notion that our lives themselves are akin to books, to investigate how we read them, and to suggest how we can read them more sensitively and thus live them more fully.

Although world and text have always been yoked together, their association has recently taken on a unique urgency as a consequence of the claim of postmodern philosophers that "being" is itself a form of text. As Jacques Derrida has expressed it, "nothing exists outside the text" (1974, p. 158). This provocative observation has been interpreted in a variety of ways. Most often, though, it has been understood as a statement that everything is some sort of signifying system. In other words, not only writing and the visual and dramatic arts, but all institutions, historical events, relationships, and actions are ultimately textual in nature. According to Derrida, in conversation with an interviewer from *The New York Times,* "'Everything is a text; this is a text,' he said, waving his arm at the diners around him in the bland suburbanlike restaurant…" (Smith, 1998, B, p. 7). The point that Derrida makes is not just that the world can be compared to text. Rather, the world itself, however ordinary, *is* text. This notion has become such a scholarly commonplace that it is now taken for granted. Indeed, it is the very sort of notion that enables us to maintain that we can read our own lives. Nonetheless, accepting that the world and everything in it is text carries some startling consequences for our understanding, not only of things that we associate with text, like authors and readers and meaning, but also of the notion of personal identity.

On the surface, the concepts of authorship and readership are clearly distinct. For instance, we can picture ourselves sitting at our desk, gradually wresting order from chaos as we sort out our thoughts and commit them to the page, thereby expressing them, and ourselves, with authority. We strive to be as clear and coherent as we can, so our imaginary readers will understand our words and grasp our ideas. The ideas are ours; the meaning is conveyed by the text that we create, but it ultimately resides in us. If the text is unclear, then a puzzled reader might ask us what we meant, but our answer would be taken as authoritative. The reader, according to this scenario, is a more or less passive participant, an empty vessel into which the meaning of the text is poured. The author produces and the reader consumes—end of story. Yet this traditional and apparently simple sense of the transmission of ideas from one mind to another is in reality not simple at all, and the complexity rests in the nature of text itself.

According to postmodern theories of text, in fact, this notion of authorship is an illusion. Ferdinand de Saussure (1974), on whose linguistics postmodern theories of text are based, defined a text as a collection of signs, each of which is composed of two elements: the *signifier,* or the word itself, and the *signified,* the concept to which the word applies. The relationship between the signifier and the signified is understood to be arbitrary, which makes sense when we consider the way that language works. By way of an example, there is no necessary connection between the letters "d-o-g" and the concept of the four-footed hairy animal that they represent in English. Evidence of this arbitrary linkage is found in the fact that the same four-footed hairy animal is called "chien" in French, "hund" in German, and "perro" in Spanish, words that clearly are not even etymologically connected with one another, let alone with "dog." When this understanding of the ways words—signs—work is applied to the infinite elements that make up our world, however, the arbitrariness undermines the meanings most of us take for granted.

For example, the notion of an author's authority over a text becomes questionable, as Roland Barthes pointed out in a highly influential essay called "The Death of the Author" (1968/1988). Barthes maintains that a text is "a multidimensional space" (p. 170) that cannot, ultimately, be deciphered: not by the reader and certainly not by the author. Why? Because "writing ceaselessly posits meaning ceaselessly to evaporate it, carrying out a systematic exemption of meaning" (p. 171). Due to the slippery, multidimensional nature of text, the author cannot possibly have the final say on its meaning: "a text's unity lies not in its origin but in its destination" (p. 171). The destination, of course, is the reader. But even the reader cannot have the final say, for according to Barthes, the reader is a concept, not an actual person: "he is simply that *someone* who holds together in a single field all the traces by which the written text is constituted" (p. 171).

When applied to the self, these theories about text, author, and reader are devastating. Of course, the concepts of selfhood, identity, and subjectivity have puzzled philosophers for centuries (and more recently, psychologists too), and we cannot hope to trace here their complicated history. Nevertheless, we can see how traditional notions of self have been undermined by postmodern ones. In ordinary life, we are used to thinking of ourselves as coherent beings who have created an identity over time. We may even think of ourselves as beings with an interior or real self that is never displayed to others—perhaps even beings with a soul. But just as postmodernist theory has dispensed with the author, so has it dispensed with the self. Because the meaning of text is so arbitrary and multiplicitous, and because neither author nor reader can be the final arbiter of meaning, the question "who am I?" loses all relevance, just as the notion of meaning itself, as something coherent and indisputable, loses relevance as well. If the self is a text, then it shares with all texts a measure of arbitrariness and instability.

While there are several ways to view the self from a postmodernist perspective, what they have in common is the conviction that there is no inner person, no real pre-linguistic *I*, no coherent identity that, in sum, is a person. Instead, the self is understood as socially constructed on a moment-to-moment basis through our discourse with others, and with our culture and society. We are completely fluid, determined by the intertextual, interpretive, conversational back-and-forth with other individuals and institutions in which, quite literally, we find ourselves. Philosopher Anthony Paul Kerby (1991), for example, describes the self as "a product of language" (p. 4), "a result of discursive praxis rather than either a substantial entity having ontological priority over praxis or a self with epistemological priority, an originator of meaning." In other words, the self is created by discourse rather than being the active creator of it: language comes first and selfhood later. As Kerby says, "Persons only 'know' themselves after the fact of expression" (p. 5). Although this perspective is theoretically coherent, it negates what most of us perceive to be the case: that there is an *I*, a self who uses language, to be sure, but a pre-linguistic, creative self who produces that language and who harnesses it to communicate meaning. Postmodern, constructionist thought suggests that this sense is naïve and incorrect and that, ultimately, all attempts to account for a coherent, individual self fall back on sheer speculation (Kerby, 1991, p. 5).

If this postmodernist vision of the self seems counter-intuitive and even nihilistic, that is because, when taken to an extreme, it is. Indeed, it is precisely the kind of vision that literary theorist Terry Eagleton (1996) is describing when he says that postmodernist thought "sees the world as contingent, ungrounded, diverse, unstable, indeterminate." It assumes, he charges, "a set of disunified cultures or interpretations which breed a degree of scepticism about the objectivity of truth, history and norms, the givenness of natures and the coherence of identities" (p. vii). Eagleton's definition supports what political scientist Pauline Rosenau (1992), in her analysis of the consequences of postmodernist thought for the social sciences, calls "skeptical postmodernism" (pp. 14–17). Rosenau says that skeptical postmodernists, "offering a pessimistic, negative, gloomy assessment, argue that the post-modern age is one of fragmentation, disintegration, malaise, meaninglessness, a vagueness or even absence of moral parameters and societal chaos" (p. 15). For them, there is no stable meaning and no truth, and they focus on "the demise of the subject, [and] the end of the author" (p. 15). If everything is socially constructed, including ethics, history, and religion, then it becomes impossible to speak of what really happened, or of what is right and wrong, good or evil. Moreover, the larger political and religious stories that compose our societies—democracy, Christianity, the notion of progress, the value of science—cease to have authority. They become no more than grand narratives, reflecting what is merely a particular point of view: influential, to be certain, but by no means grounded in "truth."

If postmodernism kills off the author and the self, and negates the possibility of truth or even of meaning, why then are we advocating it as a fruitful way of thinking about our lives? While postmodernist thought, when taken to a skeptical extreme, is pessimistic, it nonetheless offers insight into ways in which we interpret and construct ourselves—and others—that are actually quite life-giving. Perhaps the most important notion it has introduced is the possibility that identities are not fixed and unchanging, but are continually under construction, forever open to reinterpretation. Moreover, this possibility applies not only to who we think we are, but also to our understandings of the events and relationships that constitute our lives. If all the world is text (including us), with all of the multiplicity which texts invite, then we have considerable freedom to grow and change. For a number of recent scholars, such freedom is identified as *irony*.

Just as traditional understandings of author, reader, and text have radically shifted as a result of postmodernist thought, so has the concept of irony. We are used to thinking about irony as a rhetorical device, by which we say one thing when we actually mean the opposite: "Nice day," we snort, as the rain plummets and our umbrella turns inside out. Or we may think of dramatic irony, by which the audience of a movie or a play has been given some essential piece of information that the main character lacks. What both such sorts of irony share in common is contradiction. But irony is much more than a rhetorical or literary strategy. The eighteenth-century German philosopher Friedrich Schlegel defined it as "an incessant alternative of two contradictory thoughts" (quoted in Knox, 2003, vol. 2, p. 628), and much thinking and writing in the nineteenth century was devoted to achieving synthesis between competing ideas. Postmodern irony, resisting the possibility of synthesis, is different yet again. For literary scholar Linda Hutcheon (1992), for example, it is "skeptically suspended judgement": "an unwillingness to make decisions about meaning that would imply singularity or fixity" (p. 37).

This unwillingness has consequences for our understanding of both our worlds and ourselves. As literary scholar Stephen Prickett (2002) points out, "any story of the world, whether scientific, sociological, psychological or religious, will also inevitably be pluralistic, literary, ironic, tentative, and multiplex" (p. 53). Speaking of the self, literary scholar Gary Handwerk identifies irony as "a form of discourse that insists upon the provisional and fragmentary nature of the individual subject" (1985, p. viii). It "establishes the dependence of the subject's identity," he says, "on the web of social relations within which it exists" (p. 15). Not unlike Kerby, who claims that the self is a linguistic construct, Handwerk suggests that the self is a social construct, dependent on its place within a social system: "Irony is the active effort to locate one's place in the human world, in the emerging system from which one as subject emerged" (pp. 15–16).

The perspectives of Hutcheon, Prickett, and Handwerk on irony are similar to that of philosopher Richard Rorty (1989), who identifies an "ironist" as: "the sort of person who faces up to the contingency of his or her most central beliefs and desires" (p. xv). To recognize that a belief is contingent on something else is, of course, to deny ultimate authority both to over-arching stories about the world and to personal narratives. Likewise, a coherent notion of self is denied any authority: ironists are "never quite able to take themselves seriously," says Rorty, since they are "always aware that the terms in which they describe themselves are subject to change" (pp. 73–74). The ironic stance, then, is an awareness and acceptance of contradiction and multiplicity, fragmentation and contingency, in both the self and the world, and a corresponding openness to one's changing understandings.

In the chapters that follow, the theory we will be presenting clearly has postmodern roots and advocates an ironic stance. Lives are indeed fragmentary, contradictory, multiplicitous texts, we believe, and, as texts, are both linguistically and socially constructed. But we also think that we are (or are capable of being) the principal architects of that very process. Our focus is therefore not on selves as passive social constructions, but on selves as active, creative agents. In other words, a self is not merely the product of discourse but is an ongoing process of creation that is in part discursive, but also in part embodied and pre-linguistic. Like other postmodernists, we are of course skeptical of the notion that there is an a priori, coherent, "real me" inside of us, acting as a sort of stage director as we go about our lives. But we also think that most people's everyday intuitions of personal agency and coherence are too pervasive to be nothing more than wishful thinking, and are, ourselves, skeptical of postmodernism's easy dismissal of them as naïve. As narrative psychologist Michelle Crossley (2003) dryly observes, "human experience is routinely characterized by greater order and coherence than is typically suggested in postmodernist circles" (p. 294).

Intuitions of agency and coherence may be illusions. But they are based on *something*. And that something, we believe, is the constant, never-ceasing narrative activity that we carry out through perception, memory, and imagination as we exist and interact in our worlds, as we experience events, initiate actions, remember the past, and project toward the future: once again, the narrative variable. And while that variable is undoubtedly linguistic and social, it is biological as well, rooted in neurology, as we will see in Chapter 2. Postmodern theory tends to focus on the intellectual aspects of human experience more than on the physical ones. As a consequence, discussions of the body tend to concentrate, for example, on how our *ideas* of the body, or pain, or sexuality are socially and linguistically determined. In contrast, acknowledging that there is a link between the mind–body connection and the narrative nature of lived experience leads to the recognition that, to some extent, and quite apart from social influences, selfhood may precede language.

This optimistic focus on the creative agency of humanity—and the acceptance of more than linguistic and social means of self-construction—separates what we are proposing here from the postmodernist thinkers Rosenau labels "skeptical," and allies us with those she calls "affirmative" (pp. 14–17). Rosenau herself points out, of course, that her categories of "skeptical" and "affirmative" are very flexible (p. 17). Nonetheless, they serve as a useful way to distinguish between those who accept "the immediacy of death, the demise of the subject, the end of the author, [and] the impossibility of truth" (p. 15), and those like us who are contented just to "seek a philosophical and ontological intellectual practice that is non-dogmatic, tentative, and non-ideological" (p. 16). If we think of these categories as positions on a continuum, stretching from realism at one end to relativism at the other, then skeptical postmodernism is the relativist extreme, while affirmative postmodernism lies somewhere in the middle. Indeed, literary scholar Elizabeth Hart (2001) characterizes it as "a *third* epistemological position" (p. 320)—elsewhere called "constrained constructivism" (Hayles, 1993)—which "borrows from both realist and relativist positions but is, in any absolute sense, neither one" (Hart, 2001, p. 321).

Affirmative postmodernists accept that the world is text and that meanings are multiple. However, they are less quick to accept that the relationship between the signifier and signified is an arbitrary one (Rosenau, 1992, p. 35). Instead, they reserve the possibility that some ideas are of greater value than others, and are less certain that meaning is, by definition, impossible. Whereas skeptics dispense with the self entirely, affirmatives are reluctant to accept that language alone constitutes the self. Rather, as we do, they see both experiencing and our interpreting of it as constitutive of self (p. 44). Rosenau cites, for example, philosopher/psychoanalyst Julia Kristeva's notion that the modern subject is "a work in progress" (pp. 58–59), as well as other definitions of the self by scholars such as Anthony Giddens and Pierre Bourdieu who focus on the self as that which experiences (pp. 58–59). As we will see, many other scholars investigating the narrative construction of identity are doing so without losing sight of the entity who is doing the constructing, most obvious among these being Jerome Bruner, as noted already, plus the numerous thinkers who are influenced by his work.

This affirmative, ongoing process of creating ourselves is, in fact, a poetic process, especially if our lives are understood as texts. The word *poetic* is peculiarly appropriate to the process in question, for it derives from the ancient Greek verb *poiein,* which means "to make or create." Although literary scholar Gary Saul Morson (1999) correctly points out that *poetics,* since Aristotle first defined it, has often implied a finished design (p. 280), contemporary usage focuses on activity more than structure. Implicit in *poetics,* unlike other terms we might apply to aging, such as *theory* or *structure,* or even *aesthetics,* is its active, creative quality. Philosopher Paul Ricoeur (1991), for example, suggests that even plot, the most important element of poetics as Aristotle defined it, "is not a static structure but an operation, an integrating process ... the work of composition which gives a dynamic identity to the story recounted" (p. 21).

To speak of a poetics of aging, then, is to focus, not only on the activity of aging, but also on its creative agent (i.e., ourselves), and on the process of becoming. Indeed, current definitions of poetics emphasize the importance of action and agency alike. According to the Poetics Program at SUNY-Buffalo (State University of New York, 2006), which was built on the experimental poetics of Robert Creeley and Charles Bernstein, poetics is that which "stays grounded in the fact of making." Poetics concerns itself not with mere product, that is, but with process and agency: "The author is that which gives the disquieting language of fiction or poetry its unities and disunities, its knot of coherence and chaos, its insertion into the real." The author, in this thoroughly postmodern formulation, is far from dead, therefore, but vibrantly alive in the midst of creative process, responsible for any semblance of order or coherence or resemblance to reality. And this author, we believe, is us. The narrative means by which we perceive and comprehend experience is not simply a linguistic tool that we use to describe our lives after the fact. Nor is it merely a social phenomenon by which we are constructed. Rather, as we hope to make clear, it is an innate quality—both pre-linguistic and linguistic—that is integral to human existence.

AGING, INTERDISCIPLINARITY, AND NARRATIVE

At almost every turn, topics like that of text, poetics, and the self tend to cut across disciplinary lines. Coauthoring a book on the poetics of aging—in our respective capacities as gerontologist on one hand and literary scholar on the other—has therefore meant doing considerable line-crossing of our own. From start to finish, as an exploration of the psychology of aging in particular, it has been an exercise in interdisciplinary inquiry and in negotiation. Literary scholar Daniel Albright (1994) captures the challenge of blending our different backgrounds: "Literature is a wilderness," he says. "Psychology is a garden" (p. 19). That said, as Bruner (2002) points out, "psychology and literature have common roots, however different the fruits they bear" (p. xi). In fact, with the poetics of growing old, even the fruits themselves are far more related than they might appear to be at first.

Interdisciplinarity is, in many ways, the Holy Grail of the human sciences. It is certainly so in gerontology: witness the official theme of the 2005 meeting of the Gerontological Society of America: "The Interdisciplinary Mandate." The yearning for interdisciplinarity is evident in efforts to bridge the gap between quantitative and qualitative paradigms of gerontological research (Groger & Straker, 2002), and it is at work among practitioners as well. In healthcare, for instance, doctors and nurses, social workers and chaplains, therapists and specialists routinely convene to develop holistic approaches to the treatment of particular patients. Yet, inevitably, each arrives with a different set of technical language, a different model for conceptualizing the problem, and a different strategy for resolving it. Unanimity is thus elusive, and even consensus can be challenging to achieve.

Interdisciplinarity may be the ideal, in other words, but on the ground, gerontology remains committedly *multi*disciplinary (see Katz, 1996). More often than not, geropsychologists conduct their research and publish their results in isolation from social gerontologists—or, for that matter, from any number of other scholars with whom their thinking might actually resonate rather well. And overall, those coming at aging from the medical sciences, from the social sciences, and from the humanities can seem to be tackling, not merely different components of the same basic elephant, but an entirely different animal. All the while, aging itself—like life itself—is a stubbornly interdisciplinary experience. We do not age in a physical sense, cognitive sense, or social sense alone, but in every sense at once. For such reasons, it seems reasonable to approach the experience of aging from a perspective that, itself, is inherently interdisciplinary; in short, a narrative perspective. Narrativity and interdisciplinarity go hand in hand, if for no other reason than that stories themselves typically tackle a wide range of topics at once. If *War and Peace* (Tolstoy, 1865–69/2006) were not located in the literature section of the local bookstore, where would it be shelved? History? Psychology? Conflict Studies? Russian Studies? It is both the charm and the challenge of narrative that no discipline on its own can adequately account for what narrative is and does, let alone *define* it, though surely each contributes some key piece to our total understanding.

Some scholars—certainly narratologists—study the structures of stories in and of themselves. Others analyze specific narratives according to established methodologies, from the literary scholar's close reading to the sociologist's discourse analysis. Some, such as qualitative researchers, look at narrative as a form of "data"; for others, it is an approach to interpreting such data. Some compare narratives across historical periods or political groups, across cultures or genders, across age groups or ethnic groups. Some psychologists study the development of a child's capacity to comprehend narrative on one hand, and to construct it on the other—the development, that is, of an overall narrative intelligence. Some educators study narrative as a method of teaching and learning; others, as an approach to practicing medicine or social work, ministry or nursing. Some consider narrative as the modus operandi of the therapeutic process. For some, narrative activity is one of the most fundamental functions of human neurology, while others deem it integral to our emotional lives, our identities, our beliefs. And some—certainly ourselves, as the authors of this book—see it as the primary means by which we make sense of our experience through time; indeed, as the very means of self-creation. As such, it is a way of looking at life as a whole.

As a perspective on life as a whole (particularly on aging, our focus in this book) narrative is not something we can look upon from some safe, objective stance. It is something we look *through*. It is the medium of our being, its amniotic fluid. As expressed by literary scholar Wayne Booth (1988), "There can be no 'control group' consisting of untouched souls who have lived life-times without narrative so that they might study unscathed the effects on others" (p. 41). We do not just *have* narratives, in other words; we *are* narrative beings. If human life exists outside of narrative, it is impossible to imagine what shape it takes.

"Our top stories this hour…" intones the announcer, as our radio rouses us to consciousness. Around the coffeepot at work, our officemates elicit narrative responses when plying us with questions: "What did you do last night?"; then later in the day, "What happened to those widgets that we ordered last week?" At home over supper, we press our loved ones for anecdotes about their respective days, after which we retire to the drawing room to relax with a movie or novel before heading off to bed, where, more than likely, we drift away on a river of dreams—the whole lot of it, narrative activity. For many of us, then, phrases like *narrative studies* or *the narrative turn* possess an enormous intuitive appeal. They appeal to the part of us that roots for the underdog, perhaps—the part that can appreciate the irony that something as ordinary as stories, something so much under our noses that we scarcely even notice it, something so "deadeningly obvious" (Bruner, 2002, p. 3) yet so beguilingly odd, plays such a powerful role in the flow of human life.

Overall, with the topic we are looking into here—the inside of aging—an interdisciplinary approach is, not merely helpful, but utterly essential for a broad enough perspective on all that is at stake. No doubt, it is hazardous to trespass into territory different from our own, since we risk naïve conclusions based on partial understandings. Equally hazardous, however, is to ignore relevant work being done in domains other than those that we ourselves are most familiar with, as the wide range of sources—theoretical, empirical, and practical—on which we are drawing will soon make clear.

In Part One, "Reading Our Lives: Poetics Explored," we hope to lay down a conceptual foundation for our considerations in the second part. In essence, Part One amounts to an exploration of the complex process of making meaning in which all of us, at any age, are continually immersed. More specifically, Chapter 2 sets out from the neurological basis of our narrative activity, moves to the narrative complexity of ordinary consciousness, and ends with a more detailed consideration of how our life overall is like—and not like—a novel. Chapter 3 outlines what we see as the principal elements in the composing or "storying" of this novel; namely, narrative environment, narrative development, and narrative identity. In Chapter 4 we shift to literary theory to look at the intricate dynamics involved in reading literature itself, while Chapter 5 sketches the connection between such dynamics and the interpretive processes that are involved in reading life, which the remainder of the book will endeavor to elaborate.

Our aim in Part Two, "Growing Old: Poetics Applied," is to relate the perspective outlined in the first part to the psychological side, or inside, of aging. In Chapter 6, we say more on the concept of narrative foreclosure and present the process of reading a story, whether literary or lived, as one that takes us from expanding the story to examining it, and from transforming it to transcending it. With such a progression in mind, our focus in Chapters 7 through 10 will be on four large topics to which, fortunately, gerontologists have been devoting more and more attention: memory, meaning, wisdom, and spirituality. Our choice of these topics is deliberate. While valuable bodies of literature have been building around each one of them, those literatures are seldom really linked. It is just such a linkage, we believe, that narrative can provide. In the same way that any story concerns numerous subjects at once, the study of story is no respecter of disciplinary bounds. If any single perspective is capable of weaving together themes that all four of them have in common, it is a narrative one.

Two

NARRATING EXPERIENCE:

THE AUTOBIOGRAPHICAL SELF

We dream in narrative, daydream in narrative, remember,
anticipate, hope, despair, believe, doubt, plan, revise, criticize,
construct, gossip, learn, hate, and love by narrative.
    —Barbara Hardy (1968, p. 5)

The quest for a story is the quest for a life.
    —Jill Johnston (1993, p. 29)

Biologically, physiologically, we are not so different from each other;
historically, as narratives—we are each of us unique.
    —Oliver Sacks (1987, p. 111)

THE NEUROLOGY OF NARRATIVE:
FROM CORPOREALITY TO CONSCIOUSNESS

For centuries, philosophers have been arguing about the nature of consciousness, presenting us with a variety of theories that are more or less convincing. Yet emerging interdisciplinary work in cognitive neuroscience—encompassing philosophy, literary theory, psychology, and neurology, and involving both theoretical and empirical scholarship—is shedding significant light upon the matter. Evidence accumulated so far indicates that narrative activity is rooted in the most basic forms of consciousness, and that consciousness itself is a narrative process. Unlike commonsense understandings of story as a secondary activity, as simply a verbal recounting of factual or fictional events, storying, it appears, is a primary activity that actually precedes language. And unlike postmodern understandings of the self as a secondary, socio-linguistic construct, the self, it seems, exists pre-socially and prelinguistically. Moreover, its source lies in the body itself. In other words, we enter life neurologically equipped with all the tools we need to conceive of ourselves as distinctive human selves, and this conception takes a narrative form.

One of the principal researchers in this area is neurologist and psychologist Antonio Damasio (1994, 1999). Damasio's highly interdisciplinary work is widely regarded to have furthered our understanding of the brain systems that are involved in memory, language, and consciousness. For him, *self* is defined as a process: "the feeling of what happens when your being is modified by the act of apprehending something" (1999, p. 10). Likewise, consciousness is "the sense of self in the act of knowing" (p. 11). Damasio's research has led him to propose that self has three dynamic levels: *proto-self, core self,* and *autobiographical self.* Our main interest here, of course, is the autobiographical self, but as Damasio convincingly argues, it is built upon the others. No proto-self, no core self; no core self, no autobiographical self. For that reason, it is essential to consider the mind–body connections by which the latter is underpinned.

Another major theorist in this area, whose explanation of consciousness and the self, like Damasio's, points to the centrality of narrative, is philosopher, psychologist, and neurobiologist Owen Flanagan (1992). Flanagan's research is compatible with Damasio's, in that he, too, views the self as a narrative process. For him, selfhood is a spectrum extending from an unconscious state, which seems similar to Damasio's proto-self, to a fully developed self-consciousness that resembles the autobiographical self.

Damasio's proto-self (1999, pp. 153–60), or what Flanagan refers to as "informational sensitivity" (p. 56), precedes consciousness: it is merely the body's unconscious "informational pickup and processing without phenomenal awareness" (Flanagan, p. 56). Consisting of the various signals that the nervous system produces in response to various objects, the proto-self is a fluid process, changing instant by instant. It is prelinguistic, "the nonconscious forerunner" (Damasio, 1999, p. 22) of the two conscious levels: "a coherent collection of neural patterns which map, moment by moment, the state of the physical structure of the organism in its many dimensions" (p. 154). The proto-self, then, is the ever-changing physical platform upon which consciousness is based, "a collection of brain devices whose main job is the automated management of the organism's life" (p. 23).

The core self is the one that becomes aware of this dynamic management, and it is born as a result of our encounters with objects: "the object causes the organism to react, and in so doing, change its state" (p. 25). Core consciousness occurs when we become aware of ourselves as perceiving beings who are separate from what we are perceiving, in space and time alike. It is as fluid and dynamic a process as the proto-self, constantly created and recreated as the self repeatedly encounters itself in the very act of knowing. If we hear or see something, smell or taste something, feel pain or touch something, it is core consciousness that enables us to be aware of it, and to be aware of ourselves being aware of it, thus creating a sort of un-languaged, but logical story: "that of the organism caught in the act of representing its own changing state as it goes about representing something else" (p. 170).

The core self becomes conscious of itself only as it perceives and represents something else in the mind, whether it be an external object or an internal memory. The process by which it represents that something is quintessentially narrative, and displays characteristics that we have come to associate with literature. Even prelinguistically, core consciousness registers itself as a protagonist; and in being reborn in every instant, and in being aware of itself being reborn, core consciousness might also be said to engage in *emplotment.* However, it displays another quality, too, perhaps the most fundamental, and one we are used to relating to literature alone: metaphor.

We tend to think of metaphor as a literary trick, something added on as decoration or as a means of explanation or persuasion. *Metaphor,* literally, means *transference,* and, indeed, it was traditionally regarded as a mere rhetorical device that enabled the transfer of meaning from something known to something unknown. A good example is the title of a book by poet Alfred Corn (1998): *The Poem's Heartbeat.* His subject, the sound of poetry, is a highly complex matter, and many sophisticated explanations have been put forward to account for its nature, its functions, and its effects. Corn's metaphor—that the sound of poetry is a heartbeat—teases out several of these complexities. First of all, the heartbeat has a distinctive, regular, rhythmical sound, as does traditional poetry. Moreover, the sound is really a secondary effect of the beating heart itself, whose primary purpose is to pump blood, not to make its characteristic *ka-thump, ka-thump.* Likewise, the primary function of a poem is to say something, not just to make a pleasing noise. But the metaphor goes even deeper. The beating heart is an organic entity, from which it is impossible to separate its sound. Likewise, so the metaphor implies, a poem, too, is an organic entity, from which it is impossible to separate *its* sound. Building on this organic association, the total effect of the metaphor is to suggest, then, that the poem is a living thing, not merely words on a page. The metaphor ensures that the notions of rhythm, sound, and life have been transferred from heart to poem.

But is a poem, literally, a living thing? Of course not. And there we have the first traditional problem with metaphor: the notion that metaphor, a product of the imagination and not of reality, deviates from truth. On the basis of this problem, Socrates resolved to turf all the poets out of his Republic (Plato, 360 BCE/1941, pp. 324 ff.): imaginative writing was by definition untruthful and therefore untrustworthy. But this problem rests on another problem in turn: the assumption that literary language, including metaphor, is in some way different from nonliterary language. Twentieth-century scholarship on language, by contrast, suggests that metaphor regularly appears in nonliterary texts and everyday speech, and that it is in no way a special use of language. In fact, recent theorists go even further and argue that although metaphor certainly has a rhetorical expression, it is primarily a conceptual tool, integral to the moment-by-moment perception that characterizes core consciousness.

As psychologist Raymond Gibbs (1994) puts it, "human cognition is fundamentally shaped by various poetic or figurative processes" (p. 1), and metaphor is one of several such processes "by which people conceptualize their experience and the external world" (p. 1). Instead of cognition shaping metaphor, then, metaphor shapes cognition. Perhaps the best known theorist on this subject is cognitive linguist George Lakoff, who with philosopher Mark Johnson (1980) introduced the notion of *conceptual metaphor*. Metaphor exists, Lakoff proposes, "in the way we conceptualize one mental domain in terms of another" (1993, p. 203). A conceptual metaphor consists of two parts: the known thing, called the "source domain," and the unknown thing, called the "target domain" (p. 207). The correspondence between the elements of a source domain and a target domain is called a "mapping"; and a conceptual metaphor is the result of that mapping (p. 203). Lakoff argues that virtually all language has its roots in basic prelinguistic metaphors that derive from our physical nature. In other words, metaphors are embodied. And the more abstract our concepts are—"like time, states, change, causation, and purpose" (p. 203)—the more metaphorical they are. Some common sets of correspondences, or mappings, include such everyday metaphors as "more is up," or "less is down" (p. 213), or the notion that "time passing is motion" (p. 217).

In a further exploration of the deep structure of how the mind uses metaphor, literary theorist and cognitive scientist Mark Turner (1996) has convincingly argued that the foundation of human thought is parabolic. It is the creation and projection of what he calls "small stories" (p. 12)—namely, the overlaying of patterns that are familiar to us from our physical experience onto something unfamiliar. In other words, thinking is by its very nature both narrative and metaphorical: hence his concept of *the literary mind.* These small stories, or "image schemas," are "skeletal patterns that recur in our sensory and motor experience" (p. 16). For example, a common image schema is "motion along a path" (p. 17). This is the small spatial story that we project onto the notion of time, thereby perceiving it, too, as moving and linear. Such a projection results in a "conceptual blend" (pp. 57–84), an integration of the metaphor's source and target. From that blend, other blends can be born: for example, we might speculate about how the notion of time as moving and linear was projected onto the sun moving through the sky as the day progressed. In turn, this notion was projected onto Apollo, the ancient sun-god, riding in his chariot, leading to the proverbial wisdom that "time flies." Central to core consciousness, this sort of blending is "an invisible, unconscious activity involved in every aspect of human life" (Fauconnier & Turner, 2002, p. 18). It is a process: "alive and active, dynamic and distributed, constructed for local purposes of knowing and acting" (Turner, 1996, p. 57).

Enriching core consciousness is verbal ability. "In addition to the story that signifies the act of knowing and attributes it to the newly minted core self," Damasio (1999) says, "the human brain also generates an automatic verbal version of the story" (p. 185). Flanagan, along with his colleague Gillian Einstein (2003), agrees. Since human beings are languaged creatures, "the emotions, feelings, mood, and sense of ourselves as male or female, compassionate or knavish, may often be penumbral," they say. "But since we have words for these things, they can be…brought into view and become part of the narrative we can tell to ourselves and possibly share with others" (p. 212). This bringing "into view" on a moment-by-moment basis is an attribute of core consciousness. As what is brought into view becomes "part of the narrative," however, we shift into a much more complex form of consciousness—what Damasio calls *extended consciousness*—resulting in the autobiographical self.

Extended consciousness, unlike core consciousness, consists not of moment-by-moment perceptions, but of our ability to put those perceptions into a larger context, based on our memories of the past and our imaginative projections into the future. As Damasio puts it, "in extended consciousness, both the past and the anticipated future are sensed along with the here and now in a sweeping vista as far-ranging as that of an epic novel" (1999, p. 17). It is not surprising that Damasio compares extended consciousness to an epic novel, for it is precisely extended consciousness that we are most likely to think of in narrative terms. This highly developed, complex level of awareness is what enables us to have an autobiography, a lifestory. It is thus in extended consciousness that the sense of a coherent, fully-formed self develops: the autobiographical self that we construct as a result of the objects perceived by our core consciousness. These objects are both internal and external—ranging from our memories of the past to our perceptions in the present—and are influenced by a wide array of sources, inside and out: from our brain cells, hormones, and neurotransmitters, to our "innate and acquired personality traits, intelligence, knowledge, [and our] social and cultural environments" (p. 224).

The self we are at any given moment, then, is a complex, dynamic mix of the inside and the outside, of our memories of the past and the reshaping of those memories in light of the present. And our sense of who we are at any given time has consequences for our anticipation of—and actions in—the future. As long as we live, we are open-ended, never-finished texts. In Flanagan's (1992) words, the self "is subject to constant revision" (p. 205). Our agenda in the remainder of this book is to contemplate the nature of this process, and all the shifting influences, internal and external, that make us such inveterate revisers of ourselves.

THE PSYCHOLOGY OF NARRATIVE: FROM CONSCIOUSNESS TO COMMUNICATION

As we are seeing, then, the continual weaving of stories is integral to our day-to-day existence, for we never experience the world directly. We experience it only as it is filtered, shaped, and narrativized through a complex interpretive process, commencing with initial sensory perceptions and culminating in emotion, thought, and action. Without such interpreting, consciousness as most of us know it—indeed, feel it—would simply be impossible. And central to that consciousness, at the level of core self and autobiographical self alike, is reading our lives.

The bulk of this book is devoted to how such reading operates at the *macro* level of experience, and in relation to *the story of my life* as a whole. Straightaway, however, we want to say more about how it operates at the *micro* level, too—which is to say, in our moment-by-moment, even second-by-second, processing of reality. In doing so, we take our cue from the observation of psychologists John Robinson and Linda Hawpe (1986) concerning "narrative thinking." Insofar as such thinking entails "the projection of story form onto some experience or event" (the point that Turner makes as well), it can occur, they say, "as the experience is taking place, in reflecting upon the experience, or in recounting the experience at a later time" (p. 115). Thus, as a modest, somewhat playful contribution to ongoing efforts to "explain" the essence of consciousness (Dennett, 1991), and by way of beginning with what William James (1962) calls "the most concrete facts" of one's "inner life" (p. 166), reading our lives at the micro level, we can say, happens in three overall stages. For want of more sophisticated labels, we call them: *noticing and nattering, reading and editing,* and *narrating and interacting.* We say "stages" advisedly, however, because what we envision is scarcely linear. We could just as easily refer to them as "levels" or "functions" or "states." Whatever we call them, in the throes of our everyday mental-emotional activity, and certainly in the heat of our interactions with others, the boundaries between them are anything but sharp.

Noticing and Nattering

Our normal, waking consciousness is characterized by a continual swirl of images and impressions: or *noticings,* we could call them. At work as well, however, is a plethora of voices—many of them our own, many of them not—all muttering away on a number of levels and forever interrupting each other in a largely muddled manner—*natterings,* we might say. While our dreaming consciousness is no doubt muddled all the more, the difference between the two is a matter of degree and not of kind (though the subject of dreams is beyond our purview here). But in our core consciousness, not only are we quite literally talking to ourselves, but "our selves" seem to be many selves at once, no one of which appears to be "the self-in-control" (Bickle, 2003, p. 201). We are on "automatic narrative pilot" (Eakin, 1999, p. 124), in other words, and the pilot is wandering all over the map.

For evidence that this noticing and nattering are real, we need only tune into what humorist Bill Bryson (1991) dubs "my idly prattling mind" (p.289). What we hear is seldom a single, sane voice calmly recounting what we are witnessing or experiencing in an orderly, dispassionate manner. More than likely, we discover multiple voices, mumbling about multiple matters, seemingly at once: what our senses are perceiving from our surroundings in the present; what we are recalling from the remote or recent past (including countless "what ifs" or "might have beens"); and what we are expecting or fearing for the future. And most of them come out of the blue. "Why did I think of *that?!*" we often wonder. In "ballistic" fashion, writes neuroscientist John Bickle (2003), the voices pop into our heads like "unguided missiles" (p. 200), and just as quickly pop back out. As philosopher Stephen Crites (1986) observes, "many...things register in my consciousness, are perceived but not experienced, heard but not listened to" (p. 160). Such "things" can be looked upon as virtual thoughts, like the virtual particles that, supposedly, are coming and going at the quantum level, too.

In *A Life of One's Own,* psychologist Joanna Field (1934/1952) lends credence to this phenomenon with her fascinating speculations on "how my thought behaved when left to itself" (p. 116). Using phrases like "wandering attention" (p. 114), "casual everyday preoccupation" (p. 115), and the "little movements going on in the back of my mind" (p. 116), she writes at length about the "free-drifting thought" that, if watched "too obviously...would scuttle away into its hole only to appear again as soon as I turned my head the other way" (p. 115). Given the way "they silently flitted in from nowhere and were gone in a moment" (p. 116), she describes such "little movements" as "butterflies." She goes on: "I could never predict what would be in my mind the next moment, and I was often amazed," she says, "at the way these thoughts completely ignored what I felt to be important occasions. They seemed at times like the swarm of tiny beetles which skate on the surface of a pond, never diving to any real issue—an airy skimming in endless mazes" (p. 117).

Clearly, our noticings and natterings are linked. Field's "wandering attention" is effectively Bickle's "inner speech" (2003, p. 198), which takes the form of what literary theorist Peter Brooks (1985) speaks of as "an episodic, sometimes semi-conscious but virtually uninterrupted monologue" that we continually "narrate to ourselves" (p. 3). "Monologue" is a misnomer, however, because, if anything, a dialogue is taking place. Writing about "the dialogical self," psychologist Hubert Hermans (2002) refers to "a dynamic multiplicity of I-positions in the landscape of the mind" (p. 147). Indeed, given its cacophonic quality, it might more aptly be called a *poly*-logue instead, which is to say "a conversation" (Crites, 1986, p. 156)—the sort that, if others could overhear it, would probably place our sanity in question! It is not only multi-vocal in nature, but "multiphrenic" (Gergen,1992), inasmuch as many of the speakers seem to correspond to different sides of our own personalities; different "sub-personalities" (Assagioli, 1976) or "sub-Selfs" (Bruner & Kalmar, 1998, p. 320). In other words, they amount to different "interacting characters" (Hermans, 2002, p. 1) amid the assortment of subplots, chapters, and versions that constitute the stories of our lives. And of course the conversation involves characterizations of others as well. "Even when we are outwardly silent," notes Hermans (p. 27), "we find ourselves communicating with our critics, with our parents, our consciences, our gods, our reflection in the mirror, with the photograph of someone we miss, with a figure from a movie or a dream, with our babies, with our pets, or even with the flowers we care for." The result is "a complex narratively structured self," a veritable "society of mind" (p. 27).

In one instant, one voice offers the observation that "It's snowing outside," while another (that of a deceased parent, perhaps) admonishes us to "Be sure and wear your mittens." A number of our natterers, in other words, are naggers as well, some of whom reap apparent pleasure in putting us down: "You're so stupid! Can't you do anything right?" Meanwhile, another voice is busy running through the words of an old song, while another is rehearsing the pitch we aim to make to our employer to demand a raise in pay. Other voices are trotting out assorted interpretations—readings, as it were—of the grimace on a colleague's face: "What's the story?" we ask ourselves. "Is he mad at me? Is he bored? Or is he pondering some problem that has nothing to do with me?" Still another voice is on the verge of tears as we play back yesterday's run-in with our ex-; another, gushing about the roses in the garden; another, worrying about our brother in the hospital; another, mumbling about some item on the morning news; another, wondering what to cook for supper; and yet another fussing about the homework or housework that needs tackling on the weekend. Over the course of a day, an hour, a minute, much can thus be "on our minds."

But our natterers are also budding narrativists. Each of our inner voices, insists Hermans (2002), "has a story to tell about his or her own experiences from his or her own stance" (p. 1). And as for our various noticings, including the trains of thought that follow them, these, too, reflect incipient storylines. They are stories in the making. Already with something of a spin to them, they are primitive interpretive structures—"small stories" (Turner, 1996, p. 12)—through which we make sense of the details of our daily life. We do not simply see snow, for example; we see an event-in-progress: "It's snowing." "The human mind," says Turner, "is always at work constructing small stories and projecting them" (p. 12). Indeed, "if you do not have this capacity, you do not have a human mind" (p. 13). Further support for this perspective comes from psychiatrist Allan Hobson (1994) in his discussion of the chemistry of conscious states. Like Turner and Flanagan, Hobson maintains that "the brain-mind is a storyteller in all its states" (p. 117). He goes on: "The story-like strain of mental activity," which "proceeds in parallel with our minute-to-minute perceptions, thoughts, and actions," can variously be called "reflections, daydreaming, woolgathering, and fantasy" (p. 118).

Many of "these little fictions," as Hobson speaks of them (p. 118), are oriented primarily toward the past. Some will pertain to involuntary memories, explored so famously, for instance, by Marcel Proust (1927/1982): bits and pieces of remembered material that, as novelist Thomas Wolfe (1938/1983) expresses it, "return unbidden at an unexpected moment" (p. 44). Some will pertain to short-term memories, to what happened a moment ago or an hour ago, while several others will relate to longer-term episodes from the distant past. At the same time, many will be focused on the future: on what we plan to do tomorrow, next week, next year. And of course many seem aimed solely at the present: "Hey, it's snowing outside." Yet even then, any noticing in the present is done with an implicit sense of the past that preceded it ("It wasn't snowing the last time I looked out") and the future that might follow ("I'm going to have to shovel that stuff when I get home").

Worth mentioning in this connection is that, due to the essential narrativity of our noticings and natterings, they can carry considerable (not to mention, continually shifting) emotional significance. Just as stories stimulate emotions, so emotions have storied roots. They are "complex narrative structures that give shape and meaning to somatic and affective experiences" (Schweder, 1994, p. 32; see also Nussbaum, 1990; Singer, 1996). To put it simply, if we are feeling sad or mad or glad (or all of them mixed together), then it is usually because we are sad or mad or glad *about* something, a something that can only be articulated in terms of the story, or stories, through which we perceive it. As an example, suppose that we are experiencing an undercurrent of terror. Might it be because the pain we have been noticing increasingly since breakfast has activated an entire storyline about our future? Obviously, the source of our discomfort is a cancerous tumor, and we have less than a year to live!

Perhaps a journalistic metaphor can help us envision this constant internal activity. We call it *Dispatches from the Front*. In keeping with it, each noticing represents a report submitted by our senses—vision, hearing, smelling, touch, or, as Proust (1927/1982) discovered, taste—about what is happening in our surroundings, however unedited the submission may be. But even then, our senses will probably be presenting us with far more stimuli than we can properly attend to, which means that a kind of preliminary screening has already been at work: "In any situation, with its near infinite number of things that could be noticed," writes sociologist Peter Berger (1963, pp. 56–57), "we notice only those things that are important for our immediate purposes." Of course, several of our noticings would appear to possess no link whatever to "our immediate purposes," but simply be random impressions. Be that as it may, the stage we are talking about is the level of perception, yet it is more than perception alone. As psychologist Kenneth Gergen (1992) maintains, "in the very act of perception, we produce 'the events' of consciousness" (p. 91).

By "front" here, we also mean front *lines*. Many of our noticings ("It's snowing…Isn't that Frank?…It's after one o'clock") are, as Damasio (1999) has noted, already verbal events, which renders the line between noticing and nattering incredibly fine. Actual words and even sentences get uttered inside our heads. In effect, the events of consciousness represent the entry into "languageable" awareness of selected aspects of our actual existence. (Again, "selected" is the key, for by no means can we notice the whole of our existence.) Both our noticers and our natterers thus operate on the ever-shifting frontier where existence is transmuted into *texistence*.

Naturally, a number of variables is at play. How languageable our noticings will be depends on how literate we are in general, or how literarily literate, which could make the difference, for instance, between saying "Yuck! Snow!" to ourselves and "Now is the winter of our discontent"(Shakespeare, 1592/1974b, I, i, 1). How we frame our noticings will hinge as well upon our peculiar type of intelligence—of narrative intelligence, so to speak—and on the allegedly innate traits of our personality: whether we score high on, say, "neuroticism" or "openness to experience" (McRae & Costa, 2003, p. 34). Such a point bears remembering if we consider how additionally chaotic our core consciousness could be if we were afflicted with a condition such as, for example, Attention Deficit Disorder. The bottom line is that different people notice different things. Moreover, they natter about what they notice in different ways, depending as well on their particular habits or levels of competence in marshalling words to harness thoughts—habits that they have adapted from the family or culture they are shaped by, an insight we will come back to, next chapter, in discussing *narrative environment*. As for what we notice and natter about, as for what literally grabs our attention, this, too, can vary tremendously, depending on what typically most interests us, plus whatever might be happening around us and with whom we are sharing the experience. Sauntering through the countryside with a long-lost friend, listening to her muse about her life since our last encounter, what we natter to ourselves about is bound to be quite different than if we are cruising down the freeway on a summer afternoon with a car full of classmates, listening to the Rolling Stones.

Such variables (literacy, education, culture, context) determine, in turn, the range and rapidity of our noticings and natterings: whether our internal activity is comparatively sluggish and concerns but a few things at a time, or is helter-skelter and on multiple levels at once. In the case of the latter possibility, it might be said to be "saturated," which is Gergen's (1992) term for the hallmark of the postmodern self—or, more accurately, selves. For him, "each of the selves we acquire from [our relationships with] others can contribute to inner dialogues, private discussions we have with ourselves about all manner of persons, events, and issues" (p. 71). Thus, "we contain multitudes," he says; countless "possible selves": namely, "the multiple conceptions [we] harbour of what [we] might become, would like to become, or are afraid to become" (p. 72). To Gergen, such multiplicity and multiphrenia means that "committed identity," understood in terms of a singular self, is an "an increasingly arduous achievement" (p. 73). Gergen's position clearly leans to the skeptical end of the postmodern spectrum. As we will be arguing later on, however, there can still be identity amid the multiplicity. What is more, the comparative chaos of our noticers and natterers is scarcely peculiar to postmodern times. Is it not the essence of consciousness, in any era, to be "an airy skimming in endless mazes" (Field, 1934/1952, p. 117)?

Reading and Editing

Our various noticings and natterings, replete with the selves and storylines that each of them trails behind it (the vast majority of which are exceedingly short-lived), are forever vying for "our" attention. Each is endeavoring to persuade us that, however briefly, it deserves our total concentration; that the story it is telling is what is really going on. What or who this "us" is, however, is not so easy to define. Keeping in mind our journalistic image, plus what psychologists refer to as our *executive function*, the presence these voices are appealing to is analogous to a managing editor.

To this editor falls the task of maintaining a certain distance from the fray, of hovering above the rampant creativity of it all, and of reviewing, more or less judiciously, the steady stream of bulletins and fledgling editorials that are being submitted for publication in *The Daily News*—or again, a selection thereof, for there is never time to read them all. At this stage for certain, our reading is necessarily an under-reading. As editors, most of us are scrambling to keep up; and it is often on the fly that decisions get made about which submissions we accept. Similarly, it falls to the editor to determine what actions must be taken, insofar as decisions, too, are incipient storylines, plucked from the swirl and rendered substantial through our behavior in the world (MacIntyre, 1981). In this respect, our actions are guided far more by perceptions—or by stories—than by objective reality.

If nattering-noticing is, literally, brainstorming, then editing-reading is, broadly speaking, thinking. To put it another way, if in their impulsiveness or imperiousness the noticers-natterers correspond to the *id* and/or *superego*, then the reader is the *ego*: which is to say, the *I*, or simply "the conscious self" (Assagioli, 1976, p. 18). In other words, "the changing *contents* of our consciousness (the sensations, thoughts, feelings, etc.) are one thing, while the

'I,' the self, the *center* of our consciousness is another" (p. 18). In the words of Stephen Crites (1986), with James's (1962) "stream of consciousness" (p. 166) no doubt his inspiration, it is "that babbling little eddy I call my self" which "I can so readily single out" from "the great pool of intersubjective selfhood" (Crites, 1986, p. 156). As the center of relative unity and consistency amid the swirling multiplicity and flux, it is he or she who determines which, from all of the possible texts being proposed for consideration, are important enough to be readied for publication. It is he or she who determines what gets laid down as the official text for *the story of my life*, and what is available thereafter to pass along to others. To quote literature scholar and memoirist Patricia Hampl (1990): "*this*, we say somewhere inside of ourselves, is something I'm hanging onto" (p. 29). Otherwise, observes psychologist Daniel Schacter (2001), we "constantly discard what is no longer needed at the moment" (p. 28). The issue of just how complete such discarding might be is one we will return to in Chapter 7.

An example of the "hanging onto" process would be how, of everything that technically took place in our lives, certain events persist in standing out. They are, literally, the remains of the day: what gerontologists Tom Cole and Mary Winkler (1994) refer to as "the remnants of time" (p. 11). It is as if someone, somewhere, has decreed that we shall keep this, but not that. All too often, of course, events that we scarcely noted at the time managed to get registered all the same in some enduring way and, days or even decades hence, triggered by who knows what obscure cue, will suddenly resurface. The whole process is puzzling, to say the least. As religious studies scholar Ronald Grimes (1995) confesses: "Things I would like to recall I can't recall. Things I'd like to forget I can't forget. One doesn't get to choose which is which" (p. 73). Such insights raise the issues of subliminal awareness and of the relationship between our conscious activity and the various unconscious agendas that secretly we may harbor: issues that, while fascinating, are the subject of another book. In the meantime, the "somewhere" where the choices get made as to what to hang onto can be thought of as "that most human of 'regions,'" in psychologist Robert Kegan's (1982) words, "between an event and a reaction to it—the place where the event is privately composed, made sense of, ... where it actually becomes an event for that person" (p. 3). It is the inscrutable place where perception becomes experience.

In many instances, a particular noticing ("hey, an earthquake just demolished our house!") *must* be attended to. It is big news, dwarfing everything else that we were nattering about at the time. In this respect, the work of the reader can be frequently derailed, and a single, especially vocal natterer will usurp control, insisting that this and not that is essential and must be responded to at once. In short, we should not assume that the editor-reader is the dominant force. For many of us, much of the time perhaps, our readers are pushovers. The "'man-in-the-street' and even many well-educated people," notes psychologist Robert Assagioli (1976), tend to "drift on the surface of the 'mind-stream' and identify themselves with its successive waves" (p. 18). By the same token, our editor-readers may simply be particular natterers-noticers who have risen through the ranks in the society of self until they are promoted to the posh office at the end of the hall, with a marvelous vista of the avenue below.

Either way, the question must be asked: How do we know that this internal editor exists at all? Probably the most convincing evidence is that if we did not have such an aspect to our selves, however haphazard or inconsistent its functioning might be, we could not keep focused on what, for whatever reason, counts. Little of consequence would thus get accomplished. We would be driven by distraction, impulsive to a fault. We would follow our whims wherever they led, something we may be deliberately encouraged to do, in fact, when an analyst invites us to *free-associate*, to suspend our inner editor and allow our natterers freer reign. It is certainly what happens when we dream. When we dream, our editor "seems to disappear" entirely (Assagioli, 1976, p. 18). In effect, it is off duty, infinitely more relaxed than when our attention tends to wander in the middle of the day—when we *day*dream, in other words. But in our dreams we go completely with the flow. Any stream of images makes sense in its own weird way; any old storyline works. However, if we were to live as we dreamed (which some attempt to do), then we would be immobilized among competing alternatives as to which course to steer. We thus rely on our editor to actually *edit*: to rule out everything that, rightly or wrongly, seems inessential, not pertinent to the issue in question, not worth hearing of again.

In a real way, we are also reliant on our inner editor to determine what we *feel*. We saw earlier how our noticings and natterings involve imposing incipient interpretations on raw events, and inserting raw perceptions into primitive plots. And we saw how such plots imply a measure of emotional content. Insofar as the editor assesses which of the several storylines that are swirling around inside of us is most pertinent to matters at hand, the editor, one could argue, is the arbiter of our feelings. When it scuttles back and forth among the more compelling of these storylines ("she loves me, she loves me not"), then the ups and downs and endless combinations that can typify our emotional life are scarcely a surprise.

As a result of all of this inner activity, even though our reader-editor may be harder to discern than our noticers-natterers, the fact that we can function in a more or less normal manner—that we can get ourselves up in the morning, make it to work, and dispense our daily duties in an acceptable fashion—is compelling testimony to its continuing existence, or at least its ability to operate on automatic pilot. As the ambassador of sanity among the countless claims on our attention (and the emotions associated with them), it is our reader-editor who engages in the higher orders of narrative reasoning, assembling small stories into schemas or scripts that make sufficient sense to act upon, to talk about to others, and to file away for future reference.

Thanks to our inner reader-editor, then, we are able to hold our thoughts together and thus to navigate our world. But it is its ability to hold together our thoughts about ourselves—about *the story of my life*—that is of special interest to us here, for it corresponds to Damasio's extended consciousness. In other words, we mean its ability, day in and day out, to undertake a kind of "master process," as Bruner calls it (1994, p. 46), which, like the writer of an autobiography, creates a self by linking together present and past. It is on the shoulders of this reader-editor, then, that rests the task of determining what, out of everything that *might* be inscribed, *is* inscribed as the official text of our unfolding life: past, present, and future.

The implication here is that this inner text is continually thickening, an aspect of autobiographical memory we will return to in Chapter 7. Like an ever-expanding archive of previous issues of *The Daily News,* the material it contains accumulates with time, becoming increasingly substantial and itself constituting one of the primary focuses of the nattering that we do. The subject of such nattering, in other words, is very often our own remembered experience, or portions or versions thereof. It is for this ever-thickening collection of images and impressions, experiences and episodes, that we reserve the phrase *the story of my life.* That said, we use "story" in the loosest sense. What we mean is not a neat, artful, already plotted, entirely assembled narrative composition but a "rough draft" (LeJeune, quoted by Eakin, 1999, p. xxi), a living and changing collection of materials that, in the hands of the right teller (and reader), *could* become a really great story: coherent and rich, and teeming with meaning. Such a notion prompts a host of questions that constitute a backdrop to our musings later on.

For one, how might our inner reader develop over time? Does he or she acquire greater (perhaps more rigid) control over the noticing and nattering, or merely become more tired, and thus, potentially, drowned out by the buzz of different voices? What is the impact of such change on our understanding of what our story is? In turn, how does this change affect the object of our noticing and nattering? Can our reader be retrained—through, say, therapy or meditation—to attend more mindfully to the noticings and natterings and, at the same time, to step away from them, as experts in creativity might advise, and revel in the play of our thoughts? In general, can our reader assume more authority over the incessant inner activity, and not be blown about by it; telling the noticers-natterers what to do and what to look for (not the other way around); sending them on assignment to gather more relevant material? If so, what techniques would be appropriate and how can they be learned?

Still other questions we could ask are whether we can have more than one reader-editor inside of us at once. In other words, do we have certain sub-selves within the society of self who preside more regularly over the jangle of our noticers and natterers? If so, then what correspondence is there between each sub-self and the numerous environments that we move within? Do we read and edit our lives in one way with our colleagues at work, another with our spouse, and yet another with the members of our club or church? Also, as we age, do we actually become better at reading our lives at the micro level, or is it that, because of fewer distractions or interruptions, or simply less stimulation altogether, we actually have less to read in general (in the present, at least) and therefore greater time to recollect the past? Also, what is the relationship between micro-reading and *mindfulness;* that is, consciousness of the present moment? If we are not faithful in small things now (that is, in cultivating our skills at day-to-day self-reading), then how can we expect to reap the benefits of a rich life-text in later life? In general, how do our interpretive strategies and our editorial agendas change throughout our lives, and how are such changes linked to the actual experiences through which we live and—the theme we turn to now—the relationships in which we are enmeshed?

Narrating and Interacting

If only just a little, readers-editors are distanced from the bustle of incessant internal activity, pinned between the clamor of the natterers, on one hand, and the pressures encountered by the narrator on the other. If "natterer" refers to what occurs behind the scenes, then the "narrator" is the side of us that goes public, that has an actual voice we ourselves can hear—even if a host of inner voices assaults us at every point: "You can't say that!"; "That's not right!"; "You're lying and you know it!" (Some people can indeed do much of their narrating in a nattery manner, verbalizing whatever pops into their heads in the same basic disorder. Chatterboxes, we call them: motor-mouths.) In other words, the narrator's task, in close consultation with the editor, who is nearer to our inner text, is to scan the immediate environment, to divine the various agendas operating within it, and, on our behalf, to interface with others.

The narrator fulfills a distinctly social function in our dealings with the wider world, and therefore has a particular relationship with the reader. If the reader is at the mercy of the noticers and natterers, and dependent on whatever they submit (after all, a reader has to have something to read!), then the narrator is at the mercy of the reader. Narrators are only as good as the readers who feed them their material. To put it differently, readers write the speeches that narrators deliver. In the case of autobiography, paradoxically, narrator and reader effectively fuse, inasmuch as the activity of writing slows the narrating down. One becomes extra-mindful of what one is saying. One's inner editor is acutely engaged—at the same time as one is also fully aware of the audience for whom one's writing is intended.

In evaluating our countless noticings and natterings, our inner reader is, of course, far from unbiased, any more than a real editor is. In selecting—and inevitably summarizing—elements of even the most recent events to pass along to the narrator to recount, he or she is spinning them in a manner that, strictly speaking, is extrinsic to the events themselves. There are always editorial agendas, and these agendas are typically linked to the social situations in which we are placed. They are dependent on our ever-shifting perceptions of what our audience wants or needs to hear—whether, for instance, we ought to meet those needs or thwart those wants, and so on. As Bruner and Kalmar (1998) put it, alluding to the work of Erving Goffman, the narration of self inevitably involves "impression management" (p. 316; see also Linde, 1993; Ochs & Capps, 2002).

Amid the complicated, cognitive-emotive activity we blithely call "conversation," our narrator has an enormous responsibility. Involved in it is weaving selected noticings-natterings with relevant materials accessible to us through our episodic memory, as well as through our general store of knowledge (including knowledge of vocabulary and grammar), in such a way that what we say to the person(s) we are conversing with will sound coherent and sensible and will elicit the desired response. Moreover, it must accomplish this weaving more or less at once, with due attention to basic narrative structure and to acceptable formulae for recounting events. In the blink of an eye, it is his or her duty to discern what needs saying and what needs holding back. Inevitably, carrying out this duty leads not just to a quieting of the natterer, but to a certain narrowing-in of possible meaning. As sociologist John McKendy (2006) aptly words it, "Moving the words from the brain to the tongue can still the flutter of inner speech" (p. 496).

It sometimes happens, of course, that the narrator complains to the reader, "It won't go over very well if I say *that,* so give me something better to work with." In turn, the reader may need to instruct the noticers and natterers to "bring me some better material." An example of such a situation, and evidence that the narrator's function is ultimately different from the reader's function, just as the reader-editor is different from the noticer-natterer, is an experience familiar to us all. During a lull in the conversation, the person we are chatting with turns to us and asks, "A penny for your thoughts?" Instantly, our executive function is jolted out of automatic pilot and placed on full alert. Internal panic ensues: "What on earth do I say? I have so many thoughts, most of them unrelated to what we've been discussing. And some, in truth, are rather unflattering to my interlocutor. Which ones can I share that won't hurt his feelings, yet won't enmesh me in a lie?" Our answer? "I was just wondering how long it's supposed to keep snowing. Did you happen to catch the weather report this morning?"

Among the several issues such considerations bring to the surface is how reliable our narrators really are. The range of ways that narrators can be *unreliable* has understandably been of interest to literary scholars—Wayne Booth's explorations in *The Rhetoric of Fiction* (1961) being a case in point. It is clear that most of our internal natterers can scarcely be trusted to shepherd us through our day in a sane, dependable manner. Yet insofar as, inevitably, they must tailor what they say to the audience in front of us, how dependable can our narrators be as well? Another issue concerns what, a little further on, we call our "storying style" (Randall, 1995, pp. 308ff). How many such styles is each of us capable of juggling in our dealings with others, and how much might these styles change from one stage of our life to another, or one social context to the next? In turn, how are they linked to the society of selves inside of us—and to our inner reader? Are the voices that others hear us using the same ones that we employ in talking to ourselves, and which comes first? Do we natter first and narrate later, or the other way around?

Developmentally, it has been argued that the narrating self predates the nattering self, and possibly the reading self as well. The research of psychologists such as Katherine Nelson and Robyn Fivush (2000) supports the idea, for instance, that it is in learning how to talk to others that we learn how to talk to ourselves. In effect, we are social beings first and private ones second. We will come back to this notion later on. In the meantime, it is the reader mode more than the narrator mode in which most of us tend to live. Even the most gregarious of us spend infinitely more time chatting to ourselves than communicating with others (Bickle, 2003, p. 196). That said, our interactions with others are far from inconsequential, all the more so when they endure over great spans of time—as with many elderly individuals, for instance, who may well have been married to the same partner for 50 years. Our stories do not develop in a social vacuum. Directly or not, they unfold within an intricate network of narrative environments. Before we turn from the micro level of that process to the more macro level (our focus in Chapter 3), we need to say something about what, from the perspective of poetics, could be deemed our ultimate achievement.

THE NOVELTY OF NARRATIVE: FROM LITERATURE TO LIFE

"The story of my life" is no mere figure of speech. At every turn, life and story are wedded. They are "internally related," writes philosopher Guy Widdershoven (1993), insofar as life both "informs and is formed by stories" (p. 2). Certainly, the ties between life text and literary text have been acknowledged by various sources. "The structure of a person's life," observes philosopher Stuart Charmé (1984), "resembles a literary text in some important way" (p. 51). The question, however, is in *what* way. To begin with, the very category *literary text* includes a variety of narrative forms. A short story is one of them, but so, too, is a stage play or an epic poem, even an autobiography. In our view, however, a full-length novel makes a particularly helpful heuristic for envisioning the complexities of the life–literature link, inasmuch as it is the most extensive, and intensive, narrative form to date. A novel presents a vision of an entire universe, and as such is a unique way of knowing. Yet the concept of lives as novels—and the corollary idea of selves as novelists—is, in itself, not especially novel.

"Every person's life is worth a novel," observes psychotherapist Erving Polster (1987). As Jean-Paul Sartre has said of his autobiography, *The Words*, it is a "true novel," "a novel I believe in" (Charmé, 1984, p. 79). Philosopher Jonathan Glover (1988), pondering the nature of what he calls "self-creation," argues that "self-creation tends to make a life like a novel by a single author" (p. 152). The process begins early. Says child psychologist Allyssa McCabe (1997), children themselves are "emerging novelists, assembling their life stories from the numerous emotional incidents in their daily lives." As she sees it, "they are tellers of the stories they are busy assembling into coherent life histories" (p. 140). For some therapists, this line of thinking reflects precisely what they see happening in clients' lives. Mandy Aftel (1996) suggests, for example, that "in our daily lives we are ad hoc novelists. ... We are both the heroes of our own plots and their creators. In a very real sense, we are the authors of our own lives" (p. 16). Polster (1987) goes as far as to claim that the novel is "a paradigm for the therapist," one that, compared with other media, "comes closer to the scope of a person's life" (p. 11). Indeed, the novelist and the therapist share "a kinship in the deep exploration of human behavior and awareness" (p. x). Like the novelist, he says, the therapist can "sense the drama in people's lives—the plots they live through, the suspense they create, the discovery of unique characteristics and events, the microcosmic commentary each person's life offers, and the inevitably creative passage through problematic experiences" (p. ix).

For sociologist Mary Rogers (1991), who contrasts it with academic writing in general, the novel "probes the meaning of individuality, the challenge of human relationships, and the constitution of human worlds" (p. 82). Though by no means without its detractors, the novel, we feel, thus comes closest of any story-form to reflecting the intricacies of real life. For Mikhail Bakhtin, whose concept of the polyphonic novel lies behind Hermans's (2002) "dialogical self," it is "the one grand literary form...capable of a kind of justice to the inherent polyphonies of life" (quoted in Lodge, 1988, p. 137)—the very sort of polyphonies that we noted a while back. Contrasting the tightly plotted short story, of which he himself was a master, with the rambling novels of, say, Hardy or Dickens, Somerset Maugham (1938/1945) assesses the latter as "shapeless and unwieldy...huge, straggling, intimate...wandering in and out of curious characters who have nothing much to do with the theme" (p. 209). Given such an assessment, it is, overall, the *novelty* of our lives that bears closer inspection—their quality as vast, many-levelled, yet ultimately distinctive compositions, as different from one another as the novels of Dickens are from those of Maugham: a quality that, one can claim, increases as we age (see Hooker & McAdams, 2004).

To speak of the novelty of lives, however, is not to imply that everyone will automatically identify with such a notion, for clearly, there are many who—if they read at all—have an aversion to fiction in general, preferring genres that they perceive to be more factual instead, like biography or history. Nor is it to imply an exact equation between a novel and a life. Common sense suggests that, yet again, we are talking about two different orders. But the difference, we propose, is one of degree and not of kind. Between them, as between life and literature in general, lie what Freeman (2007) calls "deep continuities" (p. 223). "Human life," he says, "*pours* itself quite naturally into narrative form" (p. 236). To lay the foundation for ideas we will be working with later on, we need to spend some time considering the continuities to which Freeman is alluding. At the same time, we need to acknowledge the discontinuities, too, for while the link between lifestory and literary story is more than metaphorical, it is less than literal. It is also rather complicated, for at various points the continuities and the discontinuities would appear to come together. Perhaps some of the more obvious of the latter can serve to get us started. They have to do with space and time.

In terms of space—which is to say, its physical features—the story which a novel recounts is contained between the covers, confined to what appears upon the page. As we shall see in Chapter 4, for it to be brought to life requires the imagination and intelligence of a living, breathing reader. As a corollary, the more imaginative and intelligent the reader is, the more alive the story becomes. Morever, the more such readers read it, the more its life extends to the world beyond it. A *life*story, to the extent it is containable at all, is bound, not by a book, but by a body: the body of the person living it. It is an embodied narrative.

In terms of time, it can take us anywhere from three hours to three weeks to wade through a novel, depending on how long it is and how steadily we read. To get through our own lifestory, however, inasmuch as we are composing it and comprehending it from within, takes us…as long as it takes us. As long as we are conscious and alive, we never quite reach The End. It is continually receding from view, and with it, any definitive evaluation as to what sort of story it is. Literary theorist Gary Morson (1994) sums things up succinctly: "we can stand outside the narratives we read but not outside the lives we live" (p. 20). In other words, we never have the whole story in our possession, let alone in our consciousness, because, at bottom, we *are* the story, and are "storying" it as we go—the focus of our thinking in Chapter 3.

Shifting from time and space to internal dynamics, a novel is constituted of events and situations that are linked in what, within the fictional universe that the author is creating, is a logical manner—"story logic," one could say (Herman, 2002). Unlike in a chronicle, which is merely a listing of one thing after another, in a novel events are *emplotted,* so that basically one thing leads to another: X happens so that Y can happen so that Z can happen, and so on. Although consisting of any number of intertwining subplots, the plot as a whole thus has an identifiable beginning, middle, and end. And when we read it, we do so from the beginning—or at least from page one of Chapter One—which in some novels, of course, need not be the start of the story itself. A detective novel, for instance, is commonly a story within a story: the story of people reconstructing the story of the crime—which, if you will, is the *main* story. As famed filmmaker Jean-Luc Godard astutely observes, a story "should have a beginning, a middle, and an end, but not necessarily in that order" (quoted in Fulford, 1999, p. 143). Indeed, a characteristic of many postmodern novels and movies is a carefully contrived *dis*order that flouts the coherence we associate with "realistic" novels. In any case, when we read a novel, we read from the beginning of the book (if not the beginning of the story) toward its middle and its end: an end that is already in place, even if we have no idea what precisely it might entail. If we are familiar with the genre (romance, thriller, etc.), then we are bound to have our guesses, but unless we sneak a peek beforehand, the specifics of how everything "turns out" cannot be known until we reach the final page. Even then, and even if it is clear, for instance, "whodunit," what The End *means* may continue to exercise our minds. In fact, this is in many respects the trademark of great fiction: the story ends, but no end of meanings are capable of being gleaned from it. It is open-ended, an aspect of both literature and life-as-literature we will be revisiting further on.

A lifestory, too, consists of events and situations—millions of them in fact, of all different types, on all different levels. Yet unless we have in mind a person who is rigidly religious, it would be an enormous stretch of reasoning to insist that, somewhere behind the scenes, some cosmic Author has specifically selected them, emplotting them precisely into preplanned chapters and scenes. In the same way, a lifestory has a beginning, middle, and end, in the basic sense that "we're born, we suffer, we die" (J. Gardner, 1985, p. 43). But if we think of reading as, at the very least, following the plot, then it is clear that we do not start reading it right at The Beginning—which is to say, at birth—but only after the action is a good bit underway: in medias res. Moreover, by the time we become aware that it might indeed be some sort of story we are actually in the middle of, we are likely to be reading it at a level that is far more advanced than it would have been at the outset. And the longer we live, the more advanced that level is apt to be. One could almost say that, over time, our stories themselves teach us how to read them, and that only in later life are we finally up to the task.

But even in later life, our lifestory is, technically, still unfolding. The End has not yet been written, which means that we lack the benefit of parameters on what, in the interim, the meaning(s) of our story might be. What is more, how the ending gets written depends in no small measure on us: on the decisions we take and choices we make—of partner and residence, lifestyle and career. All of these serve to determine the genre of story that our life-course traces, at least in our own minds. In other words, how the story ends hinges on what sort of story we believe it to be: an adventure, a mystery, or a parable of something else—or, if we take the idea of sub-selves seriously, all such genres at once. In the words of Jungian psychologist James Hillman (1989), "while one part of me knows the soul goes to death in tragedy, another is living a picaresque fantasy, and a third engaged in the heroic comedy of improvement" (p. 81). Thus, the course of our life and the genre, or genres, by which we conceive it, can be uncannily connected, which takes us back to storying style, a concept we will return to later on. As Maugham (1938/1945) admits of his fiction: "I have taken living people and put them into the situations, tragic or comic, that their characters suggested. I might well say that they invented their own stories" (p. 83).

Another way novels and lives may be viewed as discontinuous is that the text of a novel is literally there: on the page, in black and white. It cannot be changed. What is more, it has been put there by an author who, in the final analysis, is outside the story, though again, what we make of that text, as readers, is in many ways up to us. With a lifestory, however, what exactly the text might be is challenging to discover. In reflecting on precisely this puzzle, Freeman (1997a) invites us to picture a book "whose words changed every time you…read it—not its meanings, but its *words*" (p. 376). Such a book, the book of life, could rightly be said to consist of the actual events of our existence, from birth to now (though minus our death), and these too, of course, are simply there, in the basic sense that what has happened, has happened. At the same time, it could be said to consist of all of the interpretations we have given those events—or at least the ones we can recall. The majority will not be memorable at all. And each time we recall those that are, we may interpret them—may literally "re-member" them—in rather different ways. As we will see more fully in Chapter 7, memory is notoriously malleable. The upshot is that, given the incessant ramblings and re-memberings of our memory-imagination, not to mention the persistent addition of fresh events, the text of our life is continually changing. At bottom, that text is us. We are *in* the novel of our life and its unfolding *is* our life, comforting or tormenting us, protecting or imprisoning us—or both.

To express such matters from a different angle, the author of a work of literature is clearly outside of the story, however much he or she was inside of it while immersed in writing it. With our lifestory, however, insofar as we could be called its author at all (a question we will come back to in Chapter 3), we are thoroughly inside of the text, and inside the story. In a very real sense, we make it up as we go. No matter how much we may rely upon habit and convention, composing a life is an act of improvisation (Bateson, 1989). In Polkinghorne's (1988) words, "we are in the *middle* of our stories and…are constantly having to revise the plot as new events are added to our lives" (p. 150)—revise our idea, that is, of where our stories are headed, our vision of what sorts of stories they yet might be. Philosopher of religion Don Cupitt (1991) goes as far as to assert that "our life is only a bundle of stories, mostly half-finished. We are, and will for the most part remain, a lot of loose ends" (p. 153). "Loose ends, missed opportunities, and mere accidents," echoes Morson (1999), "compose the very fabric of real life, as they do not do in literature" (p. 284). Lives as *stories* are notoriously "messy texts" (Denzin, 1997, p. 225).

Morson provides us with a concept that speaks to this improvisatory and, as it were, unkempt dimension of the novels we are. It is "processual" fiction (pp. 278ff), a concept arising from his analysis of works by Russian authors Leo Tolstoy and Fyodor Dostoyevsky. Like those of Dickens, these novels were published in serial form, without the authors' knowing from one instalment to the next how their central characters would behave nor how the story as a whole would conclude, and having "no possibility of altering earlier parts to make them fit with later ones" (p. 277). Processual fiction is akin, then, to journalism, in the sense that the end of the story is never in sight. Journalist Robert Fulford (1999) considers a similar link. Reflecting on how popular novelists "heading for the best-seller lists" pack their stories with events and issues that, with astonishing closeness, mirror the very events and issues with which the news bombards us every day, Fulford proposes that they are essentially "imitating journalists" (p. 79). Extending this insight, we might argue that there is a link, then, between our inner editor, struggling to adjudicate among the competing claims of our various noticers and natterers, and the author of a lengthy work of fiction, trying to assess which, from among the countless hunches and tangents that suggest themselves for emplotment, should be committed to the page—from chapter to chapter, sentence to sentence, word to word. In this respect, an author is always a reader.

The blurring of the line between author and reader is no less the case, one can argue, in the vast processual fictions that we are perpetually composing around our own unique lives. Ultimately, we read our stories from within them, in The Middle. We read not with The End already in position, merely waiting for us to get to it, but still to be decided, whether it takes forty years to get to it or only forty days. And what sort of end it will be hangs not just on what we expect it or want it to be, but on the choices we are making now. What comes to mind is the *Choose Your Own Adventure* books so popular with children, where the reader determines from page to page which twist the plot takes next, and with which of several endings the narrative will conclude. Just to add to the complexity, then, the reader and the author of a lifestory, even more so than a literary story, are the same person—as, for that matter, are the narrator and the character (or characters). They are all us, and all are integral to the entire story-making enterprise.

Another discontinuity, yet one that, ironically, turns into a continuity too, is that the story-world of a novel, by virtue of possessing a set number of characters and events and an already determined Beginning and End, is technically closed, no matter how many thoughts it may set off within us while reading it and how much its meaning eludes us long after we finish. By comparison, and as we shall consider more closely in Chapter 10, the story-world of a lifestory is as open as can be. There is simply no end to the meaning we can read into it, to a large degree because we are ultimately inside of it, meaning we never quite reach The End. If we could, then it would surely set some limits on what the story is about. As it is, that story is still under construction, and so it will be (or can be) until we die. Morson (1999) puts it this way: "In life we live our rough drafts; they are all we have" (p. 284).

Since we will be revisiting at various points the whole question of continuity–discontinuity between lived story and literary story, we will restrict ourselves for now to two somewhat less tangible dimensions of story-worlds: atmosphere and theme.

When reading a novel, it is not uncommon to find that it has a particular air about it; in other words, it stirs up certain feelings. Indeed, long after we replace it on the shelf, the mere thought of it can conjure up memories of the experience we had when we first read it. We might even recall the chair we were sitting in, or what was happening in our marriage or other aspects of our life. Naturally, as a quality of a literary work, its *atmosphere* is extremely subjective. For one reader, *The English Patient* (Ondaatje, 1992) will be wrapped in a fog of beguiling melancholy; for another, it will be just one more book about the war. Besides our life circumstances at the time that we read it, a story's atmosphere will be a function of numerous factors. Among them will be its genre, the actual events around which it revolves, its characters, and how they remind us of people we know, including ourselves. More than anything perhaps, it will be a function of the author's talents at creating a story-world that enlivens those elements in a particular style—one that may resonate, in fact, with the one(s) we use in storying our own lives. Atwood's style is distinct from Naipaul's, Hemingway's from Henry James's. It is not just that the worlds they weave concern different contexts, reflect different cultures, and wrestle with different issues, but the manner in which those issues are presented can vary enormously in terms of the actual vocabulary, imagery, and point of view that the author employs. Overall, atmosphere may be the primary reason that some of us read in the first place, as we consume novel after novel by our favourite writers. Only after we have had our fill of the feeling their stories elicit are we ready to switch to another.

A lifestory, too, can possess a distinctive atmosphere, one that can seem to have little to do with the events that actually make it up. It certainly can do so in the minds of the people who surround the individual living it—with, in their view, his or her inimitable style. Even then, that atmosphere is apt to be rather different for each of them—more or less nuanced, definable, and so forth. Some may read that individual as just plain moody. Others may say that while, true, he can be moody, he is extremely complicated as well, even tortured, and thus, understandably, has a huge cloud of sadness hovering around him. As for what is happening inside the individual himself—the main character of the story, as it were—at some pre-verbal level, he may well experience his life to have a peculiar feel to it, what McAdams (1996) calls "narrative tone" (p. 136). But it is a tone that is capable of changing from one stage of life to another, or even more frequently than that. One minute, our life seems a hopeless tragedy in which nothing—*nothing*—will ever work out in our favor. The next minute, perhaps because someone pays us a compliment or we hear a piece of encouraging news, a somewhat different tale starts coming into focus. In a twinkling, we flit from a bad day to a good day, from a glass half empty to a glass half full.

To shift to the notion of *theme*, one feature of novels that frequently attracts us is the particular insights or opinions, the messages or motifs, that run through the story and lend it a certain coherence. As with everything else about stories, such themes are bound up with multiple elements at once: the genre in question, the mode of narration, the events and characters involved, and how the events and characters interact. To put the point another way, themes are not located in particular passages. Although in some passages their presence seems especially apparent, they tend to permeate the work, and not just one or two of them but many. As novelist Diane Johnson (2001) reminds us, "any novel has lots of themes." Indeed, "the major theme of a given work" is simply "the sum of all its ideas" (p. 111). Quoting E. M. Forster, she thus sees a novel is a "'spongy tract' ... a tissue of ideas so dense and various it would be impossible to tease them all out" (p. 112).

Applied to lived story, such insights suggest a host of implications. Various researchers have proposed that lives, too, have themes. Psychoanalyst Heinz Lichtenstein (1977) speaks, for example, of "identity-themes," while psychologist Henry Murray talks about "unity themas" (1938). Gerontologist Sharon Kaufman observes that (1986), "people create themes" that "explain, unify, and give substance to their perceptions of who they are and how they see themselves participating in social life" (p. 25). Psychologists Mihaly Csikszentmihalyi and Olga Beattie (1979) refer to these simply as "life-themes." A life-theme, they propose, is "a problem or set of problems which a person wishes to solve above everything else and the means the person finds to achieve solution" (p. 48). In effect, life-themes are recurring dilemmas or "conflicts" (Erikson, 1968), which, over time, lend a distinct consistency and structure to our lives.

The point we simply wish to make for now is that factoring the narrative variable into our view of human experience, and perceiving lives as stories, renders such a concept—like that of atmosphere, character, or plot—all the more enticing to consider when probing the continuities and discontinuities between literature and life. Many of them we have touched upon already, and others we will look at later in the book. Among them are the experience of *story-time* we can have amid the two types of texts, literary and lived; the multiplicity of stories each type embodies; the notion of narrative coherence, as of meaning, and how it accumulates as the story develops; the role of the narrator in mediating the story and the reader in receiving it; plus the intertextuality of novels and lifestories alike as regards their penetration by countless other texts in turn.

What should be obvious by now is the difficulty of asserting that life-stories are—or are not—"novels." Too many conceptual complexities are at issue. We certainly cannot go down through a catalogue of literary terms and demonstrate a tidy correspondence between the two: "The 'plot' in a novel is this, while in a lifestory it is that," and so on. We are therefore in no way finished with our contemplation of the life–literature link. In the meantime, it is worth reviewing the broad contours of the intricate process whereby, day in and day out, we *story* our lives.

Three

STORYING LIFE:

THE DEVELOPMENT OF IDENTITY

We make stories about the world and to a large degree live out their plots.
    —Carol Pearson (1989, p. xxv)

"My story" can never be wholly mine, alone, because I define and articulate my existence with and among others, through the various narrative models—including literary genres, plot structures, metaphoric themes, and so on—my culture provides.
    —Mark Freeman (2001, p. 287)

The truth about stories is that that's all we are.
    —Thomas King (2003, p. 2)

In moving from the neurology to the novelty of personal narrative, we have begun laying a conceptual foundation for the poetics of growing old. What we need to do now is to take these efforts further. Having considered how, at the micro level, narrative activity is at work in our most primitive perceptions of reality, not to mention in our everyday conscious experience, and having introduced the idea of lives as novels-in-the-making, we are ready to switch to the macro level and outline the more general dimensions of *storying* lives.

While the dimensions we have in mind—environment, development, and identity—may be familiar to readers already attuned to the narrative turn, they merit some spelling out, for they are pivotal to the perspective we are pursuing throughout this book.

First, we look at the social dimensions. That this is our starting-point is instructive. People do not "narrativize" their lives as isolated, atomistic beings but in relation to an array of interpersonal environments amid which they negotiate their understandings of who they are. As core consciousness gives way to extended consciousness, a narrative model of self is preeminently a relational model of self. True, some people lead individualistic existences, whether by circumstance or choice. And as those dear to them pass on or their mobility is more and more curtailed, many older adults are obliged to live alone. Still, from a narrative perspective, none of us is an island. If nothing else, we participate in a narrative environment of one: *me, myself, and I*—once more, the society of mind. The second dimension concerns the process whereby our stories expand with time. Though this expansion—this development—takes place in concert with others, directly or not, the individual is our central focus here. Continuing even further in an individual vein, the third dimension is narrative identity. To discuss it means, among other things, to acknowledge the paradox of a self that is simultaneously author and narrator, character and reader, of the texts by which it envisions who it is.

NARRATIVE ENVIRONMENT: THE LARGER STORIES WE LIVE WITHIN

What Narrative Environments Are

A narrative environment can be understood in at least two overlapping senses. The first concerns the actual collection of written and oral narratives—of movies and novels, jokes and rumors, gossip and news—that we move within each day. This collection is continually changing, of course, and will certainly vary from community to community, country to country, culture to culture. One could also say, though (and it is the primary way we think of it in this book), that a narrative environment is simply any context in which we talk about our lives, whether to others or ourselves (Bruner, 1990, p. 94). An equivalent term, therefore, is "discursive environment" (Holstein & Gubrium, 2000, p. 228). Given that we are languaged creatures, our sense of self necessarily evolves within narrative environments. The ways in which we interact with other people, submits psychologist Robyn Fivush (2004), deeply influence our ability not merely "to construct a coherent narrative account" of a particular event, but also to articulate its significance for our lifestory as a whole (p. 89). To the extent that "a life as lived is inseparable from a life as told," as Bruner puts it (1987, p. 31), much therefore hinges on the environments that shape us. For it is not just ways of talking that they mediate; it is ways of thinking, too. As "interpretive communities," to use the phrase of literary theorist Stanley Fish (1977/1989, p. 1252), they school us—explicitly or not, consistently or not—in a vast range of beliefs and perspectives, of assumptions about the nature of reality, and of overall ways of making meaning in our lives. To participate in a particular environment is, to some extent, to accept those ways as valid.

The most immediate example is the family we grew up in: our principal "culture of embeddedness" (Kegan, 1982, pp. 115ff)—a culture that has been referred to as our "first and in many ways only coherent symbolic universe" (Csikszentimihalyi & Beattie, 1979, p. 61). From day one, in other words, we enter "a play whose enactment is already in progress," and "whose somewhat open plot determines what parts we may play and toward what denouements we may be heading" (Bruner, 1990, p. 34). Amidst this family drama, not only did we breathe in themes and tensions it can take a lifetime to decipher, but we inherited discernible patterns for talking about our actions, articulating our emotions, and conveying our ideas. We were tutored in a repertoire of "narrative practices" (Holstein & Gubrium, 2000) and "narrative templates" (Abbott, 2002, p. 7) for experiencing the present, envisioning the future, and remembering the past. We were schooled in a set of acceptable modes for applying our built-in narrative intelligence (Randall, 1999) to the complex cognitive task of understanding our surroundings, construing our experiences, and interpreting the intentions and behaviors of others. And through our pores, we absorbed, not just a certain type of narrative tone, but indeed ready-made "forms of self-telling" (Bruner, 1987, p. 16). We soaked up entire strategies for composing and editing the stories of our lives—not only the little stories about what happened on our way to the mall, but the big stories concerning our life as a whole and where it is headed. Becoming (literally) conversant with "the family genre" (Bruner & Weisser, 1991, p. 141), with its "interpretive repertoires" (Bamberg, 1997, p. 90), was an unspoken condition for acceptance as an intelligible member within it.

Powerful though it is, no narrative environment is ever static. Like our individual narratives, they are constantly changing. They are "going concerns," as narrative sociologists James Holstein and Jaber Gubrium (2000) would call them (pp. 94–95). No matter how rigid it seemed when we were growing up, our family, for instance, was not the same environment when we left home as it was when we were born. If for no other reason, the players who were central to it—ourselves, our siblings, our parents—aged (perhaps even died) in the interim. Outside and inside alike, it changed in countless little ways. Not only that, but we ourselves contributed to its transformation. In short, we shape the stories we are part of even as they shape us.

Another point is that each environment has both a history and a story. The history of our family is one thing: the objective facts of our collective existence. What we make of that history, however—the episodes that stand out for each of us and the overall myth we have composed of it inside our own minds—is another matter. The difference is between the "outside story" and the "inside story" (Randall, 1995, pp. 48–54); between actual events and our interpretations of them, or between textual features and reader constructions, a distinction we will discuss in Chapter 4. Whenever we gather with our siblings, each of us will have our own version of what "our family" is, which can make for some hilarious exchanges once we start to reminisce! ("That's not what happened." "'T is too." "'T is not.") But beside the unique chain of circumstances that distinguished ours from the family next door, each of us will experience it as having its own set of subplots, conflicts, and themes—and as casting us as particular sorts of characters within it.

What is more, we live within several such stories at once: those of the family, the community, the nation—each with its collection of characters (including ourselves) and its constituent events. Overlapping in endless ways, these constitute the intricate, multilayered setting in which *the story of my life* develops and from which it derives much of its structure, substance, and depth. In effect, such stories live within us as much as we live within them. Their characters and events, their genres and themes, are interwoven in an ever-widening web that is outside us and inside us at once—infinitely extensive and infinitely thick, threaded through with myriad story-strands that wander off in numberless directions in space and time alike. In using words like *culture* or *history*, it is precisely such networks we imply. And what a tangled web we live within.

How Narrative Environments Differ

Large or small, narrative environments can vary tremendously in terms of the history and geography, the culture and economy, that shapes them and informs them. An affluent Parisian *arondissement* constitutes a rather different setting for storying our lives than a Newfoundland hamlet on the edge of a sea whose fish are all but gone. By the same token, a city in eighteenth-century China, with its layers of cultural history and its ancestral ghosts, provided a context for storying lives that was unquestionably different from that of a coal-mining community in the hills of West Virginia in the depths of the Depression. In such broad ways, the environments in which our predecessors made sense of their lives were nothing like those in which we have been storying our own. And so it goes, from generation to generation. Somewhat less obvious dimensions for comparing narrative environments include, however, their overall atmosphere, their closedness or openness, and their unspoken rules of communication and how those rules get enforced.

For instance, some of us grew up in households that felt dull and confining. There were definite, if tacit, restrictions on who could say what and how they could say it, and dark secrets behind the scenes. Furthermore, many of the principal "family stories" that were sanctioned for telling reinforced the need for "conformity" and "unquestioning loyalty" (Parry & Doan 1994, p. 72). In consequence, our own unique "voice" was essentially "silenced" (Fivush, 2004, pp. 76–77). Meanwhile, at our friends' homes, everything seemed so open and free. In an atmosphere rife with talk, we felt we could say almost anything we wished. We felt accepted whenever we visited and were keen to be invited back. With no "company" around, of course, and no need to be on their best behavior, our friends no doubt had their own codes of conduct by which they were bound, as constraining for them as ours were for us.

Besides our family of origin, there is the family we create when we start having children of our own, and beyond that, the extended family that embraces both our partner and ourselves: aunts, uncles, cousins, in-laws—the entire clan. Viewed as an overgrown family, each community and each culture also constitute distinctive narrative environments, all the more so when they revolve around a particular language. French towns have narrative environments that can be quite unlike English ones. With different idioms and grammars, lives get talked into being in markedly different ways. Nations, too, are distinctive environments, not just because of their particular native languages, but because of their entire cultural and political heritage. Very broadly, Americans breathe a different narrative environment—a different zeitgeist—from Italians, as do Argentinians from Tibetans. Within each context, despite surface similarities in lifestyle or fashion, there can be an entirely different "feel" to how people engage with one another, not to mention a unique set of assumptions as to what a good life, and thus a good life*story*, entails.

But even within the same general culture, particular communities can possess distinct kinds of narrative environment. Visiting Manhattan from Iowa, for instance, you might think that New Yorkers talk rather funny. Not only are their expressions unusual and their accents strange, but overall they speak more forthrightly than the folks back home. Similarly, the industry or institution we work for will have its peculiar brand of communicative environment, as will our profession. Indeed, advancing from novice to insider means becoming ever more comfortable within it. On the job, English professors employ terminology that is notably at variance from that of workers in an auto plant or nurses in palliative care. Jargon—let alone jokes and slang—that make eminent sense in one situation will sound out of place in another. Not just *what* people talk about will differ, but *how.*

The same holds true for academe. Psychologists are taught to think and write, to view the world in general, in manner that is decidedly different from that of their counterparts in medicine or law, in statistics or theology. And each major religion—not to mention each denomination and each congregation that compose it—will have a specialized narrative environment. Encountering its rituals and traditions, its scriptures and strictures, people desiring membership within it will quickly learn that there are ways of talking—about one's self, one's thoughts, one's life—that are heartily supported, while others are sharply discouraged: "We don't talk that way here. You must put those thoughts out of your mind." It is similar with politics. Republicans talk differently from Democrats, Conservatives from Liberals. Buzz phrases bandied about by the faithful of one party will hardly be heard in a gathering of the other. Very broadly, gender, too, is linked to distinctive environments, distinctive storying styles. How women and men talk about their lives, how they express their emotions and listen to each other, and how "man-made language" (Spender, 1980) may generally be inadequate to articulate female experience—such questions have received their share of scholarly attention (see Tannen, 1990).

Gender, politics, religion, culture: all are examples of macro narrative environments, of *master narratives,* one could call them. All have deep roots in time and tradition, all are on some level linked, and all play potent roles in how people construe their identities, present and past. For instance, compared to people from Eastern cultures, those from Western cultures, argues Fivush (2004), "talk more about their past experiences, claim to have more memories and earlier memories from childhood, and focus more on the self when narrating the past" (p. 76)—a point that has enormous implications for how one's identity is experienced. In addition, taking the gender variable into consideration, Western adult women, says Fivush, "[tell] longer, more detailed, and more vivid stories of their past than adult men" (p. 77).

Every day, of course, we move in and out of countless micro environments as well, from the formal to the informal and the enduring to the ad hoc. Besides our family or our marriage are the clubs or classes we are members of and the circles in which we move. Within each one of them, we tell our lives and story our worlds—we talk to others and even to ourselves—in ways that are more or less unique. Even a conversation, which might last only minutes and be carried on with someone whom we never meet again, constitutes its own little narrative environment. In terms of the co-construction of storylines by which we frame the contents of our exchange, the extraordinary intricacy of so-called ordinary conversation is, once again quite rightly, the focus of more and more research. By means of discourse analysis, such research examines, among other things, the crucial "difference between telling a story *to* another and telling a story *with* another" (Ochs & Capps, 2002, p. 2; see also Linde, 1993; Bavelas, Coates, & Johnson, 2000).

Overall, each friendship we enjoy—itself, a continuing conversation—develops its own brand of narrative environment, its own rules of engagement, its own codes for talking and listening, for sharing and withholding, not to mention its own history and thus story. Between the story of me and the story of thee is the story of us. Within the friendship, not only do we share a unique set of events, but our respective ways of looking at life, our ways of making meaning, our actions and ethics even, are molded—are authored—in a particular manner (see Cottle, 2002). Depending on how mutual is the connection between us or how frequently we meet, we *coauthor* one another's lives in directions that can vary quite significantly from those that unfold in our relationships with others. Not only that, but over time, each of our friends comes to subscribe to a certain version of our story, or to safeguard certain portions of it—as, invariably, we will do for them. Indeed, swirling around inside of us at any given time will be a set of nascent storylines (or natterings) concerning what is happening in their worlds, too. Narratively speaking, our lives are intertwined.

Finally, insofar as every novel we read or movie we watch evokes in us a particular story-world, it too, as we shall be seeing in Chapter 4, constitutes a narrative environment. It fosters in our imagination a genre of self-talk, and invites the trying-on of templates for storying our lives, which we are normally oblivious to amid the other environments that we move within each day.

Why Narrative Environments Matter

Narrative environments matter enormously since what is at stake for us, at bottom, is the stories by which we live. No narrative environment is innocent. For better or worse, each has an impact, major or minor, enduring or fleeting, creative or destructive, on how we experience our selves-in-time.

Some environments—some families, as we have seen—are best described as rich. With an abundance of templates to choose from, few restrictions seem placed on how we can talk about our lives. As long as we can make ourselves understood, we enjoy remarkable freedom of speech. Within such families, children are not "seen and not heard," as the saying goes, but are encouraged by their parents to be "highly elaborative" when recounting past events (Fivush, Haden, & Reese, 1995, p. 345). As a consequence, their "memory-talk" (Eakin, 1999, p. 106) becomes detailed and nuanced. Besides parent–child ones, other relationships within such families can be wonderfully elaborative as well, with each person playing a distinct and supportive part in coauthoring others. As each individual's story thus flourishes and expands, so, sooner or later, will the stories of all. Moreover, such environments can be rich in the more literal sense still that there is a wide range of stories for their members to read or watch or hear, all the better to awaken their curiosity and broaden their respective horizons. In contrast, however, many environments can only be called impoverished, where "impoverished" need not be taken in an economic sense alone. Certainly, poverty and all that frequently goes with it—unemployment, illiteracy, abuse, despair—can give rise to an impoverished climate in a narrative sense as well. Yet abundance and affluence can be equally bleak in terms of their ability to facilitate narrative development.

Historical era is an issue here as well. Regardless of their country or culture, people today, one could argue, live their lives, and thus age and change, in accordance with rather different narrative formula than did people 10, 20, or 100 years ago. Narratively speaking, the *form* of aging and not merely its content can vary from era to era, cohort to cohort, and environment to environment in significant and unsettling ways. While certain environments are obviously restrictive in a deliberate manner—most notably, those ruled by extremist sects or totalitarian regimes where doctrinal purity is fiercely policed and members must align their stories with a single before-and-after plot (see Yates & Hunter, 2002): "I once was blind, but now I see"—many other environments are simply deficient in narrative options. Not only can families be meager in this respect, and certainly many marriages, but so, too, can entire institutions. McKendy (2006), for instance, speaks of life in prison as "discursive confinement" (p. 496). What prisoners "are prompted to say, the sorts of discursive opportunities they are afforded, the kinds of stories that are officially ratified—all of these," he says, "are severely restricted" (p. 496). Despite numerous happy exceptions, nursing homes, too, can be unthinkably bleak from a narrative perspective. Once their meals are served them, residents are consigned to their geri-chairs, installed before the television, and rarely, if ever, invited to talk at length about their lives. As a result, their stories eventually dry up, along with their reason for living (see Diamond, 1992; Kenyon, 2002).

Narrative impoverishment can take other, less obvious forms. In the majority of environments, little attention is paid to *how* we narrate ourselves, or to "the everyday technology of self-construction" (Holstein & Gubrium, 2000, pp. 101ff). The narrative practices they involve are seldom brought to mind, let alone critiqued. Instead, they are accepted as just the way things are, and reproduced with minor variations by every member in an automatic manner. While we may have some dim sense as we move from one such context to the next that we need to express ourselves in different ways, we seldom reflect upon these differences.

In a spectrum of specialized environments, however, the avowed agenda is to make us mindful of how we story our lives in whatever other environments that may shape us. At the negative end are political sects or religious cults wherein, as noted already, explicit strategies for storying members' lives are very much the norm. At the positive end is a support group such as Alcoholics Anonymous. Adherents are enjoined to rid themselves of "stinking thinking": the internal nattering that imprisons them in destructive interpretations of self and others. Instead, they coach one another in storying life the AA way, "one day at a time": in *de-storying* out of one mode of living their lives and *restorying* into a healthier, more positive one.

Within the unique environment known as therapy, however, analyzing the impact of other environments upon our lives—family, relationships, culture, gender—is often the principal agenda. Whatever their theoretical leanings, counselors are alert to differences in style and substance, content and form, in their clients' self-talk. And regardless of how they frame it, their role is to help us become more mindful of patterns of interpretation that hold our best energies hostage and sabotage our attempts to grow—themes we will return to later on, particularly in Chapter 8.

NARRATIVE DEVELOPMENT: STAGES OF SELF-STORYING

What Narrative Development Is

Development is challenging to define. Consider the synonyms that might apply, from *improvement*—in the sense of progress toward a state that is intrinsically more advanced—to mere *change,* where from one stage to the next something is not so much better as simply different, as summer is not better than spring, but merely the season that succeeds it. Between these two alternatives are terms like *process* or *journey*, words which imply that, while there is certainly movement over time, its direction, be it for better or for worse, is ultimately unclear.

Understood as process, development has numerous dimensions, and in the study of aging, we must acknowledge them all. Biological development is one: how our various bodily systems (cardiovascular, musculoskeletal, gastrointestinal) change over time, and the effect of such changes on our overall health. Social development is another: how we change in terms of our roles and relationships, not just in the family but in the countless other contexts that structure our lives.

Psychological development is a dimension as well. Though bound up with biological and social development alike, it incorporates numerous dimensions in itself. Among them are personality development, psychosexual development, ego development, cognitive development—which, itself, involves development in our ability to remember and in our capacity for learning, for creativity, and even for wisdom. Some researchers also speak in terms of spiritual development or "faith" development (Fowler, 1981), which is linked, no doubt, to moral development (Kohlberg, 1984), as well as to the development of a sense of meaning (Reker & Chamberlain, 2000). Many of these dimensions are implicit, one could argue, in narrative development. In other words, once we acknowledge the narrative variable, once we accept that whatever else we may be, we are story-making creatures, that we are hermeneutical beings as much as human beings, then the issue of how we develop in narrative terms is one we also need to face.

Narrative development can be understood in a specific way and a general way. Researchers interested in the specific way focus on the acquisition of language in early life, especially the emergence of narrative competence, as reflected in children's ability to tell and understand stories (see Bamberg, 1997): though not necessarily the stories by which they make sense of their own lives. Of related interest is the development of "narrative intelligence," a topic that has received growing attention from researchers in the area of artificial intelligence (Schank, 1990; Mateas & Sengers, 2003). If our aim is to design computers that can think like humans think, so their reasoning goes, then we must program them to tell and interpret stories. More than this, the degree of development in our overall narrative competence—from rudimentary to advanced—plays a pivotal role in our capacity to understand and to articulate our own lived experience (Randall, 1999).

For those taking a more general approach to narrative development, the focus extends beyond childhood, then, to embrace the entire lifespan. The focus is on our comprehension of our own *life*stories, and on the changes in how we compose them over time. Moreover, it is on how such changes determine, not just our self-esteem, but our self-concept, for as we hinted in Chapter 2, *self-concept* itself needs to be reconceived in narrative terms. In this second and more general sense, the study of narrative development thus overlaps with the study of extended consciousness, of autobiographical memory, of emotion and imagination, and of our overall capacity for recollection and reflection. And it is the sense in which we will be understanding it here.

How Narrative Development Occurs

Narrative development can scarcely be discussed without getting into the topic of reading life, which is our focus not just in Chapter 5, but in the whole of Part II. For now, three considerations can act as background for us later on. First, narrative development occurs within narrative environments. It is "discursively and socially situated" (Freeman, 1999b, p. 247). Next, it continues all life long, though whether it does so seamlessly or in discrete stages is an open issue. Third, it is an inherently hermeneutical (or interpretive) process, meaning it relies on introspection, a process that is inseparable from the matching processes of *retro*spection, on the one hand, and *prospec*tion, on the other.

As for the first of these considerations, we do not story our lives in an existential vacuum but by immersion, be it brief or shallow, in an ever-shifting sea of narrative environments, whether real or imagined. For instance, we can envision a person who quits school and leaves home while still a teenager and goes straight to living in a cave. There, until he dies, he is (miraculously) supplied with the basics: food, clothing, and...books. All he does, all day long, is devour an assortment of stories—indeed, the same ones over and over. Narratively speaking, his development can scarcely be expected to be as extensive as that of his twin brother, who in contrast, graduates from college, establishes a career, raises a family, and enjoys numerous relationships with others. Still, besides the memories our hypothetical hermit retains from his childhood and those that he makes on his own, the novels themselves can be said to provide a *kind* of narrative environment, in which he can experiment with a range of narrative strategies, admittedly narrow, for making sense of an otherwise stark, unstimulating life.

Many people, of course (many academics, for example), spend the better portion of their days alone, wandering among the stacks of a library: an environment bursting with potentially life-changing narrative experiences but, at bottom, still a cave. The majority of us, however, experience a comparatively wide range of narrative environments over the course of our lives, and so are exposed to multiple templates for composing our texistence. As we say, some of the most formative of these environments, such as our family of origin, may have been fairly open. While perhaps discouraged from giving vent to every last one of our noticings and natterings, we were exposed to a generally healthy selection of self-telling formulae. Furthermore, we were invited to honor our past and to think freely and creatively about our future. Above all, we were listened to in a careful, respectful manner. And as we learned to do the same for others, with air-time fairly shared, everyone coauthored everyone else to the benefit of all.

In such a family, an ideal one for sure, we could develop an appreciation for the richness and potential of our own emerging story. We could develop a sound sense of narrative agency, or authorship, for how our lives unfold, plus—as we will see in Chapter 9—a sense of our capacity to coauthor others' stories in ever-enlivening directions. Along with this could come the realization that we can make a positive contribution to the environments that have nurtured us to date, as well as to whatever other environments we might be part of in the future.

Concerning the second consideration, just as in reading a novel, where the story increases in complexity and significance the deeper we get into it, so narrative development is a cumulative and lifelong process, which begins in infancy and need never cease. However, this runs counter to an assumption often implicit in developmental circles; namely, that little significant development takes place much past adolescence. An important exception, of course, is Erik Erikson's (1968) well-known eight-stage theory of psychosocial development, the pivotal construct of which is *identity* (our focus in a moment).

At the heart of Erikson's theory is the concept of *epigenesis*, the idea that development happens gradually over time and becomes increasingly complex. Also, it is a process that takes place in identifiable episodes—as with various life-forms: egg to pupa to larva—and has its beginnings, its genesis, in some initial, seminal state, just as the oak tree is inherent in the acorn. This insight links with the commonplace concept that a story "unfolds." Novelist Henry James (1908/1963) referred once, for instance, to the "germ of a 'story'" (p. 147) that lay behind many of his creations: an idea planted in his imagination by something as innocuous as an offhand comment made by a friend or the sight of a stranger sipping soup. From such innocent events sprouted incipient storylines that blossomed into full-grown works of fiction.

Epigenesis thus contains the concept of an entity's becoming, not necessarily better, but at least something more than it was at the outset, whatever form that "more" might take. It implies an essentially organic process, a process of growth, not a mechanical one that occurs in lockstep segments, but one that works itself out according to its own unique logic: story-logic, in the case of narrative. The process therefore varies from individual to individual, as it does from species to species. Each lifestory is ultimately novel. Also, the process entails change with some sort of direction—not improvement as such, but direction. It is not inherently superior in one scene or one chapter to another, that is, but simply farther along in the course of its own unfolding.

The concept of a story's unfolding, whether a literary story or a lifestory, accommodates that of thickening as well. "Ah, how the plot thickens," we think when reading a novel, as yet another character gets introduced into the story or a further twist is threaded into the plot. As we move from the first chapter to the last, the story steadily expands. Just as the oak is bigger (though not better) than the acorn, so the story-world swells in size from beginning to end. There is more going on in it. Not only that, but events that happened near the start of it take on a deeper significance. They mean more, or at least there accrues around them in our reader's memory more *potential* meaning. The story as a whole thus becomes more meaning-filled. It possesses more substance, and thus more power. Compared to when we started reading it and may have doubted if it could hold our attention past the first few pages, we are unable to put it down. With regard to development in lifestory, a comparable process applies. As we age and change, not only does it become more unique—more novel, that is—but it gets progressively thicker. "As you grow and change," affirms psychotherapist Carol Pearson (1989), "you add themes and your life becomes fuller" (p. xxii). Accordingly, our lifestory can become ever dearer to us, and in its own way, harder to put down.

At a certain point (and we will come back to this possibility in Chapter 6), our story can begin getting thinner instead. As spouses and friends pass on, as it becomes more and more difficult for us to get around, and as fewer of our favorite activities are feasible any longer, our lifestory—on the outside at least—can begin closing in. "Our world narrows," writes Scott-Maxwell (1968). "Its steady narrowing is a constant pain" (p. 137). The scope of environments that are both accessible and stimulating can begin narrowing as well, resulting in a reduction of fresh or suitably sophisticated templates for making sense of our (technically) still-changing existence. The process is a denouement, a general winding-down, as the story strains towards its inevitable and necessary end. As we will discuss more thoroughly in Chapter 10, while there may be no end to the meanings that the story can stir up for us—indeed, the closer we get to its conclusion the more filled with meaning it can seem—the story must eventually end, or at least offer us a "sense of an ending" (Kermode, 1966). If, like a soap opera, it goes on and on, forever promising but never providing closure, it will lack satisfying coherence as a work of literary art. It will lack poetic integrity, and identity: a sense that, overall, this is what sort of story it has been.

To turn to our third consideration: development, to quote literary ger-ontologist Ruth Ray (2000), is ultimately "a narrative construction and an interpretive process" (p. 27). In asserting this, Ray is drawing on the work of Freeman (1993), who argues that "despite its customary connotations of moving *forward* in time," development "can only be predicated *backward,* in retrospect, after one is in the position to chart the trajectory of the past" (p. 9). In effect, development is "fundamentally inseparable from the pro-cess of narrating the past" (p. 9). In other words, "we can never quite say where development is or ought to be headed, not ahead of time at any rate; we can only say where it has been" (Freeman, 1991, p. 88). What is en-tailed in development, therefore, is a dynamic blend of both retrospection and prospection. Like reading itself, it involves a ceaseless back and forth between our sense of the past—in this case, *our* past—and our sense of the future: *our* future. Such to-ing and fro-ing from time past to time future (through time present) results in a continuous spiral of interpretation and reinterpretation, the sort that William Wordsworth (1798/1981) immortal-ized in his reflections on the experience (and the memory of it) that inspired his poem, "Lines Composed a Few Miles Above Tintern Abbey." At bottom, narrative development encompasses a variety of activities at once: recol-lecting, remembering, reflecting, reviewing, revising, rethinking, retelling, re-examining—all of them aspects of the process we call "reading."

Overall, however, what is the goal, or the *telos,* of narrative development? Every story has an ending, insofar as the action at some point ceases and the last word on the last page is read. Yet there can be no end whatsoever to the meanings that ending may have. Indeed, it may reverberate inside us for a lifetime. With a lifestory, however, something similar can be true, even if (or more accurately, because) we are ultimately inside of it and never quite reach its end. With narrative development, there *is* no end. "It is a potentially *infinite* process," Freeman maintains (1991, p. 90). Right up to our death, we can continue remembering, reinterpreting, and reading our lives, and thus reworking our identity. What our lifestory is, and what meanings it mediates, remains an open question, one that can inspire in us a growing sense of both irony and wonder.

NARRATIVE IDENTITY: SELF AS PROCESS AND PARADOX

Identity as Story

Environment, development, identity: all of these are linked. If our narrative development occurs in narrative environments, what develops, one might say, is our narrative identity. Yet the concept of identity, let alone *narrative* identity, calls for some definition. Developmental psychologist Dan McAdams (2001) comes at the question of identity through the concept of personality. Personality, he says, has to do with "human individuality—or the reality and the experience of the human being as an individual" (p. 3). "What is it that makes you unique?" he asks (p. 3). His answer lays out three main levels. The first consists of certain inherent "traits," which is to say "internal dispositions that are relatively stable over time and across situations" (p. 252). The second has to do with how these traits are expressed and adapted amidst the circumstances and conditions that actually constitute one's life. The third refers to how one fashions meaning from these conditions or how one interprets them and, from such interpretations, generates a story with which to understand oneself. In sum, "individuality is conveyed...through the patterning of traits, adaptations, and stories" (p. 9)—if you will, the skeleton, the flesh, and the soul of one's being.

It is to the third of this trio that McAdams has devoted particular attention. In various publications (McAdams, 1988, 1993, 1996, 2001, 2006; Hooker & McAdams, 2003), he builds on Erikson's work to advance a model of identity that centers on the notion of lifestory. The appeal of his model is rooted in common sense: we can have little idea about a person's sense of identity until she tells us something of her story, bearing in mind that the whole story and "nothing but" (that is, the outside story of her existence in its entirety) is impossible to tell. Technically, a lifestory is thus a "folk notion" (Linde, 1993, p. 36). We all believe we have one, yet what it is, or where, is another matter. "It eludes us," write Bruner and Kalmar (1998, p. 323). Still, whatever portion or version of it that someone chooses to reveal will surely tell us something about who they think they are.

Overall, a person's lifestory is characterized by two key features: it is unique to them, even if it shares themes with others' stories too, and it is still unfolding. We touched upon the first in our discussion of the novelty of lives. Gerontologists Johannes Schroots and Jim Birren (2002), who like us are interested in "growing old" (p. 51) and in "the 'inside view' of life," or in "how life is experienced and interpreted by an individual" (p. 51), reinforce this feature when they insist that "it is in the life stories of individuals that human uniqueness is most clearly expressed and may be most fruitfully studied" (p. 64). Indeed, Hooker and McAdams (2003) go as far as to insist that later life itself "provides the clearest palette on which to understand personality, as lives become more divergent from one another"—more novel—"over long periods of time" (p. P302). That said, there will obviously be a spectrum as far as the emphasis on uniqueness is concerned, with environment itself being a variable. In some contexts or cultures, for example, personal identity is defined primarily in terms of communal identity. Who "I" am and what "my" story is, as opposed to who "we" are and what "our" story is, can be difficult to delineate sharply. In other cultures, like our own for instance, the emphasis falls far more on the individual than it does on the collective—which contributes, no doubt, to what Fivush (2004) noted as a tendency to focus more on ourselves when we talk about the past.

As for the second feature, we began to see when discussing narrative environment that our lifestory is not a product so much as a process, one that is never completed. As sociolinguist Charlotte Linde (1993, p. 31) stresses, it is both "structurally and interpretively open." Regarding content, form, and meaning, it is a story-in-the-making, "never once and for all" (Bruner & Kalmar 1998, p. 322). A corollary of this, as we hinted in Chapter 2, is that we are forever lagging behind in our self-storying. Our lives are continually outstripping the stories into which we would fit them. There is always a backlog of experiences in need of interpreting, plotting, reading—an idea we will certainly be returning to in Part II.

Given such ideas, we can appreciate the variety of elements McAdams (1996) incorporates into his guiding definition. One's lifestory, he says, is essentially an "internalized and evolving personal myth" that supplies us with a sense that our lives have "unity and purpose" (p. 132). Indeed, for McAdams (2001), "Identity *is* a life story" (p. 643). In a seminal article entitled "Life as Narrative," Bruner (1987) makes a comparable claim, one with additional and even radical significance when one considers its implications for aging. Eventually, says Bruner, "we *become* the autobiographical narratives by which we 'tell about' our lives" (p. 15). For psychologist Ulrich Neisser (1994), however, such claims are exaggerated (p. 1). Our knowledge of ourselves, he says, is based not only on narrative, but on "perception, conceptualization, and private experience." Accordingly, although self-narratives make an important contribution, they are "not *the* basis of identity" (p. 1). Based on our thinking in the previous chapter, we would come to a different conclusion, insofar as the three elements Neisser cites depend precisely upon narrative activity, as primitive or semiconscious as much of that activity may be.

Narrative psychologists Jens Brockmeier and Donal Carbaugh (2001) express the point as strongly as one can: "The very idea of human identity—perhaps we can even say, the very possibility of human identity—is tied to the very notion of narrative and narrativity" (p. 15).

The aspects of a lifestory as internalized, and as providing life with unity and purpose, we have alluded to already. For now, we need to say more about its evolving dimension.

The Development of Narrative Identity

There are three broad stages, proposes McAdams (1996), into which the development of identity can be divided. Not so precise as the eight stages of Erikson, they are the "pre-mythic," "mythic," and "post-mythic."

The pre-mythic stage, as McCabe (1997) implies with her idea of children as "emerging novelists" (p. 140), runs from infancy to early adolescence. During this stage, says McAdams (1996), we are unwittingly "gathering material" (pp. 136–138) for the myth by which, in due time, we will understand who we are. In a real sense, as *it* expands, *we* expand. "Myth" here, though, is not meant as something untrue. It is meant in the sense used by scholars such as Joseph Campbell (1949), Rollo May (1991), or Mircea Eliade (1963): namely, a "powerfully symbolic narrative" or "deep story" that "animate[s] our life and imbue[s] it with meaning" (Rigney, 2001, p. 159)—so deep, in fact, that it becomes a "way of life" (Ruth & Öberg, 1996). Whether the myth in question concerns ourselves as individuals or our culture as a whole, our awareness of it is precognitive, on the borders of core consciousness and extended consciousness. It is a gut feeling more than a specific thought.

Regarding the material being gathered for our personal myth, it includes "emotionally charged images" (p. 137), says McAdams (1996), that may come to figure significantly in the stories by which we understand ourselves (p. 136). Because of the quality of our connection to significant others like our mother and father, or because of our experiences of memory-talk with them, what is also taking place during this stage is that a distinctive "narrative tone" is being set (p. 136). By this is meant the "most pervasive and identifiable feature" (p. 136) of the story of our life; namely, our "underlying faith" (or lack thereof) in the "possibilities of human intention and behavior" (pp. 136–137). Behind the scenes, of course, we can detect the first Eriksonian crisis: *Trust vs. Mistrust*. The types of tones that McAdams is referring to parallel traditional "modes of fiction" (Frye, 1957/1968), ranging from comedy to tragedy: which is to say, from naïve optimism to cynical pessimism and everything in between (McAdams, 1996, p. 136; see also Gergen & Gergen, 1984). These tones or modes can be viewed as underlying genres that, for better or worse, can structure our self-storying all throughout our lives—instilling in us deep down, for instance, a sense that "I'm competent and clever and can handle whatever life brings me," or conversely, that "I'm incompetent and stupid and will never amount to anything."

Inevitably, we stockpile more material than is needed for just one self-storyline. Although the material we assemble may turn out to have a pivotal impact on the dominant story that we compose about our lives (McAdams, 1996, p. 136), it is equally possible that it may not. Either way, *as* we are gathering it, as our inner reader-editor is laying it down inside of us, we can never quite know to what sorts of uses the total collection could someday be put. The point in any case is that from such surplus material, a wealth of surplus meanings can potentially be drawn and *re-genre-ated* stories eventually be spun—as we grow more skilled, that is, at reading our lives.

The mythic stage begins in adolescence. As Erikson, too, would claim, McAdams (1996) observes that this is a critical period for the formation of identity (p. 138). What differentiates what McAdams is doing, however, is that he views such formation as continuing well into one's 40s, 50s, and even 60s. Accordingly, it entails two sub-stages in the fashioning of one's story: "beginning" it (p. 138) and "expanding" it (p. 140). The second of these stages will be our focus in Chapter 6. But surely both of them, not to mention the post-mythic stage, can entail the continuous collection of narratable material. As long as we are having and interpreting experiences, gathering never ends. What separates what is happening from the pre-mythic stage, however, is the intense self-questioning that tends to come with puberty and the concomitant changes in our bodies and relationships.

Along with the prospect of leaving home and starting a life that is more truly our own, we begin seriously wondering "Who am I?"; "Where am I going?"; and "What's next, now that I'm not a child?" We begin awakening to the fact that we indeed *have* our own story (however much it has already been structured within larger stories still) and to a curiosity as to what sort of story it is. As our questioning intensifies, we start taking our narrative development into our own hands, explicitly imagining our future and interrogating our past in order to contextualize our experiences in the present. We start shaping our story for ourselves (McAdams, 1996, p. 140). Concerning such shaping, a few further points must be made.

First of all, the more we engage in telling about our lives, to both others and ourselves, the more proficient we become at recognizing the highs and lows and nodal points—the "nuclear episodes," as McAdams calls them—that seem most central to our emerging myth (p. 140), providing it with both "shape and substance" (de Vries, Blando, Southard, & Bubeck,

2001, p. 149). In thus beginning our story in earnest, however, it becomes additionally imperative to consolidate an "ideological setting" for our identity (McAdams, 1996, p. 140). This concept relates to those of macro narrative environments and of master narratives, and refers to underlying beliefs and values that derive, for example, from the religion in which we may have been raised (p. 140). An ideological setting, in other words, concerns the kind of world we believe we are inhabiting, the ultimate background to our thoughts and actions and concepts of right and wrong. Naturally, our sense of that world is subject to regular revision, and sometimes a radical reworking, even in later life. Nevertheless, its initial, more or less conscious establishment is essential to composing a liveable story. The mythic stage is the time in which this happens.

Besides the emergence of nuclear episodes and the formation of an ideological setting, what is also happening in the mythic stage is the development of the main characters in our story (p. 141). McAdams's term is "*imagoes*" (1993, 1996, 2001), by which he means smaller-scale selves who have their distinctive ways of seeing things, and of behaving accordingly (p. 141)—what Bruner and Kalmar (1998, p. 320) call "sub-Selfs" and gerontologist Edmund Sherman (1991) calls "myselves" (p. 111). Partly, they are creations of our own imagination and partly they are tied to the roles we play, could see ourselves playing, or were scripted into playing in our family or culture at large. In other words, they range from generalized roles such as Me-the-Child, Me-the-Friend, Me-the-Parent, Me-the-Employee, to much more personalized self-images: Me-the-Sucker, Me-the-Saint, Me-the-Admirer-from-Afar, Me-the-Silly-Klutz. We have alluded already to this dramatic complexity of "the community of self" (Polster, 1987, p. 115) when discussing the business of noticing and nattering, but we will certainly come back to it again.

As we move into midlife, McAdams proposes, we are continually expanding our stories. Much of this happens automatically, of course, inasmuch as the longer we live, the more experiences we have, and the more we learn about our world, then the thicker our stories grow; as well, the bigger the bundle of story-strands of which they are made up. Included in this bundle are the remnants of the storylines—the hopes, the fears, the fantasies—that, all life long, we are forever tossing out ahead of ourselves to pull ourselves through time. Along with this expansion, though, may come a need to reconcile time-past with time-present and time-future (p. 142), and generally to perceive unity amid the multiplicity—a concern that includes recognizing and resolving whatever conflicts might exist among our imagoes (p. 143). We also begin to project acceptable endings for our story (p. 143): in other words, for its final chapter (see Gardner, 1997). Yet not just any old ending will do. It is not sufficient, says McAdams (1996), that the ending we envision for our story fits all of its components into a neat, consistent whole. Rather, it must enable the generation of fresh beginnings. Ideally, it will be an ending that is not really an ending at all (p. 143)—a paradox we will examine more closely in our final chapter.

The emergence of this concern with endings coincides with the need to seek coherence in our story. This signals a shift, at some point at least, which naturally will vary for each of us, into the third broad phase in the development of identity: the post-mythic stage. Corroborating McAdams's thinking here are gerontologists such as Sherman (1991), for whom late life brings a "subtle but inexorable need to redefine one's self or, more precisely, one's identity" (p. 105). For McAdams (1996), though, the issue of identity is bound up with the formation of a "generativity script" (p. 143).

First coined by Erikson (1968), the concept of *generativity* has to do with contributing to the next generation in one or another of numerous ways, from actually having (or rearing) children, to teaching or healing, to generating cultural products, be they books or buildings, inventions or institutions, that will in some manner endure beyond our death. A generativity script is the aspect of our story that is focused on the legacy we bequeath to those who follow (McAdams, 1996, p. 143).

Although McAdams veers away from full-blown speculation on how our narrative identity unfolds from, say, our 60s or 70s on, he builds on the concept of a generativity script to focus on a theme that is relevant to the poetics of aging, and that we will be revisiting in Chapter 10. It concerns those who are what he calls "highly generative" (2006, p. 5). Such individuals create their lifestories in very similar ways—ways that stand apart from those whose sense of generativity is less well-developed. From childhood, they have the feeling that they are different and special. Furthermore, in storying themselves along such lines, they are inclined to conceptualize their lives as part of a much greater whole. Above all, their narratives are characterized by a persistent tendency to transform "bad into good" (1996, p. 146), to see the silver lining in otherwise negative experiences—a tendency McAdams labels "redemptive," and one he views as paradigmatic within American culture in particular (2006). In addition, they narrate stories that repeatedly reveal their humanitarian vision (1996, p. 147), which means that while others see things getting worse and worse with time, they continue to be optimistic, holding steadfast to the conviction that their actions and talents can help (as the saying goes) make the world a better place in which to live (1996, p. 147; 2006).

Overall, the very idea of a post-mythic stage is a vital addition to the collection of concepts with which to ponder the inside of aging from the perspective of poetics. Furthermore, it raises a cluster of fascinating questions. For instance, might it contain additional sub-stages within it, corresponding to the sub-stages of later life itself: young–old, old–old, oldest–old, and the like? And what differences might there be in terms of gender in the development of narrative identity? What is the relationship between post-mythic development and the development of wisdom? In addition, what marks the transition from mythic to post-mythic, and how does this transition vary from person to person, living within the unique story of his or her life, not to mention within the unfolding story of a particular family or culture? Does everyone make it to the post-mythic stage, or do some get to the mythic and advance no more? Unlike Erikson, whose schema assumes that we all move through all eight stages whether we want to or not, McAdams (1996) claims that this stage is not attained by everyone. It is not automatic (p. 136). In any case, McAdams's model, overall, is a vital contribution to deciphering the poetic complexities of later life, and provides us numerous points of reference for our thinking later on.

The Complexity of Narrative Identity

In the last chapter, we looked into some of the similarities and differences between a literary text and a lived text. To appreciate the complexity of identity from a narrative perspective, we need to return to the fundamental paradox intrinsic to the "dialogical self" (Hermans, 2002): the self as simultaneously author, narrator, character, and reader of its own story. Although we are well aware of an even broader range of constructs developed by literary scholars, including implied author and implied reader, such distinctions are not especially relevant to the line of thought we are pursuing here. Having gone a good way into the intricacies of self-as-character when talking about imagoes and sub-Selfs, and having broached the complexities of self-as-narrator in Chapter 2, we will limit ourselves at this point, then, to a few further points about self-as-author, on one hand, and self-as-reader on the other.

Self-as-Author

Mandy Aftel (1996) asserts that "we are both the heroes of our own plots and their creators. In a very real sense," she says, "we are the *authors* of our lives" (p. 16). Her conviction echoes New Age beliefs about our being the masters of our own destinies, capable of creating whatever reality we wish. Despite the appeal of such beliefs, as the authors of this book, we do not quite share them. While it is true that we can be "the authors of our own autobiographies" (Fivush, 1994, p. 136)—which is to say, of the actual texts that purport to recount *the story of my life*—it need not follow that, in some grand, ontological sense, we independently author the narrative constructions by which we understand our lives. Though, every day, we do indeed make choices that affect those lives (including choices about how to *interpret* the events that they involve), and in that sense exercise a measure of authority over how they unfold, it is ultimately a limited authority.

As we considered in regard to narrative environment, we are scripted from the start, loosely or tightly, into the story of a particular family. Almost before we are born, we can be assigned a certain role within the family plot: middle child, firstborn son, doctor-to-be. Subtly or not, we are pressed into playing it. Even though we have some say—ideally, considerable say—in *how* we play it, in how we adapt it to our peculiar personality, its imprint can linger inside of us for years. And once we leave home, our stories can continue to be authored, in content and form alike, by our participation in multiple narratives. Indeed, the lion's share of our lives, one might argue, is put in place by factors that are beyond our control: the larger systems we live within, the companies we work for, the vicissitudes of history and nature, the gender, generation, and genes apportioned us at birth. Accordingly, "we are never more (and sometimes less) than the coauthors of our own narratives," insists philosopher Alisdair MacIntyre (cited in Carr, 1986, p. 83). "Human existence," writes philosopher David Carr, paraphrasing MacIntyre, is a matter of "finding ourselves caught up in already ongoing stories" (p. 84). "My own story," he says, by means of illustration, "was underway in the minds and bodies of my parents even before my birth" (p. 84). As echoed by philosopher Daniel Dennett (1991), "Our tales are spun, but for the most part we don't spin them; they spin us" (p. 418).

MacIntyre's and Dennett's views, though not Carr's, reflect more of a skeptical postmodernist perspective than we believe is warranted. On some level, they portray human beings as narrative "dopes" (Gubrium, 2001, p. 23). Oppressive or repressive though our life-situations might be, surely we retain at least a modicum of narrative agency, and exercise *some* say in the shape our stories take. Not only that, but in storying our lives, we contribute (albeit modestly) to shaping the same larger stories that are clearly shaping us: by adding a one-of-a-kind plot line, by introducing a set of novel themes, by playing as authentically as we are able the distinctive part that we alone can play. In this respect, we agree with Carr's (1986) rejection of MacIntyre's claims, and the modified version of self-authorship that he maintains is valid. "The story which knits together and renders coherent and whole the loose strands of my life," says Carr (p. 94), "whether it is new and original or has been told and lived many times before me, is ultimately my responsibility, whether I consciously choose it or assume it by default or inadvertence." He continues: "The unity of self…is not a pregiven condition but an achievement," and a process. "Some of us succeed…better than others." Yet while "none of us succeeds totally" (p. 97), he observes, "we keep at it." It is the reader inside of us, we believe, to whom the task of "keeping at it" is assigned.

Self-as-Reader

In a lived story, the reader is right in the thick of the narrative—with its numerous characters and narrators—attempting to make some meaning while things are still unfolding, to sustain some semblance of coherence amid the whole dynamic mess. Indeed, in contrast to literary stories, readers of lived stories may have much less confidence that "the story" is coherent at all, and may feel themselves adrift on a sea of possible plots. To put it in other words, in a lived story, the text exercises far less authority over the range of plausible interpretations at which readers can arrive. Furthermore, the text is being steadily laid down, layer by layer, whether the reader is attending to it or not. A lived story is, literally, a book we cannot put down. With a literary story, as we shall be seeing in Chapter 4, an unread text is effectively a dead text. With a lived one, if our reader-mode is all but dormant, then either we are narrating it or just plain *in* it, as the character whom the story is basically about. But either way, something will still be going on. "Even if a life-story never has an author," notes philosopher Adriana Cavarero (2000) in her reflections on the link between storytelling and selfhood, "it always has a protagonist…and, sometimes, a narrator" (p. 24).

A point to be made here, of course, is that we cannot be reading our life all of the time. At least some of the time, we must be living it as well. If the unexamined life is not worth living, then the opposite is also true: the unlived life is not worth examining—which is to say, the unlived story is not worth reading. This possibility (all too real) aside, what we will be arguing throughout the remainder of this book is that the vast majority of us nonetheless tend to under-read, not over-read, our lives. Furthermore, though technically later life affords the opportunity to address this imbalance in a conscious, deliberate manner, it is by no means easy to do, given the scant schooling that most of us receive in the art—the poetics—of growing old. Not only can it be difficult, but quite conceivably it is dangerous as well, ushering us into a state of disorientation where the question "what is my story and what has it meant?" can become ever more challenging to answer, since both the text *and* its reader are continuing to change.

In reading a literary story, which can take no more than hours or days to complete, one could argue that we are the same basic person at the conclusion of the process as we were at the start. As we shall see soon enough, however, readers of literary texts, rereading the same work at sundry junctures throughout their lives will, with each fresh reading, experience its characters and themes in a notably different manner, slight though the difference might be. And in fact, this is precisely what we do in real life. In returning to the same basic passages (i.e., memories) over and over, we do so each time, physically, intellectually, and emotionally, as a different individual in the midst of a different text. With such enticing issues running through our minds, we are ready to look more closely, then, at the nature of reading as such.

Four

READING LITERATURE:

THE INTERPRETING OF TEXT

We never return to the same book or even to the same page,
because in the varying light we change and the book changes, and
our memories grow bright and dim and bright again, and we never
know exactly what it is we remember.
> —Petrarch (quoted in Manguel, 1996, p. 64)

There is creative reading as well as creative writing.
> —Ralph Waldo Emerson (1981, p. 58)

It seemed to me ... that they would not be "my" readers but readers
of their own selves, my book being merely a sort of magnifying
glass.... with it I would furnish them the means of reading what
lay inside themselves.
> —Marcel Proust (1982, p. 1089)

What we have been proposing since Chapter 1 is that reading our lives is not merely a metaphor for what we do when we think about our past. Rather, it is an actual activity we are always—and necessarily—immersed in as, day in and day out, we attempt to make sense of the texts that we have fashioned from our existence, past, present, and future. But what does *reading* mean? And how can autobiographical reflection be remotely similar to what we do with the words of a novel, written by an unknown person about events and characters that bear little or no relation to our own experience? An examination of research into the nature of reading reveals some fascinating answers.

Just as scholarship on narrative is increasingly converging from a variety of disciplines, so is scholarship on reading. Hypotheses put forward by literary theorists are now being validated by experiments in cognitive psychology and neuroscience. Evidence is mounting that reading a text, reading the actual words on a page, exploits the exact same processes of perception and comprehension, of memory and imagination, that operate in our experience of daily life. In consequence, much that has been learned about such processes has been usefully applied to our understanding of reading. As we go on to Chapter 5, we will see that the opposite is true as well. Much that has been discovered about reading works of literature can be applied to how we read our lives.

READING AND EXPERIENCING: COGNITIVE TWINS

We have all heard of "getting lost in a book," and many of us are fortunate to have enjoyed the experience on numerous occasions. Thinking back to childhood, we count among our friends not just Kathy or Bobby who lived next door, but also the Hardy Boys and Nancy Drew. Not the most complex of literary creations, admittedly, they were nonetheless characters and stories that carried us off into worlds which in many ways resembled our own, albeit peopled by different characters doing and saying rather different things than we were. Coming back to our own world was thus always something of a shock, and often the mood of that alternate world continued to suffuse our lives—until we picked up the next book, of course, and got lost in its world, too. That such armchair travelling carries on into adulthood and does not depend on our educational accomplishments or the sophistication of the stories we choose to read is demonstrated by the quantities of mass-market novels that are published every year. Mysteries, romances, and two-inch-thick thrillers figuratively fly off the bookstore shelves. Some we escape into in scattered moments, gorge ourselves on, and then promptly forget. Others, however, stay with us not just in the intervals between reading but long after we have closed the book—a phenomenon for which literary critic Sven Birkerts (1994) reserves the phrase "the shadow life of reading" (p. 97). But how can an imagined world—created by someone else's imagination, at that—seem as real to us as our own? Why do we find ourselves laughing and crying as the hero's or heroine's fortunes wax and wane? Why do our hearts race faster as the killer stalks the victim or, at last, the hero and the heroine kiss? Such are the questions that researchers of reading are endeavoring to answer.

Early researchers of the psychology of reading were more interested, however, in the micro-elements of reading, such as eye movements or word recognition. Indeed, psychologists Robert Crowder and Richard Wagner (1992) went as far as to doubt that a definition of reading was even possible, and claimed that "the proper subject of reading leaves off more or less where comprehension begins" (p. 4). By contrast, psychologists Mildred Robeck and Randall Wallace (1990) argued that "comprehension is an invariant condition of reading" (p. 25), and indeed much recent research in psychology has been devoted to exploring specific aspects of such comprehension. Increasingly, the focus has been on the intersection of its cognitive and neurological features. One of the first to look at reading from this perspective, psycholinguist Richard Gerrig (1993), has delved into how a reader gets transported into the world of a fictional narrative. "All a reader must do," he concludes, "is to have in place the repertory of cognitive processes that is otherwise required for everyday experience" (p. 239). In fact, "many critical properties of narrative worlds," he goes on, "emerge directly from the ordinary and obligatory operation of basic cognitive processes" (p. 239).

As psychologist Rolf Zwaan (2004) suggests, Gerrig's observations have been borne out by further research. The brain areas involved in the perception of actions or objects, says Zwaan, are the same as (or close to) the areas that are activated when words describing them are processed. Furthermore, in comprehending those words, we regularly experience "visual representations of object shape and orientation" (p. 35). Even the movements of our eyes and hands correspond to what they would be in the situation being portrayed (p. 35). As a consequence, Zwaan concludes, language is "a set of cues to the comprehender to construct an experiential…simulation of the described situation. In this conceptualization," he says, "the comprehender is an immersed experiencer of the described situation, and comprehension is the vicarious experience of the described situation" (p. 36). In addition, psychologist Keith Oatley (1994) has found evidence that the emotions people experience while reading are "similar to those of ordinary life" (p. 54), and, like Zwaan, suggests (1999) that when we read, we are indeed running a "simulation" in our brains. For literary scholar David Herman (2002), readers construct "storyworlds"—in other words, "mentally and emotionally projected environments in which interpreters are called upon to live out complex blends of cognitive and imaginative response, encompassing sympathy, the drawing of causal inferences, identification, evaluation, suspense, and so on" (pp. 16–17). Linguistically, visually, physically, emotionally—in all of these ways, then, a reader is transported into a text and vicariously experiences its world.

This kind of "immersed experience," to use Zwaan's phrase (2004), makes sense when we examine it in light of the process of core consciousness that we talked about in Chapter 2. Core consciousness, explains Damasio, happens as the result of encountering objects (1999, p. 25), be they internal or external in nature. In the same chapter, we explored what happens when the core self becomes conscious of itself. In this chapter, though, we want to focus on what happens when the core self becomes conscious of an external object: a landscape, another person, a skyscraper, a song, a painting, or, what interests us most here, a novel. Like Gerrig and Zwaan, Damasio (1994) proposes that, regardless of whether we are having a real experience or are simply reading about one, much the same process takes place in our brains. (One could even argue that the same holds true in dreaming about one, too.)

The key to perception, Damasio points out, is *images* (1994, p. 96), a term not to be confused with McAdams's *imagoes*, of course, and a term Damasio defines in a very specific way. Theorizing about mental images was long restricted to the domains of philosophy and literature. An image was generally agreed to be, as a popular literary handbook expresses it, "a literal and concrete representation of a sensory experience" (Harmon & Holman, 1996, p. 262), with more emphasis on the nature of the representation than on the means. When we approach images from the point of view of psychology and neuroscience, however, we see a focus on the means, and a conviction that the representation of sensory perception is a "mental pattern" (Damasio, 1999, p. 317). Images are formed in our minds "when we engage objects...from the outside of the brain toward its inside; or when we reconstruct objects from memory from the inside out" (pp. 318–319). Images are formed, then (as poets have always suspected), when our sense of sight, sound, touch, smell, or taste is triggered. Whether we see an object or a person, take part in a conversation, or read a series of words on a page, the mechanism of image-formation is seen to be much the same. "Those written words now printed before your eyes," says Damasio, "are first processed by you as verbal images before they promote the activation of yet other images, this time non-verbal, with which the 'concepts' that correspond to my words can be displayed mentally" (p. 319).

Images form when they are triggered not only by our perception of experience, but by our memory or imagination as well (Damasio, 1994, pp. 96–97). Indeed, present-day research suggests that the relationship among reading, memory, and imagination is extremely strong. The kind of memory we are referring to is not working memory or short-term memory, but rather autobiographical or episodic memory, our focus in Chapter 7: namely, memory that is accompanied by a conscious, or "autonoetic," awareness that one is re-experiencing events or emotions in the process of remembering them (Tulving, 1983, 1993). Psychologist Mark Wheeler (2000) succinctly outlines current thinking on the close link, cognitively speaking, between memory and imagination: "Individuals with autonoetic awareness," he says, "are capable of reflecting upon their own experiences in the past, present, and future. Reflecting back on past happenings is episodic memory. Related behaviors are the ability to introspect upon present experiences, and also to anticipate or imagine future experiences through imagination, daydreams, and fantasies" (p. 598).

Such a conception of memory is closely linked to reading. The areas of the brain involved when we get lost in a story—when we run a mental simulation—"are also relevant for other processes, such as the encoding and retrieval of episodic and autobiographical memories" (Mar, 2004, p. 1422). Oatley (1999) explains how this simulation unfolds. In ordinary experience, our minds regularly work both backwards and forwards, through remembering the past, inferring what might have happened in the past based on someone's present actions, and anticipating the future. Our experience while reading is remarkably similar. Our minds work forwards, "not so much predicting as understanding the range of possible outcomes that can result from actions." But they also work backwards, "inferring from trains of action the coherent set of goals and patterns of habitual planning that compose what in the theory of fiction is called 'character'" (p. 444). It is for this reason, perhaps, that story worlds and their inhabitants can seem so real to us. However, our response may also be influenced by our natural tendency to think metaphorically. As we saw in Chapter 2, we conceptualize our experience by blending what is not familiar with what is. Regularly and indeed automatically, we think of one thing in terms of another. Literary scholar David Miall and his psychologist colleague Don Kuiken (2002) argue, in fact, that "we can conceive of literary reading as a source of feeling-guided metaphors" (p. 231). The simulation we run when reading, in other words, can be seen as profoundly metaphorical: a constant, automatic blending of what we are reading with what we know.

If we consider our response just to fictional characters, we can easily see how our experience of fiction simulates our experience of real life. As psychologist Raymond Mar and his colleagues suggest (2005), "comprehending characters in a narrative fiction appears to parallel the comprehension of peers in the actual world" (p. 694). This observation echoes that of literary scholar Maria Bortolussi and psychologist Peter Dixon (2003), who propose that "readers commonly create representations of characters that are based on the same processes that are used for real people" (p. 165). For those of us who have become lost in the Harry Potter series by J. K. Rowling (1997–2005), the fact that Harry's unfamiliar world is composed of witches and Muggles is much less powerful than the fact that he is a small boy in a boarding school, surrounded by characters not unlike those who peopled our own schooldays. For young Japanese girls drawn to Lucy Maud Montgomery's *Anne of Green Gables* (1908/1942) and its various sequels (see Akamatsu, 1999), the fact that the main character is a girl growing up in nineteenth-century Canada, a context temporally and geographically very foreign to them, is not nearly as powerful as the emotional experiences they share with the maturing Anne. Such identification with a character, maintain Miall and Kuiken (2002), is an important instance of metaphorical thinking, as "the reader implicitly is taking on the embodied perspective of a figure in the text" (p. 232).

Research confirms, then, that far from being a passive activity, reading is highly creative and constructive. At the same time, it depends on ordinary, everyday cognitive talents: memory, imagination, the ability to concentrate, and most especially, perhaps, our capacity for metaphorical thought. As we shall see in the section we turn to now, literary theorists, though they have taken much different approaches, have arrived at the same basic conclusion.

READING AS CONSTRUCTIVE ACT

Despite increasing evidence to the contrary, the stereotype persists that reading is the more or less passive reception of a closed work that holds its meaning locked within it. Each year, for example, a small number of our first-year university students agonize over the "hidden meaning" of a novel or poem, as if the author has diabolically obscured the main point in order to drive the reader mad. To be fair to our students, of course, some poets and novelists have delighted in this very sort of game, but they are rare. Still, the assumption behind the students' agony is revealing. In their view, the sole source of meaning is unquestionably the text. All they need in order to be good readers are a large vocabulary and a sensitivity to a variety of literary devices: keys to unlock the words on a page. As far as they are concerned, the whole point of studying literature is to amass knowledge of as many such devices as possible and to apply them religiously to every text they read.

Upon enquiry, we invariably learn that these students have seldom, if ever, read novels for pleasure—not even mysteries, romances, or thrillers. As a result, they have never had the sense of being transported to another world through reading, and they come to class armed with the conviction that they are there to acquire information. Sadly, they are probably more typical than we would like to think. As teachers in a liberal arts institution, we tend to encounter a larger percentage of fiction readers than exist in the general population. Indeed, in a recent study that surveyed 17,000 adults, the National Endowment for the Arts (2004) reported that "less than half the adult population now reads literature" (p. vii), having dropped from 56.9% to 46.7% between 1982 and 2002 (p. ix). While 46.7% still represents a great many people, such numbers are disquieting, for as we will see through-out this chapter, the kind of activities that we undertake in reading fiction can have a significant impact on the quality of our lives: reading literature and reading our lives are intimately linked.

Scholars of literary reading have a far different understanding of the process than do our frustrated students. Perhaps as a corrective to the author- and text-focused theories that dominated literary study until the last quarter of the twentieth century, a number of theorists loosely grouped under the label *reader-response* came to prominence in the 1970s. Not surprisingly, reader-response theory, with its emphasis on meaning as constructed by the reader (as opposed to created solely by the author), developed within postmodern academic culture, which assumes that reality is not something "out there," firm and verifiable, but something we construct ourselves. Some reader-response theorists, such as David Bleich (1978) and Norman Holland (1968; 1975), went to a postmodernist extreme, proposing that the meaning of any text exists exclusively in the reader. Most theorists, however, have fo-cused on reading as the mutual relationship between reader and text. Literary gerontologist Mike Hepworth (2000) links this process to the theory known in sociological circles as symbolic interactionism. Accordingly, "reading is a process of symbolic interaction where the reader has some freedom to inter-pret the text according to his or her own ideas, emotions, and consciousness of self" (p. 3). Instead of being seen as an empty vessel into which the mean-ing of a work is poured, the reader is understood, therefore, to be part of an organic, creative process, where author, text, and reader come together in the act of creating meaning.

An early literary theorist who perceptively recognized the creativity inherent in reading was Louise Rosenblatt (1938/1976). "A novel or poem," she suggests, "remains merely inkspots on paper until a reader transforms them into a set of meaningful symbols. The literary work exists in the live circuit set up between reader and text" (p. 25). This "live circuit," or "transaction" as she calls it (p. 35), happens as a consequence of the meeting of author and reader in the reading of the text. "Through the medium of words," says Rosenblatt, "the text brings into the reader's consciousness certain concepts, certain sensuous experiences, certain images of things, people, actions, scenes. The special meanings and, more particularly, the submerged associations that these words and images have for the individual reader will largely determine what the work communicates to *him*" (p. 30). In short, the meaning of a literary work is rooted, not just in the text itself, but in the experiences, beliefs, attitudes, and memories, plus other qualities or constraints, that individual readers bring to it.

Rosenblatt's speculations on reading are similar to those of a more recent theorist, Wolfgang Iser (1978). Iser argues that "the text represents a potential effect that is realized in the reading process" (p. ix). Reading is "an interaction between the textual signals and the reader's acts of comprehension" (p. 9)—a "dynamic happening" (p. 22), as he puts it. A text may guide a reader in certain directions, but meaning is ultimately created in the process of reading itself. "The structure of the text sets off a sequence of mental images which lead to the text translating itself into the reader's consciousness" (p. 38). The reader's goal, suggests Iser, is to perceive consistency and coherence in the text. Contrary to what we might assume, in other words, coherence is not intrinsic to the text itself, but constructed by the reader through creating patterns and filling in informational gaps.

These theories of reading differ considerably from the assumptions of our frustrated students in two important ways. First, the literary text is not a complete and static repository of meaning that will reveal itself to those who possess the proper tools to break it open, whereupon meaning will simply pour into their minds. Instead, the text is but one half of a communicative process whose meaning can only be revealed when a reader actively participates. Second, this process is creative and dynamic. To use Rosenblatt's (1938/1976) term, it consists of a "live circuit" (p. 35) between text and reader. The consequence is that, paradoxically, the reader has at least as much authority over the text as the author does—a paradox not easily resolved. However appealing the notion of reading as a creative, collaborative activity may be, then, it raises some perplexing questions: how do we know what elements of meaning are inherent in the text, and what kinds of things, precisely, does a reader contribute?

Using an empirical approach to reading that they call "psychonarratology," two researchers who have gone quite far in answering such questions are Bortolussi and Dixon (2003). Defining their approach as "the investigation of mental processes and representations corresponding to the textual features and structures of narrative" (p. 24), they survey research from a variety of disciplines on the major structures of literature—namely, the narrator, events and plot, characters and characterization, perception and focalization, and represented speech and thought. Based on this survey, as well as on their own empirical research, they conclude that some of these structures have their source in "features of the text," while for others it lies in a "reader's mental constructions" (p. 24).

A textual feature is defined as "anything in the text that can be objectively identified" (p. 28): for example, events that are clearly described in the text. Bridget Jones makes blue soup (Fielding, 1998); Hamlet kills his uncle Claudius (Shakespeare, 1604/1974c); and Mrs. Bennet tries to marry off her daughters (Austen, 1813/2004). Reader constructions, on the other hand, consist of "events and representations in the minds of readers" (Bortolussi & Dixon, 2003, p. 28). Such constructions are subjective, founded not only on readers' own attitudes, beliefs, and emotional reactions to the text, but also on the inferences that they must make in order to fill in informational gaps. Depending on who is reading, then, Bridget Jones is either a silly woman—or Everywoman; Hamlet is a thoughtful, prudent man—or an indecisive coward; Elizabeth Bennet is the child of a foolish mother and a wise father—or the child of a realistic mother and a spendthrift father. Once we think about them, distinctions between textual features and reader constructions appear rather obvious. Yet as Bortolussi and Dixon reveal, some aspects of narratives that, on the surface, seem simply to be textual features actually involve reader constructions.

Contrary to what we might suppose, for example, the narrator of a text is not an objective feature of it at all but "a representation in the mind of the reader" (p. 95). Depending on the point of view from which the text is written, of course, narrators can seem more or less present within it. First-person narrators—which is to say, those who tell their own story—are always dominant, given that every event described in the text is filtered through their consciousness. Yet while such narratives have an advantage in terms of authenticity, the events presented in them are limited to those that the narrators themselves have personally experienced, and if they are either naïve or mendacious, then their story will be visibly skewed. But a narrator may be equally dominant when a third-person point of view is adopted instead, depending on the level of narratorial intrusion. In other words, whether confined to the consciousness of one of the characters in particular or broadened to have access to the consciousness of all of them, third-person narrators can either be constant presences who comment on the characters and action at every turn, or voices that are so subtle or implicit as to be almost impossible to identify.

However invisible or intrusive narrators may be, and whichever person they are, first or third, it is they who mediate between the reader and the text. It is they who are, in fact, the primary figures with whom we interact. And it is they with whom we develop a relationship the instant we enter a text. Bortolussi and Dixon propose further, though, that a narrator is constructed by two means: by "explicit attributions," which is to say the things that the author says explicitly about the narrator, and by "inference invitations," or things the author says that invite readers to make inferences—fill in knowledge gaps—about the narrator (pp. 95–96). Indeed, they liken the narrator to someone with whom we might have a conversation. Much of what we think we know about our interlocutor is rooted, not in the actual words that he or she speaks to us, but in what we infer on our own, in the guesswork we engage in regarding their motives and meanings. Inevitably, of course, the narrator we encounter in a text provides us with fewer clues than will a conversational partner. Tone of voice and facial expression, for example, are absent. The point, though, is not that a narrator is as complex as a person, but simply that the way we perceive a narrator exploits the very same processes that we employ in perceiving people.

If we perceive narrators as people, it is not surprising that we perceive characters in much the same way (Bortolussi & Dixon, p. 165). In a first-person narration, of course, the narrator and main character are one and the same, and readers make inferences about the narrator/character as the events unfold, just as we make inferences about people's thoughts and beliefs in the course of our efforts to understand their actions. A third-person narrator has the additional freedom to make observations on the appearance, personality, and motivations of the characters. And because of the apparent objectivity of the third-person voice, a reader will be inclined to take these observations at face value, much as we might accept the observations of someone we know who is describing an acquaintance. But no matter how much or how little information a narrator may provide us, our relationships with literary characters will always be as interpretive as our relationships with people. "From the perspective of human perception," insist Bortolussi and Dixon, "literary characters and real people are processed in terms of similar sense-making strategies" (p. 141).

While the relationship between the ways we perceive narrators or characters and the way we experience real people is not too difficult to see, the notion that the reader is responsible for the construction of the plot, to some extent at least, is not nearly as obvious. If we think of reading as being transported, then we are assuming that a narrative presents a story world that we interpret in much the same way as we interpret the real world. Indeed, that is precisely the conclusion many researchers have reached. On the other hand, if we think of a story primarily in terms of its language and structure, then we are assuming that the story's form determines our response to it, an assumption that underlies much of the work of literary scholars. For this reason, traditional examinations of plot have distinguished between story (the events) and discourse (the telling), and attempted to prioritize one over the other. The problem, though, is that their efforts have failed to yield much insight into how in fact we separate the two, or even if we can.

Bortolussi and Dixon seek to resolve this problem through their psychonarratological approach, arguing that although there are indeed textual features, all of the events in a narrative are, in the end, presented by the narrator. Therefore, a reader's perception of the plot is necessarily mediated: "what readers understand about the sequence of events," they say, "is not what is implied by the text, but what the narrator invites the reader to infer" (p. 119). In other words, "readers represent not the plans and events of the story world, but rather that which the narrator seems to convey concerning those plots and events" (p. 125). Often, events are not present in the plot at all, but are gaps that must be sketched in by the reader. For example, a particular passage may contain a detailed description of the hero and heroine driving down a street that is so evocative that we are able to experience along with them the spring sunshine glancing off the windshield and the scent of lilacs in the air. However, aspects of this scene are obviously reliant on reader construction. Most likely, the author failed to provide an equally detailed description of the hero opening the door, climbing into the car, closing the door, fastening the seatbelt, starting the engine, releasing the brake, adjusting the gears, and checking the mirrors, before pressing on the accelerator and pulling onto the street! We take it for granted, of course, that those things have happened; otherwise the car would not be moving. But we do not consciously recreate them in our minds, nor would we expect an author to include them in a narrative. No text contains everything: every detail of every scene, every character's thoughts, every bit of action. It is the reader who completes the text, drawing on his or her store of personal experience to flesh out the fictional world that the text is attempting to evoke. The literary experiences that are fostered by a text depend on the life experiences the reader brings to it, experiences that, in turn, are shaped by assumptions intrinsic to the environments in which the reader is rooted. As a consequence, every reading is idiosyncratic, and while textual features certainly offer guidance, the ultimate meaning of every text—as we have hinted already and will return to again—is eminently indeterminate.

We might argue, though, that some elements of a story, for example, indicators of time and place, are so objective that they can only be textual features. Yet even as a narrator indicates times or describes places, readers will naturally infer that they are in some way important to the plot, and even this inference is essentially a construction. Moreover, based on the level of detail presented in the description of a place, just as in the description of an event, readers will be more or less responsible for constructing a picture of it in their own minds. And we can be quite sure that each reader's picture will be different. Inevitably, even the spatial images created in each of our minds as we are reading what appear to be objective details will relate to our own unique memories of our own unique experiences. An example as simple, for instance, as the description of someone driving a car will evoke a picture of an entirely different street—not to mention, entirely different car—in the mind of every reader.

The frustration that our students experience when approaching an apparently impenetrable text may well have something to do with their limited vocabulary and their limited familiarity with figurative language and other literary conventions. But in our estimation, the evidence provided for the extent of reader construction provides a more powerful explanation for why they find literature so mysterious, and so difficult. Their implicit belief that literary reading merely requires the recognition of certain uses of language may, ironically, be shutting down the live circuit between reader and text that lies at the heart of such reading, and preventing them from valuing—let alone noting—its constructive dimensions. Certainly, the "literary competence" that courses in literature seek to nurture in their students focuses less on the meaning of a text than on how that meaning is achieved. According to literary scholar Jonathan Culler (1997), who introduced the term, such competence "would focus on the conventions that make possible literary structure and meaning." In other words, he asks, "what are the codes or systems of convention that enable readers to identify literary genres, recognize plots, create 'characters' out of scattered details provided in the text, identify themes in literary works, and pursue the kind of symbolic interpretation that allows us to gauge the significance of poems and stories?" (p. 62).

In contrast to this comparatively narrow definition of such competence, literary scholar Örjan Torell (2001), drawing upon his empirical research on young adult readers in Sweden and Russia, proposes that genuine literary competence is not a mastery of codes and conventions. Rather, it concerns "a field of forces, the central one being a personal and dialogical approach to the text." Instead of merely an "intellectual workout," readers, he says, are seeking "human contact." In effect, "what motivates competent reading is a constant will to understand our own selves" through "meeting 'the other'" (pp. 376–377).

While Torell comes close to defining literary competence, it is a very slippery and complex concept, and there is still more to it. Despite everything that a reader may bring to a text, despite an awareness that we approach a text not to play hide-and-seek with the author but to engage in a relationship, every reading will necessarily be an under-reading. Some of the material in any text will be scarcely processed at all, for it will exceed a reader's current store of experience. In part, this under-reading happens because readers are inevitably interested in some things more than others, whether the plot, the characterization, or the theme. But more than the particular interests that motivate the reader, the reading will be constrained by the narrative environment, or environments, out of which the reader reads. Put simply, text will be trumped by *con*text.

A key consequence of the inevitability of under-reading is that texts are always open. We may think that once we have turned the final page, a novel is finished—and so it would be if we believed that meaning lies solely in the text. But if we accept the notion that reading is a constructive act, then simply closing the book in no way closes the story. If that were the case, then we would not return to texts and find them different every time. The difference, of course, lies in us. In the most obvious sense, we are different at the last page of a novel than we were at the first because we have seen how it ends, and in hindsight, we can probably see patterns that we missed. More important, should we return to that novel, even though we know the plot, our next reading will be quite different from our first, since we will inevitably trace that pattern in a conscious manner and notice details that escaped us the first time around. Moreover, we will have moved on in our lives, with a much larger store of memories to draw from and, quite possibly, an altered view of our world in general. Reading a childhood favourite at midlife, for instance, can thus be a surprising and enlightening experience, as we revisit, not just the world of the novel itself, but our own earlier world as a child. Literature scholar Wendy Lesser (2002) puts it well: "You cannot reread a book from your youth without perceiving it as … a mirror. Wherever you look in that novel or poem or essay, " she says, "you will find a little reflected face peering out at you—the face of your own youthful self, the original reader, the person you were when you first read the book" (p. 4). Besides meaning something different to us now than it did to us before, the book reacquaints us with a self we may have long ago forgotten or discarded.

The constructive nature of reading, then, renders a text open in fascinating ways. In fact, given our definition of irony in Chapter 1 as the awareness of multiplicity and the acceptance of contingency, we could say that reading is itself an ironic act, since the creative transaction between readers and texts necessarily renders the meaning of texts fragmentary, multiplicitous, and contingent. Literary competence, we would argue, involves an awareness of precisely these qualities, and a consciousness of the ironic dimension of reading itself.

Highlighting the complicated and ironic nature of literary competence is Rosenblatt's (1978) distinction between "efferent" and "aesthetic" modes of reading. Efferent reading she describes as a focus on "the information to be acquired, the logical solution to a problem, the actions to be carried out" (p. 23). The label derives from the Latin *efferre*, which means "to carry away," the notion being that the main aim of such reading is to obtain new knowledge that can then be carried away by the reader. We read efferently when we scan the newspaper, study the directions on a bottle of cough syrup, or follow a recipe. In aesthetic reading, on the other hand, "the reader's primary concern is with what happens *during* the actual reading event" (p. 24). In addition to focusing on the words of the text, that is, such reading is aimed at "the associations, feelings, attitudes, and ideas that these words and their referents arouse" (p. 25). Moreover, "the reader's attention is centered directly on what he is living through during his relationship with that particular text" (p. 25). When reading aesthetically, the reader focuses inward as much as on the text. Not only do aesthetic readers participate in the construction of the text—they are aware of their constructive activity even as it is happening.

Efferent and aesthetic reading can be seen as two extremes of a continuum that runs from shallow to deep, and from under-reading to over-reading. Efferent reading, at the shallow end, is more cognizant of textual features. Aesthetic reading, at the deep end, is more cognizant of reader constructions. Efferent reading, then, is under-reading: reading only for the surface content, for the facts. The reader remains a passive receptacle and takes information away, making reading nothing more than a means to an end. Although such reading has its place, it is more appropriate to preparing for a multiple-choice exam than it is to savoring a novel.

Aesthetic or constructive reading, on the other hand, is a self-conscious activity. Reading is not merely a means, but is an end in itself. The object of contemplation, says Rosenblatt, becomes "what the perceiver makes of his response" (p. 31). Should the reader lose sight of the text altogether, however, and focus solely on his or her response, we are in the realm of over-reading. In such cases, reader constructions overtake the textual features to so great an extent that the text is effectively discarded, and reader and text cease to have any relationship whatsoever. We can see this phenomenon in literature classrooms, for instance, when a student insists that a poem means "anything you want it to." The most frequent way this assumption plays itself out is when novice readers encounter an image in a poem or a situation in a novel that reminds them of something in their own experience, either of life or of books. Immediately, they jump to the conclusion that the text is "about" something, and from that point on, ignore any features of it that contradict their initial interpretation—in effect, succumbing to a form of narrative foreclosure, our focus in Chapter 6. By contrast, the goal in Rosenblatt's view is to achieve a reading that balances an awareness of textual features and reader constructions, a reading that remains true to the text while acknowledging its ultimate dependence on the reader to bring it to life.

The distinction between efferent and aesthetic reading helps us appreciate what is happening to the frustrated students with whom we started off this section. Very often, they are excellent efferent readers, and can readily apply this skill to their reading of literature. As a result, they are able to follow complex plots with comparative ease and to identify endless examples of textual features. Yet despite being such proficient efferent readers—or more accurately, because of it—they often under-read. They miss the multiple meanings of a text in their hunt for "what it *really* means." And they have little or no sense of what it feels like to be transported into the story world. When asked how the story might relate to their own lives, they are genuinely baffled, because they have been unable to make a conscious connection with its world. Eventually, of course, as they are encouraged to attend to their own responses, they learn to become *aware* of the reading process—both during it and after it—instead of simply practicing it in a superficial manner. It is this very sort of deep, self-aware reading that is critical to a full experience of literature and, just as important, we believe, to a full experience of life.

READING LITERATURE TO READ LIFE

For all the discontinuity that may exist between them, life and literature are intimately connected. As we began to see in Chapter 2, where literature ends and our lives begin can often be difficult to say. Without going to the extreme of "hypernarrativia" (Eakin, 1999, pp. 130–137), where we deliberately construct our lives along literary lines, telling and living them as if they were their own dramatic productions, many of us have at some point sought to model our behavior after characters and genres that we encountered in movies, in plays, or in the story-books that we fed upon as children. It is not for nothing that we refer to a certain person as having a Cinderella complex or an Oedipus complex, as being a Hamlet or a Peter Pan. Literary motifs can be woven into the fabric of our lives so subtly that we scarcely realize how much we live our lives according to them. But again, what is actually happening inside of us psychologically and emotionally when we read a work of literature?

Poets and scholars have been endeavoring to answer this question for centuries, usually in the service of defending literature, for it has always had its detractors. Socrates banished poets from his ideal Republic on the grounds that since they were merely imitating reality and not dealing with it directly, they were not speaking truth: "All poetry, from Homer onwards, consists in representing a semblance of its subject, ... with no grasp of the reality" (Plato, ca. 380-360 BCE./1941, p. 331). Moreover, since disorder is intrinsically more interesting than order, a poet was likelier to imitate troubled people and troubling situations, thereby doing a disservice to the Republic "because he stimulates and strengthens an element [the emotions] which threatens to undermine the reason" (Plato, ca. 380-360 BCE./1941, p. 337). A few centuries later, the Latin poet Horace (ca. 20 BCE/1991) rehabilitated literature to some degree with his contention (in his verse epistle *Ars Poetica*) that it was intended both to delight and to instruct. Although their aims differed widely, the implication in both Socrates's and Horace's attitudes is that the effects of literature on readers are real—strong enough to corrupt them, on one hand, or usher them to wisdom, on the other.

During the Renaissance, the English poet Sir Philip Sidney (1595/1970) took up the argument as well, opposing the notion that poetry leads its readers to immorality, and further, claiming that its ability to create something new actually makes it superior to philosophy and history: "Only the poet," he writes, "...lifted up with the vigor of his own invention, doth grow in effect another nature, in making things either better than nature bringeth forth, or quite anew, forms such as never were in nature" (p. 14). By the Romantic period, the classical notion of the immoral poet was turned on its head. Wordsworth (1802/1981) claimed that poetry "is the first and last of all knowledge" (p. 881). Samuel Taylor Coleridge (1817/1983) assured us that the poetic imagination "brings the whole soul of man into activity" as it "dissolves, diffuses, dissipates, in order to recreate" (p. 304). And Percy Bysshe Shelley (1840/1977) maintained that "poetry is the record of the best and happiest moments of the happiest and best minds" (p. 504). Because of their superior imaginative and creative abilities, poets, by whom he meant all imaginative people, "are the unacknowledged legislators of the world" (p. 508). But by Shelley's time, the novel was in its infancy, and the early suspicion of poetry was transferred to the new form, with Coleridge (1856/1969) himself sneering that reading novels "produces no improvement of the intellect but fills the mind with a mawkish and morbid sensibility" (p. 3).

If we can make anything of this lengthy history of commentary on literature's moral value (or lack of it), it is that there has always been a recognition that literature, whether poetry or prose, exercises an enormous influence on its readers. Novels, decried at first because of their popular roots, have for over a century been considered respectable enough to be worthy of scholarly study, as long as they are not written to formula—or even if they are, if the production or consumption of formulaic fiction is the subject being studied. Outside of the academy, censorship for one reason or another still takes place on a regular basis. One striking example is the belief that the Harry Potter books (the most publicized recent target) can corrupt children's minds with occultist ideas. Despite the furor over Harry, attention is now more often focused on film (which adds performance to its potency and has itself inspired a massive quantity of scholarship) as the purveyor of untruths and disorder, from the Hollywood happy ending to less subtle scenes of explicit sexuality or gratuitous violence. Poetry, the novel, the film script: the genres and even the media may differ, yet imaginative fiction of any kind continues to inspire fear—or wonder—because of its power to affect us, for good or for ill.

The precise nature of fiction's influence is not yet fully understood, but the tendency of fiction readers to accept characters as people and the situations in books as real is being examined more and more. Psychologist Melanie Green's research (2004) suggests that if we have experienced transportation while reading a story, we are likely to accept it as realistic (p. 260). Indeed, our default approach to a fictional world is to accept it automatically as real. As psychologists Richard Gerrig and David Rapp (2004) have learned from their research, we have to work much harder at *disbelieving* a story than at believing it: "Readers must construct disbelief," they argue. "Literature will have an impact unless readers expend specific effort to forestall that consequence" (p. 280). And like Green's, their work supports the conclusion that "the probability that readers will construct disbelief is affected by the extent to which they are transported to narrative worlds" (p. 280). If we are transported, then we respond to the characters we encounter much like we would respond in reality, summing them up according to our judgement of their actions and our assessment of their motives. This automatic activity while reading, speculates literary scholar Lisa Zunshine (2006), is an example of "our tendency to interpret observed behavior in terms of underlying mental states" (p. 7). In other words, our approach to characters, like our approach to people, is essentially interpretive.

Just as Plato and his philosophical descendants suspected, practical consequences result from our tendency to be transported into a fictional world and accept what we find there as real. Mar and colleagues (2005) have determined not only that "engagement with fictional narratives can result in changes of belief and attitude" (p. 697), but that "fiction print-exposure positively predicted measures of social ability" (p. 694), in particular, empathy. This research is especially intriguing for two reasons. First, it supports the contention long held by readers and scholars alike that one of the main strengths of fiction is its invitation to identify with characters. Since we perceive characters in the same way as we perceive people, then in the identification with a character—particularly one whose mind we can see into in a way that we never could in reality—and in the metaphorical blend that takes place between reader and character, we experience affirmation of our own intellectual and emotional responses to similar issues. We discover role models to aspire to, and see the error of our ways. We recognize ourselves—or parts of ourselves—in others, and see beyond the similarities to possibilities for growth. The second reason this research is so significant is in conjunction with such growth. That fiction-readers are found to exhibit greater degrees of empathy than non-readers points to a consequence of their reading that is, by any standard, positive.

A similar conclusion has been reached by Miall and Kuiken (1995), whose comparison of the literary responses of psychology students on one hand and literature students on the other demonstrated that the latter achieved higher scores on both insight and empathy. Miall and Kuiken's further research (2002) into the self-modifying effects of literary reading demonstrates a complex connection between becoming emotionally involved in a story and undergoing personal change. As was shown by their study of feelings experienced by readers in the midst of reading, "literary reading has the capacity to alter the narratives about who we are or wish to become" (p. 229). Confirmation of the positive social effects of reading literature is also contained in the National Endowment for the Arts' study (2004) that we mentioned earlier. "Literary reading," it concluded, "strongly correlates to other forms of active civic participation" (p. xii), including "volunteerism, philanthropy, and even political engagement" (p. vii).

The notion of personal growth being possible through the reading of literature—whether popular fiction or the "classics"—is what most interests us here, given our contention that the way we read literature can shed light on the way we read our lives. Becoming competent in literary reading provides us not only with a much more extensive view of humanity than we could probably ever experience in the environments that shaped us, but it can help us become more competent at reading our own lives. This belief is the driving force behind *bibliotherapy*. As defined by psychologist Jane E. Myers (1998), bibliotherapy is "a dynamic process of interaction between the individual and literature," which "promotes the conscious recognition of clients' ways of knowing and experiencing so that both emotional and cognitive understanding of problems are enhanced" (p. 244). As the name suggests, bibliotherapy is a *therapy*—a formal, structured, guided process of self-exploration through assigned reading. But its goals can be accomplished by any of us, without the guidance of a therapist. In other words, bibliotherapy is simply a formalization of the activity readers have always carried out anyway, in a much less organized manner.

At the very least, getting lost in a book affords us a temporary respite from the demands of an overwhelming life. It is no coincidence, we suspect, that a recent study (Romance Writers of America, 2005) reports that 39.3% of all fiction sold, and 54.9% of all paperbacks sold, consists of romance novels (p. 2), notorious for their happy endings. But using literature for the purpose of escape is only one of its minor benefits. The old cliché that literature broadens our minds by introducing us to places and people, events and times that we could otherwise never experience is, like most clichés, demonstrably true, and a compelling reason for literature programs' remaining central to liberal arts curricula. Cultural critic Mark Edmundson (2004) powerfully articulates the connection between the reading of literature and personal growth. "Poetry—literature in general—," he maintains, "is *the* major cultural source of vital options for those who find that their lives fall short of their highest hopes. Literature is, I believe, our best goad toward new beginnings, our best chance for what we might call secular rebirth" (pp. 2–3).

Through active engagement with literature, we can vicariously entertain a host of alternative actions and lifestyles that we may have neither the means nor the courage to experience in real life. But if reading literature broadens our minds, it deepens them as well. In meeting characters who are similar to us and are involved in situations we find uncannily familiar, we experience the normalization, or affirmation, of our own complexities and dilemmas. We can turn off the incessant nattering in our heads to concentrate on what counts, and can discover meaningful patterns that our lives might otherwise not reveal. Moreover, reading can trigger in us the re-experience of emotions from our past. As Oatley (1994) points out in his study of literary response, "Emotion memories are not just recalled: they are relived" (p. 63). Moreover, the reliving of them can itself be transformative (Miall & Kuiken, 2002, p. 229).

As a consequence of gaining a "fresh feeling" (Miall & Kuiken, 2002, p. 229), we may be led to reevaluate our experiences, which could lead us eventually to a more extensive reinterpreting of our identities overall. Not only can we recognize parts of ourselves in the characters, but we can also see sides of ourselves of which, previously, we were but dimly aware. This, in turn, can deepen our lived experience, if not serve as an impetus for positive, perhaps radical, change. In short, if we have achieved a measure of literary competence, then reading literature can lead us to reinterpret aspects of our lives that we were not even aware required reinterpretation. Constructive, aesthetic, competent reading can lead us to deeper knowledge about the intricacies and subtleties of life, of relationships, of the world, of ourselves, rendering them far clearer than when we are living in the midst of them. Of course, as we shall discuss in more detail in the chapters to come, no novel, however complex or clever, can do justice to the inherent intricacies of even the most ordinary life. Still, when we are confused by—or lost in—our own stories, reading literature can bring us some measure of clarification, and enable us to articulate more accurately our own otherwise nascent insights and concerns. It can lay bare the essence of life's complexities and point a way through them. In Birkerts's words, "I read books to read myself" (1994, p. 102).

By far the most passionate proponent of the value of reading literature is literary scholar and bibliotherapist Joseph Gold (1990/2001; 2002). For Gold, "reading stories is the best training for making stories, especially the one central story which is the reader's life" (2002, p. xv). Gold's argument, like our own, rests on evidence that reading is both a constructive activity and an instructive one. Narrative fiction, he argues, is "translated experience" (p. 48), and an essential component of identity construction in that it "produces an inexhaustible reservoir of models of experience that can be brain-accrued for use in the encounter with life experience" (p. 288). Like Rosenblatt (1978), who argued that the deepest kind of reading, aesthetic reading, takes place when readers are conscious of their own responses, Gold believes that it is a self-conscious approach to reading that leads to the most personal growth. "The goal of reading literature," he says, "is not merely to experience the pleasure and excitement of emotion, but to cultivate an awareness of the emotion and what it can tell us about ourselves" (p. 82). One of the most valuable lessons to be gained from reading, he proposes, is that as we become part of multiple stories, we temporarily step outside of our own lives into "worlds we can occupy and live in while not leaving our real selves" (p. 127).

This simultaneous existence within multiple stories is yet another example of irony at work, and constitutes one more argument for cultivating a self-aware, ironic stance. The consequence of stepping into multiple new worlds, Gold claims, is not only fresh perspectives on our own lives, but multiple tools and strategies that can be imported into them as well. "What people read can become so woven into their knowledge, their wisdom, their residue of self-efficacy apparatus," he says, "that they cannot distinguish it from other personal experience" (p. 135). This is not to say that we confuse our lived experience with the experience of fictional characters (as our hermit in Chapter 3 may be tempted to do), but rather that we take advantage of whatever wisdom we have gained while reading and incorporate it into our own lives. The kind of reading that Gold advocates, then, is the kind that transports us out of our own narrative environments and into fresh ones. In short, it is aesthetic reading, the kind that, at its best, develops our literary competence to the point that we become *literarily self-literate*. In other words, our self-aware literary experience translates into self-aware life experience.

Let us assume, then, that the frustrated students we encountered at the beginning of this chapter have been well coached and have become well practiced in keeping track of their own responses as they read. Let us assume further that they have been required to keep journals in order to track their feelings about the moral dilemmas that the characters encounter; moreover, they have been encouraged to debate such things as whether a character chose the right marriage partner—or to what degree another character is himself responsible for his fall from respectability or power. And let us assume that they have been invited to think about whether they or anyone close to them has ever been in a similar situation; whether they have ever known anyone who reminded them of any of the characters in the book; and whether there was any passage, in particular, that expressed an experience that they had had themselves, but were never quite able to articulate. All of these techniques, simple though they are, may assist such readers—who on their own might never choose to read a novel at all—to achieve a modicum of literary competence, to develop their narrative intelligence in general, and perhaps even to be transformed from under-readers into readers who are well on their way to literary self-literacy. In the preceding chapters, we have seen that we are all, of necessity, readers of our own lives. To varying degrees, we all possess this same, essential, innate skill. The conviction we have examined in this chapter is that one of the most potent ways to enrich our understanding of our own lived experience is to grow in our ability to read literature. It is from literature to *life*, however, that we shift our attention now.

Five

READING LIFE:

THE INTERPRETING OF TEXISTENCE

The unread book is the life yet to be lived.
    —Geoffrey O'Brien (2000, p. 33)

Every true reader... is a writer and every true writer is a reader,
and every person engaged in the project of self-awareness is the
reader and writer of himself.
    —Sven Birkerts (1994, p. 113)

We are... like stories that are slowly unfolding according to our
own inner theme and plot. Each person's life is a story that is
telling itself in the living.
    —William Bridges (1980, p. 71)

THE STORY SO FAR

Reading our lives is an intricate interpretive process—a "project of self-awareness," as Birkerts would put (1994, p. 113)—and cultivating it, we believe, is central to the poetics of growing old. To grasp what it entails, however, means enlisting ideas that pertain to reading literature—literary competence, textual features versus reader constructions, efferent reading versus aesthetic reading—and applying them to the under-explored *inside* of aging.

In fact, this is our overarching agenda throughout the whole of Part II, with the themes of memory, meaning, wisdom, and spirituality as our principal points of reference. In the meantime, two themes need mentioning by way of advance considerations: the contexts in which self-reading takes place and the concept of a "good" lifestory. Before looking at each of these, it is worth reviewing where we are so far.

In Chapter 2, we saw how the narrative impulse is pivotal to our processing of reality on the most basic of levels: neurology. Narrativity, it appears, is hard-wired into our brains. Then we looked at how, on the psychological level, consciousness itself involves continuous narrative activity. Amid the interplay of noticing and nattering, editing and narrating, we transform the stuff of our lives into the stories of our lives. We turn existence into *texistence*. And moment by moment, we evaluate which events and images will get retained for *the story of my life* and which can, effectively, be forgotten. Without this constant editorial activity, this elemental narrative competence, little order is likely to emerge from the chaos inside our heads, and little would get accomplished in the world. Reading our lives, on however rudimentary a plane, is necessary for living our lives. We then began shifting from the micro to the macro level and considered the pros and cons of viewing lives overall as literary texts, as novels in the making.

In Chapter 3, we stepped back even further from the micro level of our involvement in narrative activity to look at the broader dimensions of storying lives. This led us to discuss, first, how our stories are structured through our relationships with others within an ever-changing network of narrative environments. If individuals have stories, then so, too, do families, communities, nations: any of the larger stories we live our lives within. We then considered how storying lives is not only socially shaped but is developmental as well, commencing in earliest childhood and continuing, potentially, into very late life. Lastly, we considered how the focus of this development is the emergence of a sense of identity, where "identity" is conceived as a lifestory. As we saw, however, the composition of this identity is laden with paradox: we can only compose our story, indeed can only comprehend it, from within, while its text is still being laid down. What is more, we are its (co)-author, narrator, character, and reader all at once—an inescapable complication to the very notion of a lifestory that would seem to completely deplete it of meaning. In our view, however, it merely renders it all the more enticing, and all the more pregnant with conceptual potential.

Most recently, in Chapter 4, we considered the complexities of the process we are immersed in when reading a literary work. Our guiding assumption, however, was that reading literature is only possible because we are already reading our lives—our texistence—at the micro and macro levels alike. It is the explicit form of a process of meaning-construction we are involved in all the time. As unconscious, intermittent, or inadequate as that involvement may be, reading life is the primary activity: reading literature, the secondary one. That said, a greater knowledge of the latter can only enhance our practice of the former.

We have seen, though, that much less is known about reading literature than one might think. As a complex interpretive process, it entails a continuous back-and-forth between past and future on one hand, and part and whole on the other. We understand what we are reading in the present in light of what we have read in the past, and of what we anticipate reading in the pages that ensue, right up to The End—concerning which, as we read, we will entertain a variety of hypotheses about how everything turns out. In this respect, reading is not just a retrospective activity but a prospective one as well—indeed, both of these at once. "We read in a spirit of confidence, and also a state of dependence," writes literary theorist Peter Brooks (1985), "that what remains to be read will restructure the provisional meanings of the already read" (p. 25).

In the same vein, reading involves a constant vacillation between macro level activity and micro level activity. When we read, we make sense at the level of individual marks on the page, transforming them in our minds into recognizable words and sentences. At the same time, we make sense at higher levels too, those of episodes and chapters. As such, reading involves a constant back and forth between part and whole: between the passage we are reading in the present and our sense of the story in its entirety. But we make meaning not merely in a cyclical manner. We make it in a spiral manner, too, inasmuch as the whole process transpires within an ever-widening field of understanding. Theories entertained at earlier stages concerning the significance of particular scenes or themes are never totally discarded. Traces of them will invariably remain, accumulating quietly in our minds, thus contributing to the thickness of the plot.

Reading, which Birkerts (1994) describes as "a steadily unfolding memory event" (p. 113), also requires filling in the blanks. No text contains everything that the story is about: every detail of every scene, every character's thoughts, every conceivable bit of action. As we have seen, it is the reader who completes the text, drawing on his or her collection of personal experiences to flesh out the fictional world that the text is intended to evoke. In consequence, every reading is idiosyncratic. The literary experience that a text fosters depends on the life experience that the reader brings to it. In turn, such experience is shaped by assumptions that are intrinsic to the culture, gender, and class in which the reader is rooted. In this respect, among many others, the meaning of the text is eminently indeterminate.

As we have also seen, every reading is, at base, an under-reading. Much of the material in most texts is hardly processed at all. It exceeds the reader's ability to make sense of it; it outspans his or her store of lived experience. There is always more in the text than any one reader can realize. In part, this is because readers invariably read for some things more than others, whether the plot, the characterizations, the themes, or the technical information that the story may convey. But more than the particular interests that motivate the reader, the reading is constrained by the cultural conditions in which the reader reads. As we say, text is trumped by context. To put it differently, a text is only as good—only as rich or as deep—as the interpretive community in which it is read, and by which the reader's competence is shaped. One might even go one step further, however, and suggest that each text attempts to teach its reader the very kind of competence that is needed to appreciate fully its potential for meaning—an unusual idea, perhaps, but one we will want to return to, especially in Chapter 10.

Many of the dynamics of reading literary texts have their counterparts in reading the texts of our own lives, whether we engage in that process unthinkingly, or in a mindful, intentional manner, with the express aim of shifting from efferent to aesthetic reading. In effect, Part II explores the many ways there are to cultivate this shift. Before embarking on that exploration, however, two further themes need introducing. The first, as we say, concerns the contexts or occasions in which self-reading occurs. The second concerns the concept of a *good* lifestory.

OCCASIONS OF SELF-READING:
CONTEXTS AND CONSTRAINTS

Like storying our lives, reading our lives is carried out within an ever-changing network of narrative environments, from micro to macro and from ad hoc to enduring. As a result, there are scarcely any occasions in the run of a day when we are *not* reading our lives. Each of these environments is essentially an interpretive community, with its unique spectrum of narrative practices, its preferred templates for self-interpretation, its peculiar customs for coauthoring and co-reading. And it possesses its peculiar set of attributes, as well, whether flexible or rigid, inviting or exclusive, open or closed. In addition, each will have its family of implicit assumptions about what constitutes good readings of our lives and not-so-good ones (our theme in the following section). Overriding all of these environments, of course, are the realities of gender, class, and race. In themselves, say Holstein and Gubrium (2000), these constitute "influential conditions for self-narration" and "deep reservoirs of self-construction" (p. 105). Without denying the power of such "sources of the self" (Taylor, 1989) to inform the ways we comprehend our lives, there are any number of more immediate, more concrete contexts, though, in which this comprehension occurs, some of which we touched upon in Chapter 3.

First, there is the micro-level self-reading that is essential to consciousness itself. If we were not continually monitoring the thousands of small stories that swirl around inside us in the society of self, we would barely be able to function. Nonetheless, some of us are inherently more sophisticated in this respect than others, in terms, not just of the scope of our noticings and natterings, but also of the mindfulness of our inner editing. In short, some are more self-aware in general (see Sternberg, 1998), and more aware of their various sub-Selfs, too. But insofar as such self-reading is happening whether we are aware of it or not, we can call it *automatic self-reading*.

Then there is the self-reading that we engage in more deliberately through our interactions with others, when, for instance, they invite us to try on alternative framings of some issue or problem we are keen to understand: "What if you looked at it this way?" "Had you thought about this instead?" As we mentioned in relation to telling-to versus telling-with (Ochs & Capps, 2002), our close friendships routinely inspire such self-reading, and within each one of them we inevitably envisage our lives in particular ways. Indeed, everyone we have any sort of relationship with at all will elicit a unique way, not just of talking about our lives, but of interpreting and experiencing them, too. (And in some ways, they may understand us better than we do ourselves!) Subtly or overtly, through a mixture of challenge and encouragement, coaxing and critiquing, they coauthor our identity in distinctive directions. The more varied our social circle, and the more its members stretch our horizons—intellectually, emotionally, ethically, and the like—then the more nuanced our story stands to be. Overall, this familiar yet intensely influential form of self-reading can be called *relational self-reading*.

One type of relationship that takes relational self-reading to a more intentional level still is the kind we develop with therapists or counselors. In listening to us recount our stories, they commonly encourage us to listen to ourselves: to step back from our own self-talk and contemplate the connection between what we are saying and how we are saying it—or between the story and the discourse—to reflect on how, typically, we interpret our experience, including our experience of others. As a consequence, the client–clinician interaction itself—certainly within psychoanalysis—is "a form of text interpretation" (Schafer, 1989, p. 198). Clearly, different schools of therapy will advocate different interpretive frameworks, and be guided by differing visions of the desired result. A Freudian's result may vary markedly from a Jungian's or a Rogerian's. In short, different frameworks mean different ways of reading our lives. Collectively, though, such ways can be called *therapeutic self-reading*.

Linked to therapeutic self-reading is the kind we engage in through our use of instruments specifically designed to evaluate particular aspects of one's personality. Among the countless scales that assess everything from intelligence to level of life satisfaction, certain ones, however, have come to enjoy usage outside of a research setting or therapeutic setting as such. The Myers-Briggs Personality Type Inventory (Myers & McCaulley, 1985) or the Kolb Learning Style Inventory (Kolb, 1984), even the Enneagram (Riso & Hudson, 1996), are among the better-known. The "scores" we receive when taking them become badges of our identity—*I'm an INFP* or *I'm an Assimilator*—providing us with ready explanations of our personal quirks, our relationship patterns, our attitudes and motives, our modes of moving through the world. Without discounting the value of such instruments in enhancing our self-awareness, the phenomenon is on some level akin to astrology. Once one's horoscope is read, one confidently announces "I'm a Leo," as if this designation said everything that needed to be said. Such approaches we could label *programmatic self-reading*.

A variation on programmatic self-reading, which links with therapeutic and relational self-reading alike, is what we can experience in the context of a support group, such as Alcoholics Anonymous. There, fellow members enjoin us to "work the program" according to a set sequence of steps. Followed faithfully, these will empower us to combat whatever dysfunctional life-patterns may be stunting our development. Given the millions of lives such *prescribed self-reading* has helped to turn around, it clearly has its strengths.

In a more extreme vein, there is the self-reading we are enjoined to do in a religious setting—"religious" in the sense not just of a particular faith or cult but of any context where the ideological setting we construct for our lives is monitored intensely. Drawing on their dogmas and doctrines, our comrades are only too happy to convert us, and to coach us in how to reconstrue our individual history in accordance with The Way: not the old, sinful, wasteful way we have been living hitherto, but the new, true, enlightened way, with one or another master story structuring the self-understanding with which we are urged to align our lives. We can think of this as *doctrinaire self-reading*.

A kinder cousin of doctrinaire self-reading is *disciplined self-reading*. By this we mean any school of thought, whether history or anthropology, psychology or philosophy, theology or ethics, that on some level pushes us to revise our assumptions about who we are and how we should live. The more such disciplines we are exposed to and whose concepts and theories we come to understand, then, logically, the richer and more complicated will be their impact on our capacity to read our lives, which is a classic argument, of course, for an education in the liberal arts. Related to disciplined self-reading is *professional self-reading,* insofar as commitment to a particular discipline over an extended span of time tends to intensify and internalize a peculiar mode of making sense of ourselves, as of our surroundings. Given how they earn their keep, lawyers are apt to view the world (and by extension themselves) rather differently from ministers. In a related sense, particular educational experiences, formal or informal, can inspire us to critique how, in the words of educator Jack Mezirow (1978), "we are caught in our own history and are reliving it" (p. 102). They can empower us "to become critically aware of the...assumptions that have influenced the way we see ourselves and our relationships and the way we pattern our lives" (p. 101). As this happens, we shift from academic learning to transformative learning, or *transformative self-reading,* a concept we will come back to in Chapter 9.

Transformative self-reading can be triggered, of course, by travel. But by "travel" we do not mean mere sightseeing. We mean immersion in worldviews that are sufficiently dissimilar to our own to challenge our habitual biases and inherited beliefs and to force us to view reality through different colored lenses. Travel, so defined, changes how we think about ourselves. We could call this *cultural self-reading,* keeping in mind, of course, that "culture" as a category is indefinably broad. Indeed, it can apply to practically any of the types of self-reading we have outlined up to now, beginning with automatic self-reading. So shot through is our consciousness with the modes of interpretation that are inherent in the environments we inhabit, that such self-reading is effectively *cultural* reading, too. Thus, as sociologist Peter Berger (1963) puts it, "people on the move physically are frequently people who are also on the move in their self-understanding....As we move from one social world to another, we change...our interpretations and reinterpretations of our biography" (p. 64). In an increasingly multicultural age, a world of difference makes rich self-reading a practice open to us all.

Naturally, some of our travels are undertaken vicariously, in reading about others' travels, too, or through autobiographies that trace the authors' travels across the terrain of their own lives. Whether actual or virtual, then, some of our travels take us more inward than they do outward, as we open ourselves to issues and themes in our innermost lives. Dag Hammarskjöld

(1964), former U.N. Secretary-General as well as closet mystic, described this as indeed "the longest journey" (p. 48) of all. Often associated with the therapeutic process, or with formal meditation in a spiritual context too, such self-reading can also be inspired by our encounters with works of art, whether paintings, plays, poems, or novels, all of which can seed our imagination with metaphors and images that, eventually, we can draw upon to interpret our own experience. But it can be facilitated quite explicitly, in fact, in the course of keeping a journal or of engaging in life-writing of almost any kind. The sheer act of moving the words from the brain to the pen and giving written structure to our memories and emotions pushes us to shift from merely telling our lives to actively reading them. It moves us from the *who, what, when,* and *where* of our texistence (the textual features) to the inevitably more enticing issues of *why* and *how* (the reader constructions). Insofar as it interrogates how we have textualized our lives to date, and insofar as it seeks to make sense of how we make sense, we would call such self-reading *literary self-reading.*

Still, the category is far from monolithic, any more than is literary reading as such. In literary circles, certain approaches to teaching texts are bound to be deemed better than others, depending upon the teacher. Professors with Marxist leanings may urge their students to read D. H. Lawrence rather differently from feminist ones. Similarly, formalist readings of texts will stand apart from post-structuralist ones. With such variations at work in literary reading, the concept of literary *self*-reading is not, therefore, straightforward, and its fleshing out will be our aim throughout Part II.

For now, the point to keep in mind is that each of us is capable of reading our lives in multiple ways at once, some of them more valuable than others in terms of how they contribute to, how they widen and deepen, our narrative development. Moreover, many of them will be happening more or less at once. Prescribed self-reading and doctrinaire self-reading can be tough to tease apart, for example, as can relational and therapeutic self-reading. Another point worth making is that the more modes of self-reading we are involved in, the more "nattery" it can get inside our heads. One voice is quoting Shakespeare at us, another reminding us that we are a Leo, another urging us to nurture our inner child. The extent of our internal cacophony depends, again, on the range of narrative environments that we move in and out of in any given day: from the hub-bub over breakfast, to the cut-and-thrust of office interactions, to the camaraderie of the club we belong to in the evening. The more varied the environments we are exposed to, the more muddled we may become, and the more "saturated" our sense of self (Gergen, 1992)—but at the same time, the more substantial and more interesting as well.

A possibility not to miss in all of this is that traces of the interpretations that each kind of self-reading elicits in us are never wholly lost. Rather, they take their place within the ever-thickening text that is inseparable from who we are. For evidence, we need only recall our discussion in Chapter 2 of the array of odd ideas that, out of nowhere, our natterers can suddenly come up with. That said, it is *literary self-reading,* or literary self-literacy as we called it in Chapter 4 (see also Randall, 1999), that we are keenest to consider in the remainder of this book. More than any other type, it is alert to the multitude of interpretations to which self-reading in general can lead. In that respect, it is the key to growing old, to aging in a mindful manner—a poetic manner. But this insight raises the issue of evaluation.

THE ISSUE OF A "GOOD" LIFESTORY

It is one thing to identify the kinds of contexts in which self-reading occurs. It is quite another to specify what constitutes a healthy, or optimal, or otherwise desirable self-reading. In a postmodern climate, of course, the whole question of evaluation—whether, for example, a literary work is deemed good or bad in terms of its artistic merit—is publicly addressed with the greatest of reservations, if addressed at all. Privately, however, individual scholars will surely have their favorites: works whose qualities, for whatever reason, they happen to admire. Not only that, but surely all of us can identify features that we look for in a story that seems good to *us:* whether it have subtly drawn characters, be loaded with action, or force us to think. And naturally, tastes will vary. One person's treasure will be another one's trash; what one considers high literature, the other will dismiss as fluff. But comparable considerations are involved with lifestories, too.

In numerous quarters, including psychology, sociology, and ethics, not to mention the study of autobiography itself, an assortment of criteria has been advanced for determining what constitutes a good lifestory: one that lets us live our lives in a sensible, responsible, more or less satisfying manner, whether we share it with others or keep it to ourselves. To the extent that a life is inseparable from its telling, and our story of our life is at bottom our identity, much thus rides on how we tell it—but not just tell it: how we read it. Indeed, as we shall be arguing here, the goodness of our story lies ultimately in the reading that we give it.

The criteria used to assess a lifestory hinge, of course, on our frame of reference. For instance, "each psychoanalytic theorist," writes Adam Phillips (1994, p. 70), "is telling us, implicitly or explicitly, his or her version of what a good lifestory is." What a developmentalist deems a good story may be much more comprehensive than what a behaviorist might expect (insofar as a behaviorist sees a lifestory as something worth bothering with at all), or more individualistic than a social constructionist would prefer, more self-absorbed than an ethicist would like, and so on. For a gerontologist, conceivably, a good story might not need to encompass nearly so much of our deep, dark past as it would for a psychoanalyst. Yet it could still be judged good enough to live by, broad enough and resilient enough to cope with the challenges of later life (see Gubrium, 2003). It could still be "adaptively useful" (Schafer, 1983, p. 240). Be this as it may, there can clearly be an overlap in various interpretive agendas. At some point, no doubt, a psychoanalytic agenda merges with an identity one and an adaptation one alike.

Perhaps a good place to begin is with a collection of criteria proposed by McAdams (2001). For McAdams, who maintains that we are "working on" our stories "consciously and unconsciously" all life long (p. 662), "the development of identity in the midlife years should ideally move in the direction of *increasingly good narrative form*" (p. 663). While it is impossible to crawl inside a person's head and determine if such form is really taking shape, McAdams extrapolates from what we tend to look for in stories in general to pinpoint "six standards of good life-story form" (p. 663)—as evidenced, at least, by how we actually talk about or write about our lives. They are: "coherence," "openness," "credibility," "differentiation," "reconciliation," and "generative integration." "The prototype of 'the good story' in human identity," he says—namely, "the life narrative that suggests considerable maturity in the search for unity and purpose in life"—is the one that "receives high marks on these six narrative standards" (p. 663). As will become obvious, though, such standards are closely linked. Also, McAdams's is not the only collection that has been put forward. Nonetheless, it can serve as a starting point for our considerations here, and act as a framework for additional criteria. Perhaps its greatest value lies in its emphasis less on the content of lifestories, which clearly will vary from person to person, than on their overall form.

Coherence

By this standard, McAdams means that the story must "hang together" within itself; it must "make sense on its own terms" (p. 663). It must be "followable," to use psychologist Bertram Cohler's term (1993, p. 113). It should possess Ricoeur's "narrative intelligibility" (2004, p. 243), or what Freeman and Brockmeier (2001) call "narrative integrity." Gerontologist Peter Coleman (1999) agrees. Among the four qualities of what he sees as a "successful life-story" (p. 134), coherence is also first. A good story, he insists, is not simply made up of disparate elements, but displays a "linking thread" and has "eventual goals or objectives" (p. 134). Providing such links in the case of a lifestory, he says, are "life themes" (p. 134), a concept we touched on earlier and will return to in Chapter 8. Another of Coleman's necessary characteristics, "structure," can also be seen as a component of coherence and includes "beginnings and endings" (p. 136)—notwithstanding the troublesome fact, of course, that we cannot remember the beginning of our lives; nor, given that we compose them from within, can we predict how they will end (p. 134). The issue of beginnings and endings, as well as the *sense* of an ending, we have encountered already and will be revisiting in Chapter 10.

The criterion of coherence is relevant as well to what we noted earlier about the multiplicity implicit in self-as-character. As expressed by Polster (1987), "a major challenge in the life of any person" is "to feel whole in the face of great internal diversity" (p. 115). Indeed, narrative incoherence, he says, "is often at the root of personal malaise" (p. 32).

Openness

McAdams (2001) notes, however, that "some stories are almost too coherent. They hang together so neatly that they seem too consistent to be true. The implication," he says, "is that a life-story need not make everything fit together in a person's life" (p. 663). It needs a few loose ends. "We do not need perfect *consistency* in order to find unity and purpose in life" (p. 663). Coleman (1999) claims much the same: "a life-story does not have to be consistent to be coherent" (p. 134). Such thoughts take us, then, to a third standard, openness—specifically, openness "to change and tolerance for ambiguity" (McAdams, 2001, p. 663).

While it can be argued that there is a connection here with one of the "big five" personality traits proposed by McRae and Costa (2003), namely "openness to experience" (p. 34), what is intended here is that a good life-story is resilient and flexible. Remaining open, Bruner and Kalmar (1998) maintain, is not just "culturally adaptive" and "psychologically comfortable" (p. 324), but essential. The consequence of holding on to a set story may well be the "shutting down [of] our possibilities and opportunities prematurely" (p. 324). This point prefigures our discussion of narrative foreclosure in the chapter that follows. By the same token, McAdams (2001) warns, "too much openness reflects lack of commitment and resolve" (p. 663). How a person strikes a balance between too little openness and too much is an issue we will be pondering further on. Preliminarily, though, it can be proposed that taste and tolerance will inevitably vary. Too much openness for one individual could be far too little for another.

Credibility

Next, if the furor over James Frey's (2003) purported autobiography, *A Million Little Pieces,* is any indication, one's story must not be a lie. While it may not (cannot) be totally comprehensive, it should at least be convincing. It should enable us "to re-present [our] self to others with a suasory purpose" (Fireman, McVay, & Flanagan, 2003, p. 5). While it need not (cannot) be the whole truth, it should at least *ring* true—or be as truthful as it can. Specifically, it needs to be congruent with "the facts that can be known or found out" (McAdams, 1993, p. 111) about the life it is supposedly the story of, in much the same way as reader constructions must take account of textual features. A "self-narrative," writes philosopher David Polonoff (1987) in an essay on self-deception, should possess "empirical adequacy" (p. 51). It "must be not only internally coherent but externally coherent as well" (p. 50). Certainly in a clinical context, as Polkinghorne notes (1988), "the therapeutic narrative needs to include those factual events that do exist" (p. 180). In an article in which he addresses the issue of truth in self-narratives, Neisser (1994) argues that, indeed, facts do matter. We must have "an honest account" of what actually happened in the past in order to "manage the present or survive the future." Even in the absence of such an account, he insists, "we must still *believe*" that certain events clearly happened in the past, and that those events have led to "specific consequences" (p. 1).

The criterion of credibility relates to the "coverage" of one's lived experience that one's story is able to achieve (Bruner, 1987, p. 14). A valid question, of course, is how much coverage is enough coverage. If none of us is capable of remembering everything that has happened in our lives (nor should we want to, one might say), then we cannot cover everything. It is simply "not possible for [our] narratives to encompass the full richness of our lived experience" (White & Epston, 1990, p. 40). Still, says McAdams (2001), "the good, mature, and adaptive life story cannot be based on gross distortion." Identity, he reminds us, "is not a fantasy" (p. 663).

A further aspect of credibility is that a lifestory needs to be socially accountable—not necessarily acceptable, but at least accountable. Without caving in to the pressures of the sorts of doctrinaire contexts that we talked about above, a lifestory still needs to be coherent in a cultural sense. As Gergen (1994) states, "we are scarcely free to report on our past lives in any way we wish" (p. 40). "Life stories must mesh within a community of life stories," Bruner explains (1987, p. 21). If the storyteller and the storylistener do not share a similar understanding of the "'deep structure' about the nature of a 'life'" (p. 21), they will be incapable of grasping each other's meaning. One's self-narrative must make sense, echoes Cohler (1993), "in the terms specified by a particular culture" (p. 111). In Polkinghorne's (1988) words, people's "personal stories are always some version of the general cultural stock of stories about how life proceeds" (p. 107)—in other words, some version of the forms of self-telling that are mediated by the various environments in which we live. For this reason, "the coherence of a personal story is not a simple matter of *internal consistency,*" insist Holstein and Gubrium (2000). Rather, "any one person's story may have multiple coherences" (p. 107).

Differentiation

The notion of "multiple coherences" links with McAdams's (2001) fourth standard. By differentiation, he means that the story—any story—ought to be "rich in characterization, plot, and theme." When it is, "the reader is drawn into an intricately textured world in which full-bodied characters develop in intriguing ways over time" (p. 663). Theologian Michael Novak (1971) relates this same quality to the sphere of lifestory. "The richer a life," he observes, "the more subplots the story encompasses. Interesting people are full of contradictions" (p. 49). Such an insight is reminiscent of a point made by writer Thomas Moore (1992). "A soulful personality," he says, "is complicated, multifaceted, and shaped by both pain and pleasure, success and failure" (pp. xvi–xvii). The goal of "care of the soul," to use his term, is thus "a richly elaborated life." It can be argued, however, that many of us live less elaborated lives, and thus more impoverished lives, than we need to. In effect, we suffer from what Fulford (1999) describes as "narrative depriva- tion" (p. 20). To the extent that "a good story ... is essential to a sense of self-worth," we are "story poor." Yet what we are lacking, we would argue, is not so much interesting life-events as the quality of interpretation that we bring to those we have: which is to say, the depth to which we read them.

The comment by Novak above implies that a salient aspect of differentia- tion is sheer interestingness. Again, "interesting" need not mean "exotic." One need not scale an Everest nor win gold at the Olympics to have a captivat- ing tale. Such accomplishments can help, but they are not essential. All too often, when those hailed as heroes by the media are interviewed about their achievements, their tales sound blasé and self-absorbed, or superficial to the point of boring. On the other hand, what might seem the most ordinary, most mundane of lives can contain more than enough material—properly read—for a gripping book or two. As Polster (1987) reminds us, everyone's life is worth a novel. Just as with literary stories, what renders lifestories com- pelling in the final analysis is not textual features but reader constructions.

By the same token, an element of adventure is not without its payoff. Psychologist Karl Scheibe (1986) argues that adventure plays a central role in both the composition and elaboration of "satisfactory" lifestories (p. 131). For him, a life lived "on a single plane is simply insufficient as a story—it doesn't go anywhere." For Bruner (1999), a story must have "trouble"—in other words, "an imbalance that creates the engine of the story" (p. 8). If the story lacks trouble, "it is likely to run out" (p. 9). In short, no trouble, no tale. If one is the protagonist of one's story (and not everyone is), then the point could be rephrased: no agon, no adventure. Adventures are vital, says Scheibe (1986, p. 131), to "the development, maintenance, and occasional metamorphoses of human identity." He is quick to stress, however, that "adventure" need not mean *high* adventure, as in high risk, life or death endeavors. Indeed, the range of what counts as adventure is limitless. As he puts it, "participation can be direct or vicarious, the venture can carry one no further than one's garden or to the ends of the earth" (p. 131). Included as well, of course, are the vicarious adventures we experience with books.

Another way of talking about differentiation is, once more, to say that a good lifestory becomes increasingly thick. As discussed in Chapter 3, the sheer passage of time means that there is inevitably more going on in the story—more levels and layers to it, more twists and turns—not just in terms of events themselves but of the themes discernible within them. And this increased complexity—that is to say, *narrative* complexity (McAdams, 1988, pp. 105–132)—will eventually be reflected in how we talk about our lives and in how we think about them, too. Obviously, some people will talk and think with greater complexity and subtlety than others. The impression we have in listening to them is of unspoken stories lurking between the lines. But as we shall see more clearly in Chapter 7, memory itself acquires an increasing thickness over time—a "thick autonomy," as phenomenologist Edward Casey (1987, p. 266) calls it. And as Chapter 8 will show, thickness is precisely what *narrative* therapists encourage in their clients: the deliberate thickening of self-affirming story-lines to take the place of the dysfunctional, more problem-laden ones by which they have been living (Freedman & Combs, 1996, pp. 194ff). The whole theme of thickness raises a question, though, in relation to what can transpire sometimes with age. From childhood through adulthood, our lives tend to become more complicated, true, as we take on families and careers and accumulate ever more experiences, both positive and negative. Yet with retirement from the workaday world, a certain narrowing can occur as well, leading, not to more differentiation in our stories, but rather to less.

A further component of differentiation returns us to McAdams's (1996) concept of "imagoes"(p. 141), as to Hermans's (2002) "dialogical self." Such a self, says Hermans, is characterized by a "unity-in-multiplicity" (p. 23).

Indeed, despite the twin "pitfalls" of "premature unity" on one hand and "unintegrated multiplicity" on the other, "the coexistence of unity and multiplicity is central to the multivoiced, dialogical self" (p. 24). In fleshing out Freud's image of a person as, at bottom, a "cast of characters," Bruner and Kalmar (1998) support this view by proposing that the work of a playwright or novelist is a metaphor for the unity-yet-multiplicity that constitutes our inner world. The author, they say, first "decomposes" himself or herself into the various characters that feature in the story, and then, in the course of writing it, "brings them all together." Our lives, they suggest, work much the same way, consisting of several "constituent sub-Selves" that, with differing degrees of success, our story attempts to unite (p. 321).

Reconciliation

As for this fifth standard, while the good story "raises tough issues and dynamic contradictions," it also "provides narrative solutions that affirm the harmony and integrity of the self" (McAdams 2001, pp. 663–664). Indeed, says McAdams, reconciliation is "one of the most challenging tasks in the making of life stories, especially in midlife and beyond" (p. 664)—and especially, we could add, in conjunction with trauma. Assuming that what Coleman (1999) calls "assimilation" is akin to reconciliation, the "assimilation of traumatic experience is necessary for the creation of a satisfactory life story" (p. 136). Assimilation here is to be differentiated from accommodation, a distinction of importance to gerontologists, for instance, when dealing with the topics of coping and stress (see Coleman & O'Hanlon, 2004, p. 93). From a narrative perspective, accommodation amounts to changing the event to fit one's story. By contrast, assimilation is changing, expanding, or otherwise revising one's story in order to account for the event. Without assimilation, says Coleman, one's story will suffer "ambiguity" and "fragmentation" (1999, p. 136). Surely, "fragmentation" captures the experience of the concentration camp survivors whom Lawrence Langer (1991) writes about in his disturbing book, *Holocaust Testimonies: The Ruins of Memory.* In Chapters 7 and 8 we will be returning to this dark, seemingly unassimilable side which memory surely has.

Generative Integration

McAdams's sixth standard combines two key concepts from Erikson's seventh and eighth stages of development: *generativity* and *integrity.* In Chapter 3, when considering the mythic and post-mythic stages in the development of identity, we touched on what this term means: namely, that one's self-story should eventually be oriented toward the wider world. At some point, one's quest for narrative coherence should benefit one's community, one's society. To anticipate a theme we will consider more fully in Chapter 10, one's story ought to link with the story of humanity and thus transcend itself, which is another way of saying that the discussion of a good lifestory leads sooner or later to discussions of morality. As we noted when looking at the role of literature in helping us live our lives, narratives "do moral work" (Nelson, 2001, p. 36). To put the point another way, notions of a good lifestory are inseparable from notions of a good life. "Narrative integrity," as Freeman and Brockmeier (2001) argue, "encompasses both aesthetics and ethics" (p. 76).

Additional Criteria

Obviously, there is more to McAdams's standards than meets the eye. And there is no lack of overlap among them—coherence and credibility, openness and differentiation being prime examples. In addition, the pendulum may swing between, say, differentiation and coherence. How much differentiation can we embrace before the coherence of our story is in jeopardy? And how do we balance indeterminacy with integration, or openness with structure? All of this makes the issue of evaluation that much more challenging. In addition to the six "narrative standards" proposed by McAdams, and in light of our reflections on reading in Chapter 4, four further criteria can also be discussed: *critical awareness, ironic orientation, vitality,* and *truth value.*

Critical awareness links to transformative learning. It links, too, to what adult educators call "critical thinking" (Brookfield, 1987). As narrators-readers of our own stories, we are alert to how our habitual ways of plotting our experiences and characterizing our selves, plus the themes we see as important, have been internalized from the environments our lives are shaped within—from family to community, class, and creed. We are mindful, that is, of how our strategies for self-telling and self-interpreting reflect the technologies of self-construction that are intrinsic to those environments. A good lifestory is thus one in which, while we are living it, we maintain something of an affectionate detachment from its narrative roots: in other words, we keep our (narrative) options open. If pressed to tie this criterion to one already listed, the most likely candidate is openness.

Ironic orientation is akin to critical awareness, but again by "ironic" we do not mean "cynical" or "sarcastic." Rather, an ironic stance accompanies the realization that any aspect of our lives—any portion of *the story of my life*—is susceptible to multiple interpretations, due among other things to the virtually unlimited combination of contexts in which we can read them. As a quality of a lifestory, ironic orientation has to do with the point of view from which our self-narrating and self-reading are carried out. As it were, we *see through* ourselves within the story of which we are, at once, character, narrator, and reader. Without necessarily being disillusioned, we accept the unreliability of each of the stances we occupy toward it. We also see, and perhaps even celebrate, the indeterminacy of its meaning. We understand that we do not understand; we know that we do not know—statements that point to wisdom, our focus in Chapter 9.

Vitality is one of the criteria for "adequate narratives" identified by psychotherapist Susan Baur (1994, p. 26). By it, she means "a lively openness to alternatives," making the link with openness obvious yet again. But the word contains a nuance that merits teasing out. A vital lifestory has a dynamic quality to it. It has "movement" (McAdams, 2006, p. 219). It has purpose. In effect, it has hope. It has what Polster (1987), in his own list of "qualities of a good story-line," identifies as "directedness" (p. 31). A good self-narrative goes somewhere, like we demand of any story. As with generative integration, it stretches outside itself and into the wider world, to the lives and stories of others.

A vital lifestory goes somewhere in a further sense as well. It strains toward its own restorying. It truly unfolds: outgrowing one structure and moving into another, larger one, a process that, in itself, instills in us a greater sense of irony. A good lifestory is capable of continual reconstruction, continual rewriting (Freeman, 1993). A variation on vitality, however, takes us back to the criterion of reconciliation. Polster (1987) calls it "bearability" (p. 30ff), and Polonoff (1987), "livability" (p. 50). Relentlessly assimilating the realities of our lives into the stories of our lives may be all-important. However, "whether in a novel, therapy, or everyday life," says Polster, "an acceptable proportion must be maintained…between pain and other aspects of living" (p. 33).

Lastly, we turn to truth value, which is Coleman's (1999) fourth characteristic of a good lifestory and, admittedly, the most controversial. Certainly, truth in relation to both autobiography (Pascal, 1960; Freeman, 2003b) and autobiographical memory (Neisser, 1994) is eminently debatable. Whose truth? Truth of what type? Yet while it might seem naïve even to broach the topic, it is clear that, as readers of literature, we tend to look to stories for something of enduring significance, for a message, an insight, a truth of some sort: not in a technical or historical sense so much as an aesthetic sense or narrative sense (Spence, 1982). We want the story, not just to ring true, but, as it were, to bring truth. We want to get something out of it, some nugget of wisdom to enrich our souls, both at the time that we read it and, if possible, each time that we return to it. In the poignant phrases of writer Annie Dillard (1989), we want some sense of "beauty laid bare," of "life heightened and its deepest mystery probed" (p. 72). As we will be proposing in subsequent chapters, the same could be said of lifestory. "In your own life story," insists adult educator Robert Atkinson (1995), "is where you will find your truth" (p. 43).

In discussing assimilation, Coleman (1999) refers, for instance, to our story's "central messages" (p. 138). In addition, he makes an observation which, while not without its problems, deserves consideration. A story can be judged as good, he says, not just on whether it is clear and dramatic, or whether it resolves "difficult and ambiguous experiences," but also on whether it presents a "true account" that mediates "lasting human values" in its "moral judgements" (p. 138). While such notions as "true account" and "lasting human values" are relative at best, the reference to "moral judge-ments" leads us back, of course, to the notion of generative integration.

We shall say no more for now about truth value, except to flag it for fur-ther reflection. A thought in the meantime, however, is that, whatever we may mean by it in connection with personal narrative, it is clearly linked to coherence, in the sense of comprehensiveness or coverage. And it is linked to credibility as well. What it is also linked to, we submit, is the idea that the better the story, the more it points beyond itself, or the more it is self-transcendent, like a metaphor or parable—a notion we will be looking at more closely in Chapter 10.

IT'S ALL IN THE READING

Whichever criteria we employ or imply, the very idea of some lifestories' being judged "better" than others might seem every bit as arbitrary and elit-ist as in the case of literary stories, conjuring up images of the so-called canon wars that have rocked the literary community (see Smith, 1983). Yet even if we use "good" with the utmost caution, assessment is unavoidable. Whether we admit it or not, we habitually evaluate other people's stories (if not our own) for their credibility, their coherence, and the like. Further-more, given its preoccupation with definition and delineation, evaluation is what the whole of social science, as science, one can argue, is basically about. But let us pick up on a point that was central to Chapter 4.

A story, *any* story, is only as good as the reading that we give it. How many excellent novels have languished on library shelves, their insights all but wasted on the world, because too few of us were up to the task of giving them a proper read—the unique type of reading that they alone deserve? Again, no reader, no story. When we move from literature to life, the same principle applies. The experience of our life as, indeed, a *story* requires that we engage in some degree of retrospective-prospective reflection. And in a real sense, content is irrelevant. A life filled with what, to someone outside of it, are unusual, exotic events does not, in itself, constitute a good story. Nor does "success" make a difference. Indeed, as we shall consider in Chapter 10, a life fraught with suffering and loss, a life that would be described as a tragedy by almost any measure, can still, if deeply and aesthetically read by the person who is living it, provide the stuff for a powerful story, with its own degree of dignity and integrity. How else does one explain the continuing attraction of our most poignant literary heroes, from Hamlet (Shakespeare, 1604/1974c) to Walter Mitty (Thurber, 1941/2000), and Oedipus (Sophocles, 428 BCE/1987) to Raskolnikov (Dostoyevsky, 1866/1968)? "The good story," Gubrium (2003) observes, "does not always convey good news" (p. 21).

In the end, everything hangs less on textual features than on reader constructions, on the depth of examination—the "thickness" of interpretation (Denzin, 1989, p. 101)—to which our life-texts are subjected. Discussions of a good self-story are, by definition, discussions of a good self-reading. And how well we read the "messy open-ended novel" (O'Brien, 2000, p. 3) that *is* our life connects directly to how well we age—biographically or poetically, that is. It is to the intricacies of such aging that we now need to turn our full attention.

Part II   Growing Old: Poetics Applied

RESTORYING OUR LIVES: THE NEED

FOR NARRATIVE DEVELOPMENT

It is a mistake to regard age as a downhill grade toward dissolution.
The reverse is true. As one grows older one climbs with surprising
strides.
      —George Sand [Amandine Aurore Lucie Dupin]
      (1929, p. 186)

If a person survives an ordinary span of sixty years or more, there
is every chance that his or her life as a shapely story has ended and
all that remains to be experienced is epilogue. Life is not over, but
the story is.
      —Kurt Vonnegut (1982, p. 235)

The first forty years of life furnish the text, while the remaining
thirty supply the commentary;...without the commentary we
are unable to understand aright the true sense and coherence of
the text, together with the moral it contains and all the subtle
application of which it admits.
      —Arthur Schopenhauer (2004, p. 94)

AGING AS IMPETUS FOR NARRATIVE ELABORATION

As *the story of my life* grows longer and thicker with time, so does the neces-sity of submitting it to a serious—aesthetic—reading. That, at any rate, is our thesis in this book, and there is good reason for holding it. Contrary to the stereotype of later life as a time of tranquillity and leisure, aging is hardly for the faint of heart. With it can come changes and losses, transitions and troubles, that can assault our entire sense of self—that, to put it very simply, only a good, strong story can equip us to withstand.

In narrative, of course, trouble is a must. It is the very "engine of nar-rative," the "impetus for its elaboration" (Bruner & Kalmar, 1998, p. 324). No trouble, no tale. When it comes to life-narrative, then, the same assaults that threaten to de-story the self have the potential to restory it, too. In short, elaboration is essential to development—not just to adjustment, or to coping, but to growth. If, as McAdams maintains, lifestory is a principal level of personality (the level of meaning), then as that story is expanded and deepened, our personality will presumably continue to mature. In line with such logic, one source insists that "from a developmental perspective," this is indeed "the major task of late adulthood" (Kropf & Tandy, 1998, p. 7; see also Kaufman, 1986; Viney, 1993; Garland, 1994).

In the first half of life—"the first forty years," in Schopenhauer's phrase (2004, p. 94)—so much can be happening on so many levels that it is as if we build up a backlog of "undifferentiated experience" (Sherman, 1991, p. 232) that requires sorting out. With the second half, however, can come sufficient time and, ideally, sufficient perspective to tackle this task, to examine our lives in earnest. For Cohler (1993), the task amounts to a *restorying* of our lives, insofar as, to provide ourselves with an ongoing "sense of coherence," we need "to change the manner in which [we] use time and memory to order [our] life-story construct" (p. 120). Our overarching aim throughout Part II is to consider what such self-examination, such reading, such resto-rying entails. Our more modest purpose here, however, is to consider how aging itself inspires narrative elaboration—or prompts what is conceivably its opposite: narrative foreclosure. After considering sundry reasons why some people appear to shut their stories down, we conclude with a preview of the final four chapters by sketching the sorts of emotional–intellectual stages we undergo when experiencing a story of any kind, literary or lived. To get us started, though, we need to remind ourselves of the broad types of changes that aging unfailingly brings.

Changing Bodies

One set of changes that it is tempting to think aging, as such, comes down to are those that take place in our body. Along with shifts in levels of hormones, which result inevitably in a shift in our energies overall, not to mention our emotions and our thoughts, scarcely any of our body's several systems—cardiovascular, musculoskeletal, gastrointestinal—will be spared. Whether due to free radicals interfering with operations at the cellular level, the accumulation of cross-linkages at the tissue level, or plain old wear and tear at every level, as well as hundreds of other factors that theorists have identified (see Hayflick, 1994), time takes its toll on everything that, physically, makes us tick: from our organs, to our muscles, to our bones. Even if disease and disability fail to take tolls of their own, our resiliency, immunity, and mobility are all eventually affected. "Nothing in us works well," Scott-Maxwell sighs (1968). "Our flagging bodies have become unreliable. We have to make an effort to do the simplest things" (p. 35). Naturally, so-called normal aging can vary quite remarkably from person to person. One individual at 80 could have the vigor of a 60-year-old, while another at 40 suffers far more ailments than someone 30 years her senior. Still, from a bodily perspective, the news about aging is scarcely reassuring. Notwithstanding the benefits of exercise and good nutrition, the narrative of decline that infects our conceptions of age is not without roots in reality. From the perspective of poetics, though, the story takes a somewhat different form.

Our body is never just a body. It is *our* body. It is essential to our experience of *us*. In many ways, it is the most enduring character in the story of our life, and for better or worse, plays a substantial part in how we see ourselves each day. Certainly, body-image and self-image can be tightly aligned, for men as much as for women, though perhaps in different ways. And as we learned in Chapter 2, our body is the seat of core consciousness: not only the means by which we see—perceive, experience—anything at all, but the repository of some of our deepest, most persistent memories. As author Carolyn Myss (1996) perceives it, "we are all living history books," and "our bodies contain our histories": to the point, indeed, that "biography becomes biology" (p. 40). Writer John Lee (1994) speaks, for instance, of "the dark memories lodged for years in my back, my buttocks, my chest, arms, legs, and throat" (p. 136). To express it another way, our body is not merely the housing of our life; it is the setting of our story, the main (though ever-moving) environment in which that story unfolds. It is also one of its most faithful suppliers of trouble, insofar as its functioning—or not—is all too often the target of our attention: the gout, the difficulty sleeping, the aching joints. As such, it becomes not only unreliable, but antagonistic: our nemesis almost. If our neurons are the locus of our narrative activity, and if many of our noticings and natterings pertain to what our body itself is telling us, then our physical being is at the heart of our being-in-the-world. What is more, this character-cum-setting is continually changing, and sooner or later such changes impel us to rethink our identity: "Who am I, now that I am no longer youthful or able?" Changing bodies means changing stories.

Changing Worlds

Aging brings other changes too. Retiring from a job or a career, we relinquish the role of employee or boss, including, not only the structure or status associated with it, but the sense of identity as well. More than what we do each day, such losses can determine who we *are*. Inasmuch as they remove us from the workplace, they sever us from one of the central settings of our story, one of the principal contexts in which we were used to making sense of it, and the source of many of its major adventures: the time we got promoted, the time we told off the manager, the time we got fired. Then there are the all-too-tangible losses, like loss of income, that threaten the very lifestyle we have grown accustomed to, limiting our options to those our pensions will permit.

To make up for such losses, we may take on roles that offer us comparable compensations, including those of consultant or student, or else invest more of ourselves in roles that we were playing all along, such as volunteer or hobbyist. We may also pour more of our energies into our family or our marriage—more than may be bearable, in fact. For instance, if our partner is ill or disabled, we may don the role of caregiver, becoming a supporting character in his or her narrative and, more and more, a minor one in our own.

The point is, not just physical factors but also environmental ones can have an enormous influence on the ways our story develops, and thus the themes around which it centers: no longer "making a living," for instance, or "getting ahead," but "being myself" or "waiting for death." What is more, aging brings changes, not just to our inner repertoire of imagoes, but to the cavalcade of characters besides ourselves who have featured in our story up to now. A spouse dies, or a colleague or friend, and people who for decades acted alongside us in the drama of our existence are no longer there to supply the same lines, fuel the same subplots, elicit the same selves. The side of us they habitually evoked, the identity they reinforced, fades quietly away. Bit by bit, our story-world shrinks. Our life-plot thins. Meanwhile, the wider world on whose stage we once so smartly strutted our hour, rushes madly on, leaving us estranged from the present scene, out of step, bewildered about what *the story of my life* amounts to.

Obviously, cultures and eras can differ widely in this respect; in how, generally, aging and the aged are regarded (see Keith et al., 1994). In cultures where older adults have been viewed as Elders and accorded automatic deference, the disorientation we experience might be minimal. Yet even in our own culture, the same life-changes that can leave us feeling lost harbor the potential to enliven us as well. No longer beholden to a boss, no longer subordinating our identity to that of someone else, we may feel ourselves at liberty to think what we like, say what we wish, be who we are: to claim at last our rightful authority for storying our lives.

Changing Minds

Aging brings changes, not just in the workings of memory, our focus in Chapter 7, but in other cognitive abilities as well, and not all such changes are negative. Indeed, despite prevailing stereotypes about inevitable deficits on countless levels, late adulthood can be "a period of ongoing intellectual and cognitive growth" that is "qualitatively different from childhood" (Tennant & Pogson, 1995, p. 34).

Gerontologist Gene Cohen (1999, 2001, 2005) argues, for instance, that recent research in neuroscience provides "dramatic reason for optimism for the brain's potential in the second half of life" (2005, p. 13). Along with neurologist Elkhonon Goldberg (2005), Cohen's (2005) positive assessment is based on evidence that the aging brain is much more "flexible and adaptable" (p. xv) than once believed. Indeed, its "complex neural architecture...built over years of experience, practice, and daily living, is a fundamental strength of older adults" (p. 8). Also, it "actively grows and rewires itself in response to stimulation and learning" (p. 7). Through the generation of new neurons— especially in the cerebral cortex, the area responsible for such higher (or, as we would say, editorial) functions as "reflection, planning, decision-making, and emotional control" (pp. 11–12)—our *brain*, says Cohen, is "capable of adapting, growing, and becoming more complex and integrated" (p. 28). But "our *minds*," too, he says, "grow and evolve" (p. 28). Among other things, we "experience less intense negative emotions, pay less attention to negative than to positive emotional stimuli," and are "less likely to remember negative than positive emotional material" (p. 18). Accordingly, "older people are usually calmer in the face of life's challenges" (p. 18). All things considered, the optimistic picture that Cohen paints of later life is one of "psychological development—development of insight, emotional stability, knowledge, creativity, and expressive abilities" (p. 28).

In light of our interests here, three components of this promising vision merit special note. The first is Cohen's (2005) somewhat cryptic yet compelling concept of "developmental intelligence" (pp. 29ff). Such intelligence, he submits, is revealed in "deepening wisdom, judgement, perspective, and vision" (pp. xix–xx). Furthermore, it involves awareness of our own development (p. 35). For instance, wisdom, he proposes, "is how developmental intelligence reveals itself" (p. 38). The links between developmental intelligence and narrative intelligence, not to mention reading our lives in the self-aware ways we are considering in this book, are intriguing, to say the least.

A second component, however, relates to what Cohen describes as a "rearrangement of brain functions that makes it easier to merge the speech, language, and sequential thinking typical of the left hemisphere with the creative synthesizing of the right hemisphere" (p. 23). In effect, wired into the mature brain is an "inner push" to engage in "summing up," or to find "larger meaning in the story of [our] lives through a process of review, summarizing, and giving back" (p. 75)—what elsewhere we have labelled "the autobiographical imperative" (Randall, 1995, pp. 209–33). Simply put, increased "bilateral involvement" between left-brain and right-brain activities issues in a drive toward greater "autobiographical expression" (Cohen, 2005, p. 22). One might even speculate that our built-in drive to engage in narrative thought is actually intensified with age.

The third component of interest concerns the four overlapping "human potential phases," as Cohen (1999) calls them, which in his view pick up "where Erikson left off" (2005, pp. 52–53) with respect to the second half of life. He identifies them (1999) as: "midlife re-evaluation" (mid-30s to mid-60s), "liberation" (mid-50s to mid-70s), "summing up" (late 60s to mid-80s), and "encore" (late 70s to end of life). The mere fact that Cohen proposes such a schema, though we cite it simply as background for the four phases we ourselves will be proposing, supports the view that, developmentally, later life is far more intricate than hitherto assumed. At bottom, it affords us tremendous room to grow. The argument that advancements in neuroscience support the cognitive potential of later life, as they do its narrative complexities, is one we find both heartening and persuasive.

In the meantime, aging affects more than the mechanics of the brain–mind process. It affects its contents, too. It affects not only *how* we think but *what*—in this case, what we think about our "accumulated life experience" (Tennant & Pogson, 1995, p. 34): in short, our story. Harking back to our imagery in Chapter 2, the subject of our natterings may hardly be the same as when we were young, and understandably we will be noticing different things, both inside us and out. What is more, our noticers and natterers themselves will be older, as will our inner editor, although the impact of aging on each of these functions will vary from person to person. For some, their natterers may grow deafeningly loud. For others, their editors will become more rigid, or more relaxed.

Turning from the micro to the macro level, we may experience a greater awareness of our internalized text as, indeed, *text*, plus a greater sense of urgency to grasp the structure of our life as a whole. "What is the shape of my life?" asks Anne Morrow Lindbergh (1955) in a poignant, midlife essay (p. 22). What kind of story is traced by my journey through time, her question might be reworded, and what does it mean? What can also happen is that we have a heightened sense of how dense time's passage has rendered our story: all the places we have been, troubles we have seen, lessons we have learned. By the same token, we may be stunned at what is missing, and feel compelled to fill in the blanks before it is too late—to ferret out corners that have receded from sight and coax memories to the surface that time has all but buried. We may also find ourselves striving to understand the episodes of our life, be they happy or horrific, delightful or disturbing, as exactly that: as episodes, scenes, and chapters in an otherwise coherent narrative whole—a story that has its roots, of course, in several sources and can be told from several angles. Fostered within us too, therefore, may be a growing openness to complexity, a higher tolerance for paradox, and, overall, a more ironic stance on life. And all such shifts in insight, subtle though they are, will be fuelled by the conviction that time is of the essence, that our mortality is real.

From changing bodies through changing worlds to changing minds, it comes as no surprise therefore that, for many of us, aging can carry with it a measure of narrative confusion. We lose the thread of our story; we can no longer keep it straight in our heads. Meanwhile, traces of its previous versions can taunt us for the clarity or confidence with which they once infused our sense of self. In consequence, we become vulnerable to the narrative of decline. Lacking a suitable "counter-story" (Nelson, 2001)—a narrative of "progress" (Gullette, 2004), a "remythologized" version of our life that empowers us to move forward (Bianchi, 2005, p. 320)—we run the risk of viewing aging as a way to the darkness, not the light (Nouwen & Gaffney, 1976). We run the risk of narrative foreclosure.

NARRATIVE FORECLOSURE VERSUS NARRATIVE DEVELOPMENT

According to Erikson (1968), the question all of us must grapple with, especially in our teens, is the question of *identity*. "Who am I, as distinct from my parents, siblings, peers? Who am I in relation to my future, on one hand, and my past on the other? And what has that past entailed? Are my values genuinely mine or have I merely parroted them from others?" Such questions are central to the *conflict*, as Erikson (1968) describes it, that confronts us on the border between childhood and adulthood—a period, when, coincidentally, changes linked to puberty make us take more notice of our body as indeed a central player in our story. Failure to resolve this conflict, this *crisis*, more or less successfully results in uncertainty about who we are apart from the roles we play in other people's lives.

Our argument here, as we hinted back in Chapter 3, is that issues of identity can continue into later life, when, once again, changes in our body itself are often what prompt them to return. Just when we might assume that they were settled long ago, those issues can assail us with a vengeance, reinvolving us "in the psychosocial process that dominated adolescence" (Erikson, Erikson, & Kivnick, 1986, p. 129). An acquaintance of one of us, for instance, once voiced his frustration at society's obsession with the proverbial midlife crisis. Recently retired, he found this most unfair. "What about the late-life crisis?" he exclaimed, and then went on to rattle off the ways in which Who am I? was plaguing him. *Who am I*, went the gist of his confusion, now that I'm no longer employed; now that I have all this time on my hands; now that my joints are cranky and my memory is letting me down? In his book *The View from 80*, author Malcolm Cowley (1980) sums the matter up: "Even before he or she is 80," he says, "the aging person may undergo another identity crisis like that of adolescence. Perhaps there had also been a middle-aged crisis, the male or the female menopause, but for the rest of adult life he had taken himself for granted, with his capabilities and failings. Now, when he looks in the mirror, he asks himself, 'Is this really me?'—or he avoids the mirror out of distress at what it reveals, those bags and wrinkles" (p. 7).

Identity Statuses

The late-life crisis may be no more universal, of course, than its midlife counterpart (see Willis & Reid, 1999). Yet surely how we cope with matters of identity as we age merits attention of its own. To that end, the work of psychologist James Marcia (1966) provides us with a helpful frame of reference. Expanding upon Erikson's (1968) basic formulation for the fifth stage in his model of psychosocial development, namely, "identity vs. role diffusion," Marcia identifies four possible *identity statuses* that characterize the lives of young adults: *identity achievement, identity moratorium, identity foreclosure,* and *identity diffusion.* Formulated in terms of the broad themes of exploration and commitment, Marcia's framework suggests a spectrum of approaches that older adults, too, may take when responding to the challenges of age.

Identity achievers are at the most developed end of the spectrum. Having passed through "a crisis," says Marcia (1966), they have ultimately committed themselves to "an occupation and ideology" (p. 551). They have high self-esteem (p. 557), and are independent thinkers capable of handling unexpected events (p. 551). The next group, those in a state of identity moratorium (a classic example being university students), are still in the midst of active crisis. "Bewildered," they are preoccupied with "attempting a compromise" between, on one hand, the demands of their parents and society, and on the other, their own abilities (p. 552). Not so the identity foreclosers, who instead of experiencing a crisis have adopted parental beliefs and values wholesale, notably "obedience, strong leadership, and respect for authority" (p. 557). In consequence, they are characterized by "vulnerable" self-esteem and "unrealistic" responses to failure (p. 557). Finally, the least developed of all are the identity diffusers, who are simply uncommitted, whether they have experienced a crisis or not (p. 552). Uninterested in taking up an occupation or developing an ideology, they drift aimlessly through life.

Nothing precludes any of Marcia's statuses, of course, from being possibilities for the second half of life. In fact, once one understands identity as basically multiple and not singular in nature, then conceivably the same person could occupy all four of them at once. One of our sub-selves, the one focused on career, for instance, may be basically an achiever, while another, the self that yearns to return to university, is in the midst of a moratorium on the issue, say, of what it wants in life and who it really is. Yet another is an identity diffuser to the extent that, deep down, all it really wants in life is…nothing in particular. Naturally, many older adults can be categorized as identity achievers insofar as the mere fact of holding down a steady job or managing to raise a family implies, to some degree, that they know who they are. Yet from a developmental perspective, especially a narrative one, the state of moratorium also has its merits, as will become clearer in later chapters. Given the toll, though, that the challenges of later life can surely take on a person's sense of self, and the "narrative disruptions" (Fireman, McVay, & Flanagan, 2003, p. 9) they can readily represent, it is the status of identity foreclosure, and in a sense of identity diffusion, that we wish to look at now.

Arrested Aging as Narrative Foreclosure

If identity is a lifestory, then a status that, arguably, many people come to occupy with advancing age is *narrative foreclosure*. Narrative foreclosure, says

Freeman (2000), is the "premature conviction that one's life story has effectively ended" (p. 83), that "there is no prospect of opening up a new chapter" (2003a, p. 2). Although one's life itself continues—beyond retirement, for instance—no truly new events, inner or outer, are deemed likely to occur. One settles into a holding pattern. One's story is little more than denouement, a matter of putting in time until one's death; life and story are thus torn quietly asunder. Such a narrative lacks not just coherence or credibility, though these may be at issue, too. It lacks vitality and therefore hope. It fails to go anywhere (see McAdams, 2006, p. 219).

We are not talking here about physiologically induced foreclosure due to the degeneration of brain cells—although support is in fact expanding for the idea that meaningful narrative activity can still be occurring in the minds of those who are afflicted with dementia (see Crisp, 1995; Basting, 2003). Rather, the foreclosure we are talking about is linked to a loss of imagination, not of neurons. Whether by choice or by default, it is the failure to continue working on our stories, to continue expanding them, exploring their depths, mining them for meaning. It is the refusal to keep growing in the intricate, inner manner—the biographical manner—that later life invites, an invitation that obviously not everyone accepts. As philosopher Harry Overstreet (1949) bluntly notes, "*Not all adults are adult.* Many who look grown-up on the outside," he says, "may be childish on the inside" (p. 19). "Many old people," echoes Carl Jung (1976), expressing the point even more bluntly, "prefer to be hypochondriacs, niggards, pedants, applauders of the past or else eternal adolescents—all lamentable substitutes," he says, "for the illumination of the self, but inevitable consequences of the delusion that the second half of life must be governed by the principles of the first" (p. 17).

Clearly, narrative foreclosure is not limited to later life alone. As we will see in Chapter 8, therapists can encounter clients of any age who are caught in the same old story, a story in some way deficient: too small or neat, too troubled or self-defeating, for them to live full lives. As explained by narrative therapists Michael White and David Epston (1990), "people reach out for therapy when the narratives in which they are 'storying' their experience, and/or in which they are having their experience 'storied' by others, do not sufficiently represent their lived experience" (p. 14). To put it another way, their story is out of step with their life, or at least more than it needs to be, for no story can cover a life completely. Applied to aging in particular, this predicament takes the form of what gerontologist Lawrence McCullough (1993) describes as "arrested aging." In an article on the "power of the past to make us aged and old," McCullough proposes that "time ... has the power to arrest some lives, to bring them to a stop, without death occurring" (p. 185). In such cases, he says, we lose the "ability to respond to time" (p. 186), becoming imprisoned instead in "a past that seems to allow no escape" (p. 91)—a past that contains all that really mattered and that we insist upon returning to through obsessive or escapist reminiscence, themes we will come back to in Chapter 8.

Morson (1994) employs a phrase that speaks to McCullough's point. It is "epilogue time" (p. 193). In discussing various "diseases of presentness" that afflict the characters in conventional fiction, as opposed to the processual fiction of Tolstoy or Dostoyevsky, Morson notes that "real people sometimes live as if their lives were set in epilogue time, so that no present action could make any real difference" (p. 192). In other words, "the important story is over, nothing essential will change" (p. 190). No significant restorying is likely to occur. In the most literal sense possible, one is *post*-mythic. As a consequence, "such lives are often suffused with a delicious nostalgia, a poetic sense of constant distance from a beautiful and irrecoverable past, or a painful recognition of changeless regret" (p. 192).

In arrested aging, or in epilogue time, we are living *in* the past rather than *off* the past. In effect, the past has congealed. Sweet as it may seem, it is no longer alive, no longer open to examination, to reinterpretation. It is no longer developing (Charmé, 1984). Envisioned as a form of "biographically accrued capital" (Mader, 1996, p. 43), our accumulated memories are yielding little interest. As for the insights we might be gleaning, the creativity we might be expressing, they are lost to us. More tragic still, those around us lose out, too, on the cache of "ordinary wisdom" (Randall & Kenyon, 2001) that our story potentially embodies and from which they, like us, could profit. Not that arrested aging is synonymous with emotional dysfunction, nor certainly the sole option where identity is concerned. Yet it is one we might well expect to be linked to lowered self-esteem, and even to depression. In the extreme form, when one is trapped inside a story for which there seems no hope of any more development in a positive or meaningful direction, then suicide becomes a viable, even preferable, alternative (Freeman, 2000, p. 83).

Worth mentioning at this point is a study by pastoral theologian Maxine Walaskay and psychologists Susan Krauss Whitbourne and Milton Nehrke (1983–84). The study explores how older adults deal with Erikson's eighth stage of development, in which the crisis at stake is "ego integrity versus despair" (p. 62). Four "integrity statuses," modeled on Marcia's (1966) construct of identity status, are utilized: "integrity achieving," "dissonant (in crisis)," "foreclosed (avoiding crisis)," and "despairing" (p. 61). An integrity-achiever is an individual who is characterized by self-reflection and acceptance (p. 64), which as we shall see in Chapter 9 is central to Erikson's conception of wisdom. Someone in the dissonant status is "in a state of disequilibrium...similar to the moratorium of Marcia's formulation," (p. 65), whereas a despairing person is "unhappy with his or her past and present life and fearful of death" (p. 64).

Of most interest to us here is the third group, those in the foreclosed status, who, although demonstrating "optimism and a positive state of well-being," resist "self-exploration" and reflection (p. 65) and display "denial" (p. 70). A surprising discovery of Sherman's (1991) research with older adults is that foreclosed individuals constitute the largest group (p. 47). He describes foreclosers as those who "avoid the reflective processes of crisis and life review" (p. 45). While they have "reasonably positive self-concepts" (p. 106), they tend to deny the aging process, and seem unable to accept the "losses and changes" associated with aging as "true psychosocial transitions" (p. 107). Overall, their apparently contented state of mind comes "at the expense of an integrated sense of past, present, and future," and with an absence of "any depth of insight and meaning" (p. 45). In other words, by clinging to "interpretations of things as they were in the past," they are able to deny that any change has taken place (p. 107).

We are in no way claiming that there is a direct link between foreclosure with respect to integrity and foreclosure with respect to identity, nor that the other three statuses in either case have nothing to say to us concerning the poetics of growing old. This is certainly not the situation with diffusers or despairers. Indeed, these statuses may simply be more extreme expressions of foreclosure, and therefore reasons for concern in relation to reading our lives. Accordingly, the causes of foreclosure bear looking into now.

Why We Close Our Stories Down

A variety of factors, many of them beyond our control, and many of which we have hinted at already, can contribute to shutting our stories down. To a good number of them, surely all of us are vulnerable. In other words, foreclosure is something to which everyone, in some respects, succumbs. Narratively speaking, no one is either completely open or completely foreclosed. Still, focusing on a few of these factors will anticipate strategies that we consider later on for how to "reopen" (Freeman, 2000, p. 90) a narrative that has been concluded prematurely. It will also show that to reactivate a stalled story could in fact require entering—or re-entering—a state of moratorium: a state that, while risky in terms of its potential toll on our peace of mind, could open us to the unlived life which theoretically—until our death—we have the capacity to experience.

Before getting underway, it needs to be stressed, however, that we are not talking here about the kind of natural foreclosure that comes with making choices in our lives. By opting for a career in auto mechanics rather than neurosurgery, or in teaching as opposed to acting, we clearly rule out a whole host of subsequent options: concerning our income or social class, for instance, or our prospects for lifestyle or marriage. By the same token, we open up other options instead, intrinsically neither better nor worse but simply different, and, of course, things can always change. In other words, each decision that we make in life automatically both closes and opens our opportunities for the future. While it obviously narrows our development in some respects, it enables it in others. Either way, our existence comes to acquire a certain shape. Foreclosure, as we mean it here, however, has less to do with life events as such than with the ways that we experience and interpret them internally, with what we take from them or make of them in memory and imagination—with how we *read* them. And this, we submit, makes all the difference.

To begin with, the losses that we incur through illness or infirmity can be so numerous and can come in such quick succession that, as Cowley observed above, the sense of identity we had previously established might be incapable of coping with the battering these losses inflict. And some will be so sudden or severe as to stop us entirely. Life as we have known it will grind to a halt. As scholars of narrative medicine have pointed out, our identity shifts to that of "the patient" or "the disabled," narrowing to such an extent that, in our minds, it shuts out virtually everything that we used to be (Frank, 1995). Chronic pain of any kind can take a comparable toll on narrative identity and narrative coherence (see Becker, 2001). To put it another way, if our self-image is tied too tightly to our body-image, then as the latter becomes diminished in our eyes, the former will inevitably suffer. It will succumb to the narrative of decline, supported, as that narrative surely is, by the medicalization of aging as, essentially, a sickness unto death. If our personal narrative is too thin, too simple, or too small to assimilate the challenges that we meet, then in one way or another we will shut ourselves down, cauterizing our development and retreating into a defensive, even desperate, position—the very opposite of ego integrity. On the other hand, if we were living out of a deeper, more nuanced narrative, the same challenges, rather than stunting our story, could encourage its continued elaboration.

Besides conditions in our present, events in our past can also be so traumatic, so embarrassing, or simply so odd as to be impossible to assimilate into our overall narrative. We have not yet storied them in an intentional way—the really important events, that is: the ones we suspect are pivotal to our identity yet we lack the language or courage to recount, the ones fraught with unfinished business, the ones that force us to throw up our hands and say: "How can I put this into words? Who would understand? Where would I begin?" Preventing us from beginning may be the secret realization that our present self-story is not big enough to envelop them, and that for it to do so would require radical rewriting. The prospect of the ensuing narrative up-heaval, in our own lives and quite possibly in others' lives, as well, is enough to keep us from "going there," from opening a Pandora's box of potential emotional mayhem.

Another possibility, which (paradoxically) may itself be due to the stren-gthening of neuronal pathways in the maturing brain (Goldberg, 2005, pp. 123ff), is that, because of our success throughout the years in mak-ing sense of the events of our lives in familiar and feasible ways, we have fallen into "interpretive parsimony." Philosopher Carlos G. Prado (1986), who coined the concept, defines it as "stereotypic thinking, reliance on fa-voured—and even compulsive—metaphors and constructions" (p. 9). It is "the tendency to respond to new situations in ways we have responded to old ones," with similar editorial priorities, as it were. Though he is insistent that interpretive parsimony "has nothing to do with aging as such," Prado argues that "too many of us too often respond to the world in 'tried and true' ways rather than make use of other options" (p. 9). Early on, for instance, we quietly commit ourselves to a particular genre for storying our lives and feel a certain sense of loyalty ever after to keep the faith: once a tragic hero, always a tragic hero. Indeed, the mere thought of having to respond to the challenges and complexities of life with more appropriate, more compre-hensive interpretive frameworks can, for some of us, be exhausting. We would rather not think about it. Like the foreclosers we referred to above, we would do anything to avoid changing "our old assumptive worlds" (Sher-man, 1991, p. 107). We thus succumb to a "freezing of the past...that allows no flexibility for choice or action in the future" (p. 244). At the expense of personal growth, we become conservative, rigid, set in our ways. We become, quite literally, old-timers, well before our time.

Part of the reason is that we have not learned—have not been encouraged, perhaps—to read our experiences in the variety of ways we are considering in this book, nor the variety of contexts. Like most of us with literary texts, we chronically under-read the texts that time has been gathering inside of us. To borrow from a narrative therapy perspective (Morgan, 2000), we live with "thin descriptions" of our lives and thus draw "thin conclusions" (pp. 12–13)—not just about our own identities but usually about others', too. We under-story them. We story them not as open and flexible beings, but as fixed and unidimensional, as having no narrative options other than the meager few that we assign them. We "storyotype" them (Randall, 1995, p. 57), as we do ourselves, reducing our identity to "just a housewife," "just a student," or the like.

Along similar lines, we may be subscribing to a concept of memory itself that is thin, not thick, in nature, and that rules out the element of invention. Individual recollections are taken as reliable replicas of what actually occurred. Apart from the odd flash of awareness that, yes, we sometimes embellish the facts, we have no sustained sense of the arbitrariness of memory, of the immense amount of selecting and summarizing that it typically entails. We experience it as being almost exclusively about textual features, not about reader constructions. We have little clear conception of the alternative versions into which an event might, quite legitimately, have been spun at the time, and could be re-spun now. What we remember is what took place: end of story. Armed with such a conviction, it is scarcely surprising, then, that as "benign senescent forgetfulness" occasionally besets us and our recollections of particular experiences inevitably fade, we descend into a panic that we are losing our memory, that dementia is just around the bend.

Still on memory, we may have hinged our identity on anecdotes that are ultimately rather limited in range; incidents, whether positive or negative in nature, that we take as paradigmatic of what our life has consisted of to date: moreover, that we insist on remembering in one main way, not accepting that any memory is at best a reconstruction and at worst a falsification of whatever it purports to represent. Furthermore, whenever we endeavor to write such anecdotes out, the events at their center surrender their "eventness" (Morson, 1994, pp. 20–22) to the conventions of grammar and syntax. They become freeze-framed in print. Thereafter, what we recall are not the events themselves but the polished versions that make it to the page. As author Annie Dillard (1987) warns: "Don't hope in a memoir to preserve your memories," for "it is a certain way to lose them" (p. 70). Concerning her own attempts at memoir-writing, she offers this confession: "after I've written about any experience, my memories—those elusive, fragmentary patches of color and feeling—are gone; they've been replaced by the work" (p. 71). Philosopher Georges Gusdorf (1980) refers to this dilemma as "the original sin of autobiography" (p. 41). Similarly, journal entries written during the height of an emotional firestorm can lock one into a particular interpretation of the events that sparked it off—ironically, leading to narrative foreclosure before one has even had ample time to absorb them, much less make sense of them. In general, inasmuch as our inner natterers appear to prattle on about several things at once, the effort to capture what they are saying is inescapably to edit them, more or less severely. It is to choose from among them one line of thought in particular, thereby silencing—or at least ignoring—what our other inner voices might wish to assert. For those of us whose talents lie less with writing than they do with talking, a comparable foreclosure can occur with the experiences we recount to others. What is more, our very success as a raconteur could lock us into what are ultimately rather thin, parsimonious versions of our life's events, versions that, all too easily, we ourselves begin believing. The better part of self-understanding, then, may not be speech at all, but silence.

In light of such phenomena, Freeman (2000) points out that autobiography is not entirely benign, for the very process of "narrativization" can lead to "claustrophilia" (p. 91), namely, the impulse to develop a complete and coherent story in which everything makes sense—a story, one could say, that imposes upon the past not only an artificial sense of neatness and closure, but the quality of meant-to-be. Paradoxically, narrative can be as "stifling" as it is freeing, sometimes "serving to constrict and delimit the scope of meaning" (p. 90). With respect to memoir, for example, the act of writing out our story, which on one hand enables us to expand it more fully, can force it into an unwarranted coherence. It becomes "too coherent" (McAdams, 2001, p. 663), too neat, too formulaic, too uni-dimensional. The written text fixes the internal text (see Olson, 1990), and such fixing breeds foreclosing. We will be revisiting such dangers in the chapters that follow. In the meantime, it is worth noting Freeman's (2000) observation that, if we wish to escape the "stranglehold" of narrative foreclosure, we may ultimately need to "move beyond narrative itself." But is this even possible? he wonders, as do we: "Can there be a human world apart from stories?" (p. 91).

Another factor to consider in narrative foreclosure is that the principal story by which we have identified ourselves to date has been so bound up with a particular role (Breadwinner-Parent, Super Mom, Master and Commander of the Corporation) that we are prevented from emplotting the countless situations, big and little, that fall outside its scope. We are impeded from appreciating happenings in our lives that are automatically edited out because they fail to fit the storyline by which, dysfunctional or not, we have preferred to live thus far (Freedman & Combs, 1996). In essence, we have over-invested in a subset of sub-selves, thereby closing off our narrative options just at the stage when, through retirement or the empty nest, we are cut off from the very environments and routines by which the content of these selves was regularly reinforced. As we saw in Chapter 5, the consequence of clinging to a set story may well lead to what Hermans calls "premature unity" (2000, p. 24), or what Sherman (1991) labels "an all too limited identity lived"

(p. 243). Once again, we get taken in by our own stories. Erikson (1998) speaks of what happens in such a case as "a retrospective mythologizing that can amount to a pseudointegration as a defence against lurking despair" (p. 65). Overall, we face the constant need, narratively speaking, of "keeping one's options open," of "staying loose" (Bruner & Kalmar, 1998, p. 324)—a point that underscores the criterion of differentiation.

No doubt, gender figures prominently here as well. Some men, for instance, can be so concerned with "being a Man" and with conveying the impression that they know who they are and know what they want, that their story is prematurely stifled and resistant to revision: "monothematic" in, say, its focus on career (Ruth, Birren, & Polkinghorne, 1996), or simply imprisoned in machismo. For some, therefore, retirement represents, not merely a turning-point in their lives, but the endpoint. The findings of gerontologist Brian Gearing (1999) concerning the experience of former professional soccer players are telling in this regard. Given the tight-knit community that a soccer team can be, and the surplus of fame that its members are accorded rather early in their development, when in effect a moratorium is placed for them on the task of creating an adult identity, the "particular kind of identity" that their footballing career has shaped in them "can be problematic for later well-being" (p. 42). To develop a "post-football identity" requires that they engage in what Gearing calls "re-versioning the self" (p. 51). Not just star athletes and not just retirees or veterans in general, but also the men in their 40s interviewed by Rosenberg, Rosenberg, and Farrell (1999) for their research into "the midlife crisis" could suffer a "loss of narrative coherence" (p. 68).

Also, although perhaps somewhat differently for women than for men, the body itself, its appearance and performance, can become the major protagonist of our story, indeed the *antagonist*, especially as we age. The consequence? Our story becomes less differentiated and our options less open. "Having cancer," for instance, takes over. It usurps our guiding self-narrative. It is not just a particular theme; it is the whole story, the only story. Says novelist Alice Hoffman (2001), writing about her own experience coping with the disease: "some chapters inform all the others. These are the chapters of your life that wallop you and teach you and bring you to tears" (p. 98). As the field of narrative medicine is revealing (see Frank, 1995; Charon, 2006), such chapters can determine our identities in unexpected and debilitating ways.

Gender is also linked to genre. Catherine Bateson (1989) maintains, for instance, that men have been culturally conditioned to story their experiences in accordance with "the image of a quest," which is to say "a journey through a timeless landscape toward an end that is specific, even though it is not fully known" (pp. 5–6), any frustration of which is a recipe for disillusionment and for slipping into a tragic sense of life. In contrast, an ironic stance may come more naturally to many women, whose career paths and life paths alike have tended to be much more broken up, much more diversified, given their multiple tasks and the multiple roles that, traditionally, they have filled. Their lives are composed from the outset according to a more "improvisatory" score (p. 3). In terms of a poetic approach to aging, however, this can prove a powerful advantage. Insofar as it is a recognizable milestone, retirement can constitute a new beginning as much as it can an end: a time in life to pursue one's development in earnest, and in numerous directions at once; a time to drink deeply from "the fountain of age" (Friedan, 1993). Indeed, in an era when the trajectory of a single career is increasingly the exception, "the creative potential of interrupted and conflicted lives," as Bateson says (1989), must not be overlooked—lives in which, regardless of gender, our "energies are not narrowly focused or permanently pointed toward a single ambition" (p. 9). More recently, Bateson extends this perspective even further, stressing the necessity for all of us in our fast-paced global village to envision our lives in terms of "multiple, fluid narratives" (Bateson, 2007, p. 213).

Such thinking enables us to appreciate Freeman's (2000) point that narrative foreclosure is as much a social phenomenon as it is a personal one (p. 90). Just as our identity unfolds within a web of narrative environments and coauthoring relationships from childhood on, so, too, can it be curtailed within them—be "stunted or constrained" (Rosenwald & Ochberg, 1992, p. 1). For many, all too sadly, narrative foreclosure begins more or less at birth and becomes a way of life. As we noted in Chapter 3, if the systems in which our thinking has been shaped—our family, community, culture—fail "to provide adequate narrative resources" (Freeman, 2000, p. 81); if they are unstimulating or restrictive to the point of impoverishment, with too narrow a range of narrative templates, then we will have had scant chance to story our lives in multiple ways. In the extreme case, our unique narratives are silenced altogether. But besides the boundless examples of such silencing, where the abuse is fueled even further by sexist or racist prejudice, our line of work, as well, can be associated with a silencing of sorts, not only when it is soul-destroyingly menial or repetitive, but even when it is high in pay or prestige, or keeps us in the public eye. Whether we are an athlete or a politician, a movie star or minister, people insist on seeing us in terms of our profession first, to the point that our personal identity falls prey to narrative determinism. We end up acquiescing to the typecast, larger-than-life version that our public seems bent on believing, clinging to it long after the applause has died away and the spotlight has been turned on someone else.

With aging itself, as our original social circle shrinks, a comparable closing down can happen. Not only do we lose companionship—and the comfort that comes from feeling that someone knows our story—but the sides of that story, the segments and versions, that he or she habitually elicited will retreat into the background. The possibilities contained within those versions will thus go unexpressed. And as for the individuals, however well-intentioned, who remain behind to assist us in interpreting our experiences, they may do so along thin and stifling lines, not stretching our horizons by presenting us with alternative perspectives, not inspiring us to ask new questions and think new thoughts, but the very opposite, in fact.

To shift now from the theme of particular relationships to that of the larger stories we live within, it is possible as well that, for much of our lives, we have been uncritically committed to the master narrative of a given creed, political or religious. Rather than take authority for composing a story that is authentically our own, we have defaulted to its formulae for self-interpretation, and like the foreclosing adolescents that Marcia identifies, have permitted it to dictate what our identity will be. In the same vein, we may have bought so deeply into the narrative of decline that it, itself, becomes the story through which we understand our destiny. Our image of old age is reduced to "a time in which nothing more can happen" (Coleman, 1999, p. 137) and, in our hearts, growing old is trumped by simply getting old.

A further factor in narrative foreclosure could be our difficulty coping with, let alone conceiving of, The End. The shadow it casts across The Middle and Beginning alike can be so oppressive as to obscure the meaning we might discern in our story as a whole. Accordingly, we fail to give sustained consideration to how we want the story to conclude, and so avoid the pivotal task that, for McAdams (2006) at least, midlife pushes us to undertake: composing a generativity script. Conversely, our sense of The End may be all too clear indeed. Due perhaps to our allegiance to a particular creed, with its clear dictates as to what death entails, we experience the "shutting down" of any sense that an ending other than the one we now foresee is even possible (Freeman, 2000, p. 91). In order therefore to avoid the clutches of narrative foreclosure, Freeman says, we must rewrite the future (p. 90). In Coleman's (1999) words, we must be enabled to understand that the ending of our life is not necessarily a "foregone conclusion" (p. 137). Overall, as we shall be seeing in subsequent chapters, it is questions around anticipated endings, as around time in general, that can often be at issue when our stories cease to grow.

But if endings raise problems, so too can beginnings. If we wish to restart a stalled story, we must rewrite not only the future, but also the past (Freeman, 2000, p. 90). As we age, however, we may grow anxious that to revisit, and maybe reinterpret, the past could mean getting lost in our own story. There is so much in it, so much *to* it. Our story is bigger than we are, we start feeling, and bigger than our ability to make sense of it. Better, then, to quit while we are ahead.

Lastly, it is possible that we have convinced ourselves that our narrative is simply not all that interesting to begin with, not terribly good as lifestories go. Such an attitude can often be detected when conducting open-ended interviews with older adults (Randall, Prior, & Skarborn, 2006). After ten or fifteen minutes of running through a bare-bones version of their life's events—an efferent reading *par excellence*—it is not uncommon to hear them conclude with some throwaway comment like "that's pretty much it." In fairness, a certain amount of such short-windedness could be attributed to their having, at long last, transcended their stories—or simply to having an inexperienced listener. At the same time, the propensity of some people to trot out their tales at the merest hint of an invitation may deter us from burdening the world with our own. Instead, we prefer to close the book, put it to one side, and talk about something else. A still more serious possibility may be, as Marcia (1998) observes, that "some merely carry over into adult form the identity conferred upon them as children" (p. 37). Such a foreclosed identity may be quite "serviceable," says Marcia, provided "the person remains in the same social context throughout their life." However, in "attempting to change a foreclosed identity at midlife or later," he warns, the process can be "especially painful" insofar as forming a new identity must be carried out "under conditions considerably less supportive than existed during the optimal developmental period of adolescence" (p. 37).

Our overall aim in the remainder of this book is to examine various approaches that lie at our disposal for forestalling narrative foreclosure from midlife on, for opening ourselves to the poetics of growing old. Once again, though, this does not mean that those who have, by our reckoning, shut their stories down in pivotal respects (emotionally, relationally, philosophically) cannot move into later life with some measure of contentment or of personal fulfillment. Indeed, as we saw earlier, foreclosed individuals are more likely to represent the rule than the exception (Sherman, 1991, p. 47). That said, to be "normal" in this respect does not necessarily mean to be maturing, deepening, ripening. It is only in growing old, not just getting old, one can argue, that our lives become particularly fulfilling.

STAGES OF ENGAGING WITH STORIES

Anticipating our agenda in the final four chapters, we now need to look at an idea that links back to themes we considered in Chapter 4, particularly the distinction between efferent reading and aesthetic reading. It concerns how literature elicits in us a spectrum of cognitive–emotive effects, ranging from those that are basically affirmative to those that we could call challenging or contradictory, and from transformative effects to those that are, in a word, transcendent. Thus, the deeper our engagement with a story, the more the story changes us, slight though the change might be. We enter it as one sort of person and exit it another. In short, every story restories us. Against the background, then, of a concept such as the hero's journey from separation through initiation to return, as popularized, for instance, by mythologist Joseph Campbell (1949), the following is the kind of progression that we have in mind.

Affirmation-Expansion

As we enter the story—in The Beginning—it welcomes us into its world as silent yet essential participants. It receives us with our ideas and expectations, our peculiar collection of prior experiences. In this respect, it validates us, normalizes us. It accepts us, warts and all, and invites us to think of it as our home for as long as we are reading it. And, wonder of wonders, somewhere amid its atmosphere and themes, its characters and their predicaments, we come home to parts of ourselves that no one else, we thought, could ever understand.

By the same token, no sooner do we begin relaxing into this warm, hospitable environment, than the story starts to stretch us. It opens us to aspects of our lives that we are not normally, or at least not knowingly, aware of. It transports us to places we have never yet traveled; exposes us to problems we have never had to face; acquaints us with people and situations that are by and large foreign. It confronts us with complexities of emotion which, though technically within our capacity to imagine, surpass what we have actually experienced in the past. As such, the story educates us. It expands our horizons. It leads us backward and forward in time, and outward and inward in space.

As the story displays the lives of its characters and pulls us into their thoughts and their dilemmas, we recognize sides of ourselves that are strangely familiar yet, previously, we hardly knew we had. The story "subjunctivizes" reality (Bruner, 2005), enabling us to visualize ourselves in circumstances that are otherwise outside of our experience (Brockmeier & Harré, 2001). It offers us a frame of reference, a set of images and metaphors, to galvanize convictions and formulate questions that, in principle, we have been capable of asking all along, yet that lay dormant within us until that particular story teased them out. In this respect, reading thickens us up. It renders more of our internalized text—remembered or anticipated—accessible to examination, and confers on us a heightened sense of substance, of uniqueness, of "us."

Contradiction-Examination

At some point—and for some this comes nearer the beginning than the end—the story goes beyond simply accepting us and teaching us, to unsettling us from our assumptions about the world. It shakes us, destabilizes what we thought we knew. It divests us of our views of what is what. It dis-illusions us. Indeed, ultimately, this contradictory quality may be what is necessary for a text to be deemed literature at all, may be essential to its "literariness." A novel must to some extent be *novel*. It cannot simply be the same old story, unfolding to a formula we are familiar with from countless books before.

What is more, "great fiction," says Bruner (2002), "is subversive in spirit" (p. 11). We require great stories to, at some point, stand against us, to "problematize" our world. We invite them to disorient us, to interrogate us. We expect them to be *parabolic*. We expect them to lead us into uncomfortable contexts, where what we are exposed to—a betrayal, a battlefield, an intensity of sadness or anger, evil or love—is difficult to witness. We expect them to crack the shell of our habitual perceptions and to question our tried and true patterns for making sense of our lives, of our selves. Indeed, we expect them to tear our selves apart, albeit vicariously and, in the end, safely. We expect them, though we may not *want* them, to bring us up against the more obscure, more problematic aspects of ourselves—aspects that, for whatever reasons, we try to keep from seeing.

Transformation

Such seeing requires a response. It forces us to own up to what the story is revealing—about the world, humanity, us. It pushes us to reevaluate our selves, to search for signs of self-deception. It drives us to reassess our beliefs, our values, our views of life in general: to open up to our own submerged potentials. As expressed by educator Maxine Greene (1990), writing on literature's "emancipatory potential," it drives us "to break with the

given, to arouse [our]selves from immersion in the familiar, to see afresh"
(p. 258). It challenges us to face features of our character and our past that,
in its contradictory capacity, the story invariably stirs up, yet which otherwise we might choose to ignore. It spurs us to integrate them into our
self-understanding. As such, it counteracts the dis-integration that—as
art—the best of stories are adept at effecting.

Transcendence

Given this progression from affirmation to transformation, reading brings
us out in The End, then, to a new mode of being in the world. It leads us to a
consciousness that, compared to our earlier state, is enlightened and enlarged,
imperceptible though the difference might be, whether to others or ourselves.
In crossing over into the author's world and coming back to our own, we
return from our odyssey as changed beings. Aesthetic reading ushers us into
a state of mind and heart where what we know is both less and more than
we knew at the beginning. The old us is transcended and a new us emerges:
more soulful and substantial, evolved and alive. And, overall, the story takes
on meanings that previously we were unable to predict: indeed, meanings
we may never fully fathom. In the end, the story points beyond itself.

Reading and Remembering

As we shift from literary text to lived text, our thesis becomes clear: remembering, with all of the retrospection and prospection it inevitably implies,
takes a parallel path to reading. As we venture into the realm of memory
in an intentional manner, we are entering familiar terrain, where the tracks
into the past, at least at its outskirts, are well-worn indeed. Yet as we stroll
ever further down memory lane, we find ourselves happening onto corners
of ourselves that we forgot we even remembered. Gradually, we find ourselves in a great hall. As its walls recede from us on every side, it grows ever
vaster and more vaulted, at once enticing and unsettling.

At a certain point, our inward trek takes us from what is merely a little
less familiar, then, to what is increasingly foreign. The things we see inside of
us seem the province of some other soul than ours. Yet ours they surely are,
and they command our full attention. In attending to them, owning them,
we undergo a transformation, be it quiet or dramatic. A reconfigured "us"
emerges, modest though the change may be. The same events as were there
all along, acknowledged or not, are there still. But the pattern that connects
them is not the same. It is more inclusive, revealing a bigger, deeper picture
of what our life encompasses.

THE STORY FROM HERE

Using these stages as an over-arching framework, we turn our attention now to the intricacies of reading our lives from midlife on. This means considering four broad processes that, in our view, are tightly intertwined: *expanding our stories,* which will take us into the mysteries of memory; *examining our stories,* which will move us deeper into the question of meaning; *transforming our stories,* which will lead us to think further about the concept of wisdom; and finally *transcending our stories,* where we ponder the poetics of spiritual growth.

Before we continue, two points need stressing. The first point is that, in real life, the process we envision is not nearly so neat, certainly not nearly so lockstep, as these four divisions might imply. Furthermore, the movement from expansion to transcendence is one that, on some small scale, our stories undergo each day. Reading and rewriting the self is a continuous activity—a fluid, subtle, organic process that, for the most part, for most of us, takes place just beneath the level of conscious awareness. What we have in mind here, however, is a more mindful, more macro-level version of this same basic progression, one that aging itself invites us to experience.

The second point is that the emphasis on *process* is deliberate, as it was when we looked at the concept of identity or the self. To the extent that psychologists attend to the inside dimensions of aging, their tendency is to organize the discussion into topics that are deemed more or less discrete: in this case memory, meaning, wisdom, and spirituality. But although identifiable literatures certainly exist for each, these topics are bound up so intricately with one another—when viewed, that is, from a narrative perspective—that to treat them fairly requires approaching them, not as separate subjects, but as intertwining processes. So treated, our sense of each of them thickens and deepens in fascinating ways.

Seven

EXPANDING OUR STORIES:

THE MYSTERY OF MEMORY

When we speak to our children about our own lives, we tend to reshape our pasts to give them an illusory look of purpose.
   —Mary Catherine Bateson (1989, p. 17)

Our memories are the fragile but powerful products of what we recall from the past, believe about the present, and imagine about the future.
   —Daniel Schacter (1996, p. 308)

The charm, one might say the genius of memory, is that it is choosy, chancy, and temperamental: it rejects the edifying cathedral and indelibly photographs the small boy outside, chewing a hunk of melon in the dust.
   —Elizabeth Bowen (1955/1996, no. 8021)

REMEMBERING OUR LIVES:
THE NECESSITY OF MEMORY

As with reading literature, so with reading life. In the continual interplay between past, present, and future, the process of reading involves more than just remembering. That said, surely the lion's share of the text that is the object of our reading—our *texistence,* as we call it—consists of what our inner editor has laid down *in* and *as* "the past." Although the relationship between the past and our remembrance of it is anything but obvious, it is from memory that we must begin when setting out to examine our lives. "Before passing judgement," writes Malcolm Cowley (1980) at the beginning of his autobiography, "we have to untangle the plot of the play." Accordingly, "the first step is simply remembering" (p. 72).

Memory may be our primary text, yet what memory has preserved of the past is only a portion of what we actually experienced. To express the point another way, the inside story is but a fraction of the outside story: the totality of our actual existence. Smaller still is the portion of that inside story we can readily recall. Indeed, much of the past that we have managed to retain is so tightly compacted within us, so deeply buried beneath subsequent layers, that it is impossible to recollect it in anything resembling its original reality. In a word, it is thin. Memory-wise, many of us thus operate with a rather thin sense of who we are, or at least much thinner than it needs to be. As for the challenges of later life, this presents a problem. To face them squarely, we need more of our past to work with in the present. We need to widen our awareness of what our lives have actually involved. We need "an enlarged understanding of Self" (Freeman, 1993, p. 30), a self more fully "re-membered" (Myerhoff, 1992, p. 240). In short, we need a good, strong story. "Expanding the story," as McAdams (1996, p. 140) would put it, is pivotal to reading the life.

When we speak of expanding our stories, though, it is not the past alone that is the object of expansion. It is the future, too: the stories we envision about what awaits us up ahead—our hopes, our fears, our worries. But inasmuch as memory is its primary object, it is memory of a particular type that is most at stake—not memory for how to do things, or procedural memory; not memory for general knowledge, or semantic memory; and not implicit memory either, although, as we shall see, each of these plays its role in the type we have in mind. Rather, it is *autobiographical* memory.

Autobiographical memory, writes psychologist David Rubin (1995), "is what we usually mean by the term memory in everyday usage" (p. 1). At once "one of the oldest and most complex areas of psychological inquiry," it is in fact "the basis of many of psychologists' ideas about memory in general" (p. 1). Unless otherwise specified, it is what we mean by "memory" here. It is memory of us and for us, memory we have of ourselves over time. It is memory, not of the past as such, but of *our* past (Wheeler, 2000). Broadly speaking, it is long-term memory, and insofar as it is memory of events, it is episodic memory. More specifically, it is memory of episodes with a measure of personal meaning. It is the sum of the material we have been amassing since infancy, however unwittingly, for the evolving narrative that is our unique identity. Casey (1987) puts the matter succinctly: "we are what we remember ourselves to be" (p. 290). More succinctly still: "I remember, therefore I am" (Beike, Lampinen, & Behrend, 2004, p. 3).

Clearly, then, memory is never just memory. It is no passive repository of impressions of the past, no mere warehouse of dead images. It is an active, purposive, creative capacity, "not far removed from invention and imagination," notes literary scholar James Olney (1998, p. 59), well known for his scholarship on autobiography. Above all, it is a process and not a thing. The object (memory) is inseparable from the activity (remembering). To modify the words of William Butler Yeats (1928/1996), the dance and the dancing are one (p. 217). Moreover, it is a process that already leans toward meaning: meaning for the remembering self. As psychologists Susan Bluck and Tilmann Habermas (2000) express it, "autobiographical memories are linked to the self through emotional and motivational significance for one's life" (p. 122). Inasmuch as memory and meaning are therefore connected, expanding our stories and examining our stories can be seen as two sides of one basic coin. While the meaning side will occupy us in Chapter 8, the memory side is our principal focus here. To the extent that we can tease the two apart, it is with contents more than meanings we will be concerning ourselves first—with events more than interpretations, that is, or with textual features more than reader constructions.

Before moving on, we need to reiterate the importance of a "good" memory, both from an ontological perspective and from a political–ethical one as well. Setting aside the thorny philosophical issue of whether someone with advanced dementia technically possesses a self, memory is essential for at least a *sense* of self (see Neisser & Fivush, 1994; Beike, Lampinen, & Behrend, 2004)—a sense that is vibrant and varied, substantial yet subtle. "Memory and the self," states psychologist Mark Howe, "exist in a symbiotic relationship" (2004, p. 46), which is why for those suffering from dementia, in the opinion of scholars such as Sherman (1991), self-memories must be "amplified, made more vivid, and dramatized for fear of losing the self" (p. 7).

Yet there is something of a paradox in this. Memory, notes Howe (2004), "may not be a particularly dependable base upon which to build our self-concepts" (p. 45). One could even argue that our self-concepts are founded on leftovers: that our identity is rooted in exceptions to the rule. Memories are in many ways anomalies. They are centered around incidents that depart from the routine, the mundane, the day-to-day. They are "violations of the expected and ordinary," or *peripeteia* (Bruner, 2005, p. 57): incidents that are problematic or painful or otherwise important, that are not merely noticed but that cannot be ignored. It is as if our memory had a mind of its own. This, our inner editor decrees, is something I simply *must* remember, something that requires more reflection, more work. Psychologist James Pennebaker (1990) proposes, for instance, that what we tend to dwell on most in our memories, thoughts, or dreams are events or situations that are somehow unresolved: situations where something went wrong, where our plans went awry: events that harbor some measure of outstanding business, be it practical or personal in nature. Once that business is dealt with, though, we are free to let the memories go, a theme we will return to Chapter 10.

Ambiguously though memory may be linked to self, it is nonetheless crucial for a sense of personal power. Hampl (1999) reminds us, for instance, that if we fail to create our own sense of the past, then "someone else will do it for us" (p. 32). A corollary of this is that memory is vital for a responsible sense of history, insofar as "what is remembered is what becomes reality" (p. 32). "If we 'forget' Auschwitz," Hampl asks—if we do not find a way to include it in *our* story too—"what then do we remember? And what is the purpose of remembering?" Memory thus has a moral dimension. Insofar as we can place ourselves inside the lifeworlds of our fellow human beings by remembering incidents from our own lives that resemble what they appear to be experiencing now, memory is also what inspires our empathy and compassion. It is our principal resource in learning as well, above all in learning from experience. In addition, not only is it our primary "data base for talking-cure psychotherapy" (Rubin, 1995, p. 1), but overall, it is essential for our experience of such things as spirituality and generativity, and for imparting our wisdom to the world we leave behind.

MINDING THE GAPS: THE SCARCITY OF MEMORY

Memory, it appears, is eminently important. But what exactly is it? Memory, writes T. S. Eliot, consists of "the few meagre arbitrarily chosen sets of snapshots ... , the faded poor souvenirs of passionate moments" (1933/1975, p. 91). Cynical though this assessment sounds, any consideration of the necessity of memory must own up to its scarcity as well. A few words concerning that scarcity are therefore warranted before tackling our two main topics for the remainder of this chapter: the complexity of memory and the retrievability of memory.

The gaps in memory's text are many. There is much more between the lines than on them. Just as the events that are presented in a novel never include the countless specifics of what "actually" took place, our memories are invariably summaries—often quite severely so. Not only do most of us tend to forget much more than we remember, but the things we never noticed in the first place, and therefore never wove into some wider fabric of meaning, are basically lost. It is water beneath the bridge in the relentless flow of minutes, days, and years that constitute our lives. And even with the vast amount that we *did* notice, we did so only for an instant at the fringes of our awareness, after which it was either reduced to a shadow of its original eventness and then laid aside for future reference, or else dispensed with altogether as unworthy of retention. Granted, traces of it might still be lurking in dusty files in a corner of the archives, but, by and large, it is gone.

"Each moment in a person's life hosts an endless number of events," Polster (1987) notes; however, "considering the abundance of this treasure, relatively few stories emerge" (p. 21). On the surface all of this seems like such a waste: so much time, so few memories; so many events, so few remains. Yet whether or not our forgetting is forever, let alone complete, it is just as much of a necessity as remembering. In *The Seven Sins of Memory: How the Mind Forgets and Remembers,* Schacter (2001) discusses a form of forgetting called "transience," namely the tendency for remembered material to fade with time. Transience, he says, is probably "the most terrifying" (p. 40) of memory's many failings. By the same token, it is also its salvation. Paradoxically, we need to forget in order to remember—to remember what is most important. To express it another way, we need not mind the gaps with which memory is inevitably riddled. No gaps at all and memory would be prevented from doing its work. This claim, however, requires some explanation.

Psychoanalyst Adam Phillips (1994) wonders, for instance, "what the completely remembered life would look like" (p. 69). Considering how a good lifestory should be not just credible but bearable, we can appreciate Phillips's point. Says Holocaust survivor Elie Wiesel (1988, p. 254): "I would lose my mind if I remembered everything." But even from a more pragmatic perspective, "life in any true sense is absolutely impossible," insists Casey (1987), "without forgetfulness" (p. 2). "What if all events were registered in elaborate detail...?" Schacter (2001) asks. "The result would be a potentially overwhelming clutter of useless details" (p. 190). By way of example, he cites the case of famed Russian mnemonist Solomon Shereshevski, who "formed and retained highly detailed memories of virtually everything that happened to him—both the important and the trivial." Nevertheless, "he was unable to function at an abstract level because he was inundated with unimportant details of his experiences—details that are best denied entry into the system in the first place" (p. 190). This insight accords with philosopher David

Novitz's (1997) observation that a viable sense of self is only possible if we "regard some of the events in, and facts about, [our] life as more prominent than others" (p. 147). In other words, without some measure of narrative emplotment, "there is simply no way of emphasizing some events, marginalizing others, and at the same time relating all in a significant whole" (p. 147).

Schacter's conclusion concerning memory's "sins"—which, besides transience, include for him absent-mindedness, blocking, misattribution, suggestibility, bias, and persistence—is, therefore, that they "are not merely nuisances to minimize or avoid" (p. 206). Quite the contrary: rather than representing the failures of memory, they are precisely why it serves us as successfully as it does. Thanks to them, memory "draws on the past to inform the present, preserves elements of present experience for future reference, and allows us to revisit the past as well." In sum, "memory's vices are also its virtues, elements of a bridge across time which allows us to link the mind with the world" (p. 206).

Given Schacter's thoughts on the matter, perhaps we can understand the comment made by writer Graham Greene. "A novelist," he once remarked, "has a greater ability to forget than most men. He has to forget or become sterile. What he forgets," says Greene, "becomes the compost of the imagination" (1973, p. 160). In turn, the imagination, Coleridge reminds us (1817/1983), "dissolves, diffuses, dissipates, in order to recreate" (p. 304). Oscar Wilde joins the chorus: "The great enemy of creativity is a good memory" (cited in May, 1991, p. 68n). Even in writing this book, we have at some point had to curb our reading of relevant material (of which there is no end!) and start laying out our own ideas, trusting that what we have absorbed of that material will emerge when needed, duly distilled. But Greene's and Wilde's insights lead us to a further thought.

Talk of memory "files," such as we indulged in a page or so back, conjures up the image of an office—a newspaper office, for instance, or perhaps the office of a novelist. But it also suggests a computer. Computation is far and away the dominant model by which memory has come to be conceived. Indeed, seeing memory in terms of "operating systems," as of "encoding" and "storage" and "retrieval," has aided us tremendously in deciphering its complexity. However, it does not necessarily tell us the whole story of memory.

Memory cannot be conceived of without resorting to metaphor, and different metaphors reveal (and conceal) different features of what memory is and does (see Draaisma, 2000). Among the more familiar, more longstanding candidates are memory as bank, in which the past is kept secure; as lane, which can be wandered down at will; as an artist who takes liberties with the facts; and as a trickster who is not to be trusted. Greene's comment, however, points to a metaphor that we have hinted at already and that, in our view, holds particular conceptual appeal. Indeed, it is one that psychologists of aging (especially narrative psychologists) might do well to consider for the way that it can accommodate, among other things, how the events of a novel and the meanings we assign them tend to accumulate within us—to thicken—as we read. It is memory as a *compost heap* (Randall, 2007). A quick synopsis can set the stage for some of our thinking later on.

Though much less sleek or chic than a computer, the humble compost heap moves us away from the mechanical connotations that accompany a computer. It offers a framework not just for the communal quality of memory, which is often overlooked, but for its organic dimensions as well, the fact that it is in its own way alive, and is a veritable seedbed for creativity and growth. In addition, it recasts the fallibility of memory as a strength and not a sin. And it honors what is in many ways the messiness of memory (Bruner, 1990), its quality as a "spongy tract" (Johnson, 2001, p. 111), its density and depth—what Casey (1987) calls its "thick autonomy" (pp. 262–287). Above all, it provides us with certain reference points for thinking about the complexities of memory and remembering from the perspective of poetics. Instead of "computer-speak" (Draaisma, 2000, p. 159) such as encoding, storage, and retrieval, that is, one could speak perhaps of *laying it on, letting it be, breaking it down, stirring it up,* and *mixing it in.*

Laying it on links with the idea that we introduced in Chapter 2 about the texts of memory being laid down continually inside of us as, quite literally, the remains of the day, the things we "refuse" to forget. And it addresses memory's compacted dimension as well, its layeredness and thickness. *Letting it be,* something every compost heap demands, speaks to the sense that for memory to do its work—of, say, incubating insights or fostering "soul" (Moore, 1992)—it needs fallow time, dreaming time, time for just sitting, time for settling quietly inside of us. *Breaking it down* relates to transience, to the fact that, sooner or later to a greater or lesser degree, a good many of our memories simply "decay" (see Bower, 2000, p. 13), becoming fuzzy at their edges and eventually merging with others. In effect, they decompose. Yet breaking down is not the tragedy it might seem. Far from being a sin, one could argue, it is actually a necessity for composing (or composting) our life as a coherent, narrative whole. For its part, *stirring it up* is what happens when our memories get triggered by various means, as we shall see in a moment, so that things that were long since buried are lured to the surface. Lastly, *mixing it in* is about sustainability, about spreading the compost around. It is about sharing our memories and experiences, and the insights they have led us to, for the benefit of others, and for the sake of their growth, too.

ENTERING THE THICKET OF THE PAST: THE COMPLEXITY OF MEMORY

As patchy as our memory seems when we consider all it *could* contain, it is still incredibly vast. There is far more to it than most of us realize, and thus a much thicker self to be experienced. A simple one-word exercise, like that devised by psychologist Herbert Crovitz, following the lead of Sir Francis Galton (see Schacter, 1996, p. 73), reveals just how complex and crowded our memory can be, certainly how powerful—and pliable—in a social sense. We use a form of it in our classes, in fact, as well as in workshops with older adults.

The ABCs of Autobiographical Memory

One at a time, a series of simple, everyday words—*apple, bike, cat* (hence: ABCs)—are projected on a screen. As participants recall a story from their own life that each word sparks, they are invited to share it with the group—a short story, we hasten to stress, so as many as possible can speak. Within seconds, the hands start going up.

Take *apple.* One person might say, for instance: "That reminds me of when we were growing up on the farm. We had this orchard behind the barn and, every fall, my brothers and sisters and I would collect the ones that had fallen on the ground. We'd have the most amazing rotten apple fights. What a mess!" Another person might follow with: "When our kids were little, we used to take them picking apples at this U-Pick place. What a great family-time that was!" Another: "My granny made the best darned apple pies. I can smell them even now! One of my best memories is the time she showed me how to make one myself." Another: "In Grade 2, we had this horrible teacher named Miss McGillicuddy. One day, I brought her an apple because someone told me that's what you should do. But she accused me of bribing her and gave me the strap. To this day, I can see her swinging that big leather belt onto my little red hands!" Yet another: "Speaking of rotten apples, I remember when my buddies and I would go swimming at the lake. As we ran for the shore we'd always shout 'last one in's a rotten egg'!" Another still: "I couldn't think of an apple story when we started, but one just popped into my head. I've really never liked apples, and there's a good reason. During the war I was in a prison camp, and we were constantly hungry. I can still see the guards jeering at us this one January afternoon, as we scrambled over top each other in the freezing cold trying to grab a piece of moldy old apple that they'd tossed in the snowbank outside our barracks."

We keep extra words in reserve, of course, in case the group runs out of steam (which it never does), not all of them as innocent as *apple* or *cat*. Some are quite loaded in fact, like *divorce* or *war;* and some more abstract, like *religion* or *love.* In any event, after a few turns around the room with each of them, we conclude with some open discussion on a few basic questions: Why did particular recollections get triggered at particular points? What types of memories were shared, and what types were not? How did others' stories inspire our own? Why, generally, do we remember what we remember and forget what we forget? Invariably, the discussion is intriguing, and in a manner of minutes it sets off a swirl of observations.

The process works, not just pedagogically, but emotionally as well. A great deal of energy gets generated in the room and participants report a broad array of feelings: from curiosity to excitement, and sadness to surprise. Scarcely anyone finds it boring, and the majority find it fun, for what gets fostered is an empathetic environment in which the stories themselves appear to pull the group together—if you will, the tales that bind. But at the same time as it pulls people out of themselves, it also transports them into their pasts, where they can almost feel the original events: the taste of the pie, the sting of the strap, the smell of Grandma's kitchen. It is as if they feel more *themselves* in the process, too. As expressed by participants in a life-writing group facilitated by gerontologists Tom Cole and Kate de Medeiros (2001): "there's something more to *me,* and I want to find out what that is"; "I'm peeling back the layers of the onion."

In a sense, the exercise reveals as much about the narrative complexity of social interaction as it is does about memory itself. It becomes obvious, for instance, that stories serve a variety of functions for the people who tell them, whether to gain acceptance or to get a laugh, to entertain or to edify. It is clear, too, that stories tend to breed stories, often in ways that stray from the appointed path. As one person holds forth, a word will be used or an image thrown out that, for another, evokes a memory only tangentially connected to apples: "When I first saw the word, I couldn't think of a single apple story. But when Bob told about his grandma making apple pies, I suddenly remembered my Uncle Homer butchering a pig, and then getting Aunt Betty to bake us a *pork* pie for supper." In turn, this could remind another person of the butcher shop his or her parents used to go to; another, of the wild pigs that roamed the countryside that they hitchhiked through in Asia years ago. Overall, the entire meandering process is testimony to memory's complex system of "cross-indexing" (Schank, 1990, pp. 84–113).

What also stands out is that, while many of the anecdotes people come up with are stories that concern themselves alone, others are more about family and friends. Still others possess broader, historical significance—a greater degree of *back-text*, one might say. They are as much about life during the Depression, for example, as about the life of a particular individual. Some are firsthand memories ("I was there and that's what I saw"), while others are hand-me-downs ("my dad told me one time that *his* father once traded a basket of apples for a pair of boots"). Some concern quite specific things, while others concern the sorts of things we *used* to do on repeated occasions—what Neisser calls "repisodic" memory (1986, p. 79).

Typically, too, there is a spectrum of sophistication, from poetic to prosaic, and eloquent to halting, in the actual language with which recollections are conveyed—in the storying style, that is. Some will be loaded with pathos and move everyone to tears; others will sound comical or corny and send ripples of giggles round the room. While some stories are told in faltering tones, others will roll off their teller's lips as if they had been recited on countless occasions before. Some stories are related clearly and coherently, with the scene suitably set at the start, then a steady progression to an obvious point, with too-good-to-be-true precision in terms of details, dates, and dialogue ("he said—she said"). Others come tumbling out in stops and starts, with all manner of side-plots and self-interruptions, whose chronology is impossible to follow.

Not only are some members more articulate than others, more talented in the narrative arts, but their memories seem richer to begin with. They reek of back-text, of under-story, of things left purposely unsaid. With others, however, the meaning is right on the surface: what you hear is what you get: "That's what happened; that's what I did—end of story." In some stories the tellers position themselves as heroes whose savvy saved the day, while other tellers portray themselves as fools, whose stories are as much *on* them as about them. Furthermore, some stories are eminently believable, while others smack suspiciously of embellishment. They are tall tales. Some stories spring from just the day before; others, from the deep, dark past, with their tellers shyly confessing, "I've never told this to anyone before..." or "I haven't thought of that in years." Finally, certain stories we will probably have forgotten by the time we make it home, whereas others, our own or someone else's, could keep haunting us for days.

In its own fashion, then, each insight participants express illustrates an aspect of memory that scholars themselves have noted. From the perspective of phenomenology, for example, Casey (1987) notes that "to remember...is to become enmeshed in the thicket of the past" (p. 266), an image that lends legitimacy to the metaphor not just of getting lost in one's story, but also of memory as a compost heap. Among the characteristics he sees connoted by the adjective *thick* are: "a depth not easily penetrable by the direct light of consciousness"; "resistant to conceptual understanding"; "sedimented in layers"; "having 'historical depth'" and "temporal density"; "concentrated emotional significance"; "closely packed or 'thickset' format"; and "a compression of objects or events, ... or condensation" (pp. 265–266). From the perspective of cognitive science, on the other hand, Rubin (1995) notes four "components" of memory that researchers repeatedly cite: the "social nature" of its formation and communication; its visual "imagery"; its emotional dimension; and the role of "verbal narrative" in articulating and sharing it (pp. 2–3). In their own way, participants testify to every one of these components—especially its narrativity. If we make meaning in terms of stories; if we perceive, think, converse, decide, and act in terms of stories, then it should come as no surprise that we remember in terms of stories, too, that memory is "story-based" (Schank, 1990, p. 119). From a narrative perspective, memory's vast complexity can be looked upon from four overlapping angles: *time-wise, truth-wise, self-wise,* and *other-wise.*

Time-wise: The Temporal Dimension

The Levels of Time

Memory is complicated in terms of both levels of time and modes of time. Beginning with levels, memory researchers have identified at least three broad categories of memory-units that appear to be "nested" (Neisser, 1986) within one another in a roughly hierarchical manner: *lifetime periods, general events,* and *specific events.*

Lifetime periods, writes psychologist Martin Conway (1995), who actually prefers to speak of autobiographical "knowledge" rather than autobiographical memory, are "the most general, most abstract, or most inclusive" units of such knowledge and "denote time periods typically measured in units of years" (p. 67). Examples would be: growing up on the farm, college days, first marriage, life in London. For any given stretch of years, however, there may be many lifetime periods; for example, "when I lived with Y may overlap in time with when I worked at X" (p. 69). However, "the thematic knowledge of the two time periods may index different parts of the autobiographical knowledge base" (p. 69). In other words, any given life-theme—relationships, family, work—will be linked with more than one lifetime period. Also, embedded in our memory of any one of them—in a sense, glueing it together—are all manner of procedural memories and semantic memories, too, which means that the categories of "autobiographical," "procedural," and "semantic" are essentially impossible to tease apart. The period "growing up" consists, not just of the events we lived through at the time, but of the numberless things that we learned how to do, like riding a bike or tying our shoes, and the immense amounts of information we ended up absorbing, like the days of the week or the months of the year. That said, surrounding such knowledge could lurk traces of the particular episodes when acquiring it first occurred: the time Miss McGillicuddy taught us the colors of the rainbow or Mother showed us how to brush our teeth.

Next, within each lifetime period will be any number of general events. For Conway (1995), these are "typically measured in units of months, weeks, and days" (p. 67), and can "encompass both repeated events...and single events" (p. 69). The period when we lived in London, for example, could contain any number of event-clusters: riding the Tube, friendship with Brian, working at the bank. Conway calls these "mini-histories" (p. 69). Insofar as many of them represent "repisodic" memories (Neisser, 1986, p. 79), then "general event" implies a hierarchy of generality. At the lower end of that hierarchy lies event-specific knowledge (Conway, 1995, p. 67). This consists of our most vividly recallable episodes, some of which (though not all, necessarily) are "nuclear episodes," as McAdams (1996, p. 140) calls them, events that can almost stand on their own: the time the bank was robbed, the time Brian's mother came to dinner.

Given the existence of such episodes, we have the option of entering the thicket of the past from more than one direction. On one hand, we can begin with the particular apple fight when we hit Jenny in the head and caused a concussion, and then work our way up through playing in the woods (general event) to growing up in Maine (lifetime period)—no doubt scooping up other memories in the process. Or we can enter from another direction instead, beginning with the broad trigger of "growing up" and recalling progressively more specific events as we go along. Either way, the concept of levels ranging from overarching time frames down to particular incidents addresses a central dimension of memory's temporal complexity.

Above the level of lifetime period, perhaps, is "the most superordinate unit of thinking about the past"—what Bluck and Alea (2002, p. 71) refer to as the lifestory, also called the "lifestory schema" (Bluck & Habermas, 2000). At the lowest level of all, skulking at the edges of both specific events and general events, as of entire lifetime periods, can be countless snippets of remembered material that resist easy retrieval just by projecting a word on a screen; moreover, that resist incorporation into a larger, more tellable story-unit. *Narrative debris* is what one might call such material (McKendy, 2006, p. 473); or "floating fragment-memories," to use the phrase of novelist Esther Salaman (1982, p. 63); or "butterflies," as Joanna Field says (1934/1952, p. 116). In keeping with the journalistic metaphor, we can think of them as the scattered remnants of dispatches from the front, which were noticed for the briefest of instants and then officially rejected. Yet at the oddest of times, cued to consciousness by who knows what, they can reappear at the back of our minds or on the fringes of a dream. For Schacter (1996), such material constitutes "a subterranean world of nonconscious memory and perception, normally concealed from the conscious mind" (pp. 164–165), a type of *implicit* memory: the stuff between the lines. Famous for the thinly veiled reminiscences that saturated his novels, Thomas Wolfe (1938/1983) refers to such stuff as "all the things [a man] scarcely dares to think he has remembered" (p. 44): "those hundreds and thousands of things which all of us have seen for just a flash… a voice once heard; an eye that looked; a mouth that smiled" (p. 42).

The Modes of Time

"In coming to terms with my past," writes Freeman, "I can only do so from the present" (1998, p. 42). The sole way we can think of the past at all is to re-present it—not totally or even accurately, of course; and obviously, we can hardly do so in the past itself, but only in the present, when how things turned out is a fait accompli. Quite literally, we remember back. For Paul Ricoeur (1981), therefore, "recollection inverts the so-called natural order of time. By reading the end in the beginning and the beginning in the end, we learn also to read time itself backward" (p. 176). In effect, The End is now. Brockmeier (2001) refers to this same phenomenon—odd when you think about it, yet as familiar as breathing—as "retrospective teleology" (pp. 248ff), where *telos* means "end" or "goal." Odd or not, it is integral to what Olney (1998) calls "the tangled and fascinating, dull and symbiotic matter of memory and narrative" (p. xi). In effect, it is pivotal to "narrative time" (Freeman, 1998, p. 43), and runs through every occasion of remembering.

At the same time, our sense of *now* is inseparable from our sense of *not yet:* of the future, short-term or long, toward which the present appears to be leading. As such, the future (or any number of envisionable futures) is as present as the past (or any number of rememberable pasts). Each act of remembering is thus "about the simultaneity…of all three modes…of human time" (Brockmeier, 2001, p. 250). This insight is as ancient as Augustine, who writes of "a present of past things, a present of present things, and a present of future things" (397–398/1961, p. 269). We will return to such insights in Chapter 10, where we consider how advancing age itself inspires the transcendence of time as normally experienced. Meanwhile, all of this need not suggest that the past as such has no existence (the future is another matter), or that it, plus memory, is an illusion, as some would insist (Tolle, 1999), simply that our only access to it is by means of the present. In a parallel way, our only route into the story that we encounter in the text of a novel is, technically, through the words we are reading at the moment.

Two intriguing implications arise from the simultaneity of time's main modes—implications that inspire a variety of metaphors. First, given the role of the present in our experience of the past, yet the fact that the present itself is changing with every second, the past is a "moving target" (Robinson, 1995, p. 214). To employ the image of the compost-heap, we stir it up simply by talking about it, or even just thinking about it. Each time we remember when the teacher gave us the strap, we do so from the midst of a different present and from a different stage in the history of our self. The same is true for all subsequent recollections. However slightly, their significance is refracted from what they were for us last week, or will be tomorrow. It is the Uncertainty Principle applied to time: the observed is altered in the act of observation.

A second implication is that our experience of time—not linear time but narrative time, story-time, or, simply, the time of our lives—is made even more complicated, as Freeman notes, reflecting on the "narrative fabric of self," by the countless "'shuttlings' between the various modalities of time operative in memory" (1998, p. 43). These shuttlings are frequently what feed our inner nattering, as we mutter to ourselves about, now the past, now the present, now the future—or, more accurately, about the past viewed in light of this particular (hypothetical) future, the present haunted by that particular version of the past, and so forth. Furthermore, says Freeman, quoting Brockmeier, the temporal complexity of memory is due, not just to the interweaving of time's three modes, but to the "different 'temporal orders'" that can be associated with "natural, cultural, and individual processes," which in turn engender "'all kinds of splittings, flashbacks, flash-forwards, associations, reconciliations, overlappings'" (1998, p. 43). To put it more simply, no two of us are ever the same, because no two of us are shaped within the exact same network of narrative environments, and each such environment instills within us slightly different (perhaps significantly different) attitudes toward the nature of time itself. In consequence, the permutations and combinations in our experience of narrative time are essentially endless, underscoring all the more the novelty of lives-as-texts. In both telling and reading those texts, time's arrow points us every way at once.

Earlier, we mentioned Augustine's reference to the presence of things past. Freeman (2002c) offers a soulful illustration of just such an insight as he recalls a visit that he had with his father on the way home from college at the end of his sophomore year, not long before the man's untimely death. Despite a rather frosty father–son relationship up until then, they fell into a four-hour conversation in which Freeman finally began to feel that, all things considered, the man truly believed in him and, in his own way, loved him. "In nearly everything I've done since," writes Freeman, especially things he might have shared with his father or things that would have made his father "proud or happy, he is right there, missing" (p. 173). In effect, Freeman still feels "the presence...of his absence" (p. 173). Reflecting further on the incident, Freeman observes how, in the same sort of way that poetry "deals with what's not there and there at the same time" (p. 174), so memory deals, not only with "what's happened," but also "with what didn't happen and what couldn't happen" (p. 173). For this reason the event continues to be "filled with a kind of diffuse, unspecified potential" (p. 174). Freeman's words speak to the reality of memory's virtual dimension, the richness of what might have been. Also, although a fuller discussion of the memory–emotion connection is beyond our scope here (see Nussbaum, 1990; Schweder, 1994; Singer, 1996), his reflections point to the poignancy of nostalgia and regret, of melancholy, of wistfulness: emotions that are rooted in memory's immense complexity and integral to its power. Its complexity time-wise, however, is tied to its complexity truth-wise as well.

Truth-wise: The Imaginative Dimension

The issue of truth, both in autobiographical memory and in autobiography itself (see Pascal, 1960), is far too thorny to do more than make note of it here, even though we have alluded to it already in conjunction with a good lifestory. It is problematic for at least three main reasons: the backward gaze of time, the tendency to condense the past, and the definition of "truth" itself. Before touching on each of these in turn, we must acknowledge that the idea of memories being literally true is probably not one most of us would insist on. Memory's sins are no secret. We can even be downright affectionate toward them, making light of how our memory "isn't what it used to be" or how we "sometimes get things wrong." Despite this intrinsic acceptance of memory's many failings, there is ample reason why, technically, it ought not to be trusted.

The Backward Gaze of Time

Where memory is concerned, time itself is the enemy of truth. Looking back on the past from the standpoint of an ever-shifting present, we inevitably falsify it. We experience it, not for what it was, but for what we interpret it to have been, always in light of our current editorial agendas and our present theories on where our life is headed. The subjective dimension of memory thus determines what we perceive as the objective contents of the past. The problem in this—if problem it is—lies in retrospective teleology. In the very act of telling, or even just thinking, about a remembered event, its end is implicit in its beginning. In other words, we get it all backward. Morson calls this "backward causation," or "backshadowing," which is to say "foreshadowing after the fact." In other words, "the past is treated as if it had inevitably to lead to the present we know" (1994, p. 13). Not only does remembering re-present the past, therefore; it *mis*-re-presents it, too. Roquentin, antihero of Sartre's (1965) philosophical novel *Nausea*, gives this insight sarcastic expression. Troubled by the chronic disjuncture between living and telling, Roquentin concludes that "when you tell about life, everything changes; only it's a change nobody notices; the proof of this is that people talk about true stories. As if there could possibly be such things as true stories; events take place one way and we recount them the opposite way" (p. 62). Remembering, echoes Ricoeur (1981), reverses the "natural order of time" (p. 176). The only view of the past we can ever have is the one we have in hindsight.

Condensing the Past

Given our continuous inner editing, memory misrepresents the past at the very instant we start laying it on. From the field of possible events that surround each moment we remember, Morson (1994) explains, "a single event emerges," such that "the other possibilities usually appear invisible or distorted." In this way, he says, "a field is mistakenly reduced to a point, and, over time, a succession of fields is reduced to a line" (pp. 119–120). What ended up happening—out of all that *might* have happened—is seen as somehow *needing* to have happened. We got a feeling for this phenomenon when discussing the dangers of narrative itself in relation to narrative foreclosure. But not only are most of the might-have-happened pasts thereby ruled out, huge portions of what *did* happen are also largely ignored: a fact easily demonstrated when comparisons are made among eyewitness testimonies to an accident or crime. And as for the much smaller portions that we manage to retain, all but the most persistent of them submit sooner or later to the sin of transience. Compressed beneath subsequent layers of the compost heap, they are flattened and thinned until only the slimmest remnant of the original occurrence is left, and even this may eventually fade.

Fading (or decaying) is understandable in the case of our more distant memories, but even our recent ones are no more than condensed versions of what technically took place. Once more, the paradox is that they have to be. If memory retained every detail of every event, if it did not "smooth" some things, maybe most things, over (Spence, 1986), if it did not in fact fix the past to some degree, then it would be useless to us in navigating our daily lives with a feasible sense of self. The case of Shereshevski aside, we simply cannot hold onto all the details of a given event in all of its eventness, replete with the countless might-bes and what-ifs, the possibilities and contingencies, that encircled it at the time, and with its subsequent outcomes not yet in place. Rather, we ever-so-surely distort, or at the very least, refract, what actually happened: not just through exaggeration (did they *always* say "last one in's a rotten egg"?) but, in general, by playing down some aspects, elevating others, and jettisoning the rest.

So, then, far from being a kind of recording of the past exactly as it happened, in all its detail and uncertainty, memory is at best a matter of *faction*. It is impossible without the element of imagination. One might even argue that it is merely imagination by a different name, which is the very sort of argument that led Neisser to quip that the concept of autobiographical memory is ultimately "best taken with a grain of salt" (1994, p. 8). For such reasons, and insofar as its dynamics inside of us are analogous to those of the past of a story itself, as we experience it when reading a novel, autobiographical memory could fairly be defined as story memory.

Theoretical, Technical, and Textual Truth

"In talking about the past," writes the late editor William Maxwell (1980), "we lie with every breath we draw" (p. 27). That talking and lying are linked is perhaps bad enough, although with the pressure upon our narrators to impress or persuade our listeners it is scarcely surprising. Embellishment is unavoidable, and bad faith is a fact of life. But even in just thinking about the past, memory proves the trickster. That said, while out-and-out confabulation can certainly occur, with some of us patently deluded about the realities of our past, memory does what it needs to do—equip us with a workable sense of self—with, all in all, considerable success. "Our memory systems," Schacter (1996) insists, "do a remarkably good job of preserving the general contours of our pasts," making them "potent determinants of how we view ourselves and what we do" (p. 308). While memory may be far from perfect, then, it is more than good enough. But such an assessment is, itself, not good enough. Unless we are content with settling for second best, we need a deeper conception of truth, for it is upon such a conception that our verdict on memory hangs. Understanding memory as a quasi-literary composition which is less factual than factional in nature suggests a conception that may be of some assistance. Instead of a technical direction—where Memory X corresponds directly to Event X—it takes us in a textual one.

According to philosopher Alexander Nehamas, the technical direction leads us nowhere anyway. "Choosing, selecting, and simplifying do not amount to falsifying what is before us," he writes, "unless we believe that there can be a representation of the world that depends on no selection at all and that this representation represents the standard of accuracy" (cited in Freeman, 2002a, pp. 17–18). For Nehamas, such a standard is meaningless. The supposed contradiction between "true" and "story" is therefore misleading. A life remembered in excruciating exactness is scarcely a life at all. If memory is a liar, it is a necessary one.

In what is widely regarded as a seminal essay, Bruner (1986) distinguishes between "two modes of cognitive functioning, two modes of thought" (p. 11): namely, the logical or "paradigmatic mode" (p. 13) and what he calls the "narrative mode" (p. 13). Each of these, he says, provides "distinctive ways of ordering experience, of constructing reality." Stories, for example, operate differently from logical arguments. Whether "true" or "fictional," a story is evaluated by different kinds of criteria from what we use "to judge a logical argument" (p. 12). One of his key contentions is that the preoccupation of Anglo-American philosophy with the "epistemological question of how to know truth" stands in contrast with the "broader question of how we come to endow experience with meaning." Such a question, he notes, is what "preoccupies the poet and the storyteller" (p. 12).

Contrasting truth, defined in logical–theoretical terms, with meaning, the province of poiesis, is one way of carving out a conception of truth that is "more comprehensive and expansive" (Freeman, 1993, p. 32), and at the same time more "serviceable" (Freeman, 2001, p. 297), in the sense of more appropriate to memory. Another is to draw on the distinction that psychoanalyst Donald Spence (1982) has made between "historical truth" and "narrative truth." Spence critiques the "archeological model" of Freud, the central aim of which is to reconstruct the history of the patient by "uncovering pieces of the past," particularly those that are repressed. In this manner, one "come[s] as close as possible to what 'really' happened" (p. 32). For Spence, this model is naïve. The aim of analysis, he says, is not *reconstruction* but *construction*. It is "to turn the patient's life into a meaningful story" (p. 123). It is to confer on what is otherwise mere "case history" a kind of "narrative intelligibility" that enables the patient "to see his life as continuous, coherent, and, therefore, meaningful" (p. 280).

In their respective ways, Bruner and Spence thus nudge us from notions of logical–theoretical truth, on one hand, and historical–technical truth on the other, toward what one could call *textual truth*. Though this is a controversial notion in itself, as noted in Chapter 5, there is nonetheless a type of truth that many of us believe we encounter "in the make-believe of fiction" (Bruner, 2005, p. 55), and it is a type we will be giving more attention to later in the book. Except possibly in the case of historical fiction, such truth has little to do with verifiable facts. It is a truth less of facts than of feelings, less of events than of insights. It is "emotional truth" (Barrington, 1997, p. 65); it is aesthetic truth: truth as a kind of coiled potential for meaning—truth of which memory, we submit, is undoubtedly the medium.

Self-wise: The Individual Dimension

According to Howe (2004), it is widely accepted in research circles that "personalized memories for experiences" and a "cognitive sense of self" develop early in life "in a symbiotic relationship" (p. 46). There are grounds for our claim here, then, that an expanded memory is critical to coping with the assaults on self that later life can bring. But this memory–self connection runs in two directions at once. Just as our sense of self is rooted in what we remember ("I remember, therefore I am"), so what we remember depends upon our sense of self—or, more accurately, on the selves that do the remembering, with the various interests and agendas to which each will be committed (Lampinen, Beike, & Behrend, 2004, p. 255). As such, two themes need to be considered: *defining self* and *multiple selves*.

Defining Self and Self-Defining Memories

In their introduction to an important collection of articles entitled *The Self and Memory*, psychologists Denise Beike, James Lampinen, and Douglas Behrend (2004, p. 4) admit frankly that "no single definition of the self [can] cover all the senses of the self that are relevant for this volume." Everything we are saying in *this* volume, however, leads us to agree with Bruner (1994) that, whatever else it might be, "self is a perpetually rewritten story" (p. 53). In effect, we remember what we need to in order to keep the story going. Quite literally, memory is self-serving. With psychologist Carol Feldman, Bruner (Bruner & Feldman, 1995) refines this thesis further by arguing that autobiographical memory is "dominated" by a "narrative pattern" that appears to be controlled by a "self schema" that, in itself, "undergoes evolution" with the passage of time. In other words, the self-schema—a concept it is impossible not to link with lifestory schema—"is not a 'free-standing' or self-contained procedure for interpreting text, but is itself constituted by those acts of interpretation." To put it another way still, the same self who "constructs the past is changed by the outcome of its own construction" (p. 292)—the Uncertainty Principle again.

Against the background of this back-and-forth between self-schema and autobiographical memory, we can contemplate a class of memories that psychologists Jefferson Singer and Pavel Blagov (2004) label "self-defining." Earlier we talked about signature stories and nuclear episodes, which can be taken as alternative terms for the same essential category. And we all have our private collections—the things that stand out, the turning points and "branching points" in our lives (Birren & Deutchman, 1991, pp. 67–69), the often-anomalous incidents to which our identity is tied. Such memories, say Singer and Blagov (2004), have five main characteristics: they are "vivid," "affectively intense," remembered "repetitively," connected to "other similar memories," and based on an "unresolved conflict of the personality" or some otherwise "enduring concern" (p. 119).

As for vividness, self-defining memories have a "strong sensory quality," as if people had a "movie inside their heads" (p. 119). Besides sight, in other words, sounds, smells, and even tastes may stand out as well. The second and third characteristics correspond to the fact that such memories are "touchstones" in people's lives, offer "information about what they want or don't want," and thus act as "reference points" that supply "guidance or reinforcement" in present-day life situations (p. 119). Polster (1987), for instance, would call them "highly charged stories," or "life-lighting stories" (p. 69), and proposes that they could almost have titles and stand on their own as distinctive narrative units. Often, they concern firsts—first day at school, first date, first apple fight, and the like. The fourth characteristic is that they are linked to other memories with which they share "goals, concerns, outcomes, and affective responses." Finally, they tend to point to continuing—perhaps lifelong—areas of "concern or conflict within the personality"(Singer & Blagov, 2004, p. 120), which is why the mention of a broad life-theme, such as love or money, family or faith, is commonly so successful in evoking recollections.

As central as they may be to our repertoire of remembered material, however, self-defining memories are not cast in stone. Rather, they are open to reinterpretation, depending on the self-schemas through which we view them, for these, too, are forever changing. Indeed, the continual reinterpretability of self-defining memories will be a central focus in Chapter 8. In the meantime, two comments are in order before moving to the notion of multiple selves.

First, researchers studying reminiscence have determined that many of our most vivid recollections are rooted in the period between, roughly, 18 and 30 years of age. "Things learned early in adulthood are remembered best," say Rubin and his colleagues, psychologists Tamara Rahhal and Leonard Poon (1998). During this period, most of us are immersed in the process of leaving home, establishing a career, starting a family—each of which involves any number of identity-determining events. "Turning-point episodes," says Bruner (2001), "are critical to the effort to individualize a life" (p. 31). Such episodes "represent a way in which people free themselves in their self-consciousness from their history, their banal destiny, their conventionality" (p. 32). Depicted on a time-line, the density of memories formed around such turning-points is commonly an upward spike: the so-called "reminiscence bump" (Neisser & Libby, 2000, p. 318).

Recalling our earlier point about the body itself as both the setting of our story and its most abiding character, the second comment is that many of our more self-defining memories are embodied ones. Positive or negative, obvious or insidious in nature, they are memories of us-in-this-particular-physical-form: breaking a leg, making love, winning a race, enduring pain. Thus, time and again, themes like "health" or "illness" will open up broad avenues into the thicket of the past.

Multiple Selves: Remembering and Remembered

In the study of biography, it is a commonplace that multiple versions of a person's life can be woven around the same basic set of facts (see Runyan, 1984). With autobiography, the same holds true. "There are many stories of self to tell," writes Eakin (1999, p. xi), "and more than one self to tell them." Neisser (1994) agrees, suggesting that instead of one enduring self, there are actually several (p. vii). In terms of their relationship to a given past event, he distinguishes, for instance, among the "historical" self, the "perceived" self, the "remembering" self, and the "remembered" self (p. 2). To express this complexity another way, and to pick up on our line of thinking in Chapter 2, the "I," argues Hermans (2002, p. 147), "is essentially a collection of storytellers....The self," he says, is "a dynamic multiplicity of relatively autonomous I positions in an imagined landscape." Moreover, each "I" "has a story to tell about its experiences from its own stance," which leads Hermans to see the self as a polyphonic novel: a complex story with multiple versions. Overall, McAdams (2001) echoes, "a lifestory is the product of many different authors—many different I positions....The person," he says, "is endowed with multiple storytelling selves, each in dialogue with others" (p. 671).

All of this is not to propose that we are suffering from Multiple Personality Disorder; simply that, memory-wise, we are multiple selves in multiple ways. Moreover, there are multiple ways to explain how this is so. We can begin with the selves that feature in autobiographical consciousness in general. In the same essay in which he talks about retrospective teleology, Brockmeier (2001) considers the narrative complexity of "autobiographical time" that is evident in our everyday involvement in remembering. Even in just talking about our lives in normal conversation, "autobiography always is an account, given by a narrator in the here and now, about a protagonist bearing his name who existed in the there and then." Moreover, "when the story terminates," the narrator and protagonist have "fused" (pp. 250–251). Past and present, subject and object, "I" and "me" have—paradoxically—converged.

There is another way to talk about the distinction between I-as-narrator in the here-and-now and Me-as-protagonist in the there-and-then. The self who presided when a given event was originally encoded—or the inner editor who determined what would be worth hanging onto from all of the stimuli that accompanied the event at the time—is not the same self that we are each time the event gets retrieved thereafter—that is to say, each *remembering* self. Constantly confounding research into memory, then, is the fact that, as Rubin (1986) puts it, "a college sophomore may be asked to recall an event encoded by a 6-year-old" (p. 69)—or, one could add, an 80-year-old is asked to remember something that happened to her 20-year-old self. Indeed, the recalled event is scarcely the same event anyway, inasmuch as each act of retrieval has a formative-interpretive impact upon what gets retrieved: the Uncertainty Principle yet again. Inevitably, we commit the sin of "bias," whereby "our memories of the past are...rescripted to fit with our present views and needs" (Schacter, 2001, p. 138). Hindsight is tantamount to blindsight, and the remembering self might just as accurately be termed the "oblivious" self (Neisser, 1994, p. 8). Built into all remembering, therefore, is a degree of self-deception. Not just in telling about our lives but in thinking about them too, we do indeed lie with every breath. Self-deception, states Crites (1979), is "the normal pathology of everyday life" (p. 125).

The distinction between selves-then and selves-now concerns the multiplicity of the self over time. However, *within* time—not just a lifetime period but the time of a specific event—it can be argued that we have access to "a small squad of Possible Selves," as Bruner (1994) calls them, "each based on a somewhat different working over of the past: what we would *like* to be, what we *fear* becoming." In addition, there is "a Now Self (or Selves) who carry out the mundane transactions of daily life" (p. 46). Distinguishing between an ideal self, feared self, and now self is another way, then, of talking about the multiplicity of selves. As we will remember from Chapter 2, Bruner and Kalmar (1998) write about our having many "sub-Selfs," a concept we have connected to our capacity to play a variety of characters, or imagoes, in the novels that we are. Yet of those novels, besides self-as-narrator and -character, we can talk about self-as-author as well, plus self-as-reader—the side of self that interests us the most throughout this book.

In the end, we are obliged to agree with cognitive psychologist Craig Barclay (1994) when he asserts that there is no one "unique remembered self" (p. 56). Rather, "autobiographical remembering is largely an improvisational act" (p. 70). Amidst "the improvisational activities that are characteristic of autobiographical remembering," what get created, he argues, are "remembered selves in the making" (p. 70). This insight lures the discussion of memory's great complexity in an even more intriguing and, in the end, more liberating direction. Because each act of remembering requires—and conjures up—a slightly different *remembering* self, and in the process conjures up any one of several *remembered* selves, as well, the pathways into the past are infinite. The greater the range of contexts in which we read our lives, then the more such selves we can be open to, so our thesis runs, and thus the more fully *ourselves* we can become. A quick point in passing, however: "fully ourselves" is not the same as "full of ourselves." An expanded story need not mean an expanded ego. If anything, it may serve as an antidote to egotism, a theme we will appreciate all the more in Chapter 9 when we consider the ironic stance as an essential dimension of wisdom.

Other-wise: The Relational Dimension

From the outset, we have stressed that lives are not storied in a social vacuum but amid a complex web of relationships with others. We can discuss memory's complexity, *other-wise,* in terms of two key themes: how relationships elicit selves and how environments evoke memories.

Relationships Elicit Selves

An exercise like the ABCs confirms just how much stories stimulate stories. Other people's recollections tend to stir up memories from levels within us—lifetime periods, general events, specific episodes—that might not be nearly so accessible if we were just sitting by ourselves, musing on the past. And we can never know in which direction the process could lead us, nor how far back in time, nor into what strange corners. What is more, place us in a different group of fellow reminiscers, or with the same group on a different day, and even with the same triggers (apple, bike, cat) there is no way of predicting which parts of our past will be brought to the fore.

That stories breed stories leads to the idea that there is something about interpersonal interactions in and of themselves that elicits certain memories, even as others are silenced. As we touched on when talking about self-reading contexts, different relationships invariably elicit—and inhibit—different remembered and remembering selves, different protoselves and sub-selves. In turn, these different selves open up alternative pathways into the tangle of the past, taking us back to particular lifetime periods and, with them, to particular modes of experiencing ourselves. For example, when we visit an aging parent, avenues into our past will open that are likely to be closed when visiting a colleague or a friend. Given our instinctive sense of the version of our story that only she possesses, an hour in the company of our mother can pull us right back to when we were tugging at her apron strings. Deep down, we feel once more the acceptance and excitement, or anxiety perhaps, that characterized that early chapter of our life. Indeed, with every person in our circle, we share a distinctive history, and running through that history is, inevitably, a distinctive set of themes. Moreover, we will have laid down memories not just of ourselves but of ourselves with that particular individual.

On one hand, then, some of our central memories are strictly about us, and to that extent could be secrets. On the other, many concern our experiences with others; so much so that, with the passage of time, where our life begins and their life ends is somewhat difficult to say. In fact, our stories can often get so mixed up—so intertextually intertwined—that we find ourselves wondering if a given recollection is really our own memory at all, or rather their memory of us—one they have recounted on so many occasions that it feels like *our* memory of us: "Is that your story of me based on my memory, or my story of me based on yours?" In consequence, the sins of both misattribution and suggestibility can easily beset us, especially if our take on the event is in any way challenged: "'That's not what happened.' 'T'is too.' 'T'is not.'"

Excellent examples of this process of collaborative memory-making are couple stories. Over time, partners build up a stock of coauthored anecdotes about events they have gone through together. They are relationship-defining memories, signature-stories-for-two: "the first time we met," "the time we went apple-picking in Ireland," "the crazy thing we did on our honeymoon." And often they are contested, with each person viewing the events through a different lens, not to mention through different stories of the relationship itself (see Sternberg, 1998). Indeed, the contested dimensions could come to be central to the telling, and a selling-point for listeners on the lookout for a bit of entertainment: "'I never said that, and you know it!' 'Did too.' 'Did not.'"

Narratively speaking, the boundaries between selves, and thus the memories that define those selves, can be blurred in intricate ways. Inasmuch as "memory is where social constructionism and developmental psychology meet" (Neisser, 1994, p. 11), such intricacies characterize, not just our adult relationships, but those we enter at birth. Accordingly, children's stories can be hopelessly enmeshed in parents' stories (and vice versa, too), in part because parents will often coach their offspring in what experiences are worth remembering and in how they can encode them—experiences, perhaps, that the parents themselves particularly value due to the editorial priorities that are guiding their own lives at the time. But there can be notable variations where gender is concerned.

Research on memory-talk by psychologists such as Fivush, whose work we touched on in Chapter 3 and who has an added interest in "the gendered socialization of memory" (Fivush, 2004, p. 77), shows, for instance, how "parents talk more about the past with girls than with boys" (Fivush, 1994, p. 153). Furthermore, it is mothers more than fathers who tend to do the talking. Conversing about everyday events, they will encourage their young daughters to construct memories that are more richly detailed, more elaborate, and more emotionally nuanced than those that their sons are invited to form. Indeed, for boys, "the past is not talked about as much nor as richly" (p. 154). In consequence, even into adulthood, women, "on average may have slightly better memory for life experiences than men" (Neisser & Libby, 2000). Not only do they "recall more events" but "they encode more detailed representations in the first place" (p. 322).

Overall, such differences in how our habitual avenues into memory get laid down across the life span—how they develop and perhaps deepen with time—have profound implications for the poetics of aging (see Pillemer, Wink, DiDonato, & Sanborn, 2003). As Reese and Fivush (1993) conclude, "daughters may very well grow up to value reminiscence more than sons and to produce more elaborate personal narratives" (p. 605). If it is true that "reminiscing begins very early in childhood" (Fivush, Haden, & Reese, 1995, p. 341), then is it possible perhaps that women end up becoming, by socialization if not by nature, more adept than men at reading their lives in the mindful ways that are of interest to us here?

Environments Evoke Memories

An extension of the complexity of memory from a relational perspective concerns the subtle ways in which particular environments evoke particular recollections. Once again, the process is unpredictable. It is impossible to know beforehand how a specific setting will prompt specific memories to rise to the surface, whether of events that we ourselves experienced *in* that place, or of events related to some other place of which, for some reason, the present place reminds us. Once again, Freeman (2002b) offers an example that takes us in what could seem, at first, an unorthodox direction.

In an essay on what he calls the "narrative unconscious," Freeman reflects on a disconcerting form of place memory that he once experienced while visiting Berlin, one that links with implicit memory of a certain sort, on one hand, and shared history on the other. While riding through the city on a bus, he became unaccountably overwhelmed by an "intense experience of *history*" (p. 197). It was as if all the standard tourist sites—the Reichstag, the Brandenburg Gate—had suddenly become a "living, breathing presence" (p. 197). Everything was transformed "from *monument* to *memory*," steeped in dark stories, leading him to experience "a deep grief, a mixture of sorrow and horror" (p. 197). As he told someone later, "it was as if death was in the air." Indeed, the whole strange incident left him wondering whether terrifying past events could "leave traces" (p. 197), whether the past could in some respects remain "alive and operative" (p. 198) in the present.

Freeman's experience of the narrative unconscious, of memories that were not his personally but, as a Jewish person, *might* have been, argues for the reality of that vast realm of social memory or cultural memory that, along the lines of Jung's concept of the "collective unconscious" (1976, pp. 59–69), underlies our sense of self. In a quiet but certain way, such a realm suffuses our personal story with the conflicts and complexities of larger stories still, and with something of their overall narrative tone, which conceivably becomes an undertone in our individual construal of the world. And some places, some contexts, make us more mindful of this suffusion than do others: more aware of our roots.

The complexity of memory from a social or collective perspective could lead to the conclusion that the self is "saturated," to use Gergen's term (1992)—so riddled with the textual traces of the stimuli that swarm around us in our hectic postmodern lives that it has no distinct center that makes us uniquely *us*. As should be obvious from everything said so far, however, and which Freeman's experience in a strange way corroborates, the view we take here is that, self-wise, the glass is by no means half empty. It is half full—and more. The saturated self is also the open-ended self, the expanded self: whose roots run deep, whose substance is unthinkably thick, and whose potential for meaning extends in every direction at once.

PIECING OUR STORIES TOGETHER: THE RETRIEVABILITY OF MEMORY

Appreciating the complexity of memory from these numerous angles confirms, then, how tangled our past can be, and thus how puzzling is our "passage through the maze of the inner life" (Cole, 1992, p. xxxii). By the same token, it offers a relief map of the areas we venture into once we set out to expand our story—a process that, we reiterate, is essential to our narrative development. Again, the thicker the text, the richer the read. Yet too often we operate with simplistic assumptions about what memory actually entails. So as not to lose our bearings, then, it is imperative that we accept just how intricate a realm, how textual a realm, memory really is. And how unique a realm as well, for it is in the contents of memory that we are at our most novel. Who else but us harbors the exact same collection of lifetime periods, of general events and specific events, not to mention of narrative debris? Cataloguing that collection in some detail is the first step in reading our lives, much as attending to its textual features—certainly not ignoring them—is critical to the experience of a literary work.

For many of us, the routes we habitually take into memory, insofar as we do more than putter at its fringes, are needlessly narrow. Many of them would appear to end in a cul-de-sac, as if the thicket were a maze. But if memory is a maze, then it is an odd one for sure, since any path at any time can lead to its center—or, more accurately, to any center, for just as the same memory can be triggered by multiple prompts, so memory as a whole possesses multiple centers, accessible by multiple means. Our goal in what follows is to look further at what some of those means might be. Before we get to them, however, we need to review how, on the physiological front, aging complicates memory beyond simply adding more and more events to be remembered, or putting more layers on the compost heap. While biographical aging thickens what we remember, in other words, biological aging affects *how* we remember it.

Changing Memories

The main impact on memory of so-called normal aging (senile aging is another matter) is due to an overall shrinkage in the mass of the brain itself by as much as 10% per decade as we move into our 60s and beyond. Despite great variation from one individual to another, hardest hit in this shrinkage are the frontal lobe regions, a change that Schacter (1996) stresses has "far-reaching consequences" (p. 291). "Frontal lobe functions," echo Woodruff-Pak and Papka (1999), "are central to the understanding of the neuropsychology of aging" (p. 118).

Among the tasks that depend largely on frontal lobe functions are those that concern recall more than recognition. For example, we may recognize Helena as the capital of Montana if presented with more than one candidate (Billings, Missoula, Helena), or if given a suitable clue ("it's a woman's name"). Yet asked straight out "what is the capital of Montana?" the answer could prove far harder to come up with—unless Montana is our home! Performing poorly on a geography quiz may not be too serious an issue, of course, but not being able to recall which pill we ought to take at bedtime is potentially far graver.

Frontal lobe damage is also linked to the sin of misattribution, insofar as it interferes with *source memory*—remembering a particular fact, that is, but not who it was that told us. Such problems become embarrassing if someone has entrusted us with a juicy bit of information about a common acquaintance, yet we forget both who that someone was and the fact that they had sworn us to secrecy. To put it simply, failure to recall the sources of our memories can lead to "illusory recollections" (Schacter, 2001, pp. 88ff).

As for semantic memory, it "holds up well with age" and "on balance...is less affected than episodic memory" (Schacter, 1996, p. 291). Indeed, "our abilities to call on our enormous networks of facts and associations are generally well preserved" (p. 291), a fact that contributes, no doubt, to Casey's (1987) "thick autonomy" (pp. 262–287). It also sheds light on May Sarton's (1977/1995) observation (p. 231) that "as life goes on, it becomes more intense, because there are tremendous numbers of associations and so many memories"—an experience related, no doubt, to changes at the neuronal level, such as we noted in Chapter 6.

By the same token, procedural memory is more adversely affected. Insofar as frontal lobes "inhibit thoughts and associations that are irrelevant to carrying out the task at hand," it can happen that "some elderly adults are plagued by extraneous thoughts and associations that distract them during demanding tasks" (Schacter, 1996, p. 293). Being plagued by extraneous thoughts explains the sin of blocking: the *tip-of-my-tongue* phenomenon. Clearly, it contributes to absentmindedness as well (Schacter, 2001, p. 42).

Regarding the formation of episodic memories, because frontal lobe changes tend to interfere with working memory, they are therefore at work in our difficulties with "recalling and pulling together the diverse elements that constitute an everyday episode: what happened, when it happened, and who said what" (Schacter, 1996, p. 289). Compared with younger adults, then, older adults' recollections of recent experiences tend to be less detailed and less "vivid," more "sketchy and incomplete" (p. 289), leading them to "rely more on general feelings of familiarity" (p. 294). As a consequence, they "often prefer to focus on events from the distant past" (p. 294). (Incidentally, aging reduces the incidence of "flashbulb memories" [p. 293] too: those intense recollections we can have of what we were doing when, say, we first learned about the assassination of John F. Kennedy, the fall of the Berlin Wall, or the horror of September 11th.)

Overall, it is due to this generally greater focus on the past that gerontologists have placed more emphasis on the role of reminiscence in later life,
one of our central topics in Chapter 8. For the present, we can revisit the
idea of the reminiscence "bump." The "rule," says Schacter, is that "memories
become gradually less accessible with the passage of time" (p. 298). In other
words, transience always takes it toll. The exception is the "enhanced memo-
rability of experiences from late adolescence and early adulthood" (p. 298).
Such memories are often "extensively rehearsed and elaborated" (p. 299),
and appear to wield special power in "the psychological landscape of the
elderly" (p. 299). In other words, they are self-defining, and constitute "the
core of the emerging adult life story that we carry around with us, largely
unchanged, for the remainder of our adult lives" (p. 299). Precisely how unchanged, and unchangeable, is an issue we will return to soon.

The bottom line, in any case, is that "when older adults focus on the past,
there need not be any pathology involved" (p. 283). There is no dramatic
"across-the-board decline in all memory functions" (p. 283). True, older
adults are more prone than younger ones to memory's various "sins." Yet
these are ultimately the "by-products of otherwise adaptive features of memory, a price we pay for processes and functions that serve us well in many
respects" (p. 184). This is encouraging. Nonetheless, we would go one step
further and, in sympathy with the optimistic perspective of Cohen (2005)
or Goldberg (2005), propose that the features at issue are more than merely
"adaptive." What memory may lose in efficiency of functioning, in other
words, it more than makes up for in thickness of substance and richness of
potential for meaning.

Barriers to Remembering: Emotional and Relational

Rather than being roadblocks to entering our pasts, the effects on memory
of changes to the aging brain may actually make our journey more exciting. Still, two other possible barriers, emotional and relational, need noting
before we proceed.

As for emotional barriers, the memory–emotion connection concerns
feelings that are aroused by particular memories, or, conversely, memories
that are triggered by particular moods. But it also concerns the feelings we
may harbor toward memory itself. Ambivalence or indifference is one such
feeling—the attitude that, as Henry Ford presumably remarked, *history is
bunk*: "Why bother with the past? Thinking about it won't change it. No use
crying over spilt milk." Or we may feel that the past is simply uninterest-
ing; that there is no big deal to it: "I haven't done much," we insist. "I've led
an ordinary life, nothing special at all." Behind such expressions may lurk

the fear of getting lost in our story; fear of dredging up pieces of the past that could prove difficult to handle, that we have never properly articulated, let alone reflected on—that could overwhelm us if we let them out, becoming not just one story among many but the only story of our lives, the main event. For some, whether because of a temperament that is nonchalant about the past or a past pain of which they do not care to be reminded, indifference hardens into disdain. "I [do] not wish to be a rememberer; I cannot see the reason for it," literary scholar Carolyn Heilbrun (1997) stoutly maintains, going on to stress "my impatience with memory, and my scant portion of nostalgia" (p. 122).

The emotional barriers that deter us from going more deeply into memory—beyond the corners of it that we frequent on a regular basis—are often bound up with relational barriers. Inasmuch as different relationships elicit different selves, and different selves have access to different memories, or to the same memories from different angles, the people we interact with every day can have a major impact on the rapport we develop with our past. Contact with the same old interlocutors can mean staying stuck in the same old stories. It can mean losing touch with the sides of ourselves that are buttressed by memories that, otherwise, are buried beneath the narrower, more formulaic memories that contact reinforces.

To the degree that others coauthor our stories, there is a quiet tragedy in all of this. As they regularly censor certain sides of us, as their style of listening intrinsically dissuades us from telling and reading ourselves with anything approaching our capacity for narrative development, that development is needlessly inhibited. More tragic still is if we have no real listeners at all, or are confined to an institution where we are talked to and listened to in a condescending manner, as patient first and person last. On the other hand, the listeners who have previously let us talk liberally about our lives can also become internalized, so that even though gone, their voices—or more importantly, *our* voice, which they habitually empowered—can still sound inside our heads, keeping alive those more self-affirming versions of our lives that they had a knack for bringing out. Alternatively, we may have cultivated such a voice on our own—say, through keeping a journal, a practice that, though on one hand can be a factor in narrative foreclosure, as we noted in Chapter 6, on the other can strengthen our inner reader, nurturing the noticers and natterers who are, so to speak, on our side.

Ultimately, relational barriers are a function of environmental barriers. As we have seen, such environments range in scale from that of a particular friendship to that of a family, a community, or an entire culture. And each will mediate its own set of assumptions about the nature of the past, both personal and social, and how we are to use it. This fact is eminently relevant to the poetics of aging. An environment in which the past seems widely devalued and the future is essentially all—a society like our own perhaps—may place scant importance on memory in general. Conversely, the more open to the fullness of time an environment is, the more expansive its constituents' stories can be.

Avenues of Entry

We move now from the complexities of memory in general, and from these various barriers to remembering, to the more practical issues of how many memories we can actually retrieve, and by what means. How are we to set about "mining for stories," as Polster asks (1987, pp. 68–96)? "How might we begin our census of the contents of the mind?" inquires psychologist Marigold Linton (1986, p. 52). To start with, a vast portion of those contents lies outside our field of view in any given moment. We are simply not conscious of them. Indeed, this is one way of defining the unconscious: the unconscious is to the conscious as what we *can* remember is to what we *do* remember. In computer terms, what appears on the screen is only a portion of a particular file, although several such files may be open at once. Yet even they are but a fraction of the thousands that are stored away inside us. How, then, do we take stock of what is normally unconscious, what is not currently on the screen, nor sitting in those relatively few files that we work with everyday? Switching metaphors, how do we access what lies deeper in the compost heap? Accessing all of it at once, having our whole life pass before us, is probably impossible. What is not is a more expanded version of it.

Expanding our stories is the critical first step in a full-scale reading of our lives. But it needs to be distinguished from *life review* (Butler, 1963; 1996)—a process we will come back to in the following chapter. Crudely put, the difference between retrieving our memory and reviewing our life is the difference between a store-wide inventory of the stock on the shelves and an audit of the books: the weighing of mistakes against accomplishments and sorrows against joys to determine to what, on balance, our life has amounted to. Such a tallying clearly has its place, yet there is always more material tucked away in memory than meets the conscious mind, and some of it, perhaps much of it, holds unspecified potential for meaning that a life review as such could easily overlook.

Besides the ABCs above, and besides composing a memoir (which we will come back to in Chapter 8), what we want to look at here are a few broad strategies that we can utilize in doing our own census of the contents of our mind, strategies that are disarmingly simple: indeed, well within our reach.

Some, we can use on our own; others work better in the company of others. Either way, they are *sitting, looking, listing, listening,* and *talking.*

Sitting

A common practice in schools of meditation is to *just sit:* to observe dispassionately whatever bubbles up inside us (Field's butterflies again), note any emotions that might accompany them, and let them go. Rather than get drawn into the dramas and agendas of our various noticers and natterers, we are urged to stay centered in the self who presides behind the incessant internal activity. Very often, though, this activity represents shuttlings between different modes of time, and each shuttling can have traces of memories attached to it. Linton's term for such a strategy is "memory watching" (1986, p. 52), since what we are watching for most is where, in our past, the butterflies are coming from. Sitting can be surprising. It might hit us, for instance, that the tune that has been running through our head since breakfast is the same one that our father used to hum to us when putting us to bed. In fact, it was sounding in the wings of our dreams as recently as last night. Why might we be recalling it now, for our father has been dead for years? Memory-watching thus inspires an element of wonder at the unpredictability of our past, not to mention at the intricate, if elusive, links between our memories and our dreams.

Looking

If looking inside ourselves has merit, then so, too, can looking around. An obvious option in this regard, one we can pursue while just sitting, of course, is to allow our eyes to wander round the room. That faded photo on the wall: Who is in it? When was it taken? What was happening on that particular day? Then there are the snapshots in the albums by the window, the letters on the top of the filing cabinet, the dusty diaries sitting on the shelf, replete with all the poems we once, so passionately, composed: Who were we when we wrote them? What was happening in our world? Who were the people in our circle? What did our life look like and feel like at the time—socially, emotionally? What memories were at that point uppermost in our minds, and what futures did we envision? Other objects, too, could qualify as "reminiscentia" (Casey, 1987, pp. 110–111; Sherman, 1991, pp. 127–130). Indeed, technically, every single thing in our lives has some sort of story behind it. The dresses in the closet, the tools in the basement, the toys in the attic—someone at some point brought them home, or some one or other of our own many former selves. Which one? Where was I at in my life when I did? What was I thinking, feeling, dreaming?

Listing

One strategy is a variation on what many of us do anyway—which is, to make lists. Not lists of what to do in the future, but of what we did—said, experienced—in the past. Different individuals will make different sorts of lists. A participant in one of our workshops once experienced a *"Eureka!"* moment when it dawned upon him halfway through the day that the most fruitful means of drilling into the layers of his own past was to list the various houses he had lived in since his birth. The image of each of them in front of him, he was certain, would release a flood of memories from an entire lifetime period.

If no such route leaps to mind, then making lists of broad general categories could also be effective, with more specific ones suggesting themselves to us as we go along: in essence, a *who-what-when-where* approach. Who are the people who have been part of our lives across the years? What activities have we been involved in? What jobs and hobbies have we had? What possessions have had particular significance for us—what clothes, cars, books, toys? Where have we traveled, and in what places have we lived?

Such an approach can be followed in relation to our life as a whole, to broad lifetime periods, or to particular parcels of datable time—1950 to 1960, 1980 to 1990, and so on. Correct chronology need not be essential, of course, for our memories are bound to be cross-referenced in all manner of arrangements. Even with a predetermined time frame, for example, the names we might jot down (of classmates, teammates, neighbors) could surprise us by how helter-skelter they come to mind—or that they come to mind at all: Who *were* those people? What did we do with them? What sides of us did they evoke? By considering such questions, certain episodes or incidents may start standing out for us as particularly intriguing, and as worthy of the kind of close examination that is our focus in Chapter 8.

Listening

Listing could take longer than we think, and turn up all manner of items that, for whatever reasons, our inner editor chose to tuck away. Another broad strategy for entering memory, then, is simply listening—not only listening to music, which is a potent memory-trigger in itself, but listening to what others around us are saying, and noting which of our memories their words awaken. The ABCs exercise illustrates the unpredictable directions into which individual words can lead on their own, apart from what they might suggest within the context of a given sentence: nouns (apple, bike, cat), names (Melvin, Mildred, Mexico), verbs (flying, fishing, skiing), adjectives (angry,

tired, sad). But every conversation holds equal potential to stimulate remembered material, as we listen out of the corner of our minds for images of our
past that the words of the people we are talking with could revive—again,
depending who they are. Certain of them will tend to employ certain ways
of speaking to us, use certain expressions or phrases, and, as we have been
saying, evoke specific sides of us, including the memories to which those
sides habitually have access.

Talking

Talking in general, then, is a path into the complexities of memory. Within
this category, one strategy is requesting our friends to ask us questions about
our lives, and there is no limit to those they might use to prime the pump:
Where did you go on your first date? Did you ever give away a secret? What
sort of perfume did your mother wear? Again, the mere act of talking with
particular people will prompt particular sorts of memories. In this connection, family members can be vital. Very often, they hold within them some
of our most salient reminiscences, not to mention reminiscences of us that
are totally outside our ken, because we were merely infants at the time. By
the same token, *how* they hold those reminiscences may be problematic, for
rather than corroborate our own memories of our lives, they might just as
easily contradict them—in the process undermining our confidence, not
only in the accuracy, but in the very occurrence of the events that are supposedly behind them. Of course, having one's parents still alive provides ample
opportunity to revisit—and, as the case may be, revise—one's past. However, there is a for-better-or-worse dimension to such revisiting, for it can be
unsettling not to know whether what we think took place in our childhood
will be supported by their memories, too. Still, once they are dead, access to
the portions of our past that they routinely afforded us will in many ways be
sealed off, and we may never know for certain what took place.

Then there are the pathways into our past that we can tread with people
who have never known us at all, whose version of us is not confused by
restrictive "storyotypes" but dependent solely on what we share with them
today. The proverbial stranger-on-the-train is a case in point: the traveling
companion we never met before and will never meet again, yet to whom we
find ourselves divulging the most intimate details of our past, the obscurest
corners of our inner world. Another example is a professional listener—a
therapist, for instance—who asks us questions and responds to our answers in ways that can lure us into our stories more deeply than familiar
listeners can, who, competent and compassionate though they may be,

ultimately know our story—or *their* version of it—far too well to be of much assistance.

Another strategy we can try, with others or ourselves, is to free-associate using certain broad life-themes, such as love, finances, or family—a strategy that is central, in fact, to "guided autobiography" (Birren & Deutchman, 1991). But it could run through a therapy session as well: "Today, it might be helpful if you talked about the theme of 'rejection' in your life. Can you think of any times when you felt you were not being accepted for who you are? When someone disappointed you or pushed you away?" And linked to such questioning could be the use of metaphor: "In what way does your life feel like a game of chance? a battlefield? a merry-go-round? a journey?"

We will be returning later on to the role of metaphor in reading our lives. For now, by proposing this very basic and, admittedly, broad approach of *stop, look, and list(en)*, our assumption is certainly not that it will suit every-one's needs as a tool for retrieving the past. The point is not *how* we engage in such a process, but that we engage in it at all. In stirring up the past by whatever means we choose, we are not merely expanding our stories, but taking a critical step in the direction of examining them as well.

Eight

EXAMINING OUR STORIES:

THE QUEST FOR MEANING

I am a man telling the story of his life.... Like the world-evolution, it is endless. It is a turning inside out... with the result that somewhere along the way one discovers that what one has to say is not nearly so important as the telling itself.
    —Henry Miller (1941, p. 20)

I can't give you any advice but this: to go into yourself and see how deep the place is from which your life flows.
    —Rainer Maria Rilke (1986, p. 7)

Inquire within.
    —Anonymous

MEANING IN MEMORY

In shifting our focus from expanding our stories to examining our stories, what ought to be clear is that memory and meaning are inseparably connected—as are memory and the self. While the past as such may have "no ready-made meaning of its own" (Charmé, 1984, p. 30), our memory of it is about nothing if not the making of meaning, from the instant that our senses seize upon some incident or item for particular attention.

Continuing with our newspaper analogy, our noticings and natterings are seldom straight reporting. They are already alive with incipient significance. And as for those that get chosen for inclusion in our official inner text, that are transferred to longer-term storage, they invariably reflect the agendas and priorities and overall self-schemas that guide our internal editor. These priorities themselves, however, are constantly evolving, as is our editor, and as are our noticers and natterers. Indeed, as time goes by and life inside of us becomes thicker and thicker with accumulated experience, reflected on or not, the paper as a whole will clearly be expanding. More departments will be established, more sections inserted, more customers included in its circulation. This expansion of our inner operations hosts some intriguing implications for our relationship with memory as a whole.

As we become more aware of the primary stories our identity has revolved around, we might wish, for example, that we could go back and notice different details about the events that we held onto, if not register alternative events entirely. If we knew then what we know now about how our life has unfolded, in other words, we might prefer to have gathered rather different material than we did—happier events and more positive details, instead of the string of hard-luck tales that we ended up collecting, and that tempt us continually toward narrative foreclosure. As we hope to show in this chapter, though, it is not really different material that we need so much as different interpretations, different storyings, different "valuations" of the material that we have (Hermans & Hermans-Janssen, 1995, pp. 17–18). It is not what we have retained that is the problem but what we *make* of what we retain. It is not the textual features of the novel of our life that are at issue but our reader constructions.

And yet, the kind of memory inventory that we considered toward the end of Chapter 7 could lead us to the discovery that we have retained a good deal more material than we might suppose, from the level of general events right down to that of narrative debris. Furthermore, as we think about all of the material we did not retain, we get an inkling of how each bit of what we did is, in its own way, there for a reason. It is *about* something. Everything in our lives may not *happen* for a reason, in the sense of being integral to some grand design, but everything, one can argue, is *remembered* for a reason. Out of "the incalculable number of impressions which meet an individual," says psychologist Alfred Adler, "he chooses to remember only those which he feels, however darkly, to have a bearing on his situation" (Ansbacher & Ansbacher, 1956, p. 351). What sticks in memory, one might say, is whatever possessed significance for the self (or selves) out of which we were operating at the time that a given event took place. In turn, this becomes fodder for such further significance as we may fashion in the future, from the standpoint of other selves. Clearly, then, discussions of remembering are impossible apart from discussions of meaning (see Robinson, 1995), as will be obvious all the more when, later in the chapter, we talk about dynamic reminiscence. And it is in relation to lifestory that the two sets of discussions converge.

As we saw in Chapter 3, our lifestory is both "structurally" and "interpretively" open (Linde, 1993, p. 31). In light of the thesis we are developing here, we can refine this insight as follows: in a structural sense, our story—as memory—is much more open than we think. Both its contents and its organization are much more flexible than fixed. In an interpretive sense, however, our story—as meaning—is infinitely open. Indeed, it is this dual openness, structural and interpretive alike, that is inspiring our hunches about the poetics of aging. For even as time takes its toll on our body, it intensifies the benefits we stand to gain from reading our experience. Our memories, says Sherman (1991), can be imbued with "a richness never experienced before" (p. 245). To put it simply, the longer our life, the greater the potential and capacity for meaning, and the greater our need for it as well.

MEANING IN LIFE

Despite its widespread use in daily speech, the term *meaning* is "notoriously vague" (Cole & Gadow, 1986, p. 4). What we mean by it depends on our frame of reference. In general, philosophers can be expected to use it differently than psychologists will. That said, existentialist philosophers could mean different things by it than philosophers of history, while humanistic psychologists will understand it differently than cognitive ones. In turn, linguists will have their own range of takes on the topic; literary scholars, the same; and so on.

As for what we mean by it here, it is not the meaning of specific events that is of interest to us, nor events themselves as being somehow meant to be. And neither are we interested in any central way in ultimate meaning, or the meaning *of* life. What interests us is meaning *in* life, otherwise known as "existential meaning" (Reker & Chamberlain, 2000). Furthermore, the particular approach we take to such meaning comes out of a conceptual space where existentialist psychology meets literary theory. In short, human beings need meaning, and literature mediates meaning. Naturally, they need other things in life besides meaning, nor is meaning the only thing for which literature is the medium. Still, this basic twofold formulation provides a helpful reference point as we ponder, respectively, the *necessity, nature,* and *narrativity* of meaning.

The Necessity of Meaning

Gerontologist Harry Berman (1994) insists that "the essence of human being is making meaning" (p. xviii). Indeed a "central tenet" of the human sciences "is that humans are self-interpreting animals" (p. 21). For this reason, he stresses the need for a "hermeneutical gerontology" (p. xxiv): an approach to the study of aging that focuses on the self-interpreting, meaning-making dimensions of human existence, on the fact that human beings are, at bottom, hermeneutical beings, and—as we would put it—are continually reading their lives. Fellow gerontologist Sharon Kaufman (1986), who employs a symbolic interactionist approach in her research into what she calls the "ageless self," views the self as basically "the interpreter of experience" that "maintains continuity through a symbolic, creative process." In other words, "the self draws meaning from the past, interpreting and recreating it as a resource for being in the present" (p. 14). Developmental psychologist Robert Kegan (1982) shares a vision similar to both Berman's and Kaufman's, but carries it even further. It is "not that a person makes meaning," he says, "as much as that the activity of being a person is the activity of meaning-making." "Human being," he argues, "is the composing of meaning. We literally make sense" (p. 11).

A corollary of this is that some of us make more sense than others do, or at least we are more intentional about it, or we make sense better. How much sense we make and how well we make it—which is to say, both the quantity and the quality of the meaning that we fashion—will naturally vary from one individual to the next, as will the least amount of meaning that we can tolerate yet still get by. Given our differing needs for structure in life, some of us may be quite comfortable living amid circumstances where, to someone else, for instance, the meaning of things is chronically unclear, where chaos and confusion seem to reign. The issue of consistency figures here, as well. Some of us may find certain interests or activities to be meaningful in ways that contradict the meaning we find in our other interests or activities. Such variations aside, *that* we make sense, moreover that we need to make at least *some* sense, can be taken as a given. And nothing less than our sanity may be at stake. As expressed by psychologist Dominique Debats (2000, p. 99), "the less the sense of meaning, the greater the severity of psychopathology."

For McAdams, as we will recall from Chapter 3, meaning constitutes the third and, in a sense, highest level in the structure of personality, the first being that of more or less stable traits, and the second, our adaptations of these traits amid the circumstances of our day-to-day lives. In the end, that is, it is the making of meaning that is necessary to complete—literally, to inform—our sense of identity. Insofar as identity *is* a lifestory, meaning-making is inseparable from story-making. In short, the necessity of meaning is tied to the narrativity of meaning.

If constructs like *personality* and *identity* need defining in terms of meaning, then no less so does *development*. For Freeman (1998), development does not take place in accordance with a preprogrammed plan that is, at base, physiologically determined, and has only a future trajectory. Instead, it depends upon what we make of the past. We can only be said to develop, in other words, to the extent that we are growing in our understanding of our past, and this process, he insists, is a "*hermeneutical* project" (p. 42). While our hermeneutical development commences with the emergence of consciousness itself, it continues with special intensity (or it needs to, if it does not) well into later life, not unlike how a novel becomes more engrossing, more meaningful, the closer we get to its end. This stands to reason. The more memory we acquire (or recover), then the greater the need to make some sense of it all.

May Sarton, whose published journals document the complexities of living the examined life in one's later years, complains in more than one place of having "too much experience and too little time to sort it out" (1980, p. 178)—too much "undifferentiated experience," as Berman (1994) would put it, that "has not been thought about or expressed in language" (p. 231). Compared to most of us, Sarton, for whom (as a writer) expressing thoughts in language amounts to a raison d'être, may be speaking from an unusually low tolerance for internal disorder. Still, a robust sense of meaning, one could argue, is essential for us all. We can withstand almost anything if we can find some meaning in our suffering. "The disposition to increase the meaningfulness of life," claims philosopher Herbert Fingarette (1963), "is fundamental to human being" (p. 26). Framing the point in narrative terms, Cohler (1993) argues that "well-being is associated with enhanced preservation of meaning, expressed as a purposive and coherent life-story." The inability to sustain such a story, he warns, may result in a decrease in psychological well-being and "a sense of personal depletion" (p. 108).

The tragedy for many of us as we age, however, is that our reservoir of meaning is in danger of depletion at the very phase in our lives when, really, it ought to be at its height—a possibility that contributes, no doubt, to the late-life crisis. "The crisis of old age," suggests one source, is "a crisis of meaning" (Missinne, 2003, p. 113). Yet it is not so much that we need *more* meaning (as if meaning could be measured), but meaning of a deeper, more satisfying kind—moreover, not meaning in general, but meaning for our own unique lives. To the extent this need is left unmet, the result, one could argue, is narrative foreclosure. The life continues, but the story has effectively concluded: under-told, under-storied, and under-read.

"Most of us," admits Sherman (1991) frankly, "do not live a fully examined life" (p. 231)—an understatement if there ever was one, for such a life is probably no more feasible than the fully remembered one. Yet the consequence of the basic disjuncture between our need for meaning and the available supply of it can, for many as they age, be a sense of *anomie*, of what existential psychologist and Holocaust survivor Victor Frankl calls "noogenic neurosis" (cited in Debats, 2000, p. 95)—a condition it seems reasonable to link to depression as well. Depression, claims Kegan (1982), is "necessarily" bound up with "a threat to meaning" (p. 269). A discussion of the links between mental health in later life and a healthy degree of meaning—links that can be argued from a variety of angles (see Reker & Chamberlain, 2000)—is well beyond our scope. What we would propose, however, is that the richer the meaning we can make, or the more intentionally we can cultivate the examined life, the more resources will lie at our disposal to cope creatively with the challenges of age.

The Nature of Meaning

Meaning is not ready-made. Nor does it inhere in things themselves, any more than it inheres in the past itself, or in the marks and squiggles that greet us on the pages of a book. It is not a quality such things possess in some once-and-for-all fashion, but is created or attributed in the very process of perceiving them. In short, meaning is a process, a continual making and re-making. It is an active noun, a gerund. It is, literally, mean-*ing*.

In consequence, the same events or objects will mean different things to different people. A couple goes through what, to friends looking on, is the exact same event. Yet each partner could well construe it and recount it in a markedly different way—a comedy for one, while a tragedy for the other. Indeed, such disagreement may be a constant feature of the narrative environment that their union represents. Again, to one person, two planks spiked together in the shape of a cross will symbolize the death of a first-century carpenter, plus an entire theology on the destiny of humankind. For another, it will be nothing more than...two planks spiked together: same object, different meaning. Moving from events to things to people, the same principle applies. Someone might sigh, for instance, that "she means the world to me," while of the same individual, someone else, or possibly the same someone at a later date, could equally claim that "she means nothing to me at all." Like beauty, meaning resides in the eye of the beholder. The slipperiness of meaning as a concept, then, underscores the need for a map of the territory into which thinking about it leads us. In this regard, gero-psychologist Gary Reker (2000) proposes four overall aspects of meaning that bear consideration here: the "structural components" of meaning, and the "sources," "breadth," and "depth" of meaning.

Structural components concern how meaning is experienced, whether in primarily cognitive, motivational, or affective terms. The cognitive component has to do with our overall "belief system," while the motivational one concerns our personal "value system" (p. 42). For its part, the affective component involves the "satisfaction" that we derive in trying to live by such systems. Obviously, these components are related, and all three are required in the construction of meaning (p. 42).

The aspects Reker calls "source" and "breadth" refer to the contents of our experience of meaning. Depending on our social or cultural background, not to mention our developmental stage, we draw meaning, he says, from numerous sources: among them relationships, religion, art, money, leisure, humanitarian causes, material possessions, and nature. In fact, research indicates that only a very few people are limited to one such source alone (p. 44)—moreover, the wider the range of them, the greater our sense of "fulfillment" (p. 44). Conversely, the narrower the range, one could add, then the greater will be our chances of narrative foreclosure.

Depth of meaning, which is the most pertinent feature for our purposes here, concerns the value of the meaning that we derive—in other words, whether it be "shallow, fragmented, and superficial" or "deep, integrated, and complex" (p. 44). Reflective of the difference between efferent reading and aesthetic reading, there are four levels, writes Reker, according to which the experience of depth can be categorized. The first is a desire for "pleasure and comfort"; the second, the attempt to fulfill "personal potential." The third is a belief in a "larger societal or political cause," while the fourth is the possession of values that "transcend individuals" and are concerned with "cosmic meaning and ultimate purpose" (p. 44). In this respect, the fourth level correlates with *ultimate* meaning, or the meaning *of* life. But each of these levels, Reker suggests, serves as a "horizon" or "background" for our construction of meaning (p. 43). The implication is that as we mature from lower levels to higher ones, we are able to cope with "contradictions, conflicts, and absurdities" by transcending them, by seeing them as part of a bigger, broader picture (p. 44).

Besides the fact that what we call reading our lives partakes of all but the first of these levels, the idea of them as horizons that are more or less comprehensive corroborates adult educator Jack Mezirow's (1978) concept of "meaning perspectives." In turn, such an idea links with the definition of growth itself put forward by fellow educator Laurent Daloz (1986): namely, as "a series of transformations in our ways of making meaning" (p. 137). In Chapter 9, we will return to these ideas in conjunction with wisdom—as, among other things, a matter of transforming our stories. For now, four additional features of meaning need mentioning, we feel, in view of our focus on the poetics of aging. Though implicit in everything said so far, such features pertain less to the structure of meaning than to its dynamics, to meaning as something we are continually creating. Specifically, it is *developmental, retrospective, contextual,* and *cumulative.*

Meaning-making is developmental in a few different senses. First of all, we tend to find meaning in different sources to different depths at different life-stages. When we were children, we made meaning as children do. But in adulthood—early, middle, and late—we might not make it in the same manner at all, nor from the same sources. More specifically, our ways of making meaning may vary with respect to numerous other aspects of our lives, or other structural components, which can themselves be discussed in developmental terms: the development of "moral reasoning" (Kohlberg, 1984), for example, or the development of "ego" (Loevinger, 1976), or of "faith" (Fowler, 1981). Finally, meaning is developmental in the basic sense that it builds over time. For such reasons, some textbooks on the psychology of aging devote entire chapters to "the growth of meaning" (Bee & Bjorklund, 2004).

The retrospective dimension of meaning should come as no surprise, for it links with what we said in Chapter 7 about memory and the backward gaze of time. To paraphrase Kierkegaard's (2003) famous dictum, we live life forward but we make sense of it backward (p. 263). But in addition to "reading the past backward" (Schiff & Cohler, 2001, p. 116), we do not make meaning from nothing, nor from sources that exist solely outside of us. Rather, just as the composing of our lives is done from within them, so meaning-making takes place inside of us as well, with (and this is the point) our own remembered experience as the principal material on which the process hangs. In all its vastness and complexity, memory is one of our primary sources—perhaps *the* source—of meaning in life.

As for the contextual dimension, we do not make meaning—we do not read our lives—in isolation, but in terms of an endless array of coauthoring relationships, narrative environments, and interpretive contexts. And running through such contexts are all manner of meaning systems and meaning perspectives that are absorbed by osmosis into the stories by which we live. In effect, then, no one has "total control over the meanings in his or her life" (Drewery & Winslade, 1997, p. 35). But meaning-making is contextual in the further respect that, as we make sense of an event that has happened in the past, we invariably adjust our memory of it in the present. As we revisit the memory from within the more extensive background that is opened up by the passage of time itself, which distances us from the original occurrence a little more each day, then it becomes, effectively, a different memory. It is literally "recontextualized" (Schachter-Shalomi & Miller, 1995, p. 20). At work yet again is the Uncertainty Principle, plus the hermeneutic circle. "Meaning is contextual," Berman explains, to the extent that "interpretation occurs within a circle in which parts are always interpreted within some understanding of the whole" (1994, p. 4). As an example, we read the peculiar grin on the face of our spouse not just as a random arrangement of facial muscles but as an indication of her response to our comment about "how far we have traveled" since we first got married.

Concerning the cumulative nature of meaning-making, old or outworn meanings, which we fashioned around events that were lived through within previous horizons, are never entirely discarded. However imperceptibly, they attach themselves in trace form to our memories of those events. Thus, the more events we experience with the passage of time, and the more times that we remember them, then the more such traces, the more "layers of significance" (Charmé, 1984, p. 38) and "layers of pastness" (p. 46), will accumulate within us—as they do, of course, when reading a literary text, where "meanings that had emerged earlier both contribute to and are retroactively transfigured by what occurs later" (Freeman, 1999b, p. 247). One has the sense of the story being increasingly gripping as one follows it from beginning to end. Applying this to the domain of lived text, "the meaning of the past," says Charmé (1984), "develops throughout life" (p. 40). Artist Anne Truitt (1987, p. 17) captures what many of us thereby come to feel: "My life has accumulated behind my own back while I was living it, like money in the bank"—like biographical capital (Mader, 1996). Not just memory-wise but meaning-wise, our inner text—whether we examine it or not—grows thicker and thicker with age.

The Narrativity of Meaning

These four extra features of meaning (that it is developmental, retrospective, contextual, and cumulative) underscore how existential meaning—meaning with respect to our unique, evolving self—cannot be comprehended without appreciating the narrative complexity of human life in general. Yet, as with wisdom, spirituality, and even memory, treatments of meaning in the psychology of aging have been shy about taking that complexity into account.

The compulsion to compose stories about our lives and to navigate our world by means of narrative knowing—the entire narrative variable—has largely been absent from conceptions of meaning. For that matter, so has memory. As an example, the index to Reker and Chamberlain's (2000) otherwise valuable collection, *Exploring Existential Meaning*, contains no references whatever to memory, despite the insistence of memory research pioneer, Francis Bartlett, that "memory and interpretation [can] not always be so easily separated" (Lampinen, Beike, & Behrend, 2004, p. 257). What is more, only two references are made to narrative. While these omissions are hardly surprising given the comparatively brief time in which the "inside" of aging has even been up for discussion (Ruth & Kenyon, 1996), they leave insights into the nature of meaning somewhat thin. Insofar as it is "the primary form by which human experience is made meaningful" (Polkinghorne, 1988, p. 1), then narrative itself is a dimensional feature of meaning, at the micro and macro levels alike: from the development of core consciousness itself, through our endless noticing and nattering, to our intentional reflection on the novel of our lives. Just as autobiographical memory can be looked upon as story-memory, so existential meaning is analogous to story-meaning. On this point, let us remember the proverbial chicken–egg relationship that story and meaning share.

We go to stories *for* meaning and we derive meaning *from* stories, so much so that we may read the same stories, or watch the same movies, over and over. Also, we expect stories to *have* meaning and, indeed, be structures for meaning, to consist of words and images that depict events that are connected in meaningful sequences—in con-sequence, one might say. Because of this, stories help us make meaning amid the events and circumstances of our own unfolding lives. In Birkerts's view (1994), the very process of reading stories "keep[s] alive the dangerous and exhilarating idea that a life is not a sequence of lived moments, but a destiny" (p. 85). As readers, he says, "our lives feel pointed toward significance; we feel ourselves living toward meaning, or at least living in the light of its possibility" (p. 90). On the other hand, as we saw in Chapter 4, we impose meaning *onto* stories, or read meaning *into* stories, on the basis of the story of our own particular life. Indeed, without doing so the story in itself will have no meaning whatsoever. What we experience as the story's meaning is the product of its constant interaction with the meanings that we bring to it from our own ever-changing story-worlds. As such, the richer our own lived story—which is to say, the more richly we read it—then the more we stand to profit from reading the literary one.

Charmé (1984) assumes this whole complex connection between narrative and meaning in his exploration of what Jean-Paul Sartre refers to as "existentialist psychoanalysis" (p. 1). Intended as a reaction to Freudian psychoanalysis, which, to Sartre, wrongly employed the language of "mechanisms," not "meanings" (p. 2), in its conception of human nature, existentialist psychoanalysis is a "method for interpreting the meaning of a particular human life" (p. 1). Indeed, for Sartre, as Charmé puts it, "every human being is a source of meaning" (p. 2). Sartre's application of existential psychoanalysis was focused on interpreting four lives in particular—those of French authors Genet, Baudelaire, Flaubert, and himself, using their respective fictional and autobiographical texts as evidence. The implication running through Charmé's book, however, is that the same basic method can be enlisted in the analysis of our own lives—understood, that is, as texts.

According to Charmé, Sartre believed that what "undergirds the meaning of every person's life" is the "fundamental project" (p. 2). Not to be confused with something one pursues in a conscious, deliberate manner, like rearing a family or building a career, such a project is essentially "the cumulative structure of meaning that unfolds slowly in the course of life and links together a person's past, present, and future into a coherent whole" (p. 2). Accordingly, narrative comes immediately into play, insofar as the "essential form of the self" on which this concept is premised is that of a "retrospective story that creates order out of the chaos of experience" (p. 2)—an ever-evolving, unifying, and organic "structure of meaning" made up of all the aspects and activities that constitute a person's life (p. 35). Such qualities suggest that a fundamental project is sufficiently similar to a lifestory, at least as defined by McAdams (1996), to warrant drawing further on Sartre's ideas.

Paralleling our juxtaposition of textual features with reader constructions is Charmé's (1984) interpretation of Sartre's distinction between the "'content'" of the past, which for Sartre is "unchangeable," and the "'meaning'" of the past, which he deems "'eminently variable'" (pp. 30–31). This variability is in line with the perspective we are proposing here, especially in view of the conviction that the fundamental project is to be construed on "a more or less literary model" (p. 46). Just as with a literary text, where "words have already been written," so with a lived text: "events have already occurred." However, "their meaning is not fixed"; it "depends on how they are 'read'" (p. 50). As Polster (1987) echoes, "there is no given proportion in personal existence between an event and its meaning" (p. 102).

This unfixedness of personal meaning is inherent in the parallel with literary meaning: "the reader can always create [meaning] more profoundly," says Charmé (1984). As a result, "a work is inexhaustible, capable of being interpreted by the reader in multiple ways" (p. 50). A literary work is inexhaustible, of course, both after it is read and, in a different way, while the reading is still being done. In life, however, we can read the text only (from within it) while it is still unfolding, still being composed. As we saw with memory, this makes for all manner of shuttlings and circlings amid the meaning-making enterprise: between self-now and self-then; between life-time periods and specific episodes; between past, present, and future.

"Initial experiences and impressions," says Charmé (1984), "are revised at later times to fit in with new experiences or new stages of development" (p. 33). Moreover, "each new dialectical movement" between the old and the new "turns back on the past synthesis, absorbs it, and adds new layers of significance" (p. 38). At the same time, "by placing a later event in the context of an earlier one, both events are enriched and grasped in a new light" (p. 41). As a result, "an experience may be lived through naïvely, while its significance does not accrue until a later date" (p. 32). In sum, "the significance of any part of a life is tentative and awaiting further development" (p. 45). Such insights into both the retrospective of meaning-making and its cumulative dimensions apply, not just to existentialist psychoanalysis, but to the entire interpretive process in which, to varying degrees, each of us is continuously involved. Bringing that process to awareness is often the aim of therapy, an approach to making sense of our lives that, overall, is so thoroughly narrative in nature that it could fairly be referred to as *therapoetic.*

MEANING-MAKING AS THERAPOETIC:
THE NEED FOR NARRATIVE REPAIR

"All therapies are narrative therapies," states psychologist John McLeod (1996) in his overview of the therapeutic field (p. 2). Narrative therapists, in particular, of course, operate with a distinct perspective on what therapy is and does, central to which is "the text analogy" (White & Epston, 1990, pp. 9–13) for understanding subjective experience, and the assumption that it is clients themselves (not therapists) who are the principal experts in their own lives. Yet narrativist or not, "whatever you are doing, or think you are doing, as therapist or client," McLeod (1996) explains, "can be understood in terms of telling and re-telling stories" (p. x). Though each school of therapy will be guided by a particular therapeutic *metanarrative* (p. 22), as well as by particular criteria for what constitutes a good lifestory, the core of the therapeutic endeavor can be captured by a variety of terms: not only "retelling" a life (Schafer, 1992), but also "re-authoring" (White & Epston, 1990, p. 16), "re-biographing" (Rotenberg, 1987), "re-versioning" (Gearing, 1999), or simply "restorying" (White & Epston, 1990, p. 14; see also Kenyon & Randall,

1997). Regardless, though, of which metaphor one employs, why do people seek therapy in the first place?

The stories by which we come to tell and live our lives possess a power that is not merely "formative" but "sometimes deformative" in nature (Rosenwald & Ochberg, 1992, p. 1). It is in relation to the latter possibility that therapy plays a role. According to White and Epston (1991), as we will remember from Chapter 6, people seek therapy when the narratives by which they are storying their experience "do not sufficiently represent their lived experience" (p. 14). Indeed, "significant aspects of their lived experience ... contradict these dominant narratives" (p. 15). Granted, any one of a huge range of real-life issues—chronic or acute, individual or marital—can prompt a person to knock on a counselor's door. Still, White and Epston's assessment expresses what, at bottom, perhaps, is being sought. It is "narrative repair" (Sarbin, 1994, p. 29).

Philosopher Hilde Nelson (2001), in whose book *Damaged Identities* this notion plays a pivotal role, positions her thinking within a perspective that is compatible with our own. "Identities," she says, "are complex narrative constructions consisting of a fluid interaction of the many stories and fragments of stories surrounding the things that seem most important, from one's own point of view and the point of view of others, about a person over time" (p. 20). With this premise in mind, she considers how identities become "damaged" and thus demand "repair." Focusing on groups that are in various ways marginalized, she argues for the need of *counterstories*. By this, she means "a revised understanding of a person or social group...that define[s] people morally, and [is] developed for the express purpose of resisting and undermining an oppressive master narrative" (p. 8). Nelson's approach bears noting in view of the narrative of decline by which, among other influences, the lives of older adults can all too often be oppressed.

Admittedly, the term "repair" is problematic. Not only does it conjure up images of mechanisms more than meanings, but it implies that something is broken and ought to be fixed. What Nelson is careful to stress, however, and what she shares with narrative therapists, along with theorists such as Spence (1982), is that what needs fixing, or at least what needs attending to, does not have to do with us ourselves, in some essential sense. It has to do with the narratives through which we interpret us and experience us. Simply put, our story is deficient. It is not working. It is problematic. But insofar as the two can be pried apart, it is our story that requires healing, not our self. "The person is not the problem," goes the mantra of narrative therapy; "the problem is the problem" (see White & Epston, 1990, pp. 38–76). This shift in emphasis, though next to impossible to appreciate when the problem has us firmly in its grip, is from the ontological to the hermeneutical. The real problem is one of interpretation, not of being. Accordingly, the goal of therapy is "to facilitate the renegotiation of the meaning system within which 'the problem' exists" (Gergen, 1992, p. 251).

Once more, of course, *the story of my life* does not reside inside our heads in some transparent, accessible fashion. It is not a concrete thing to which we can readily point, nor does it bear a necessary relationship to the "brute data" of our actual existence (Novitz, 1997, p. 153). Rather, it is an "imaginative construct" (p. 151): a vague, though powerful idea, an evolving myth in the back of our mind concerning what our life entails—past, present, future. It is our self-concept extended in time and invested with emotion. It is a gut feeling about who, deep down, we really are. It is not something that we can ever tell straight out, but only indirectly and incompletely, in an anecdote here or a *précis* there. Even a full-blown autobiography is, in the end, no more than an extended metaphor for the ever-elusive "whole story." To the extent we can see that story at all, it is only out of the corner of our eyes, on the edge of our awareness. It is a sensing more than a seeing. We are, after all, inside of it. As our fundamental project, it has us more than we have it. It "lives us," one might almost say (see Parry & Doan, 1994, p. 44). For better or worse, we experience our world in terms of it, in many ways setting up our interactions with others in order to confirm the storyline to which we cling about who we really are: "I'm a loser, and sooner or later everyone rejects me." We become open to therapy, then, or indeed to any interpretive context in which we can tell and retell, read and reread, our lives in relative safety, when our stories are too constraining, when they are not serving us sufficiently, when "they close down possibility or...are heading for tragic endings" (Gardner, 1997, pp. 212–213). But again, the insufficiency at issue is experienced less as a specific idea than as a general emotion. Things just don't feel right. In essence, we *feel* the need to re-*think* who we are.

In understanding therapy as the renegotiation of meaning, or as "meaning-reorganization" (Fingarette, 1963, p. 30), and our stories themselves as both sources of and impediments to the meaning that we make, three overlapping categories suggest themselves for how—perhaps especially as we age—our stories can turn into problems. By way of furthering our earlier reflections on both narrative foreclosure and a good lifestory, one could argue that our stories need narrative repair to the extent that they become *dominated, disjointed,* or *disrupted.*

Dominated Stories

Pressured by dominant narratives that story our experience for us, the versions we live by grow shallow and small, constricted and narrow. They grow thin—as, all too likely, will the versions we view others through as well. The problem can exist at the level of the broadest environments that shape our lives. In several respects, our modern, technology-driven culture fails to supply us with sufficient "narrative resources" to live "meaningfully and productively" (Freeman, 2000, p. 81). But domination occurs on more immediate levels, too, from memories, to relationships, to roles.

Perhaps there is one particular period in our lives, or even just a single event, on which it feels our entire identity depends: fighting in Vietnam; missing out on a promotion; being betrayed by a partner; some secret, deep and dark, that holds us hostage; some grudge, regret, or guilt that denies us peace of mind and keeps us spinning in "vicious circles" of anger or despair (McAdams, 2006, pp. 209–240). That one story has become our *whole* story. We cannot see around it, cannot move past it, and cannot construe it in any other way. We over-read it in one way alone. On another level, the narrative of someone else may have overtaken our own. We live in its shadow. We are a pawn in that person's fundamental project, a minor character in his or her unfolding drama: the battered wife, the henpecked husband, the dutiful daughter or son, the faithful sidekick to a "friend" whose agenda we permit to take precedence over our own. Huge aspects of our inmost self must thus be placed on hold, kept hidden in the closet. The relationship shapes us or stories us, yes, but in a coercive, not coauthoring, way. Less dramatic but still worth noting is the woman whose sense of self has been wedded so tightly to her husband's through the years that, once he dies, she succumbs to "identity foreclosure" (van den Hoonaard, 1997)—a phenomenon that could pertain equally, of course, to husbands losing their wives.

Often a certain social role—caregiver, partner, parent, employee, soldier, boss—will usurp our sense of self. The death of the person cared for, the divorce from the spouse, the children leaving home, the retirement from the job—these can leave us wondering: who am I? Another role is that of "sick person," where "having cancer" or "being depressed" becomes the determining, indeed totalizing story by which we envision who we are (see McKim, 2005). The story has *us*—and *is* us. A strain of interpretive parsimony infects us so severely that, basically, there is no other story to be told: I *am* arthritis, I *am* diabetes, I *am* migraine, I *am* depression, I *am* old. Indeed, the "medical model" itself enforces such domination. Through the procedures we are subjected to and the diagnoses we are assigned, we are scripted all too quickly into the character of "patient," until we experience ourselves no longer as bona fide persons with particular histories but rather as passive displayers of particular symptoms. We are not Bill Randall or Beth McKim, with memories and feelings peculiar to us alone, but "the gall bladder in 13B"—a problem to be fixed.

A third form of domination is when the larger story we identify with most closely, whether our family or profession, our clan or creed, squeezes us into straitjacketed patterns of experiencing ourselves. So enslaved is it, in turn, to the myth of its own heritage and destiny that the stories of the individuals who actually people it cannot be properly expressed. Far from being the heroes of their own stories, they are mere players in a grander, more important pageant. One is, most of all, a Harvard Man, a Democrat, a Doctor. One is, first and last, a member of The Royal Family. Conversely, one might be a member of "that family from across the tracks," from the wrong side of town. Either way, it can be tough to live one's legacy down. In more extreme instances, we are de-storied through the policies and practices of a repressive regime, or, in our zeal to find meaning in life, through impaling our distinct identity upon the dogmas of a cult. Finally, we can become addicted to the myth of our own self—the unsung genius, the perfect Mom, the self-made man, or, alternatively, the failure, the victim, the fool: a myth that, despite all data to the contrary, we insist upon believing. Moreover, it is not an evolving myth, but a static one, a rigid one: a form of self-telling and self-interpretation that excludes all possible alternatives.

By any of these means our own unique narrative, in all its intricacy and depth, is eventually eclipsed. It atrophies and dies a slow and undramatic death. The several selves who we otherwise might be, and the countless storylines associated with them, are weeded down to the meager few that are permitted to exist, propped up by a far more limited range of self-defining memories than those that are technically at our disposal. Under such conditions, if our fundamental project stands a chance of flourishing at all, it is only by retreating underground. There it might lie dormant for decades, if not forever, awaiting in silence the right environment and encouragement—the right counter-story— to empower it to reemerge. In the interim, the story we are left to live on the surface lacks openness and differentiation. It lacks vitality. It is emaciated, thin. In such a predicament, we can be tantalized, of course, by foretastes of a far fuller self-story through our sporadic exposure to environments that, however briefly, evoke it. Intermittent bursts of narrative development thus punctuate what, otherwise, is continuous foreclosure, teasing us cruelly with the vision of what ("if only...") we might yet be—or might have been.

In fairness, being overshadowed by narratives other than our own is something to which, in certain situations, we might willingly consent. In the give-and-take of intimate relationships, we may gladly lay aside our personal agenda for the sake of our partner, our children, our aging parents. Similarly, in committing ourselves to a particular life-path, or in yearning for a grander, more meaningful narrative to which we can subscribe, we may willingly subordinate our personal development to the dictates of our profession, the doctrines of our faith, or the destiny of our nation. It will feel like rebirth, like coming home to our true self. That said, one person's salvation could be another one's undoing. Once such commitment is experienced as oppressive and no longer redemptive, then restorying our lives, through therapy or not, could well be something that we reach for yet again.

Disjointed Stories

Our stories can become disjointed—or at least can *feel* disjointed—in a variety of ways. Occasional periods of disjuncture are common, of course, in all our lives and, in moderation, can even be welcomed as invitations to narrative elaboration. That said, we are obviously in the clutches of a disjointed story when the version that we believe about ourselves is at odds with the life that others see us living. Or our brain tells us one main story about who we are, which our behavior, or body, belies. People witness us stumbling around, eyes glazed, every day of our life, yet we stubbornly maintain, "I don't have a drinking problem." We are in denial, in the grip of self-deception. Or, at work, we are a respected executive, praised for our commitment to equal rights, yet at home we are a spouse-beating tyrant whose children are seen but not heard. The story we are living is split down the middle, lacking coherence and credibility alike. It fails to ring true.

Another way our stories can become disjointed is when our overriding version of ourselves is incapable of assimilating what, by any standard, would be judged significant occurrences in our past. While, technically, we remember them, they remain outriders to our innermost identity. We simply do not know what to do with them. The self-story that is preponderant in our memory/imagination is not big enough to cover them, not flexible enough to include them. Of course, no self-narrative can assimilate all of life. No matter how good it might be, our evolving myth cannot keep pace with the task of processing our actual experience, and what we retain is forever but a fraction of what takes place. Life itself, with its steady flow of fresh events, continually outspans our attempts to story it, which is precisely why our myth must keep evolving. In the kind of case at issue here, however, what exists between our remembrance of the past and our perception of the present is a disturbing and arresting disconnection, one we ourselves are probably the last to see.

A further example would be people whose stories—in their own minds, at least—consist of so many bits and pieces, little more than narrative debris. Insofar as they sense their existence to possess some internal consistency or structure, it is not that of an unfolding novel but, at best, of an anthology of short stories, all by the same author, presumably, but not, in the end, an aesthetic whole. It lacks narrative integrity. Novelist Ursula Le Guin (1989) outlines the consequences: "An inability to fit events together in an order that at least seems to make sense, to make the narrative connection," she says, with embarrassing frankness, "is a radical incompetence at being human" (p. 43). Indeed, "stupidity could be defined as a failure to make enough connections, and insanity as severe repeated error in making connections—in telling The Story of My Life" (p. 43). As Eakin (1999) would argue, "narrative disorders and identity disorders go hand in hand" (p. 124).

Yet another way of understanding disjuncture is that there are significant gaps in our story—as, technically, there are in any text. But entire chapters seem strangely missing from our self-accounts. Concerning what, to others looking on, should be eminently memorable events, we are afflicted with amnesia. Or, events that do not quite square with the dominant version that we tell ourselves are largely, or at least temporarily, unavailable. In the grip of an "I'm a failure" story or "I'm so stupid" story, which may well be one that those around us (parents, spouses, colleagues, "friends") insist on our believing, we have difficulty remembering, let alone valuing, those times in our lives, in other environments, when we experienced significant success—at work, at school, at home. To the extent we can recall them at all, it is only by denigrating their relevance, assessing them as aberrations with no enduring meaning. For all intents and purposes, they go "unstoried" (White & Epston, 1990, p. 12). As a consequence, the story by which we are living and by which, deep down, we define our identity is deficient in the criterion of reconciliation. For narrative therapists, such outstanding incidents constitute "unique outcomes" (White & Epston, 1990, p. 41), which clients are urged to flesh out more fully, and to build around them thicker, more self-affirming versions of their lives.

Novelist and memoirist Sharon Butala (2005) provides a touching, indeed troubling, illustration of a life-narrative that is disconnected from the reality that surrounds it. It concerns her own mother and what Butala perceived—obviously, with bias—as the woman's need to write "a new story" (p.43): a version of her life, in other words, that to Butala looking back, fit better with the facts. Her mother, she observes, "clung" to a single story all throughout her life. Central to it was that she was descended from an aristocratic, wealthy family, which instilled in her a feeling of "superiority." In reality, however, not only was the family no longer wealthy, but she herself did not, in her view, marry well, and ended up with "too many small children and no money." Although "not personally diminished by her circumstances," writes Butala, the woman nonetheless "saw herself, all her life, as living the wrong life, a tragic life" (pp. 43–44).

Disrupted Stories

Our stories undergo "disruption" (Fireman, McVay, & Flanagan, 2003, p. 9) when they are cut short or cut off, or important subplots are abruptly aborted, leaving us stranded in a state of narrative incoherence. Like a novel we cease reading midway through, so that we eventually lose the thread of its plot and grow fuzzy on its characters and themes, our life no longer quite makes sense to us. We lose our place in it. The causes can lie in any number of circumstances, from external to internal, and from the mundane to the horrific: from our partner walking out on us, to some sudden revelation that throws our world into disarray, to the devastation of our community by a hurricane or fire. Old age itself, of course, brings an abundance of situations that can make us feel "stagnant, stuck, immobilized" so that we "cannot move forward" (McAdams, 2006, p. 220)—clearly, depending on the person. For one who all life long loved nothing more than to get behind the wheel of a car, the onset of glaucoma and the consequent surrender of his license is a crisis of unimaginable magnitude: "Who am I if I can no longer drive? What is the point of living?" Life as he has known it is effectively finished. The same fate for another individual, though an enormous inconvenience, is scarcely the end of the world, for her meaning is derived from multiple sources and not merely from her ability to drive. The death of a spouse can be equally disruptive, as can a terminal diagnosis. A doctor announcing that "you have cancer and only six months to live" is a sentence on one's story as much as on one's life. But even if not faced with so terrifying a fate, the transition into retirement itself and the potential erosion of our professional identity is, for many, an enormous disruption. The post-mythic stage feels more like the post-mortem stage.

Frozen in epilogue time, the urge to look backward intensifies. We escape into reveries of yesteryear, of a past that looms glamorous and glorious in contrast to the present. In his research with the aging footballers, men whose careers, like those of many athletes, have peaked in their 20s and 30s, Gearing (1999) observes that "for some it was the most important thing that had ever happened to them...something you can never replace"

(p. 56). Though most of those he interviewed, in fact, "don't live in the past but appear to draw strength from that earlier stage in life" (p. 56), for many the opposite will be true. Their story is split quite clearly into Before and Since, where Since pales before the splendor or the pathos of *the good old days*. Writer Ronald Blythe (1979) speaks of the retired soldier for whom, for instance, "The War remains the moral pivot of all his experience, attitudes and dreams." Indeed, "the older he gets, the more the trenches call" (p. 132; see also Shaw & Westwood, 2002).

Our stories can be far more dramatically disrupted, "shattered" even (McKendy, 2006), and our plots more "contaminated" (McAdams, 2006, pp. 209ff), when we are confronted by trauma of one type or other. An elderly friend of one of us, a widower in his late 80s who had made his way to Canada from Europe as a "displaced person" in the wake of World War II, had his house of 30 years broken into, with him still in it. Beaten up and then tied to a chair, he watched with horror as the vandals ransacked his surroundings. Despite everything else he had suffered and survived to that point in his life, the poor man's world was shattered so soundly that, until his death, he remained in a state of permanent confusion.

The impact of trauma in the present is, for many, more than matched by what they went through in the past as victims of crime or abuse, terror or war—as far back as childhood perhaps. In an essay on the "silenced self," Fivush (2004) considers the persistent impact of trauma in early life, when significant others such as parents, for instance, actively discourage the child from voicing his or her feelings. The result is that, even into adulthood, the victim can find it difficult "to construct a coherent life story" and thus an "integrated sense of self" (p. 88). Some individuals may have been subjected to such violence for years, in fact: the consequence being an entire lifetime period that sits blackly in their minds, at once dead and alive. It is not just that their stories are lacking in reconciliation or in generative integration; they are split, in time and space alike. Asked if she still "lives with Auschwitz," survivor Charlotte Delbo replied: "No—I live beside it. Auschwitz is there, fixed and unchangeable, but wrapped in the impervious skin of memory that segregates itself from the present 'me'" (quoted by Langer, 1991, p. 5).

Individuals who come through ordeals this ghastly can possess, not just the two broad sets of selves that all of us do—remembered and remembering, selves-now and selves-then—but, in a sense, two entire memory streams, one amenable to the fashioning of narrative coherence, the other not (Schiff & Cohler, 2001). As Langer (1991) explains, there is, on one hand, the "common memory" (p. 5) of their lives both prior to the horror and following it—memory of their childhood, and then, after the war, of marrying and raising a family. On the other hand is the "deep," "anguished," "humiliated," "tainted," and "unheroic" memory associated with their existence in the camps. Without constituting schizophrenia as such, the split—with which, somehow, they manage to continue living—has ramifications for their experience of self. For Langer, each such mode of "ruined memory" is linked with a particular type of self: the "buried" self, "divided" self, "besieged" self, "impromptu" self, and "diminished" self, respectively.

This overview of some of the main manifestations of narrative disrepair, though in no way intended to be exhaustive, points again to the multitude of factors that can stunt our narrative development, retard our fundamental project, and make narrative foreclosure, to some extent, a foregone conclusion—for all of us at any time no doubt, though particularly perhaps in later life. It also prepares us to appreciate the power of reminiscence, especially *dynamic* reminiscence, in restarting stalled narratives and inspiring richer, more meaning-filled stories by which we might live.

NEW MEANINGS FROM OLD TALES:
DYNAMIC REMINISCENCE AS DEEP READING

Memory, Rubin reminds us (1995, p. 1), is our primary database for therapy. Broadening that base requires intentionally entering the thicket of the past. It requires making a deliberate and mindful effort at expanding our stories: a necessary, though still not sufficient, condition for narrative repair. Equally important is examining our stories, a process to which, both literally and literarily, there is no known end. While there might well be a limit to how much memory we are capable of retrieving, there is none whatsoever to the meaning to be made from what we do. As far as memory is concerned, meaning-in-life is indeterminate in nature.

Prior to outlining what dynamic reminiscence is and does, we are reminded of the comment of psychologist Jean Houston (1987). "Many of you are in the helping professions," says Houston, "and have listened for thousands of hours to neurotics. And what do you hear?" she asks point-blank. "The same old story over and over again. Your work is clear. It is not to change the story, for this is to deny it; it is, rather, to expand and deepen the story, thus releasing the energy bound within it" (p. 99). Deepening the story—which narrative therapists refer to as "story development" (Freedman & Combs, 1996, pp. 76ff)—is fundamental to deep self-reading. By no means, though, need it be done with the aid of a therapist alone. We do it ourselves, in fact, every single day of life, amid the numerous "naturally therapeutic contexts" (Kegan, 1982, pp. 255–296) that we experience across the life span in relationship with parents, partners, colleagues, and friends. Such relationships, says Kegan, "spontaneously support [us] through the sometimes difficult process of growth and change" (p. 256). In sum, central to making meaning-in-life is making it through our connections with others—a theme we will be returning to in Chapter 9.

Reminiscence as Reading Our Lives

Before looking at dynamic reminiscence in particular, we need to say a few words about reminiscence in general—another vast topic that, oddly enough, has not often been linked to the discussion of memory itself (Bluck & Alea, 2002). Sherman's definition serves as well as any to get us started: "The process or practice of thinking or telling about past experience" (1991, p. 257). This simple definition is helpful, for reminiscence is clearly a mode of remembering, yet not all remembering is reminiscence. As we saw in Chapter 7, we remember many things other than past experience: facts about our world and how it works, or semantic memory, plus how to perform a multitude of tasks, or procedural memory. If autobiographical memory already tends toward meaning, however, then reminiscence is remembering that tends toward meaning-*making*, or to use our central concept here, toward reading our lives (Randall & Kenyon, 2002). But reminiscence-as-reading includes a number of types, ranging from those in which the meaning-making is comparatively minimal to those where it is both more intentional and more intense. Of assistance to us as a frame of reference is a typology proposed by psychologist Paul Wong (1995). Wong categorizes reminiscence according to whether it is primarily "narrative," "obsessive," "escapist," "transmissive," "instrumental," or "integrative" in nature.

Narrative reminiscence, he says, is essentially "descriptive," not "evaluative" (Wong, 1995, p. 27), and it often serves a social function (see also Wallace, 1992). It is more or less straight telling, whether thick or thin, embellished or bare-bones: "I was born in the Depression, I grew up on a farm, I left home at 12." Plot-wise, it comes out as "And then ... and then ... and then...." When conducting lifestory interviews with elderly participants, as we noted in Chapter 6, much of what one hears at the outset falls into precisely this category. It is the mode they default to automatically when talking about their pasts (Randall, Prior, & Skarborn, 2006). With respect to the degree of self-reading it represents, narrative reminiscence is efferent reading and thus under-reading, with scant stretching of one's horizons of self-understanding. Insofar as what we hear is what countless other listeners have heard before us, it is, quite literally, the same old story.

The essence of obsessive reminiscence is reflected by the expression: "To this day, I can't understand why...." Wong defines it as "persistent rumination on unpleasant past events" (p. 27). It, too, is the same old story, only over and over and over. As McCullough (1993) writes of arrested aging, we are caught in a "past that seems to allow no escape" (p. 191), victims of what Heilbrun (1997) calls "torture by recollection" (p. 119). Often, such reminiscence is well hidden from others. It happens silently, broodingly, inside of us, in corners of our memory that defy assimilation, lurking in the shadows, running on a parallel track in the manner that Langer has described. It is a blend of reminiscence and rumination for which Casey (1987) reserves the term "ruminescence" (p. 46). As for reading our lives, it represents the over-reading of certain passages in our story and the under-reading, if not misreading, of the rest. Concerning identity, it is linked with narrative foreclosure, and even, one might argue, with narrative regression. "That's my story," the reminiscer is insisting, "and I'm sticking to it."

Escapist reminiscence is similar to its obsessive cousin, but as essentially "nostalgic reminiscence" (Chandler & Ray, 2002), it entails returning to a place and time that seems "better than the present" (p. 77). Whether they are former footballers, old soldiers, or anyone in fact, escapist reminiscers, says Wong (1995), use statements that "glorify the past and deprecate the present" (p. 26). Operating out of epilogue time, they don the role of old-timer, pining after the way (they think) things used to be: "Oh, for the good old days...." Living in the past, they engage in "boasting exaggeratedly about past achievements" (p. 26), or about how great things were in days gone by, possibly to buffer themselves against the pain or bleakness of the present. Alternatively, it can also be a matter of boasting about how *bad* things were, as in the *Monty Python* skit (Chapman, Cleese, et al., 1982) where everyone tries to outdo each other with how hard life was when they were growing up. As a form of self-reading, then, escapist reminiscence is not especially advanced. Like obsessive reminiscence, it is a combination of over-reading certain passages from the past yet under-reading the rest. Indeed, there is nothing *but* the past: the life is not over, but the story might as well be.

Transmissive reminiscence includes aspects of narrative and even escapist reminiscence, but its principal purpose is "instructing or entertaining the listener" (Wong, 1995, p. 25). A phrase like "when I was your age, we used to..." catches its essence. Transmissive reminiscence is teaching reminiscence, meaning that in certain respects it is linked to generativity: passing our knowledge, our experience, our learning on to others. In terms of reading our lives, however, it is more likely to be efferent than aesthetic. What is more, it could ultimately amount to an under-reading of one's life-text overall, insofar as it focuses primarily on the parts from which one feels other people could learn. Accordingly, though important for posterity, it does not necessarily foster narrative development for the reminiscer. Instead, it could be associated with narrative foreclosure—unless it overlaps with instrumental reminiscence.

Instrumental reminiscence, which is characterized by a comment like "At the time it was hard, but I've learned from it that…," is one of two types which Wong calls "adaptive" (p. 25). It involves "drawing from past experience to solve present problems" (p. 25). It is the type of reminiscence, therefore, that the mindful educator, aware that past experience can be both "a base for new learning and…an unavoidable potential obstacle" (MacKeracher, 1996, p. 36), is wise to facilitate, to assist the learner in grasping new ideas. Through close reading of situations in our past that are reminiscent of issues before us in the present—"critical incidents," as educators call them— we make a connection and say, "Ahh, I handled that situation in that way then, so I can try handling this situation in this way now." If transmissive reminiscence is teaching-reminiscence, then instrumental reminiscence is learning-reminiscence. Like transmissive reminiscence, it, too, is related to generativity—and also, perhaps, to "successful aging"—to the degree that it enhances our sense of competence. In this respect, it serves not just to buttress our sense of identity but to expand it as well, and so contributes to our continuing development.

The second adaptive type is integrative reminiscence. While not everyone may care to engage in it, nor be able to, it is clearly linked to life review, a topic we will come back to in Chapter 9. Wong reminds us, though, that life review is an "active, ongoing process" (p. 30) more than it is a "structured process" of self-evaluation using preset themes (Burnside, 1996, p. 253). Though structured forms of life review clearly have their place, integrative reminiscence, too, is an ongoing process, with the emphasis on integration more than integrity as such. Indeed, it involves a number of activities that, from our discussion in Chapter 5, are conducive to a good lifestory, among them, believing that one's past is "significant and worthwhile"; being able to accept and integrate "negative past experiences"; identifying experiences that have helped develop "personal values and meaning"; and being able to create "coherence" between present and past (Wong, 1995, p. 24–25).

Of all of these types, then, integrative reminiscence comes closest to an aesthetic reading of *the story of my life*. In a sense, it endeavors to avoid under-reading and over-reading alike. It is intent on minding the gaps in our story, and on dealing with the backlog of life-events that beg more time from us to ponder them. As such, it is most likely to further our narrative development. It involves absorbing the stuff of our lives into the story of our lives, reassessing segments of our past that have not yet been sufficiently assimilated. At the same time, it positions us to accept our "one and only life cycle as something that had to be and that, by necessity, permitted of no substitutions"—which, for Erikson at least (1963, p. 268), is a cornerstone of wisdom. Perhaps the spirit of such reminiscence is expressed best in the words of Florida Scott-Maxwell (1968), with which we prefaced Chapter 1: "When you truly possess all that you have been and done, which may take some time," she says, "you are fierce with reality. When at last age has assembled you together, will it not be easy to let it all go, lived, balanced, over?"(p. 42).

The Dynamics of Dynamic Reminiscence

The reality, of course, is in that in any single session of reminiscence most of us will probably shuttle among a number of types at once. Yet often without realizing what we are doing, not a few of us will occasionally engage in a further type of reminiscence that holds immense therapoetic potential. Rather like an apple among the oranges, it is *dynamic* reminiscence. Drawing on their work with life-writing groups of older women and men, literary scholars Sally Chandler and Ruth Ray (2002) make a point of distinguishing it from "fixed" reminiscence (p. 77). Fixed reminiscence, which can characterize any of the less adaptive types that Wong has laid out, including transmissive reminiscence, is essentially what we engage in when reciting set pieces, those well-rehearsed stories that most of us have caught ourselves recounting on numberless occasions—"the one about the time I ... got kicked by the cow, was chased by a grizzly, or mistook my wife for an old flame." We mean the sort of "frozen anecdote," as Heilbrun (1997) describes it, that is "no longer vital and, because forever encased in the amber of repetition, unable to offer to us as we recall or recount it any new rewards" (p. 115). Set pieces are, in effect, neat narrative nuggets that elicit predictable responses from our audience, and in a sense, answer their own questions. Not only do they tend to be recounted in the same basic manner every time, but they often contain a "moral or homily" that supports the values shared by the group as a whole (Chandler & Ray, 2002, p. 77).

Dynamic reminiscence is a different story. It is "more change-oriented" (p. 77)—change facilitated through the creation of a climate within the group whereby members can mull over their memories with a measure of safety and support. Naturally, some will tell and retell stories that change little with each retelling. From the outset, though, others tell more "reflective stories"—stories that, through the telling and the retelling, gradually expand in both breadth and depth. As a consequence, later tellings are "more detailed and troubling" than earlier ones (p. 85); they are less and less naïve. Reflective stories are those we have in relation to episodes that, even if years have elapsed since their original occurrence, continue to be emotionally charged. They are so fraught with issues and implications that require sorting out, and have so much backstory behind them, that we hardly know where to begin when recounting them. It is important, says Sherman though, to "work through" such "troublesome" memories, as he calls them—not just to resign ourselves to them, but to reinterpret them, so that we can "repair old wounds" and develop a "more viable current conception of self" (1991, p. 7).

To illustrate how reflective stories work, Chandler and Ray (2002) describe the approach to reminiscence taken by one participant as "speculative," since it is articulated in bits and pieces that appear to gain coherence only through "interactive group response" (p. 90)—through telling-with, that is, as opposed to telling-to. As the members of the group ask questions, ponder possible interpretations, and interject their own "parallel stories," the participant is prompted to re-version the piece as a whole (p. 92). Given how stories breed stories anyway, not to mention the complexity of memory in a social sense, group dynamics themselves, then, can transform a story that has been told hitherto in the same basic manner. The same old story is always "potentially reflective" (p. 92), which suggests that fixed reminiscence is dynamic reminiscence simply waiting to happen, provided the right environment. Yet the impact of environment, note Chandler and Ray, has thus far been "underexamined" in research on reminiscence (p. 89).

Here again, gender plays a role. While both men and women in Chandler and Ray's groups exhibited fixed and dynamic reminiscence, the men generally tended to talk more (p. 92). Consequently, their stories received more attention from the others in the group, led therefore to more self-reflection, and resulted in more instances of dynamic reminiscence. Once more, though, we encounter an under-examined area: how the different "conversational styles" of men and women affect not just the "content and purpose of reminiscence" (p. 93) in which they each engage, but their respective levels of personal development as well (see also Tannen, 1990). Despite the tendency of men to take up more air-time, however, Chandler and Ray conclude that the differences between genders "enhance emotional development" in reminiscence groups rather than curtail it (p. 93).

Dynamic reminiscence may be looked upon as meaning-making in the moment, the "storying moment" (Randall & Kenyon, 2001, p. 95), and not just in the therapeutic moment either. Although at the heart of any therapy that seeks to be restorying, it can occur in an ordinary moment, too. In every interpersonal encounter in which memory is lured to the fore, dynamic reminiscence is a real possibility. This is especially the case to the degree that each audience to whom we tell some part of our past inevitably evokes different remembered and remembering selves, resulting in our emphasizing some aspects of the incident in question while downplaying—or even omitting—others. Indeed, such differences characterize our self-telling every day of our lives. Yet we seldom pay attention to them. As we do, however, we pry the activity of the telling from the content of the told. Philosopher Jonathan Glover (1988) captures the potential for self-discovery, and for growth, that is actually inherent therefore in conversation of any kind: "When we talk together," he says, "I learn from your way of seeing things, which will often be different from mine. And, when I tell you about my way of seeing things, I am not just describing responses that are already complete." Indeed, "they may only emerge clearly as I try to express them, and as I compare them with yours. In this way, we can share in the telling of each other's inner story, and so share in creating ourselves and each other" (p. 153).

Dynamic reminiscence can be prompted by nonverbal means as well, of course, including memorabilia or *reminiscentia,* as mentioned last chapter (see also Habermas & Paha, 2002), plus other modes of artistic expression like drawings or paintings or poems. In fact, a medley of such approaches is central to a form of dynamic reminiscence developed specifically for use with older adults who are depressive. Called "creative reminiscence" (Bohl-meijer et al., 2005, p. 302), its goal is to encourage such individuals "to create and discover metaphors, images, and stories that symbolically represent the subjective and inner meaning of their lives"—for instance, my life as a battle, a pilgrimage, a roller-coaster ride. In the "multi-form" life-writing group designed by Tom Cole and Kate de Medeiros (2001), participants experience something similar when exploring poignant personal events by means of an assortment of genres: a first-person memoir, a letter to someone else (per-haps a deceased parent), a short story, a poem. In the manual accompanying the workshop, de Medeiros and Lagay (2000) stress how "using different forms [to explore the same episode] opens up different possibilities for the narrator and allows different types of stories to be told" (p. 14; see also de Medeiros, 2007). It allows different selves to do the telling. This observation points to another under-examined area, which could easily take a book of its own to properly consider: how specific written forms enable us to read specific experiences to differing degrees of breadth and depth—not to men-tion how writing our lives, in general, differs in this respect from telling our lives to (and with) others, or from thinking about our lives in the privacy of our own minds. In terms of their capacity to promote reflective experience, how do external self-texts (spoken or written) differ from internal self-texts (thought or remembered), and what is the interaction between them? How do the former enable the elaboration of the latter, and how might they freeze them instead?

By whatever means we engage in dynamic reminiscence, it represents simultaneously the stirring up of memory and the breaking down of our tried-and-true habits of interpreting the past. It is a way of both expanding and examining our stories at once, one memory at a time. Each memory that is not just remembered but is actively reflected upon—that we literally "turn over" in our mind—changes our relationship to memory as a whole. Quite simply, our memory comes alive. Dynamic reminiscence is remembering that leads to the discovery of something new inside of us, through a reconfiguration of the relationship between our past and our present, and between specific episodes and *the story of my life* as a whole. And it is the very sort of activity that feeds the process Sartre and Charmé intend when they speak of the meaning of past events being continually under revision in light of present ones (and vice versa)—not unlike how details or incidents in the early chapters of a novel are seen to have grown quietly in significance when alluded to in later ones. They have been "reframed within a larger life context" (Sherman, 1991, p. 7); or as Fingarette explains, "construed within a pattern of meanings which makes more of a unity than the meaning patterns we had formerly used" (1963, p. 36).

As a form of what we referred to in Chapter 1 as "reflective meditation" (Assagioli, 1974, p. 223), dynamic reminiscence is thus what facilitates "the process of meaning-evolution" (Kegan, 1982, p. 274). It is what furthers the growth of the myth by which we understand ourselves, stretching it this way and that way to embrace the complexities and subtleties of our remembered experience, and to articulate the possibilities within it as well. It diminishes the distance between past and present, "raising the possibility that multiple (even contradictory) selves might coexist in memory and experience" (Chandler & Ray, 2002, p. 78). We thus forge a revised relationship not just with time and memory, but with our life and our self. In the words of participants from the Cole–de Medeiros workshop (2001) referred to earlier, we have the sense of "getting under our own skin," of "digging into the past," and of really "dealing with the past." We have the sense, as one source expresses it, of "releasing and recycling the past in the present" (Rainer, 1978, p. 233).

In such respects, dynamic reminiscence enables us to experience what religion scholar Eugene Bianchi (1996, p. 2) calls "the harvesting" or "the

204 GROWING OLD: POETICS APPLIED

mining" of memory. It helps us get at what educator Peter Alheit (1995) calls "the surplus meanings of our biographical knowledge" and "the potentiality of our *unlived lives*" (p. 65). To the extent that such reminiscence represents a "more active and creative reconstructing of the past" (Sherman, 1991, p. 228), and indeed the "creation of new meanings" (p. 26), then through it, says Sherman, we become "someone who is a little different from the one we took for granted in the past" (p. 231). "After self-examination," echoes Gusdorf (1980), "a man is no longer the man he was before" (p. 47).

Dynamic reminiscence is thus the mode that Sherman (1991) seems to have in mind when he argues that reminiscence is the "key ingredient in the 'examined life'" (p. 5). For Chandler and Ray (2002), who maintain that it is precisely what is needed if people are to undergo growth in later life, dynamic reminiscence is a telling and a retelling of one's story that, at the same time, is a reading and a rereading—a second reading, a third reading, and so forth. In effect, expanding and examining, telling and reading converge, which means that of any of the types of reminiscence it runs closest to aesthetic self-reading. It is literary self-literacy in action. Amid it, we instinctively experience our life as an open text, and therefore avoid overreading. It is reading in which we are conscious not just of *what* we are reading but of what we are *not* reading—also, of *how* we are reading, and how we might read differently instead. It is, so to speak, reading ourselves reading. And it is reading that can most appreciate the literariness of our lives, the open-ended eventness of remembered events, the structural and interpretive openness of our past. It opens the way to deeper stories within us, to backstories and larger stories behind the ones we have retained (and even to the links between our memories and our dreams), thus giving us a glimpse into more profound, more comprehensive modes of interpreting our lives. Accordingly, it most promotes our narrative development, for it is carried out at the cutting edge of our emerging identity.

In this respect, dynamic reminiscence is not about summing up or tallying up our lives, which certain approaches to life review can seem to assume, so much as it is about opening up—opening what Kegan (1982) calls "portals to growth-work" (p. 276). It is not about evaluation and integration so much as examination and interrogation. It is not about finding answers so much as creating a context around a given memory (and by implication, every memory) in which we can re-experience some of its initial indeterminacy, an experience that Morson (1994) calls "sideshadowing" (p. 5)—a context in which we can ask different questions of it than we do in just expanding it; in which we can question it, period. Dynamic reminiscence is concerned less with what happened, therefore, than with what the "what happened" means, and with the fact that we remembered it at all. It is concerned less with the who, what, where, or when of the remembered experience than with the how and the why. In a sense, then, it is not merely different from integrative reminiscence but, in many ways, its opposite. By opening up the past and examining both the content and the meaning of our memories, we are engaging less in integration than in dis-integration. Indeed, we are working our way toward a different understanding of integrity altogether—not in terms of neatness and completeness, one might say, but of "openness and boundlessness" (Freeman & Brockmeier, 2001, p. 94).

In *Beyond Nostalgia,* which provides a more extended sense of what such reminiscence is and does, Ray (2000) observes that "life-story telling carries an infinite potential for transformation and growth"—or at least (barring the onset of dementia)—"for as long as we can remember" (p. 128). The book outlines the life-writing work engaged in by a group of older women which Ray facilitated, and the sharing that took place around what each member of it wrote. For Ray, "writing and sharing life stories in groups is valuable from a developmental perspective because it makes public our interpretive strategies, and seeing and hearing others' life stories broadens the scope of interpretive possibility for our own lives" (p. 128). Again, the dynamics of the group itself are vital to encouraging dynamic reminiscence: so much so, that in the words of a participant in the Cole–de Medeiros (2001) workshop, "the sharing is bigger than the writing." As for Ray, she connects her reflections to wisdom, our focus in Chapter 9. "'Wise' people," she says, "watch themselves tell life stories, learn from others' stories, and intervene in their own narrative processes to allow for change by admitting new stories and interpretations into their repertoire" (p. 29). To anticipate our discussion of wisdom later on and to recall what we said in Chapter 6, we could say that wise people are attentive, therefore, to their own narrative development.

Dynamic Reminiscence in Action

"Memory and imagination," observes Bruner (2002), "supply and consume each other's wares," and effectively "fuse in the process" (p. 93). In a provocative essay, memoirist Patricia Hampl (1999) illustrates precisely this insight with an excellent example of dynamic reminiscence that she herself experienced. Although the experience took place, not within a group, but within her own mind, aided by pad and pen, it captures the quality of dwelling with the texts of memory that we associate here with reading our lives. Worth noting, though, is the fact that the memory Hampl works with is memorable only for its innocence, its innocuousness. It is anything but dramatic, at least no more so than most of the material that any of us have gathered from the early years of life. Indeed, it is not so much a story, she admits, as "the beginning of what could perhaps become a story" (p. 24). What is exciting, however, is that if dynamic reminiscence can be applied in "spot-lighting" (Polster, 1987, p. 128) what is otherwise narrative debris—a snippet of our past that could easily have escaped the editor's eye—then there is no end to the meaning we are capable of unpacking if we applied it to our more self-defining memories as well. Beneath their well-polished surfaces may lurk all manner of unexplored possibilities, and thus of unlived life. Viewing them through memoirist's eyes, we can see them as brimming with interpretive potential.

"When I was seven," Hampl (1999) begins, and then proceeds to describe her first piano lesson. In a matter of three pages, she fleshes out the details that supposedly surrounded the original event. Among them is the fact that it was her father who took her to the lesson and that the venue for it was a church basement, where they were met by a certain Sister Olive (p. 21). One of her peers from grade school was there as well, a little girl named Mary Katherine Reilly, who was "playing something...more sophisticated than my piece" (p. 23), she says. In addition to Hampl's recollection of being "given a red book, the first Thompson book," is an image of Sister Olive taking a sneezing fit, which somehow coincided with the woman's pulling down the window shades. When the fit was over, Sister Olive offered what felt to little Hampl like an explanation: "The sun makes me sneeze" (p. 23). And in what could be deemed the center of the memory, Hampl says, "I remember thinking, Middle C is the belly button of the piano, an insight," she continues, "whose originality and accuracy stunned me with pride. For the first time in my life I was astonished by metaphor" (p. 22).

Figuring that there must be an explanation for retaining such a vivid memory of this odd little incident, Hampl sets out to analyse what she has just finished laying out, treating it, essentially, as a literary text. With a mixture of curiosity, playfulness, and wonder, she critiques the memory carefully, sorting it out into its constituent components. In effect, she cross-examines it—in the process, discrediting it as an accurate recollection of a bona fide event that actually occurred. Her reflection on the process yields an impressive range of insights into memory's many sins—among them, transience for certain, but also suggestibility, misattribution, and bias. It also exemplifies how the act of writing, in itself, can lure us into the thicket of the past more deeply, and more meaningfully perhaps, than does mere telling.

Among Hampl's realizations are that, frankly, "I had told a number of lies," not the least of which concerns Sister Olive, of whom, in fact, she had no real memory whatsoever. Rather, "She's a sneeze in the sun and a finger touching middle C" (p. 26). Also, although her father *may* have taken her to the lesson, she is ultimately unsure (p. 25). "Worse," she says, "I didn't have the Thompson book as my piano text" (p. 26), since she can distinctly recall coveting the books that other children had. As for Mary Katherine Reilly, they could not yet have even met, she realizes, for it was only "in high school" that they first became acquainted (p. 26).

Such revelations compel Hampl to critique the concept of memory itself. Memory, she concludes, is "not a warehouse of finished stories, not a gallery of framed pictures" (p. 26). Instead, in our zeal to fill in the gaps and to fashion a tellable tale, we—quite simply—invent things (p. 27). Memory, she says, in words that echo Bruner's (2002), "impulsively reaches out and embraces imagination" (Hampl, 1999, p. 31). Thus, a dreamlike quality inevitably results. Yet to Hampl this is far from the problem it might seem. It is an invitation to rethink what memory really is. If we are naïve enough to think of memory as something that is "logged like a documentary" inside of us, then we fail to appreciate both its "beauty" and its "function" (p. 33). That function, she states, is "to transform experience into meaning" (p. 32). And it is through memoir, she believes, that this function is made explicit.

Despite stereotypes of memoir as snooty bragging about one's achievements in the public realm, memoir can be the road to genuine self-discovery and self-creation. As "the intersection of narration and reflection, of storytelling and essay writing," it is able, says Hampl, to "present its story *and* consider the meaning of the story" (p. 33). In other words, the meaning of the story is not something that is predetermined and then merely tacked onto the story by the writer; rather, it is "revealed" (p. 31). In the course of the writing itself, notes fellow memoirist Sharon Butala, truth starts to "percolate through the psyche" (2005, p. 48). For such reasons, Hampl (1999) speaks of what she has written as merely a first draft (p. 28), as possessing a potential for meaning that only time can fully unfold. "The piece hasn't yet found its subject," she observes; "it isn't yet about what it wants to be about" (p. 29). This leads to what is perhaps her most important point: "If we learn not only to tell our stories," she says, "but to listen to what our stories tell us...we are doing the work of memory" (p. 33). To do "the work of memory" is, in our view, to read our lives. Once the first draft is committed to paper, she says, "I can read this little piece as a mystery which drops clues to the riddle of my feelings, like a culprit who wishes to be apprehended." The culprit is the "narrative self," as she calls it, who "wishes to be discovered by my reflective self": in other words, "the self who wants to...make sense of a half-remembered moment about a nun sneezing in the sun" (p. 29).

Another example that highlights the re-creative possibilities inherent in dynamic reminiscence comes from research that Sherman (1991) and his colleagues conducted with a group of older adults in an attempt to improve their "social supports and...morale" (pp. 2–3). As for morale, and as we ourselves have found with an exercise as simple as the ABCs, such reminiscence generated considerable energy, both in the group at large and in the individuals who made it up. As for the introspective process to which many of the participants attested, Sherman describes it as a shifting between present and past, with each giving meaning to the other and both providing meaning for the future. "This iterative process can be an ongoing one," he says, "like a perpetual hermeneutic circle of interpretation of a life" (p. 205). In view of our interest in the poetics of aging, and of Sartre's insights into the workings of our fundamental project, what is exciting about Sherman's findings is how "this fine-tuning," as he puts it, can be "a thoroughly satisfying and aesthetic experience," when past, present, and future, imagination and reality all "fit harmoniously into the larger tapestry of a person's life." Accordingly, "meaning is both created and experienced with a consummate kind of artistry" (p. 205). One participant in particular articulates the element of discovery that Hampl, too, experienced. "I can...go back and forth from then to now," the woman says, "and I always seem to come up with something new...something a little different from a new angle. Things seem to fit together a little different," she goes on, "and it always gives me satisfaction...even if I think about bad memories, because now they fit. I see where they fit...but they didn't before. It's like...they *had* to be that way...for the whole thing to make sense. Does that make sense? Or does it sound crazy?" (pp. 205–206).

INQUIRING WITHIN

The idea of the pieces of the past, present, and future fitting "harmoniously" together may be overstated, and possibly misleading, unless we allow for the fact that today's synthesis is likely to be undermined by further fine-tuning tomorrow. Compared to instrumental or integrative reminiscence, in other words, dynamic reminiscence is not about tying up the loose ends of one's life into a complete and tidy package. As a "perpetual hermeneutic circle" (Sherman, 1991, p. 205), it is far more about untying instead, about stirring things up. It is about undoing the abbreviated versions of particular occurrences that memory, of necessity, composes. It is about problematizing the remembered past, defamiliarizing the texts by which we have hitherto made sense of it, and coming up with something new, including a new appreciation for the complexity of our self as such. It is about reopening the closed time into which memory necessarily compresses the past, both recent and remote, and restoring some semblance of the field of possibility that encompassed the original event in all of its eventness, as it was still "unfolding." To that extent, it "recreates the fullness of time as it was," to use Morson's language (1994, p. 120). Given the "more accurate picture of the past" that thus results, he says, "the significance of present configurations might look quite different" (p. 119). In short, dynamic reminiscence "subjunctivize[s]" memory (Bruner, 1986, p. 26), subjecting it to "counterfactual" speculation (see Ferguson, 1997): "What might have been? What might yet be?"

Just as there are many means of entering memory in the first place, so are there many ways of exploring our surroundings once we find ourselves in the thick of things. As a counterpart to the stop-look-listen strategy for expanding our stories that we proposed in Chapter 7, various clusters of questions (which ask "why" and "how" more than "who" and "what") can be asked when examining them as well, whether at the level of life-time periods, specific pieces, or even just narrative debris. The examples from Hampl and Sherman, as from Chandler and Ray, provide us with a glimpse of how many different directions the lines of questioning could lead. But before listing just a few of the countless possibilities, a word is in order about questions in general.

As in science or philosophy, so in life: the quest for meaning proceeds by means of questions. In narrative therapy, for instance, where therapists respect clients as the authors of their own lifestories, asking questions is the core of restorying: which is to say, of "deconstructing problematic stories, identifying preferred directions, and developing alternative stories that support these preferred directions" (Freedman & Combs, 1996, p. 118)—in short, "generating a possible version of a life" (Epston, cited in Freedman & Combs, 1996, p. 113). Every time we ask a question of our own stories as well, the same thing happens. Each question affords us some distance (ideally, affectionate) from our past as presently remembered. Memory by memory, story by story, question by question, alternative versions of our lives begin coming into focus, and with them, the fullness of our lives begins to be experienced.

Emplotment

What sort of plot-line runs through the story? What genre is it: adventure story, sob story, tragedy, comedy? What seems to be its main message or point? Its principal themes? In selecting and summarizing the event at its center, how might I have veered from what actually happened? How has historical truth been overtaken by, been smoothed by, narrative truth? Which details do I emphasize when telling it, and which are clearly missing?

Characterization

How do I portray others in the midst of this story? How do I portray myself? What sort of role do I play: the hero, the fool, the observer, the victim? What sort of "me" was "I" when this event was initially committed to memory, and how is it different from who I feel I am at present? What was the story of my life that, deep down, I believed that I was living at the time? What future did I imagine for myself? And how does this memory fit with the story I see myself living now? What assumptions about life in general, and about my life in particular, does it imply, and in which of my allegiances or formative environments are those assumptions rooted?

Narration

How do I feel whenever I tell this story, and what sorts of feelings might it evoke in those who hear it? Do I tell it in different ways with different listeners? If so, what might such differences say about the motives that it serves me in my relationships with others? Insofar as I can conceive of what "my life" was like back then, what else and who else were part of it? What relationships and commitments did I have at the time, and how did they shape my life? How much background do I need to provide to my listeners to set this story up? Have I always told this story in the same basic manner, or has my approach to telling it changed across the years? Do I tell it less frequently than I did a decade ago? And if so, why? What side of myself has the telling of it served me in the past, and how has this side changed?

Interpretation

How would I feel if I learned that this story was not true? And what is behind it? What backstory lurks between its lines? At bottom, what is this story about? What is its significance for my life? To what issues or themes, what conflicts, what unfinished business, does it point in my guiding personal myth? What can I learn from it about how I experience myself and my world? How might my concept of my self at present differ if this story were not in my repertoire, if it had never been "storied" to begin with? Why, after all these years, am I still clinging to this story? Why, of all the other things that must have been happening in my life at the time, is this what I ended up retaining? In the past, how in general have I tended to read it? And as I see how strange a story it is in many ways, what alternative readings of it might be possible for me now?

LIFESTORIES AS MEANING-FULL

Memory is an open text. To any portion of our remembered past, there is no end to the questions we can pose. As with works of literature that we experience as "great," there is no end to the meanings that our memories, as quasi-literary texts, are capable of yielding. Meaning-wise, they are un-fixed, indeterminate, amenable to multiple interpretations, which means we can always create meaning more profoundly. But indeterminacy of meaning does not mean lack of meaning. It does not mean meaninglessness. If any-thing, the opposite is true. "Inquire within" and we find that "within" con-sists of worlds within worlds, stories within stories. To borrow from Polster (1987), who as we will recall insists on the parallels between what novelists do and what therapists do, we "will never run out of material" as we "seek to turn old meanings around or add new meanings that have been over-looked" (p. 113). This is what dynamic reminiscence accomplishes. This is its therapoetic effect. It opens memory up. It breaks down the clumps into which time has congealed it and stirs up possibilities that eluded us before. Anecdote by anecdote, draft by draft, it effects a "loosening of the hold of the old story" (Monk, 1997, p. 13) that may have overruled our lives. It gets our stories going again, so that we can resume the journey of narrative develop-ment. It sows the seeds of transformation to a renewed relationship—with ourselves and with our world.

Seeing our memories themselves as sources of meaning enhances both the breadth and the depth of our meaning-in-life. What is more, which-ever sources we normally draw upon, it is inside of us, and in terms of us, that those sources are ultimately understood. They are woven into our iden-tity. In turn, our identity is inseparable from our fundamental project: *the story of my life.* Experienced as multilevelled, ever-thickening texts, our lives are therefore meaning-filled. It is time now to extend these insights to the time-honored topic of wisdom.

Nine

TRANSFORMING OUR STORIES:

THE UNFOLDING OF WISDOM

*Is this not our destiny as human beings, to learn, to grow, to come
to know ourselves and the meanings of our life in the deepest, most
textured way possible? If we do not know the self, what can we
know?*
   —Michael Brady (1990, p. 51)

*We make our lives bigger or smaller, more expansive or more
limited, according to the interpretation of life that is our story.*
   —Christina Baldwin (2005, p. ix)

*It's very simple. As you grow, you learn more....Aging is not just
decay, you know. It's growth.*
   —Morrie Schwarz (Albom, 1997, p. 118)

COMING OF AGE: FROM MEMORY TO
MEANING TO WISDOM

We have been seeing just how tightly memory and meaning are linked.
Not only do we remember what is meaningful for us, but memory, in general, is one of our primary sources of meaning-in-life. Wisdom, we believe,
is the extension of this fundamental tie. Whatever else it might be, it is

meaning-making in an intensive, in-depth manner. It is meaning-plus. And reading our lives, which aging itself invites us to do more fully, is what connects the three.

By way of review, to read our lives is to make sense of our lives in two main ways. It is to assess events provisionally at the time that they occur, interpreting what our inner natterers are noticing in the present in terms of some version of our past and future alike. But it is to make sense retrospectively, as well: after the fact, when events are available only through memory and thus in abbreviated, partially interpreted form. Either way, to one degree or other, we are reading our lives all of the time. A valuable analogy for this twofold process is the experience we have when lost in a novel, both while we are reading it and afterward, as—or if—we reflect on what we have read. As with literature, that is, so with life: there is reading and there is *reading*.

In efferent reading, we read what can be read off the top of the text. We read for information, for escape, for the plot, for who did what to whom. Aesthetic reading goes deeper. Though by no means oblivious of the contents of the story or the features of the text, it does not stop there. Aesthetic reading seeks a sense of the story as a whole, in all its complexities and depths. Drawing on the range of our interpretive talents, it seeks what lurks between the lines. What is more, aesthetic reading is self-conscious reading. Readers are attuned to their changing thoughts and feelings, even as the story unfolds. For the efferent reader, then, the story is essentially closed. For the aesthetic reader, it is open, and its meanings are continually developing.

Concerning the stories we are, efferent self-reading is happening all the time. As our inner editor knows full well, it is essential to survival. And yet at some point, all of us engage in aesthetic reading, too. Even the dimmest among us, even those of us whose development seems the most arrested, the most foreclosed, have moments when we dwell with memory more profoundly or probingly than usual—moments of intensified awareness, moments when the who-what-where-and-when of our lives take a back seat to the wherefores and the whys. In such moments, moments that we taste, for instance, amid experiences of dynamic reminiscence, we catch a glimpse of our story as something evolving and unfolding deep beneath the flux of daily life. We catch a vision, however fleeting, of an open field of meaning-potential that is unique to our texistence. And cultivating such self-reading—supplying "the commentary" as Schopenhauer says (2004, p. 94)—is vital to our growth. It is our principal task in the second half of life. It is virtually a moral imperative. Otherwise, we may squander the treasure that time has been silently amassing inside us, wasting the cache of wisdom that is peculiar to us alone.

Happily, recent decades have witnessed a renaissance of wisdom as a focus of scholarly inquiry (see Sternberg, 1990; Goldberg, 2005). Wisdom has come—again—of age. Given the ancient understanding of wisdom as the knowledge of how little we know, the timing of this development is no accident. Insofar as modernism, as epitomized by science, has been about knowledge, prediction, and ultimately, control, and has framed aging in general in terms of a narrative of decline, then despite centuries of revering wisdom as the pinnacle of human development and the automatic concomitant of age, it has become something of an embarrassment: a nostalgic holdover from pre-industrial times. In a postmodern era, however, we have become more open to the fallibility of our knowledge and to the limits, if not failures, of our efforts to rein the world in—technologically, ecologically, militarily. Wisdom, too, resists reining-in. It is not tidy or neat, nor can it be rolled off an assembly line, shiny and new. It is not arrived at by following some formula for "mental fitness" (Cusack & Thompson, 2003) or a recipe for aging "smart" (Rosensweig & Liu, 2006)—as valuable as such programs no doubt are. Wisdom is more than smartness. And it takes time—indeed, a *life* time—to emerge from the compost of memory and experience.

The turn toward narrative that has affected several fields permits an appreciation for dimensions of wisdom, however, that are otherwise overlooked, for want of a suitable conceptual framework. The framework being elaborated here, we believe, helps address that lack, revealing wisdom to be a possibility accessible to us all. In factoring the narrative variable into the discussion of it, we see that wisdom, too, has its storied dimensions. For, ultimately, it is not things—objects, behaviors, ideas—that we deem to be wise. It is people: the people who create those objects, exhibit those behaviors, advance those ideas. And people, as inveterately meaning-making beings, experience their lives in terms of stories: stories of which they are (co)author, narrator, character, and reader at once, and stories they are forever composing within a complex web of environments and relationships. But wisdom not only has a narrative dimension; it *is* a narrative *process*. It is not an achievement, a once-and-for-all virtue, but a steady unfolding, a journey—a "quest" that is "never completed" (Ardelt, 1997, p. 16).

Our agenda in this chapter, then, is to approach wisdom from a narrative perspective, and to see our stories themselves as its primary source. First, though, we need to position our approach in relation to dimensions of wisdom that others have already noted—in particular, wisdom as self-knowledge. But since such knowledge is, inevitably, narrative knowledge, this means revisiting the concepts of life review and a good lifestory. Finally, after looking at wisdom as transformation, and after considering the ironic stance as, in fact, one of its hallmarks, we conclude with some reflections on the types of interpretive environments in which, potentially, it can thrive.

WISDOM ON WISDOM: INSIGHTS AND ISSUES

To do justice to this most venerable of concepts would mean making our way from antiquity to the present, culminating in the emergence of gerontology as a field in which, ideally, it is a topic of great interest. It would mean noting what scholars down through the ages have pronounced on the subject, the broad differences between Eastern understandings of it and Western ones, and how folk notions about it will obviously vary from culture to culture and era to era (see Robinson, 1990; Labouvie-Vief, 1990). What is more, to tackle the task properly would mean crisscrossing the largely uncharted border where philosophy meets both theology and psychology, and where education meets both ethics and the arts. Included in the list would be literature as well, of course, insofar as "the experience of literature," in Birkerts's words (1994, p. 6), "offers a kind of wisdom that cannot be discovered elsewhere." Overall, such a task is simply too grand to be undertaken here, nor need it be. But even in confining ourselves to the social sciences, research into this "complex and illusive construct" (Coleman & O'Hanlon, 2004, p. 56) confirms that "there are many difficulties inherent in defining, measuring, and capturing" it (p. 56). Similar to memory and reminiscence, there are inevitably different types of wisdom as well; moreover, those we highlight will hinge on the framework that we use.

A sociologist, for instance, might approach the study of wisdom with a focus on interpersonal behavior, on how responsibly one acts in one's involvements with others, or on how different societies assume different understandings of it in the first place—or different genders for that matter, or age-groups. Comportment deemed wise among men, for example, might be dismissed by most women as patriarchal posturing. What is wise in the eyes of a teenager might look silly to a centenarian—and vice versa. What a North American entrepreneur hails as wise counsel, a Tibetan monk might well find utterly inane.

For their part, educators are apt to emphasize the relationship between wisdom and learning, as well as wisdom and knowledge, or even intelligence, in which case certain questions immediately arise: How much education does one require in order to be wise, and how much knowledge, not to mention education of what type (formal or informal) and knowledge of what kind (book knowledge, street knowledge)? At what point does an increase in knowledge eventuate in wisdom, or conversely, in wisdom's being lost? And as for intelligence, how intelligent must one be to qualify as wise, and intelligence of what variety: crystallized or fluid, mathematical or linguistic, emotional or narrative?

The aspects of wisdom a psychologist sees as most salient will be linked to the branch of psychology with which he or she most identifies. Developmentalists may see wisdom—or the equivalent of it within their respective theoretical schemas—as a desirable consequence of development. Yet how that consequence is envisioned will be linked further to how development itself is defined, or on which dimension of it the emphasis is placed: moral development, faith development, intellectual development, and so on. For Erikson, for instance, one of the comparatively few psychologists to single out wisdom for serious consideration, it is the ultimate *potential* in his eighth—and final—stage of psychosocial development, and entails a balance between the twin poles of integrity and despair. From such a perspective, wisdom is achieved only after involvement in a process of life review, in which we attempt "to gather the experiences of a long and eventful life into a meaningful pattern" (Erikson, Erikson, & Kivnick, 1986, p. 288), as well as "to accept the inalterability of the past and the unknowability of the future" (p. 56). At bottom, wisdom is "detached concern with life itself in the face of death itself" (p. 37).

One definition of wisdom that embraces many such aspects at once has been proposed by gero-psychologists James Birren and Laurel Fisher (1990). For Birren and Fisher, wisdom is the "integration of the affective, connative, and cognitive aspects of human abilities in response to life's tasks and problems." It is a "balance between the opposing valences of intense emotion and detachment, action and inaction, and knowledge and doubts." While it "tends to increase with experience and therefore age," it is "not exclusively found in old age" (p. 326). A measure of commentary on this definition may help to tease out features of wisdom (inevitably overlapping) that, to us, a narrative perspective is uniquely equipped to accommodate.

"The integration of the affective...and cognitive..."

Wisdom is not a completed achievement in which the loose ends of one's life are tied neatly together and a solidity of character is clearly acquired. It is a process, for which, like development itself, there is no pre-determined end—a process of "sage-ing," as one source calls it (Schachter-Shalomi & Miller, 1995). Wisdom is less about integrity than about integration. With wisdom, one is always on the way toward integrity, never in firm possession of it. One can always be wiser.

Integration also suggests congruence, but again as an ongoing process, not as an ultimate attainment. It is a matter of seeking (though not always succeeding) to synchronize one's actions with one's attitudes and talents, and to do so across the board. One can scarcely be "wise" at work yet violent at home, "wise" on the tennis court yet insufferable in one's friendships, "wise" in one's profession yet a scoundrel in one's marriage. Congruency implies an ethical consistency among one's various involvements.

The term "affective" suggests that wisdom is neither sterile nor cerebral. It concerns what psychologist Daniel Goleman (1995) calls "the rich sea of emotions that makes our inner life and relationships so complex, so compelling, and often so puzzling" (p. 49). To be wise, one might say, is not just to have greater "emotional stability," as Cohen (2005) puts it, but to be "emotionally intelligent" or "emotionally literate" (p. 28). It is to "have a greater complexity of emotional understanding" (Kimble et al., 1995, p. 7). It is to be attuned to our feelings, aware of our reactions in assorted situations, and open to the full range of our emotional nature. Still, wisdom is not about emotional maturity alone. It is about emotion in congruence with cognition (Fields & Norris, p. 102), about "increasing emotion-cognition integration" (Labouvie-Vief, 2000, p. 366)—or, simply, intuition. For Mihaly Csikszentmihalyi and Kevin Rathunde (1990), therefore, wisdom needs to be understood as a "holistic cognitive process" (1990, p. 30).

As a category, cognition concerns both content and activity, both knowledge and knowing. With respect to knowledge, wisdom involves not merely book knowledge, but knowledge of life in general. And it involves self-knowledge, too. Yet despite the ancient Delphic injunction to "know thyself," reference to this possibility is relatively absent in research on wisdom, except when the focus is on "wise persons" (Orwoll & Perlmutter, 1990), perhaps because such knowledge is both hard to observe and even harder to measure. In any case, to be wise is to be cognizant on a number of levels and in a number of directions at once, more or less congruently. It is to be actively accumulating—and coordinating—knowledge. It is to be open to lifelong learning. It is to possess what one educator calls "the inquiring mind" (Houle, 1963), plus the accompanying qualities of curiosity and wonder. But ultimately, the link between knowledge and wisdom is ambiguous. Wisdom, we could say, is about the quality of the relationship one has with one's knowledge more than the quantity of one's knowledge itself. More knowledge does not mean more wisdom.

With respect to knowing, or wisdom as a "way of knowing" (Csikszentmihalyi & Rathunde, 1990, p. 28), wisdom is "an awareness of the limits of one's own personal knowing" and "the general limits of human knowing" (Kitchener & Brenner, 1990, p. 215). Partly, this is because it involves "interpretive knowledge" more than "descriptive knowledge" (Ardelt, 1997, p. P16). In other words, it involves awareness of the multiple perspectives that can be taken on any one subject, including one's own self. As such, it involves a "deeper comprehension of contradictions," and correspondingly a greater tolerance for paradox and ambiguity—indeed, a greater cognitive complexity all around (Ardelt, 1997). This increased complexity is linked to the emergence in adulthood and later life of what is referred to as *post-formal thought.*

Post-formal thought brings the cognitive and affective domains closer together, and it encompasses the pragmatic domain as well. As Kramer explains, wisdom is at once both "more practical and concrete, and more detached and abstract" (1983, p. 97). In their "evolutionary interpretation" of the psychology of wisdom, Csikszentmihalyi and Rathunde (1990, pp. 30–31) identify some of the features that characterize post-formal thought. These include: the recognition of the "relativity of various formal systems through life experience" (p. 30) and of the "interrelatedness of all experience and the inevitability of change and transformation" (p. 31); the ability "to assume contradictory points of view" (p. 30) and to adopt a more "reflective and integrative approach to thinking" (p. 31); and finally, the capacity to make "choices with commitment to a certain course of action" (p. 31). Cohen (2005) notes many of these same features as integral to his idea of developmental intelligence, something that, as we saw in Chapter 6, he considers as a synonym for wisdom (p. 38). He defines it as "the maturing of cognition, emotional intelligence, judgement, social skills, life experience, and consciousness and their integration and synergy" (p. 35). Such intelligence, towards which, we would argue, changes in the aging brain itself incline us, is characterized by three related kinds of thinking. They are: "relativistic thinking," which means "understanding that knowledge sometimes reflects on our subjective perspective" (p. 36); "dualistic thinking," which is an "ability to uncover and resolve contradictions in opposing and seemingly incompatible views" (p. 37); and "systematic thinking," or "being able…to take a broader view of the entire system of knowledge, ideas, and context that are involved" (p. 37).

"In response to life's tasks and problems…"

The theme of wisdom as awareness of the relativity—and often inconsistency—of formal systems of knowledge in the light of life experience suggests that wisdom does not unfold in an ivory tower but in the real world. For gerontologists Paul Baltes and Jacqui Smith (1990), for example, wisdom is "a highly developed body of factual and procedural knowledge and judgements" having to do with the "fundamental pragmatics of life" (p. 87). Even though losses are expected in the "hardware-like" aspects of intelligence, a comparable loss is by no means inevitable in the more "software-like" aspects (p. 94)—a theme that resonates loudly with what we have heard already. Insofar as, in their view, it entails knowledge of both "the conditions of life and its variations," as well as "about strategies of judgement and advice concerning matters of life" (p. 95), wisdom is thus a central element in (not-so-common) common sense.

But to the extent that "life pragmatics" about life problems implies problem-*solving*, wisdom can be about problem-*finding* as well, about seeing complexities where others see none—a point that links the wisdom process to the creative process. As educator Patricia Arlin (1990) proposes, "wisdom may be more a matter of interrogatives rather than of declaratives," of "questions rather than answers" (p. 230). It is less about answering our questions, so to speak, than about questioning our answers. Given such a view (which, as we say, suits what science itself entails: namely, ongoing inquiry, and which dynamic reminiscence is about as well), wisdom is "recognized not so much by the problem solution but rather by the question or problem that is found" (p. 230). It is "the means by which one discovers, envisages, or goes into deeper questions" (p. 230)—a perception that underscores wisdom as continuing quest and as a balance between knowledge and doubt.

"Balance between...opposing valences..."

Balance, like congruence and integration, is to be understood dynamically, not in static terms. Erikson qualifies his definition of integrity accordingly: "We certainly do not postulate a total victory of Integrity over Despair and Disgust, but simply a dynamic balance in Integrity's favor" (1978, p. 26). Balance, in this sense, means balancing *act*, for the opposing valences in question are living, changing elements in our day-to-day existence. Weighing these opposites in the balance, as it were, involves a continual shuttling back-and-forth, never quite settled: "On one hand," one says, as one strains to make sense of one's world, "but on the other hand...." If balance implies equanimity, then it is equanimity, not in a naïve bubble, but with antennae fully extended amid the complexities and contradictions of our worlds, our relationships, our selves.

"Intense emotion and detachment, action and inaction..."

As we saw with post-formal thought, the challenge with wisdom is to maintain a balance. On one hand, it involves a passionate engagement with the world—at least, the urge to be so engaged. Scott-Maxwell (1968), for example, wants "to put things right," and indeed admits to being "so disturbed by the outer world and by human quality in general" that "I burst out with hot conviction" (pp. 13–14). On the other hand, the matching urge is to pull back from the world, to disengage, not for lack of caring (or even energy) but in order to take a longer view, to ponder and reflect, and this urge feeds the first. To quote Scott-Maxwell again, "now that I have withdrawn from the active world I am more alert to it than ever before" (p. 5). The wise person is not emotionless, therefore, but capable of profound feeling, and, furthermore, is *aware* of this capacity—is emotionally intelligent (Goleman, 1995). Nonetheless, passion is tempered by perspective, by the sense that it has ever been thus. Action is grounded in reflection, and involvement is rooted in both introspection and retrospection, in insight and hindsight alike.

"Knowledge and doubts…"

Wisdom is beyond knowledge. It is neither ignorant nor uninformed, but it is not reducible to knowledge—to book knowledge, say, as distinct from knowledge of the pragmatics of life. It is the continuing realization that knowledge as such is not enough: "Of making many books there is no end," moans the Preacher in Ecclesiastes, acclaimed for his wisdom (12:12, King James Version), "and much study is a weariness of the flesh." Wisdom senses the contingency of all our knowing and the cloud of unknowing that surrounds every certainty we hold, including our certainties about ourselves (Baltes & Smith, 1990, p. 103). As such, it monitors our memories and our motives for evidence (never far removed) of self-deception, of "blindsight." In essence, wisdom always harbors doubts, indeed depends upon them: the backdrop of "yeah, buts" and "so whats" that hangs behind many of our convictions and decisions, not to mention many of our recollections, as Hampl has clearly shown: "Did that really happen, and what does it mean, whether it happened or not?" Wisdom demands such doubt, not in a manner that cripples our will and hobbles responsible action, but that humbles us at every turn. Such humility is essential. The minute we believe ourselves wise, wisdom has slipped our grasp.

As a process, wisdom is a juxtaposition of questions with convictions, and of self-analysis with self-acceptance, including acceptance of one's overall lot: "of one's one and only life cycle as something that had to be," writes Erikson (1963, p. 268), and that "permitted of no substitutions." To accept ourselves, we could also say, is to acknowledge the range of our beliefs and biases, idiosyncrasies and contradictions, virtues and limitations, and the complexities of our nature overall. Yet it is not to be arrogant or dogmatic because of what we know. For it is to know that for all the changes that we have undergone we are not necessarily any better as a person—thicker, yes; more experienced, yes; but not better as such. It is also to know that all our knowledge is incomplete, that—as dynamic reminiscence clearly reveals— there is still much to be learned about ourselves, still discoveries to be made, still experiences to be fathomed more fully.

If wisdom is about learning, then it is about un-learning, too. It is, as McAdams (2001) might say, to be a "searcher" (p. 571). However familiar we may be with our inner terrain, an area of mystery persists. "The older I have become," confesses Jung (1961), "the less I have understood or had insight into or known about myself" (p. 358). Yet we are not troubled by the seeming contradiction: obvious to ourselves yet, at the same time, enig-matic. On the contrary, it keeps us open, curious, wondering, in a state of comparative moratorium: "trying to find a shape or pattern in our lives," writes Malcolm Cowley (1980, pp. 70–71); "even if they are hard to discern." Where self-knowledge is concerned, therefore, wisdom is characterized less by knowing than by meta-knowing, by knowledge of our knowledge (or lack thereof), by "awareness of awareness" (Olney, 1980, p. 45). The result, as we shall consider a little later, is the ironic stance and, with it, ideally, a healthy sense of humor.

"Tends to increase with experience and therefore age…"

On one level, it seems self-evident that wisdom increases with age. It is diffi-cult to imagine a three-year-old as "wise." Clever, cagey, quick—but wise? On another level, the claim that wisdom increases with experience brings up the question of what "experience" means. When we say "experience is the best teacher," what we mean is certainly more than the mere passage of time. It is linked somehow to knowledge: in particular, "rich procedural knowledge" of life problems (Baltes & Smith, 1990, pp. 100–101). What we take "experience" to mean here is the combination of accumulated memories—of the ups and downs we have endured and the more self-defining of our life-events—and the interpretations and reinterpretations which we have given them. It is the steady piling up of all the little insights that we have quietly acquired throughout the years. To speak of experience, therefore, is to speak of the compost heap—the mulch with which wisdom is nourished—and surely this does increase with age.

But the transformation from raw material to examined material, and hence to meaning-plus, is just as surely not a certainty. Some people experi-ence it; some people don't. To the degree it entails a sifting and sorting, a breaking down and a letting be of the layers that lie inside us, it invariably takes time. If anything, however, time is exactly what later life affords us. "Age," observes Scott-Maxwell (1968), "is a desert of time—hours, days, weeks, years perhaps—with little to do." One has "ample time," she says, "to face everything one has had, been, done; gather them all in: the things that came from outside, and those from inside. We have time at last to make them truly ours" (p. 41).

"Not exactly found in old age..."

On the other hand, wisdom does not come automatically with the advance of years. For one thing, wisdom can be lost. Wisdom-as-process can be aborted. "Many people simply do not complete the life cycle," states psychologist Vivian Clayton (1975, p. 123). "They die uncommitted, unresolved and frustrated, never having arrived at the stage where they could fully integrate and utilize their accumulated years of experience and knowledge" (p. 123). We have touched on this possibility already in our reflections on narrative foreclosure, and also on the unclear link between wisdom and knowledge, certainly knowledge that is divorced from understanding, knowledge un-accompanied by awareness of its fallibility. Wisdom, as psychologist John Meacham (1990) argues, consists not in the content or nature of the knowledge one has accumulated, but in how one uses it (p. 187). As we say, it lies not in the quantity of our knowledge but in the quality of our relationship to what we have.

Contrary to the stereotype that wisdom comes inevitably with age, Meacham goes as far as to say that life experience can actually thwart wisdom, above all if it "leads merely to the accumulation of information, to success, and to power" (p. 209). Thus, the wisdom that, in his opinion, all of us possess as children often dissipates with age (p. 198). By way of example, in several of his poems Wordsworth explores the notion that wisdom is the province of the child, and ironically his own life demonstrates exactly that. Notwithstanding his many insights into the complexity of memory in such celebrated works as "Tintern Abbey" (1798/1996) and "Intimations of Immortality" (1807/1996), it seems he did not always practice what he preached. In the final version of *The Prelude* (1850/1979), the epic poem in which he set out to trace the growth of his own mind, and which he revised numerous times across the years, the more he rewrote it, one could argue, the thinner became its record of his growth. In the words of feminist writer Betty Friedan (1993), he "grew stale" (p. 124). Given the perspective guiding us in this book, we find ourselves agreeing with Meacham—if not that everyone is "wise to begin with," then at least that aging is not synonymous with wisdom (p. 198). Our agreement is rooted in our argument that many older adults—too many, one might say—end up succumbing to narrative foreclosure. Stuck in stalled lifestories, they become set in their ways of knowing, hobbled by their biases, and imprisoned in static constructions of their selves and their world. Defaulting, wittingly or otherwise, to meager modes of self-telling and to an interpretive parsimony that narrows their options for making meaning-in-life, they suffer from what psychologist George Kelly (1963) diagnoses as "hardening of the categories" (p. 294). It is at softening such categories that this book is aimed.

WISDOM AS SELF-KNOWLEDGE: A NARRATIVE PERSPECTIVE

Which aspects of wisdom one emphasizes depend on one's perspective. One of the most prevalent perspectives is an ethical-pragmatic one: wisdom as sound judgment, in other words. But certain pieces of the wisdom puzzle can be understood more helpfully, and more thickly, we feel, when looked at from a narrative perspective: wisdom as ongoing process, wisdom as concern for others, and wisdom as self-knowledge. It is the third of these we wish to focus on here, however, for in many ways the other two are bound up with it. Like wisdom in general, self-knowing—or "self-wisdom" (Tobin, 1991, p. 9)—is a continuous process; there is no end to it. At the same time, it is a process that, sooner or later, reaches out to others, a theme we will revisit in Chapter 10. To set the stage for understanding wisdom in more narrative terms, however, it is worth reviewing what those terms entail.

The Narrative Perspective Restated
Objectively speaking, our life is the sum of all the events on every level, from the molecular to the social, that have constituted our existence since the moment we were born: the *outside* story, in other words (Randall, 1995). Subjectively, however, it is not those events themselves. It is what we make and remake of them through memory and imagination—or more precisely perhaps, what we make and remake of those comparatively few events that have managed to catch our notice. We transform such events into rudimentary narrative texts, and our existence itself into texistence. This continuous, creative transformation is what we mean by *poiesis,* hence the poetics of development in general and of aging in particular.

Understood as text, our life is infinitely intricate and continually thickening with age. On the surface, of course, the process can seem more like a thinning, with less and less happening in terms of external occurrences. Yet on the inside, precisely the opposite is potentially the case, as we employ our naturally increasing cognitive complexity to reflect on our accumulated experience from ever more comprehensive horizons. Indeed, such reflection in itself, one might say, intensifies that complexity all the more. Overall, this ever-thickening inside text amounts to our evolving personal myth: the unfolding story of which we are author, narrator, character, and reader at once, and which we compose within a web of larger stories still.

In saying that our lifestory "unfolds," however, we do not mean that its plot (whatever it might be) plays itself out in some preprogrammed manner from an original plan. As philosopher John Dewey argues, taking issue with the "classic Aristotelian formulation" of *potentiality* and, in a sense, anticipating McAdams's (2001) critique of the concept of traits as determinative of our personality: "potentialities are not fixed and intrinsic," he stresses, "but are a matter of an indefinite range of interactions in which an individual may engage" (1940/1962, p. 155). By *unfolding*, then, we do not mean that the author somehow knows all along where the story is going. Rather, we have a more improvisational, more meandering process in mind: a process that, over time, changes in both direction and form in the face of life's vicissitudes. An analogy can be made with a piece of jazz. Its effect on us, as listeners, accumulates through the gradual weaving of multiple variations on a central, initial theme. In a similarly intricate way, our lifestory is a creative work-in-progress, an ever-evolving "structure of meaning" (Charmé, 1984, p. 35). Restricted to some extent by the range of interpretative strategies that are mediated by our narrative environments, and vulnerable, certainly, to the eventualities of the natural and human worlds alike, we make it up as we go. At the same time, we make *sense* of it as we go. That is, we read it as we go, whether we under-read—which most often, of necessity, we do—or over-read, which we sometimes do as well.

This ever-extending text that is us, and that we are obliged to read to at least a minimal degree if we are to function at all in the everyday world, is a quasi-literary text—"quasi-" due to one or two evident exceptions. The first, once again, is that we are inside that text. The second is that, as its author-reader ourselves, we have a measure of power to change its plot, and even perhaps its genre. Such an idea makes little sense where literature is concerned, except in the case of a Choose-Your-Own-Adventure. But with lifestory, restorying is forever taking place. Even *radical* restorying is possible, if not at times imperative (Kenyon & Randall, 1997, p. 155).

These exceptions aside, the text we are is tantamount to a novel: to a rambling yet ultimately unitary story, with its countless overlapping plot lines and interlacing themes, to which we bring the expectation that it will hold some personal significance for us and that, however slightly, we will be transformed in the activity of reading it. Like the novel that we find between the covers of a book, this novel that we are, lengthening and thickening within us even as we speak, is also fraught with meaning, all the more so as we age and have that much more backlogged material to process, ponder, plot. That is, assuming that we have the time—which, ideally, later life allows. Yet as May Sarton (1980) bemoans, hyperaware of the disjointed quality of her own lifestory at times: "Too much is happening all at once and I have no time to sort it all out" (p. 216). "I feel cluttered," she writes in another place, "when there is no time to analyze experience," cluttered by "the silt," as she describes it, of "unexplored experience that literally chokes the mind" (1973/1977, p. 160).

The quality of fraughtness here is key. Lifestory does not "have" meaning, at least not in some segments to the exclusion of others. Rather, like a literary story, it *means*. It does not mediate one main meaning that is hidden within the text and must somehow be deciphered, so much as it is pregnant throughout with meaning-potential, a potential that grows with time, a potential Sarton herself (1980) seems mindful of when she comments that "the deeper the experience, the more time is required to sort it out" (p. 173). Not, of course, that certain experiences are deeper than others in some intrinsic sense; rather, the "depth" of an experience depends on how deeply we read it. The more deeply we do, then the more of its potential we stand to realize—at the level not just of particular events but of our life as a whole, almost regardless of its contents, its textual features. Theoretically, there is no end to what we can get out of our stories, no end of meaning we can harvest from them. Overall, it is into such ways of envisioning lives that discussions of wisdom must increasingly be nudged, if they would honor the internal complexity of human existence when viewed through a narrative lens.

Self-Knowing as Narrative Knowing:
Life Review and the Good Lifestory

Self-knowledge is no less complicated a concept than any of the others we have been considering throughout. What kind of knowledge is it, and what is the self of which it is knowledge? When urging us to know ourselves, ponders philosopher David Hamlyn (1977), "what was Socrates asking of us?" (p. 173). What we take as our departure point here is the assumption that self is inseparable from story. As Polkinghorne (1988) insists, self "is not a static thing nor a substance." It is "a configuring of personal events into a historical unity which includes not only what one has been but also anticipations of what one will be." It is therefore better understood as a "self-story." Seeing the self as "a single unfolding and developing story" (p. 150) means, then, that to know one's self, whatever else it might involve, is to know one's story. Self-knowing is narrative knowing: the expansion and, indeed, enrichment of our fundamental narrative intelligence. What is more, self-knowing is knowing oneself as both author and narrator of one's story, and as reader of it, too. To the degree that "selves are constructed through storytelling" (Holstein & Gubrium, 2000, p. 21), then selves, one could argue, are understood through story-reading. By extension, the closer we read our stories, the deeper our self-knowledge. As self-knowing, therefore, wisdom is acquired neither independently of our stories nor in spite of them. Insofar as any novel is a unique way of knowing the world, wisdom is *in* our stories (Randall & Kenyon, 2001). It is not some elitist ideal that only a few rare souls are capable of attaining. As *our* wisdom, unique to our particular history and our particular strategy for storying experience, it is within our reach, right under our noses—provided we have the eyes to read. But if the self is "a narrative in process" (Polkinghorne, 1988, p. 154), then self-knowing is no once-and-for-all achievement. It is a matter of continuing development, of keeping one's story open—ever-expanding, ever-evolving. A key means by which that development is enabled—and foreclosure avoided—is life review.

Life Review

First proposed by Erikson in relation to his seventh stage of development and as a prerequisite to wisdom, life review was introduced into the mainstream of gerontological thinking by psychologist Robert Butler (1963). For Butler, it is "a normal developmental task of the later years characterized by the return of memories and past conflicts, which can result in resolution, reconciliation, atonement, integration, and serenity" (1996/2007, p. 67). As we noted in Chapter 8, this task can be can undertaken "spontaneously" or it can be "structured" (p. 67). People can be engaged in spontaneous life review when keeping a journal, when talking quietly with a confidant, or when just sitting, sorting things out. Structured forms, on the other hand, run the gamut from scrapbooking to family genealogy, and from guided autobiography to life review *therapy* (see Garland, 1994; Haight, Coleman, & Lord, 1995; Burnside, 1996).

Structured or not, according to Butler (1996/2007), life review possesses a "moral dimension" (p. 70), meaning that it involves the evaluation of one's behavior over time. If such scrutiny issues in a recognition of guilt, then it must be acknowledged and acted on if one is to achieve a sense of "atonement and reconciliation" by life's end (p. 70). In a sense, therefore, life review involves what Schachter-Shalomi and Miller (1995) label "life repair"

(p. 116). That life review is about making amends links to Butler's belief that it has an urgency about it. As psychologist Jeffrey Garland (1994) explains it, life review is "prompted by the realization of approaching dissolution and death, and the inability to maintain one's sense of personal invulnerability" (p. 21). That said, it does not occur solely in later life. People can be involved in it at any age and on multiple occasions, whenever they reflect upon the significance of life's challenges and changes in relation to the course of their life thus far. Still, Butler (1996/2007) insists, life review is most common amongst the aged. Old age, he argues, is the time when we are in a uniquely favorable position to assess our entire lives.

The stress Butler (1963) originally placed on life review as normal, and not "pathological" (1996/2007, p. 68), pushed the gerontological community to see reminiscence in general not as a symptom of senility but—at least in its integrative mode—as a positive, indeed formative activity. However, his initial claim that life review was universal, that everyone undertook it to some degree, has since been debated. As we saw in Chapter 6, evidence suggests that not everyone engages in it, nor even feels the need to. Psychologists Paul Wink and Brian Schiff (2002) have argued on the basis of their own research, for instance, that "although many older adults who are highly satisfied with life appear to have reviewed their lives, an equal, if not higher, number have not" (p. 46). What is more, life review is not an automatic route to peace of mind. As Butler (1996/2007) has stated more recently himself, while it "potentially proceeds toward personality reorganization" (p. 68), it can also—depending on the intensity of the conflicts one is wrestling with—lead to fear, depression, and even suicide. "The most tragic situation," he says (p. 68), is the recognition that one has not truly lived one's life at all, that one's years have in many ways been wasted. In this respect, life review can be the route, not to reconciliation but to regret, not to serenity but to despair, not to writing a satisfying ending for one's story but to shutting it down. Still, whether or not it issues in serenity, life review, claims Butler, enhances our self-knowledge, which is a "virtue" in itself (p. 72).

Compared to structured forms of life review, which as we suggested last chapter could, in some cases, pressure us too quickly toward reconciliation, spontaneous life review comes closer to what we mean by "reading our lives." For reading our lives is no one-time activity but an overall attitude to the texts of our lives that, ideally, persists through time. Expressed succinctly, reading our lives is habitual life review. To read our life is to *live* the examined life, not to have that examination prescribed for us by others and administered in a regimented manner, as if it were one more procedure in a program of medical care. Life, as we say, is not an easy read. There can be dense, impermeable passages within it, demanding extended spans of time to properly digest. To read our lives is to keep working at that challenge, to dwell thoughtfully with our accumulated experience on a more or less regular basis—though, again, not a constant one. If the unexamined life is not worth living, then the opposite is true to some extent as well: the unlived life is not worth examining.

In linking reviewing to reading, though, we do not mean reading our lives as such, since our lives are never available to us directly, only as our life-*stories*. Reviewing our lives means bringing these stories—particularly their storying—more fully to mind. It is "achieving consciousness," as Bruner (1996, p. 147) would say, "of what we so easily do automatically." Such consciousness, we propose, is precisely what wisdom entails. "A person is truly 'wise,'" writes Ray (2000), "when she is able to see life as an evolving story and to create some distance between self and story by reflecting on it from multiple perspectives" (p. 29). But if we take Butler at his word, reviewing our life means evaluating it, too.

The Good Lifestory Again

To put it in the simplest terms, a wise person is one who seeks to live a good, strong story. Indeed, in later life, with all of its challenges and changes, doing so is all the more a must. As we saw in Chapter 5, however, an assortment of criteria can be invoked to assess what sort of story such a story is. Given the idea of wisdom as narrative self-knowing, some refinements of at least a few of them are in order for us now.

Coherence   The criterion of coherence, it will be recalled, means that our story should make sense on its own terms, should be intelligible, should hang together—more or less. In other words, a coherent story is not necessarily a consistent story, or at least not so much so that it is "too consistent to be true" (McAdams, 2001, p. 663), a point that links to the criterion of differentiation, as of openness, our focus in a moment. Whether we examine it or not, our self-story has a built-in coherence anyway, of course, by virtue of the fact that it is a "single unfolding and developing" entity (Polkinghorne, 1988). Like any story, that is, it represents a dynamic integration of the affective and cognitive domains. It is the vehicle, not only of our thinking—about ourselves and our world—but also of our feeling, our valuing, our acting in the world. It is not that we hold *it* together so much as it holds *us* together. Dysfunctional or not, examined or not, our stories live us.

With respect to wisdom, it is this dynamic dimension of our stories that is crucial to consider, insofar as self-knowing involves the ongoing effort to sustain narrative coherence amid the chaos of our noticers and natterers, the flux of daily life, and the swirl of larger stories that would construct that coherence for us. Once again, David Carr (1986) words the matter this way: "The story which knits together and renders coherent and whole the loose strands of my life," he says, "…is ultimately my responsibility, whether I consciously choose it or assume it by default" (p. 94). Wisdom takes the conscious route, embracing this responsibility head-on, continually seeking, if never quite attaining, integration. Yet it keeps working at it. Wisdom keeps struggling to "feel whole in the face of great internal diversity" (Polster, 1987, p. 115)—or as Scott-Maxwell expresses it, to "face everything one has had, been, done; gather them all in" (1968, p. 41). That said, gathering them in does not mean tying them up: freezing *the story of my life* into a fixed, consistent package. In short, wisdom is about keeping our story open, not closing it down.

Openness   As we saw in Chapter 5, and in our discussion of post-formal thought at the beginning of this one, openness is about tolerance for ambiguity and receptiveness to change. This implies flexibility. It implies keeping one's options open—in this case, one's narrative options. Self-knowing thus entails continually stepping outside of oneself. It is not a static state but a continual self-transcendence—a continual expansion of our horizons of self-understanding (Berman, 1994; Mezirow, 1978; Daloz, 1986). As we have seen with the example from Hampl (1999), and with dynamic reminiscence in general, such expansion can happen merely in peering closely into one or two episodes from our past, however innocent they might seem. Each act of self-reading, if only of a single event, takes us to a new place, to a new sense of *the story of my life* as a whole. One self-defining memory, one signature story, one set piece subjected to careful, aesthetic reading and reinterpreted from alternative perspectives, stirs things up. It pries us away from too tight a commitment to versions of our lives that need reconfiguration, that could benefit from narrative repair. However little, it alters our sense of our story overall, and awakens our sense of the meaning-potential that is integral to our other memories, too. Restorying one episode—opening it, unpacking it, rethinking it—sets off a reaction through the rest of our inner material, whether we follow it up or not. Remaining open to doing so is central to the wisdom-process.

Differentiation   Applying the criterion of differentiation to the discussion of wisdom, a wise person is one who acknowledges that there is more than one story behind a given event, more than one angle from which to construe it. A wise person engages in side-shadowing, in sidesight, mindful of the penumbra of possible causes and outcomes—of counterfactuals—that encircles every situation, present or past. Viewed from a narrative perspective, wisdom involves differentiation in two further senses as well. First, it involves opening ourselves to a variety of self-reading contexts, such as we identified in Chapter 5. Each will permit us to appreciate our stories from a particular and uniquely transformative angle. Second, it is about honoring our difference from others as storied beings: honoring our novelty, that is—indeed, growing into that novelty all the more with time. In other words, it entails "individuation" (Jung, 1923). As self-knowing, wisdom is "idiosyncratic" in its expression (Randall & Kenyon, 2001, p. 12). It is therefore *extra*-ordinary, not because it is attainable only by gurus or sages, but because each individual's story entails a unique sequencing (and interpreting) of life-events, a unique storying style, a unique set of coauthoring relationships, and a unique network of narrative environments in which it is rooted and composed. And just as each novel, we can say, teaches its reader how it should be read, so each lifestory asks that it be understood on its own unique terms by the person who is living it.

Generative Integration If it is to be moving in the direction of increasing completeness, or "increasingly good narrative form" (McAdams 2001, p. 663), then self-knowing must not be concerned with one's own life alone. It must reach out to others, in two or three senses. To know ourselves is to know ourselves-in-relationship, to be mindful of how others' lives and stories have influenced our own—whether directly, through family and friends, or indirectly, through our antecedents. Wisdom, as the process of self-knowing, is about understanding ourselves in socio-historical context. Ultimately, it is about seeing our individual story in relationship to humanity as a whole, a vision for which, yet again, the process of aging masterfully prepares us. As Schachter-Shalomi and Miller (1995) invite us to view things in their book *From Ageing to Sage-ing,* the goal of aging is "an ever-widening expansion of consciousness, and a growing sense of unity with life" (p. 15)—a theme we will certainly be returning to in Chapter 10. In the meantime, the wisdom-process is a self-transcending process in that, sooner or later, it connects us and commits us to future generations. To put it bluntly, wisdom should be shared.

A further point on this theme is that self-knowing possesses, not merely an inner direction but an outer one, too. It involves knowing both the texts *in* our lives and the contexts *of* our lives. It is not enough to concentrate on one's own life-text alone, as engrossing and essential as that process clearly is. One must seek to read the larger texts with which it is intertwined—the texts of our family and community, of our culture and creed, of the world at large. Reading the world, with all of its intricacies and issues, its tensions, its history, and processing that history in terms of one's own, as Freeman was stimulated to do through his experience in Berlin—this, itself, is a huge and never-ending task. Yet, once again, it is one that later life positions us to undertake more broadly and deeply than we could when we were young. What is more, deep world-reading and deep self-reading are ultimately two sides of a single coin. One may begin with whichever side one wishes, for at some stage the two sides converge.

Truth Value   As we have been hinting since the outset, each lifestory, like each literary story, is the vehicle of its own wisdom, the medium of its own "central messages" (Coleman, 1999, p. 138). It is a unique way of knowing, just as a novel is a unique way of knowing. As self-knowing, wisdom involves recognizing and contemplating our ongoing life-themes: the peculiar patterns of questions and conflicts, tensions and troubles, that thread through our story and fuel its plot. Just as the issues it wrestles with define the soul of a novel, so our personal issues—the recurring quirks of character, the dilemmas that beset us in our relationships or our work—define our evolving myth, our fundamental project, the novel that we are. In that respect, we need them. Without them, we would be storyless. "The serious problems in life," insists Jung (1933/2001), "are never fully solved." Indeed, "if it should once appear that they are, this is the sign that something has been lost. The meaning and design of a problem seem not to lie in its solution, but in our working at it incessantly. This alone preserves us from stultification and petrifaction" (pp. 105–106)—from foreclosure, one could say. What Jung is implying, we submit, is a deep acceptance of our "problems," not in the sense of acquiescing to them, nor of denying our need for narrative repair because of them, but of acknowledging them, even honoring them, as the unresolved chords in the haunting tune that rings through our life alone, that constitutes our truth—our textual truth, that is. What he is implying is, in Rilke's phrase, that we "live the questions" (1986, p. 32). Wisdom, as gerontologists Fredda Blanchard-Fields and Lisa Norris (1995) sum things up, "is living the uncertainty and celebrating it" (p. 116).

WISDOM AS TRANSFORMATION

Openness, differentiation, truth—these are not static standards by which the stories of our lives are to be judged and found wanting. They are

invitations to narrative development. Such development, and by implication wisdom, entails continuing transformation, a notion we have introduced already but now need to flesh out more fully. First, though, we need
to remind ourselves of the tight connection between transformation and
narrative in general.

In stories, says Ricoeur (quoted in Berman, 1994), "unexpected events
become transfigured into narratively necessary events." To put it simply,
"chance becomes fate" (p. 179). What is, is transfigured—is transformed—
into what had to be. But stories not only entail transformation; they also
incite it. As we saw in Chapters 4 and 5, the transformation can be to varying
degrees and assume a variety of forms, among them catharsis, illumination, epiphany, alleviation—which is to say, escape from our immediate
concerns. Whatever the form, in our encounter with a narrative, something
gives within us. We enter its world through The Beginning and emerge at
The End with a different experience of our own world. Short-lived or shallow though that difference might be, the literary experience is invariably
life-altering.

Coming at the theme of transformation from another angle, to be worth
telling at all, a story must deal with transition. The End—whether it means
solving the murder, winning the war, slaying the alien, or generally calming
the trouble that a story, as a story, requires—must be different from The
Beginning. Otherwise, there is nothing to recount. Happy beginning, happy
middle, happy end makes for a boring tale. The movement from beginning
through middle to end is a qualitative one, not quantitative. It is not just a
matter of adding more events. In other words, transformation is not mere
change. It is fundamental change: change, for instance, in how the hero (or
heroine) experiences reality. Indeed, for Joseph Campbell (1949) transformation lies at the heart of the hero's journey, what he calls the "monomyth"
(pp. 3–46)—the primordial plotline of separation, initiation, and return
that, he believes, all our lives embody and that constitutes the center, not
only of every religion, but indeed of every tale. The story of "the loss and
regaining of identity," writes Northrop Frye (1963, p. 21), "is the framework
of all literature." Paralleling McAdams's (1996) notion of the pre-mythic,
mythic, and post-mythic stages of development, educator Laurent Daloz
(1986) explains how the process unfolds.

"The journey tale begins," says Daloz, "with an old world, generally simple and uncomplicated, more often than not, home. ... The middle portion,"
however, "is characterized by confusion, adventure, great highs and lows,
struggle, uncertainty"—the midlife "muddle," as fellow educator Robert Atkinson (1995, p. 30) would dub it. Daloz goes on (1986): "the ways of the old

world no longer hold, and the hero's task is to find a way through this strange middle land, generally in search of something lying at its heart." Then, "at the deepest point, the nadir of the descent, a transformation occurs, and the traveler moves out of the darkness toward a new world that often bears an ironic resemblance to the old." In essence, "nothing is different; yet all is transformed" (pp. 24–25). Experienced as journeys, then, narratives are transformative in two main ways. They trace transformation in the lives of their characters, and they stimulate transformation in the minds of their readers. As for the narratives we ourselves are living, though, particularly since we are character and reader alike, the same holds true: No transformation, no story; no story, no transformation.

In broad terms, the way of wisdom is the way of transformation. It is not just a matter of change, and it is not just the automatic consequence of added life-events. It is a significant shifting in how we interpret and experience our world. Such transformation can be prompted by numerous means, from the intentional to the everyday. Among the more obvious, as we saw in Chapter 8, is what happens in a therapeutic setting. For instance, psychoanalysis, notes one source, "is overwhelmingly concerned with the production and *transformation of meaning*" in the client's life (Bowie, 1993, p. 97; emphasis ours). Drawing on their work with a depressed individual in her eighties who was dominated by the vision of herself as fundamentally a failure, gerontological social workers Nancy Kropf and Cindy Tandy (1998) show how, through the use of narrative therapy, the woman's sense of self was significantly reconfigured from "I'm a failure" to "I'm a survivor." The use of terms like "restorying," "retelling," and "re-authoring" only confirms that such transformation—transformation of self, in the final analysis—is at the heart of the therapeutic enterprise. But religion is about transformation, too. Recounting the story of Jesus or Moses, Mohammed or Buddha, has prompted for millions the profoundest of personal change. Scales have fallen from eyes and lives have been converted, revitalized, reborn.

Education, as well, is ultimately not about imparting information but about inspiring transformation. For John Dewey (1916/1944), education, properly so-called, concerns the "continuous reconstruction of experience" (p. 80). For adult education in particular, especially perhaps since Jack Mezirow (1978) profiled the concept of "transformative learning," learning "involves more than the mere confirmation of experience" (Tennant & Pogson, 1995, p. 151). Rather, "experience has to be mediated and reconstructed (or transformed) by the student" (p. 151). In discussing "the transformational power of adult learning experiences," Daloz (1986) ties the concept of transformation directly to that of growth. Growth, he writes, "is not simply a matter of quantitative increase"; it entails "a qualitative kind of change as well" (p. 130). Growth, he goes on, "means transformation and transformation means the yielding of old structures of meaning-making to new" (p. 140). Indeed, this is how growth may be best defined: "a series of transformations in our ways of making meaning" (p. 137).

Life review itself, plus autobiographical reflection of any sort, are means of opening ourselves to such growth and such learning—to "autobiographical learning," as one source calls it (Nelson, 1994, p. 391). As we began to see last chapter, dynamic reminiscence in itself clears a path for this sort of learning by playing with alternative interpretations of pivotal passages from our past. In this respect, it illustrates what Schachter-Shalomi and Miller (1995) describe as "the power of recontextualization" (p. 94). Essential to "sage-ing," they stress, and a key "tool" for "harvesting life," as well as for "life repair," is the need to "open old files, relive them, recontextualize them for deeper meaning, and then refile them in the 'plus' files," to use their phrase, "free from their negative emotional valences" (p. 117). Such recontextualization, one could say, amounts to *re-genre-ation*—to the transformation of "perceived failures into successes," or of the tragic into the romantic: a process characteristic of McAdams's "redemptive self" (2006).

Schachter-Shalomi and Miller's vision might seem unduly optimistic, underestimating the resistance to reliving, repairing, and refiling that certain memories can surely mount, not least the kind that Langer (1991) implies are ruined to the point of being unredeemable. Nevertheless, it is not out of step with the view of Berman (1994) in his analysis of elderly diarists such as Sarton and Scott-Maxwell. Drawing upon the work of hermeneutical philosopher Hans Gadamer, Berman explains how their journals epitomize the ways in which "we make sense of the present in terms of our working theory of the kind of story we are in the middle of" (p. 180). As our "horizon of self-understanding shifts," however, "it may become apparent," he says, "that we were not in the middle of the story we thought we were in the middle of." For example, "perhaps we thought our life was a tragedy and all along, unbeknownst to us, it was a romance. Or perhaps we thought our life was almost over, at least in terms of the future holding anything new, and it turned out there was a lot more to it" (p. 180). Thus, says Berman, offering his own take on the issue of narrative foreclosure: "even in later life, the movement of that horizon can lead to a reconfiguration of the events of the past and a radical rewriting of the story of one's life" (p. 194)—a "radical restorying," as it were (Kenyon & Randall, 1997, p. 120). The fact that the diarists whom Berman discusses are women raises an enticing possibility, however, which we have hinted at already so will simply mention here in passing. If women tend to develop richer, more emotionally nuanced memories to begin with (as we saw in Chapter 3), might they then be inherently more open than men to restorying their lives, and thus to wisdom, too: more open to the poetics of aging in general? If so, then might this not, in itself, play some small role, however unexamined, in women's greater longevity overall?

If transformation is true for life review, for dynamic reminiscence, or for writing in one's journal, then it is true for remembering of any kind. Much of what ends up in memory in the first place are images of events that transgress our expectations, that depart from the run-of-the-mill, that are not the same old story. Thereafter, though, each act of remembering is invariably a transforming of the event in question, insofar as the context in which we recall it, not to mention the self who is doing the recalling, is sure to differ from the context we were occupying at the time it initially occurred. We have seen repeatedly the impact of context on memory at the social and cultural levels, the level of narrative environment. But even at the neurological level, its impact is experienced. Neuroscientist Elkhonon Goldberg (2005) insists that "every time you activate a previously formed memory, you change it ever so slightly by embedding it into a new context prompted by the unique circumstances of the mental activity at hand." Indeed, "as they are being called upon…memories undergo constant reconstruction" (p. 141). Psychiatrist Susan Vaughan (1997) reinforces this insight from a therapeutic perspective. In her reflections on the restorying that therapy entails, she explores how what she calls "the talking cure" effects an actual "rewiring" of neurons in the brain. "When such rewiring occurs on a grand scale, through repeated experience and work on specific patterns," she says, "particular parts of the brain are permanently altered" (p. 18). The arguments of both Goldberg and Vaughan call to mind the image of the compost heap, perhaps, in which memories are quite literally "turned over" in our minds. In sum, each recalling is essentially a rereading, transforming our relationship to the original event.

On every level, then, it seems that the push of life itself—resisted or not—is to effect a continual reconfiguration of the contents of our memory and a transformation in our horizons of understanding, thus a continual outgrowing of outdated versions of the stories by which we live. This continual outgrowing is in many ways a metaphorical process, insofar as, in Freeman's (1995) words, "a new relationship is being created between the past and present, a new poetic configuration, designed to give greater form to one's previous—and present—experience"(p. 30). Polkinghorne (1988) adds support to such a view: "experience makes connections and enlarges itself," he says, "through the use of metaphoric processes that link together experiences similar but not exactly the same" (p. 16). As we saw in Chapter 2, our ability to make such metaphorical connections is at the heart of our capacity to learn new concepts, and as we saw in Chapter 8, it plays a potent role in reminiscence, above all in its more dynamic, more creative forms. As Sherman (1991) observes, "metaphor enables us to take experiences and construct them into larger meaningful wholes," leading "to valuable new linkages or integrations with other life experiences" (p. 87). With each such linkage, not just in formal memory work but, indeed, in our everyday remembering, the metaphorical suggestibility of memory is revealed, therefore, as endless. Memory is infinite in its metaphorical potential. The gradual enlarging of experience and the steady stretching of our horizons that tapping into that potential explicitly effects is surely a form of Kegan's "natural therapy" (1982, pp. 255–296).

As with the chambered nautilus, elevated by poet Oliver Wendell Holmes (1895/2005) to a metaphor for personal growth, development proceeds, then, by pressing past the stages we occupy at present—cognitively, affectively, spiritually—and spiraling toward ever more inclusive ones instead. Kegan (1982) writes, for instance, about revisiting "old issues...at a whole new level of complexity" (p. 109). Whether or not we are open to it, encourage it, or are even aware of it, the process takes place beneath the surface all life long. For this reason, wisdom has been seen so often as the province, automatically, of age. Certainly, advancing years "supply the means to it," as one source says, "whether or not the means is consciously used" (Blanchard, 1967, p. 324). Wisdom as such, however, is about working deliberately with the mass of accumulated material that lies at our disposal, engaging in the journey of transformation in a conscious, mindful manner.

WISDOM, NARRATIVE, AND IRONY

If we view wisdom as self-knowing, and the wisdom-process as a matter of continuous transformation in awareness (including awareness of awareness), then an attitude—or a narrative tone (McAdams, 1996)—that is uniquely characteristic of a wise individual is *irony*. Congruence, curiosity, common sense: these may be characteristics as well, but as we noted when discussing the nature of a good lifestory, an ironic orientation—a hallmark of postmodernity—is also key. If midlife coincides for many (many men, at least) with the emergence of a "tragic sense of life" (Levinson, 1978, p. 225), through the realization that death thwarts all of our attempts at immortality, then conceivably, from midlife on, a certain mellowing occurs as a more ironic sense arises. Again, this does not mean *ironic* in a superficial sense:

saying one thing and meaning another, or circumstances unfolding in ways that contradict our expectations. Rather, we have something deeper and more positive in mind, something beyond tragedy, and something intrinsic to self-consciousness as such, something of which wisdom—understood in storied terms—represents the heightening.

In Chapter 1, we saw how a postmodern conception of irony has to do with fragmentation, openness, and multivalence. But irony has also been associated with narrative itself, as a necessary consequence of storying, story-telling, and, by implication, story-reading. Irony, says Prickett (2002), is "endemic to narrative" (p. 38). As observed by literary scholars Robert Scholes and Robert Kellogg (1966), "the narrative situation is ineluctably ironic." Indeed, "the quality of irony is built into the narrative form as it is in no other form of literature" (p. 240). In his discussion of narrative irony, literary scholar and novelist David Lodge (1992) reminds us, for example, that "all novels are essentially about the passage from innocence to experience, about discovering the reality that underlies appearances" (p. 179). As with novels, so with lives, especially when lives themselves are experienced as novels in the making, of which we ourselves are the authors and narrators, the characters and readers. It is "in the relationship between the teller and the tale, and…the teller and the audience," say Scholes and Kellogg (1966), that one finds "the essence of narrative art." Indeed, "our pleasure in narrative literature itself" is "a function of disparity of viewpoint": a disparity, in other words, between "three points of view—those of the characters, the narrator, and the audience" (pp. 240–241).

Clearly, expressions of narrative irony will be as numerous as the novels in which they appear. What is more, some novels will be additionally ironic in that they make irony itself their modus operandi, with their authors regularly interrupting the narration to insert some self-reflexive aside aimed at sharpening the reader's appreciation for the text's rhetorical complexities. But as we saw in Chapter 4, even without such interruptions, reading itself, whether efferent or aesthetic, is inherently ironic. And reading the texts that are *us* is more ironic still, since we are composing them from within. In effect, the teller and the tale—and in a sense the audience as well—are one and the same. Overall, the ironic stance is rooted in the complexity of our self-narratives in a range of inter-linking ways: time-wise, self-wise, other-wise, and meaning-wise.

Time-wise

Though our sense of it is typically implicit, there is a built-in disparity about our experience of daily life inasmuch as it is only through the present that we have access to the past. Furthermore, our perspective on the present (and thus the past) is influenced by the future toward which we perceive ourselves advancing. In coping with our mother's illness today, for instance, our memory may be flooded with recollections of the relationship we had with her as a child, which in turn are rendered all the more poignant by the awareness that, tomorrow, she could well be gone. As Charmé (1984) is right to remind us, then, "retrospective interpretation necessarily proceeds with a kind of dramatic irony" (p. 123). On some level, we always know that the past itself was never exactly as we recall it. Extrapolating from such an insight, Bruner and Weisser (1991) go as far as to propose, in fact, that "lying is the origin of consciousness" (p. 132): consciousness that arises amid the recognition that there is a difference between the event itself and the myriad ways in which one might recount it.

Our experience of time also undergirds an ironic perspective in that it is associated with our implicit knowledge that we are forever in the middle of our story, poised between a beginning we can barely envisage and an ending that has yet to be determined. Due to this predicament, our image of the genre our story might belong to—tragedy, romance, comedy—can be chronically unclear (some days it feels like one, some days another). And this lack of clarity in itself only buttresses the ironic stance. Our sense of irony increases apace as well, one could argue, with our sense of the disparity between the actual *quantity* of time that remains to us and the *quality* of time that we require to "face everything one has had, been, done" (Scott-Maxwell, 1968, p. 41)—in short, to *read* our lives.

Self-wise

Even in as primary a state as core consciousness, where we become aware of ourselves being aware, a distance exists between "us" as observer and us as observed, between "I" and "me." Additionally, insofar as irony concerns disparity of understanding, then living within our stories themselves (at the macro and micro levels alike) provides abundant opportunity for irony to emerge. We experience our stories through several selves at once—self-as-narrator, -character, and the like—and each will have its slant on what our stories really are. Immersed in conversation with someone whom, for whatever reason, we do not quite trust, we can quite acutely experience an awareness of our awareness. With one side of ourselves (the editor–reader), we can hear another side (the narrator) recounting a story about something that we (the character) accomplished in the past that reflects a distinctive spin, that intentionally skirts some details while exaggerating others. Meanwhile, an inner natterer is certain to be nagging: "that's not how it happened, and you know it." Either we can exploit such situations and indulge in outright lying, or we can take heart, remembering, as Ray (2000) says, that wise people "watch themselves tell life stories" (p. 29).

But even with someone whom we trust, someone with whom we can let down our guard and tell it like it is, the awareness of what our "narrative self" is up to (Hampl, 1999, p. 29) never fully fades. Rather, we catch ourselves embellishing this bit and downplaying that bit, in view of the overall version of events that we want our listener to confirm. As honest as our telling might strive to be, our left hand always knows what our right hand is doing. Even in explicitly autobiographical activity, it can be a struggle to strike the right voice. The reality, as Butala (2005) admits, is that even in the memoir, where presumably we seek to be as honest as we can, "the literary 'voice' and the writer are not one and the same" (p. 49). The more intentional we are about exploring our story, in other words, the more ironic our sense of self will grow.

Continuing in the same vein, the greater our realization that the past as it was is never available in raw, uninterpreted form, that the self (as-narrator) with which we recount a given event is never the same as the self we were at the time (self-as-character)—i.e., "I" versus "Me," self-now versus self-then, or "oldest self versus past selves" (Gullette, 2004, p. 150)—then the greater our sense of irony will become. In consequence, says Margaret Gullette (2004), the less "age-naïve" our "life storytelling" will be: a quality that characterizes what she calls "age autobiography" (p. 154). An ironic attitude will also be intensified the more we become mindful of the spectrum of sub-selves or selves-as-characters that operate inside of us. It will be intensified, too, as we become aware of the several "possible lives—real or imagined, narrated or enacted, discovered in one's past or projected in one's future"—i.e., the might-have-been, might-still-be lives—that are "a constitutive part of our selves" (Brockmeier, 2002, p. 462). "While one part of me knows the soul goes to death in tragedy," writes Jungian psychologist James Hillman (1989) by way of illustration, "another is living a picaresque fantasy, and a third engaged in the heroic comedy of improvement" (p. 81). Such a multiplicity of inner storylines, past and future, contributes to the unimaginable complexity and often baffling contradictions of our emotional life (another underexamined area in gerontology). It contributes to our sense of empathy as well, and mitigates our tendency to "storyotype" by enhancing our capacity to imagine that the inner worlds of our fellow human beings are every bit as intricate and as baffling as our own. Such considerations take us to how the roots of the ironic stance also lie in our interactions with others.

Other-wise

First of all, irony is intensified as we experience the many different sides that, like us, the others in our lives possess, sides that may well have led us to become disillusioned with them and even to delete them from our circle. But our sense of irony also increases with our awareness of how everyone whom we have interacted with across the years has elicited sides of *us*—or evoked characters in our story—that inevitably differ from the sides or characters that others have evoked. Inasmuch as self-knowing involves knowing ourselves in relationship to others, it involves a heightened awareness of such differences in a way that enables us to laugh—above all, at ourselves. In other words, the ironic stance is fundamental to most forms of humor, perhaps especially those that can accompany later life—again, an underexamined area. A certain amount of such humor relates to our ability in the present to understand some problem that preoccupied us in the past within a more comprehensive framework of meaning—our ability, that is, to look back and laugh at the person we were back then, a person who let something so silly bother us at all. But much of such humor also concerns the disparity between a willing spirit and a weakening flesh—as screenwriter Nora Ephron (2006) wryly observes about her increasing wrinkles and sags: "I feel bad about my neck." The body becomes the "other," the would-be main character of our story, who sabotages our attempts to act as if we were still a teenager. The upshot is that wisdom involves keeping an affectionate distance—from ourselves. It involves seeing through the self-legendizing (or self-minimizing) to which we could otherwise be tempted. It involves not being taken in by the various characters we can play (however commanding our performance) but remaining cognizant that none of them represents the *whole* story of us. Once more, wisdom entails being aware of ourselves' being aware of ourselves.

The ironic stance is intensified as we move, not just from one individual to the next, but from one self-reading context to the next. It is intensified as we realize just how differently we tend to story our experience in each; and how the people whom we encounter in each call forth different overall versions of our lives by coauthoring us in distinctive directions. It is intensified as we appreciate how each context entices to the fore of self-consciousness particular chapters, episodes, or themes in our lives thus far. It is intensified as we learn to read ourselves both more deeply and more widely; again, as we learn to read ourselves reading ourselves—the essence of aesthetic reading. Here again, the discipline of keeping a journal, or indeed of engaging in any form of autobiographical exploration, can enhance our ironic sensibilities. It can heighten our awareness of the inevitable "slippage" (Spence, 1982, pp. 82–83) between our thoughts or feelings and the language by which we would give them form, the inevitable gap between signified and signifier. It can intensify our awareness of the challenge of achieving a point of view that suits what we are seeking to express, and the side of ourselves that is seeking to express it. And in keeping with the greater complexity of post-formal thought overall, it can sharpen our awareness of the infinity of ways there are to articulate and understand virtually anything about our lives.

Meaning-wise

The ironic stance is bound up with the realization that every memory is in the end a work of faction; moreover, a faction that has been filtered through the agendas of the various internal editors by which we have recalled it since the event at its center first occurred. Again, though, it is not that we are inveterate self-liars or are hopelessly self-deceived. This is how memory works. It *has* to fail us, it has to sin, in order to fulfill its mission (see Schacter, 1996, 2001). Also, the ironic stance is sensitive to the possibility that the remembered event was retained for a reason, that it holds some meaning in our lives, that it can tell us something significant about ourselves. If at times it has seemed to become forgotten, it is only because its meaning has become temporarily less critical to hang onto; either that, or the self-reading circles in which we were moving at the time did not encourage its recollection and examination. In other words, different remembered events can hold different meanings for us for different reasons in different situations, including situations in the future—situations we have not yet experienced but that, like metaphors we have not yet met, could tease out depths of significance that, at present, are impossible to imagine. Charmé (1984) refers to this phenomenon as "the determining of the past by the future" (p. 33). The phenomenon is one that historians, of course, have recognized all along and, indeed, has spawned an entire approach to literary studies known as "new historicism."

The ironic stance is also strengthened as we grow more aware of the gap between the vast array of memorable events that lie within us and our capacity to read them, let alone recall them, as extensively as they deserve. Irony is rooted in the realization that our story never quite covers our life—just as no story can completely cover any event. Thus, even for the sincerest among us, it never quite rings true, if for no other reason than that our life itself is still unfolding, still being storied. At the same time, our story continually outstrips us too, for we are, after all, inside of it. Moreover, the more conscious of it we are, in all its novelty and vastness, the more mysterious it becomes to us, the more pregnant with unspecified potential, and the more we realize that any kind of "complete" reading is fated to elude us. The injunction to "know thyself" simply cannot be met. "There is always more to be said," concludes Prickett (2002), "further questions to be asked, more of the story to be told" (p. 257). Rather than have us throw up our hands in despair, however, might such a situation not lead us to wonder all the more—and, sooner or later, to laugh?

Overall, an ironic attitude (which some of us exhibit more naturally than others, clinging less tightly to our own evolving myth) is the only appropriate attitude for the intrinsic indeterminacy of *the story of my life*—not just in relation to specific stories that are as yet untold, but to the additional meanings that beg to be deciphered in those that we have been telling all along. There is *always* more than one side to every story. Accordingly, there is no end to "the potentiality of our unlived lives" (Alheit, 1995, p. 65). Our unlived lives are not merely the "might have beens," the alternative avenues along which our stories could have unfolded if we had turned right rather than left, joined the army instead of hiking in the Alps, and so on. They are the "might still be's": the corners of our experience that we could experience more fully; the sides of ourselves that fresh storying environments, fresh self-reading contexts, fresh relationships could still call forth; the significance embedded in memories, painful or pleasant, that rereading and recontextualizing could even yet reveal. McAdams expresses it concisely: "when it comes to our lifestories, nothing is ever final. Things can always change" (1993, p. 278).

CULTIVATING WISDOM ENVIRONMENTS

A good lifestory is one that is not kept to ourselves but—in some form, by some means, at some point—is passed along to others. Accordingly, the pursuit of wisdom pushes us beyond ourselves. It pushes us to impart our learning and our wondering, our questions and discoveries, our knowledge and doubts, both to those who are around us and to those who come after us. But it is not merely that others need *our* wisdom; we need *theirs* to help us to grow. As we saw with dynamic reminiscence, sharing is the key, and the cultivation of environments—of "sacred spaces" (Turner, 2006)—in which such sharing may occur is what we need to look at now.

Meacham (1990) concludes his reflections on the loss of wisdom with some comments on the conditions that may prevent that loss from happening. Wisdom can be achieved, he suggests, only through particular sorts of experiences. Those he has in mind take place within a "wisdom atmosphere." By this he means a "framework of supportive interpersonal relations in which one may safely discover and reveal the limitations of and doubts regarding what one knows" (p. 209). Factoring the narrative variable into Meacham's line of thought, the sharing of our knowledge and our doubts sooner or later involves sharing our stories—which is to say, telling them and having them listened to, respectfully and openly, by others.

Storylistening is in fact no less intricate an art than storytelling (see Kenyon & Randall, 1997, pp. 130–141). Moreover, no matter how much we might benefit from it, good lifestory-listening can be challenging to find, especially with advancing age. That said, such an ideal is clearly what inspires many support groups, including groups devoted to "guided autobiography" (Birren & Deutchman, 1991) and to dynamic reminiscence (Chandler & Ray, 2002). In the life-writing groups that Ray (2000) has been part of, much the same process is at work. For her, that process is all about wisdom. Again: "'wise' people...learn from others' stories, and intervene in their own narrative processes to allow for change by admitting new stories and interpretations into their repertoire" (p. 29). Wise people are involved instinctively, that is, in narrative elaboration.

But the same more or less mutual coauthoring and co-reading of one another's stories, of telling-with as opposed to telling-to, is a potential in any friendship, or indeed any relationship, however rarely or fleetingly that potential is fulfilled. Any conversation—and we can never predict in advance which one—can become a "biographical encounter" (Kenyon & Randall, 1997, p. 168) in which we learn from each other's way of seeing things; in which we unwittingly coach each other in our biographical development (Alheit, 1995); and in which a genuine expanding, examining, and transforming of our respective narratives can therefore occur. Educational encounters in which autobiographical reflection is encouraged could be included here as well. Indeed, says educator Wilhelm Mader (1995), there is theoretically "no educational material, no subject matter, that would not be able to trigger" such reflection (p. 245). In a somewhat one-sided way, a therapeutic encounter encourages such reflection as well. In other words, the therapeutic relationship itself acts as a "developmental milieu" (Gutmann, quoted by Eisenhandler, 1994, p. 137) or "a culture to grow in," or a "holding environment" (Kegan, 1982, p. 276, 115), as the client reaches out for healing or repair from stories that are disjointed, dysfunctional, or otherwise foreclosed—albeit "repair" as defined in terms of the therapeutic master plot with which the therapist may be working.

There is always the chance that larger collections of people, from book clubs to church groups, and from families to entire cultures, may be transformed into wisdom atmospheres—or "story spaces" (Baldwin, 2005, p. 28)—in which people can contemplate their lives to a depth that is reflective of the self-reading we are proposing in this book. Even nursing homes, it has been suggested, could be reconfigured as wisdom environments (Kenyon, 2002), and in that regard, better embody the ideal of "home." Indeed, it is tempting to slide into reverie about a world in which, at every level, wisdom environments are the norm. What sort of world would it be? What growth would be fostered and what compassion unleashed? What respect for each person's uniqueness—and commonality—would pervade our interactions, regardless of our age?

Developing a wisdom atmosphere for the world as a whole is as fanciful a likelihood as the physical atmosphere itself suddenly coming clean, the ozone layer healed, and global warming stopped. But does it hurt to move as much as we can in that direction? Surely, the injunction to "think globally, act locally" is as valid in relation to wisdom as it is to world peace, or to anything else worth struggling for. Our conviction here, in fact, is that the quest for wisdom and the quest for such other goals eventually converge. Thus, inquiring within is always a worthy place to start. A wisdom environment is something one can cultivate within oneself.

We have alluded repeatedly to the value of keeping a journal in expanding, examining, or transforming our stories. Indeed, numerous authors have catalogued the benefits of doing so, notwithstanding the drawbacks that such practices may have when it comes to narrative foreclosure, as already noted. One strategy, however, appears to accomplish all three of these processes at once. Pioneered by depth psychologist Ira Progoff (1975), it is what he calls the "intensive journal" method. While the language he employs to lay out this method has almost a mystical tone with which few psychologists, even narrative ones, are likely to be comfortable, his guiding insights resonate well, we feel, with those of McAdams (1993) concerning lifestory as an evolving personal myth, of Sartre with his vision of the "fundamental project" (Charmé, 1984, p. 2), and undoubtedly of diarist Anaïs Nin (1981), given her musings on "the personal life deeply lived" and the diary itself "as an instrument for…creating ourselves" (p. 158). Progoff refers routinely, for instance, to "the inner myth that has been guiding our lives unknown to ourselves" (p. 11); to "the unfolding meaning of our life as a whole" (p. 294);

to a process that is "self-enlarging" (p. 156); to "the Tao of growth" (p. 14); and to "the implicit wisdom of a life" (p. 41).

Supposedly, "without imposing any external circumstances or intepretations or theories on the individual's experience"—that is, without any therapeutic master plot structuring the process—the intensive journal, Progoff writes, "plays an active role in reconstructing a life" (p. 9). The goal of his method is to invite the individual to experience a "dialogue" with his or her own inner life through a variety of reflective techniques. This in turn "draws him further along the road of his own life process" (p. 9). One such technique, which in effect extends what occurs amid dynamic reminiscence, entails "entering the details of particular experiences, drawing forth their significance, and opening the possibilities of their still unexpressed contribution to our lives" (p. 129).

Good candidates for such an intense examination are what Progoff calls "steppingstones." By these he means "significant points of movement along the road of an individual's life" (p. 102). Steppingstones, one could say, parallel McAdams's nuclear episodes, Bruner's turning points, Birren's branching points, not to mention self-defining memories and, in some respects, set pieces and signature stories. But even "the very act of listing our steppingstones," he says, "reshapes the context of our life and thus draws us a step further into our future" (p. 118)—a point that accords with what we said in Chapter 6 about the value, in and of itself, of expanding our stories. More important than listing such events, however, or indeed listing any other episodes that our memory has retained, is "re-entering our past from the inside" (p. 126), a process Progoff refers to as "time-stretching." Time-stretching, which can be taken as an equivalent to side-shadowing (Morson, 1994), entails the contemplation of "intersections," of "roads taken and not taken" (p. 139), in order to "draw from our life history those seeds that have not grown in our past but can grow very meaningfully in our future" (p. 139). It is one of a number of ways in which, as we practice intensive journaling, we can engage in "opening out the contents of our lives with an open curiosity" (p. 102), and thus in "balancing and directing our growth" (p. 14). With the compost heap implicit in the background, Progoff celebrates how, by means of the intensive journal, "the soil of our lives is loosed and softened. The solid clumps of past experience are broken up so that air and sunlight can enter...soon the soil becomes soft enough for new shoots to grow in" (p. 100).

This sort of "re-entering our past," he says, permits a "transvaluation" (p. 114) of our life experiences and gives us the opportunity to "explore possibilities contained in the unlived aspects of our lives"—"seedlings of potentiality" (p. 148), as he calls them—and thus "open avenues to our future while we are reentering the experiences of our past" (p. 131). In the end, "our total life history is progressively recrystallized" (p. 292). Overall, the point of intensive journaling, one can say, is not to live *in* the past at all but to live *off* the past; to experience it as biographical capital by which, in the present, our lives may be enriched, rendered deeper, more substantial, more filled with meaning. Besides organic imagery, Progoff uses aesthetic imagery, as well, to celebrate how "our ultimate artwork is our life itself" (p. 180), and how the intensive journal is the "inner workshop" where "the creative shaping" of that work of art takes place. The conclusion of his vision, grand though it might seem, is ultimately not unlike the one that has led us to inquire into the poetics of growing old. "The potential for growth in a human being is as infinite as the universe," Progoff says; "not physical growth but the qualitative growth of persons" (p. 296).

The idea of a wisdom environment of one—of a wisdom atmosphere within ourselves—might seem to undermine all that we have said so far about how our lifestories are coauthored and co-read in our relationships with others. Be that as it may, it is both the beauty and the burden of being human—in part, *because of* our relationships with others—that we have a relationship with ourselves, as well. If we ignore the fact of that relationship and the nurturing of it, too, then our narrative development cannot help but be jeopardized, and foreclosure could well become a way of life. Such a possibility is additionally relevant when one considers that the further we journey into the second half of life, the narrower our circle of relationships is likely to become, and thus the lonelier we might feel. In nurturing our relationship with the society of self, however, loneliness can be transformed into solitude (Payne & McFadden, 1994). Such a transformation is ultimately impossible to articulate, of course, insofar as it pertains to "that most human of 'regions'...where meaning is made" (Kegan, 1982, pp. 2–3)—where, one might say, our noticers, natterers, and inner reader-editor continually confer and where quietly, secretly, mostly un–self-consciously, we go about composing our lives. The vast, sprawling, yet ultimately idiosyncratic entity that results from this ceaseless composition deserves at some point to be soulfully examined. But the activity of doing so is no narcissistic enterprise. It is not, as the saying goes, navel-gazing. It is *novel-grazing*, the searching and savoring of the stories that we are. And its cultivation is crucial, we submit, for our wisdom to unfold.

Ten

TRANSCENDING OUR STORIES:

THE POETICS OF SPIRITUAL AGING

Those who do not have power over the story that dominates their lives, power to retell it, rethink it, deconstruct it, joke about it, and change it as times change, truly are powerless, because they cannot think new thoughts.
    —Salman Rushdie (1992, p. 432)

Our lives... [are] like richly ambiguous texts to be interpreted and understood...whose meanings are inexhaustible, whose mysterious existence ceaselessly calls forth the desire to know, whose readings cannot ever yield a final closure.
    —Mark Freeman (1993, p. 184)

[Age is] a growing, deepening, knitting together of your life, a consciousness of what you have lived needing to come together in a whole picture, as if you had to prepare for the sloughing off of the body, as if in age the soul is getting ready to take off—the big adventure.
    —Suzanne Wagner (cited in Friedan, 1993, p. 575)

SPIRITUAL AGING AS NARRATIVE ENDEAVOR

From wisdom to spirituality is hardly a huge leap. Even more than with memory and meaning, it may simply be misleading to treat them as separate topics. The development of wisdom "is a spiritual pathway," insists one source (Blanchard-Fields & Norris, 1995, p. 114). Acknowledging the link between them is what starts us, then, down the path we will be pursuing in this chapter. Our first step is to look at the relationship between spirituality, on one hand, and aging, religion, and narrative, respectively, on the other. Following this, we consider how the prospect of death—conceived as The End of our story—constitutes both a challenge and an opportunity for spiritual growth. Not only that, but the very fact of it has crucial implications for notions of "successful aging." Next, we touch on the role of master narratives—religious ones, especially—in shaping our experience of spirituality, after which we return to an idea we have hinted at already, that of our stories themselves as sacred texts—indeed, as parables of sorts. This will lead us to explore gerotranscendence, generativity, and genealogy as means by which we let our stories go. To conclude, we discuss how, just as irony is a hallmark of wisdom, so wonder is the companion of spiritual growth.

Spirituality and Aging

If wisdom and spirituality are connected, then aging itself is what binds them together. For gerontologist Robert Atchley (2000), for instance, growing old has been perceived in a variety of cultures down through the ages as a "profound opportunity for spiritual growth and wisdom" (p. 329). In the view of literary gerontologist Barbara Fay Waxman (1997, p. 175), "our later years are a time of rich intensity and opportunities for psychological and spiritual growth." For Thomas Moore (1992), author of the popular book *Care of the Soul,* "growing old is one of the ways the soul nudges itself into attention to the spiritual aspect of life" (p. 214).

It is not that the middle of life is of no consequence, of course. Many would claim, ourselves included, that the midlife years are in fact critical to the development of both spirituality and wisdom alike. Atchley (2000) notes the evidence, for instance, "that spiritual concerns, experiences, and development are increasingly important in mid and later life" (p. 324). For McAdams (1993), "the 40s can be a time of reassessment...and involve significant changes in self-understanding that may have profound implications for mythmaking" (pp. 198–199). The 40s, he continues, mark a move from a "youthful, passionate perspective" to "a tempered, refined, philosophical orientation" (p. 199). And Eugene Bianchi (1982/1995), who devotes over half of his book, *Aging as a Spiritual Journey*, to "the challenges" and "the potentials" of midlife, speaks of "the unique opportunities that [it] offers for deeper spiritual growth" (p. 39). By then, he says, "the chastened self is ready for the religious journey" (p. 40). Not only that, but "if we do not begin to grapple with our own aging in mid-life," then "we may find it much harder in later years to turn our losses into gains in terms of spiritual development" (p. 58). Certainly in terms of the framework we are advocating here, the practice of reading our lives ought to be cultivated early in life rather than later—*too* late, in other words.

Nevertheless, our later years are accompanied by development that, it has been argued, is "qualitatively different" from what we experience in our middle ones (Tornstam, 1994, p. 204). Gerontologist Harry Moody (1986) maintains, for instance, that "old age is not simply one more stage but the final stage, the stage that sums up all that went before" (p. 16). Not that it "inevitably bring[s] spiritual development," as Atchley (2000) explains, but it "alter[s] the conditions of life in ways that … can stimulate interest in a spiritual journey" (p. 335). While interest in that journey can begin far earlier, of course, it naturally intensifies with time. Says Scott-Maxwell (1968), therefore, "the last years may matter the most" (p. 112). Aging itself, it might be said, is an inherently spiritual process—a "natural monastery," in Moody's words (1995, p. 96), making *spiritual aging* every bit as critical to ponder as cognitive aging, social aging, biological aging, and the like. Yet, oddly enough, until quite recently at least, the study of spirituality and the study of aging have "remained highly isolated from one another" (Atchley, 2000, p. 329).

Spirituality and Religion

All such observations raise the question, of course, of what exactly *spirituality* means. Like the majority of themes we have been dealing with so far, it is a complicated construct. It takes many forms and is expressed in many ways: from attendance at church, to private reflection, to mystical experience. However, despite Bianchi's (1982/1995) conviction about "the chastened self" being "ready for the religious journey" (p. 40), the increasing number of people who take pains to describe themselves as spiritual but not necessarily religious suggests that the relationship of spirituality to religion, like wisdom's link to knowledge, is ambiguous at best.

We can see this ambiguity in the range of approaches researchers tend to take. Some approach spirituality in terms of explicit involvement in organized religion, one of the main sources of meaning that we noted in Chapter 8, seeing a positive correlation between participation in religious activities and various measures of mental and physical health, life satisfaction, and the like (see Koenig, 1995). Others, however, are more skeptical, concerned that "much of the literature on the relation between religion, spirituality, and well-being is flawed by problems of defining and measuring variables" (Kimble et al., 1995, p. 5). And some separate spirituality and religion even further. Moody (1995), for instance, focuses on mysticism and later life, and on experiences of transcendence that span the frontiers of particular traditions. For his part, Moore (1992) sees spirituality as essentially anything to do with "soul," one of whose "chief functions," he says, using imagery that is reminiscent of Progoff's, is "to transfer material of the outside world into the interior" (p. 204). Working with a metaphor not unlike that of the compost heap, Moore proposes that "just as the mind digests ideas and produces intelligence, the soul feeds on life and digests it, creating wisdom and character out of the fodder of experience" (p. 205). While spirituality may include religion, then, it seems by no means bound to it. In effect, spirituality *transcends* religion.

Spirituality and Narrative

However we define it, spirituality is a narrative endeavor. Key to seeing it in narrative terms is its link with meaning. Atkinson (1995) argues that "everything we encounter as adults that gives us a new and deeper meaning in life is spiritual" (p. xiii). Gerontologist Stephen Weiland (1995) reinforces Atkinson's insight in a somewhat all-embracing definition of spirituality as "the timeless and universal human search for 'meaning' and the desire for 'wholeness' or an integrated self thinking, feeling, and acting in the presence of the 'numinous'" (p. 589). Besides its reference to meaning, Weiland's definition alludes to an assortment of themes that recall our various discussions of a good lifestory, not to mention of autobiographical learning and, in general, of reading our lives. Thus, to approach spiritual aging from a narrative perspective—a perspective that views aging "as narratively complex and open to re-storying" (Holstein & Minkler, 2003, p. 788)—makes eminent sense for a variety of reasons.

For one, telling a story is by nature a spiritual act. Through the dynamics of emplotment and theme, in other words, it represents both the seeking and the finding of meaning, and is predicated upon the conviction that events are connected to one another with intrinsic significance—that life can be "lived and known as a unified whole" (Birkerts, 1994, p. 94). This is especially the case with the kind of deep storytelling, and story-reading, we are envisioning in this book. "Telling our stories is an act of transcending the personal," stresses Atkinson (1995, p. 11), "and entering the realm of the sacred." Stories, he says, "awaken a feeling of wonder and reverence toward life" (p. 11); they "connect us to the soul of life, to its depths and heights" (p. 11). In the view of psychologist Charles Simpkinson and journalist Anne Simpkinson (1993) in their introduction to a collection of essays entitled *Sacred Stories,* "telling one's personal or community story authentically is a religious event" (p. 2). Taking such points further, Bianchi (2005) maintains that all religions are based on "the dreadful and wonderful stories of human existence." Indeed, "religions are more significantly immersed in stories than in philosophical abstractions." Storytelling itself, he claims, "is a spiritual act, a quest for personal meaning at deeper levels" (p. 321). Echoes autobiographer Alfred Kazin (1981), the writing of "personal history is directly an effort to find salvation, to make one's experience come out right" (p. 35). Making this effort becomes particularly imperative, perhaps, in the face of events that drive us to despair. Writes theologian John Shea (1978), "we turn our pain into narrative so we can bear it." In short, "we tell our stories to live" (p. 8).

A second reason that spirituality needs to be approached from a narrative perspective is that, to the extent it has to do with making meaning, what we make meaning from, and through, are ultimately the stories in terms of which we understand our own lives. This observation links spirituality, not just with meaning, but, once again, with memory. We do not practice spirituality in a vacuum. We do not meditate, we do not pray, we do not have mystical awakenings, except in reference, sooner or later, to our own internalized text. In listening to a sermon in a synagogue or church, what moves us most (if anything) is what the speaker's words illuminate about our particular life-situation: how they relate to—how they offer metaphors for—what lies within our personal horizon of understanding. Nor do we ponder theological doctrines or absorb the words of sacred writ in a clean intellectual space abstracted from our peculiar accumulation of memories and experiences. And insofar as the spiritual journey is an inward journey, then what do we get entangled with the moment we embark upon it but our own remembered past, interwoven in infinitely intricate ways (self-wise, other-wise, time-wise) with the present as we interpret it and the future as we anticipate it might be? The inward journey, writes author Richard Stone (1996, p. 204), is "the journey into story"—our story. We make that journey *through* our story, not despite it. It is all we have, all we are. It is not some impediment to be steered around, not a needless complication to somehow be ignored. It is the lens through which we perceive where we are going, the medium in which we move.

This theme runs counter, however, to what some exponents of spirituality would propose. In the opening line of his bestselling book, *The Power of*

Now: A Guide to Spiritual Enlightenment, Eckhart Tolle (1999) asserts, for instance, that "I have little use for the past and rarely think about it" (p. 3). Throughout the book, he urges us to let go, to have "no buildup," of "psychological time" (p. 56). By *psychological time* he means "identification with the past and continuous compulsive projection into the future" (p. 56)—in essence, what we are calling story-time. What is pivotal, he says, is that we "do not unwittingly transform clock time into psychological time" (p. 57). Tolle's philosophy, which he maintains is a "timeless spiritual teaching" and "the essence of all religions" (p. 10), undoubtedly has some merit, especially in light of what we said in Chapter 8 about being imprisoned in dysfunctional versions of our lives. Not only is it too starkly pragmatic, but it renders the notion of lifestory almost irrelevant, much like the advice proffered by the aged shaman Don Juan to anthropologist Carlos Castenada (1975) to "erase all personal history" (p. 30). While, to us, erasure is tantamount to foreclosure, with no sense whatever of memory as biographical capital, to Tolle, such an assessment merely testifies to the tyranny of psychological time, which is fueling the delusion, the striving, the lack of "inner connectedness with Being" (p. 29), he says, that is the curse of the human condition. On the other hand, clock time "includes learning from the past so that we don't repeat the same mistakes over and over" (p. 56). And it involves "setting goals and working toward them." Still, apart from certain practical advantages of a healthy sense of clock time, "the enlightened person's main focus," he insists, "is always the Now" (p. 57). By keeping clear that "the present moment is all you ever have" (p. 58), you "continue to use clock time but are free of psychological time" (p. 57).

Somewhat less ardently, meditation teacher Jon Kabat-Zinn (1994) advances a similar perspective, though one that in an odd way is more compatible with that of narrative development through reading our lives. In a book on "mindfulness meditation" entitled *Wherever You Go, There You Are,* he urges us to awaken "to the fact that our lives unfold only in moments" (p. 4). Alluding to the continuous noticing and nattering that we noted in Chapter 2, he warns that "if we are not fully present for many of those moments, we may not only miss what is most valuable in our lives but also fail to realize the richness and the depth of our possibilities for growth and transformation" (p. 4). All too often, however, "we lock ourselves into a personal fiction that we already know who we are, that we know where we are and where we are going, that we know what is happening." In effect, we narratively foreclose. "All the while," he says, we remain "enshrouded in thoughts, fantasies, and impulses, mostly about the past and about the future, about what we want and like, and what we fear and don't like, which spin out continuously, veiling our direction and the very ground we are standing on" (p. xv).

Setting aside our stories—and story-time—in the way that Tolle advises us is easier said than done, as the majority of therapists would probably agree. And even if possible, it could ultimately be counter-productive. From a narrative perspective, our stories—multilayered and infinitely dense, filled with unsolvable problems and unspecified potential—constitute the fodder on which spirituality feeds. Spirituality is not about brushing those stories aside, for rightly or wrongly, for better or for worse, they are all we have. They are who we are. Instead, it is about looking so deeply *into* our stories that, in effect, we see through them—"see through" in the sense both of understanding by means of them and of recognizing their limits.

A third reason for viewing spiritual aging through narrative lenses is that, with age, comes an inner push toward, not just greater cognitive complexity, but, as we have been seeing, greater narrative complexity, too. If we experience and express our spirituality *through* our stories and not in spite of them, then this increased complexity clearly needs consideration. We need to bear in mind, in other words, what Bruner (1987) calls the "development of autobiography" (p. 15)—which is to say, how our modes of storying our lives—our styles of self-storying—change over time. One manifestation of this increasing complexity is the change that can be traced from childhood to adolescence in our competence at making sense of narrative materials (see Bamberg, 1997). Extending such research into later life, psychologist Giselle Labouvie-Vief (2000) has found that, compared with young adults, older adults "render different readings of stories such as those of fairy tales, myths, and parables." Specifically, they focus more on "the inner and psychological meaning of the information; what it reveals about the general condition of being human" (p. 368). One way of explaining such differences is to say that older adults bring a thicker internal text to the task of deciphering the external one. Also, and in keeping with the sorts of changes to the aging brain that we noted in Chapter 6, older adults work within a broader horizon of self-understanding, tend to make meaning at subtler levels within themselves, and are more open to the metaphorical resonances between the story they experience in the text and the stories by which they understand their own texistence.

In all, the dynamics of spiritual aging cannot be adequately grasped without factoring the narrative variable into our calculations. Whatever else it involves, spirituality is not detached from our narrative development but is integral to it—quite possibly, its zenith. Spiritual aging is about expanding, examining, and transforming our stories so fully that eventually we transcend them. As the transcending of our stories, spirituality, like wisdom, is thus not a product but a process. What is more, if wisdom can be conceived of as meaning-plus, then spirituality can be conceived of as wisdom-plus, with narrative as the constant in each equation.

THE SENSE OF AN ENDING: SUCCESSFUL AGING AND THE NECESSITY OF DEATH

An awareness of the fallibility of knowledge is what marks the beginning of wisdom. Likewise, awareness of our mortality, which can chasten us at any stage, is a spur to spiritual development. "Encountering one's own mortality," writes Bianchi (1996), "is a crucial aspect of spiritual growth" (p. 324). As "going over the top" looms nearer in our sights, to use a euphemism from one of the veterans interviewed by Ronald Blythe (1979, p. 146), it sets in motion profound internal shifts. Not only does it help to push us into post-formal thought, which educator Armin Grams (2001, p. 101) reminds us "requires accommodating ambiguity and uncertainty, irony and contradiction," but it has an impact upon our experience of time itself. Compared with when we were children, time-past is greater than time-future, and growing greater by the day. The question of how best to use the days that remain to us—what Heilbrun (1997) calls "the last gift of time"—can increasingly consume us. In all, the prospect of death presents the profoundest of challenges and, ironically, the greatest of opportunities—when approached, that is, from a narrative perspective.

The Prospect of Death:
Implications from a Narrative Perspective

A central challenge with which death confronts us is how to make it *our* death—in other words, how to assimilate it into the story of our *life*. For death as such is inconceivable. In terms of our story, however, it is in many ways the main event, the one towards which all other events are leading. It is their *telos*, their end. This need not mean that our lifestory is ultimately a tragedy ("all's unwell that ends unwell") but simply that, in the final analysis, a lifestory is just that: a story. Accordingly, it demands an ending, which death, by definition, brings. To the degree that, like a soap opera, a lifestory goes on and on, with no overall conclusion to its multiple plotlines, we could say that it lacks meaning. We need to have "an ending in mind," says Freeman (1997a); otherwise, "there could be no story, but only a series of events, experiences, moments, valued not only for their pleasure or their avoidance of pain" (p. 388). The key, one could argue then, is not to ignore death but, in a sense, to embrace it, even to befriend it. "Learn how to die," says Morrie Schwartz, subject of the book *Tuesdays with Morrie* (Albom, 1997), "and you learn how to live" (p. 83). In many ways, biologically, ecologically, but above all, narratively, death is a necessity. It is as essential to a life—understood in terms of poiesis—as The End is to a novel.

That death is essential to life-as-story does not make accepting it any easier, for it presents us with a paradox, and thus another source of irony. On one level, it is the raison d'être of our story; on another, it is its undoing: the great de-storyer. The mere thought of it can so dominate our narratives, so disrupt them and render them disjointed, that we surrender to narrative foreclosure. Our life is not over, we say somewhere inside us, but our story might as well be. By the same token, the prospect of death can act like any deadline. It can motivate us, get us moving. It can serve as a stimulus to narrative elaboration, creating "new conditions of thoughtfulness, memory, and desire," as Mary Gergen and Kenneth Gergen word it in their reflections on *positive aging*, "that are inaccessible to those oblivious to the passage of time" (2003, p. 223).

Once again, with lifestory, we are inside of things far more radically than we are with literary story. When reading a novel, we are inside of the story in the basic sense that (unless we have read it before) we do not know exactly how it will end. But the end itself has already been put in place by the author, meaning that, as reader, we are really only half inside the story. The author occupies the other half. With lifestory, however, our situation is rather more extreme. We are in the process of composing the story from within it: making it up as we go, knowing *that* it will end, but never quite *how*. How it ends depends in many ways on us. The reader of a novel always knows that how it ends is outside of his or her control, and except in the case of a *Choose Your Own Adventure,* must accept that this is so. As for us, unless we subscribe to a grand master narrative whereby both the timing and the form of our demise is predestined by a higher power, the prospect of death instills in us a measure of responsibility. We have to do something about it. We have to wrap our minds around it. We have to incorporate it into our story in advance, so that we can bear it.

If we think endings are curious entities where life-narratives are concerned, then we have good reason to. In narrative generally, observes literary theorist J. Hillis Miller (1978), "the notion of ending is inherently 'undecidable'" (p. 3). No narrative, he says, "can show either its beginning or its ending." Rather, "it always begins and ends still *in medias res*" (p. 4). To assist us in our thinking here, however, we can invoke a vital distinction: between *ending* and *closure*. A story possessing what narratologist Shlomith

Rimmon-Kenan (1983) considers "the *minimal* requirement" of "temporal succession" (p. 18)—this happened, then this, then this—may have an ending in the sense of the termination of that succession. But it may possess little by way of closure, of some sort of point: some sense of its thrusts and themes converging in a satisfying manner—a manner that *feels* like The End. The story concludes, that is, but we have no "sense of completion" (p. 18).

What differentiates a mere ending from a sense of completion, of course, is not just how the author has written the story but how the reader reads it. Readers with minimal narrative competence may labor their way from start to finish through a work of complex, subtly crafted fiction, yet might experience the events depicted in its final pages as The End only in the sense that they happen to appear on the final pages of the *book*. In other words, they will experience little sense of closure to the *story*. That said, different readers will experience the same text as having different degrees of closure. As literary scholar Ibrahim Taha (1998–99) is right to remind us, the role of the reader "in determining...closure is central and indisputable" (p. 6).

But there is a further distinction to consider: between *closed* closure and *open* closure. Closed closure is what we normally think of as The End. It is characterized, explains Taha, by "well defined...solutions to all the questions and problems" that the story raised (pp. 4–5). Such closure, he says, "leaves no room for more questions. The text is closed since there is nothing to add to it." On the other hand, "open closure" (p. 5)—or what Morson (1994) labels "aperture" (pp. 169–170)—is "the absence of answers and solutions to questions and conflicts" introduced in the story (Taha, 1998–99, p. 5). Given our focus on the challenge that death represents for the middle of lived story, how do we make sense of such insights?

Living in a therapeutic era, we have come to accept that people possess the need for closure when a key chapter in their lives, for instance an intimate relationship, comes suddenly to an end. The conclusion of the relationship without a healthy, or at least bearable, sense of closure is a recipe for discontent. By this, though, is meant closure that is not *too* neat, that leaves room for further reinterpretation, that allows for the mining of meaning that may only become apparent once enough time has elapsed to grieve our loss (if not "heal all wounds") and our horizon of understanding has sufficiently expanded to make sense of it within a broader, more comprehensive context. Overall, however, achieving a sense of closure is a retrospective process, assimilating the loss into our story after the fact—or expanding our story itself in order to encompass it. In facing the end of our life as a whole, and thus our lifestory, the achievement of a comparable sense of closure may be equally important, though yet again, easier said than done. Because we compose our stories from within them, such closure can never be achieved retrospectively, only prospectively.

All autobiographers engage in just such a prospective process insofar as they must determine how to end, not their story as a whole, but their version of it to date. As Bruner reminds us, "no autobiography is completed, only ended" (2002, p. 74). Indeed, most autobiographers end their narratives on a largely positive note, implicitly assuming that the standpoint from which they are writing in the present is more enlightened than any of the standpoints they have occupied in the past. There is a built-in imperative to tell their stories in such a way that everything "comes out right" (Kazin, 1981, p. 35) in the end—or at least promises to. In this respect, autobiographers end up "redeeming" remembered experience, turning bad into better (McAdams, 2006; Brady, 1990). In the less formal type of autobiographical activity that we experience in life review, of course, the same prospective process is at work, inasmuch as one of our implicit tasks is to compile an acceptable ending to our story—which is to say, a generativity script (McAdams, 1996, p. 144). As we saw in Chapter 9, the drive to undertake that task is triggered by the awareness of our mortality, which means, though, that we are in the paradoxical position of trying to read the ending, trying to contextualize it or make some anticipatory sense of it, before it actually arrives. The degree of sense we seek, or with which we can be content, raises intriguing possibilities.

The point of life review, one could argue, is to take a life that, on some level, is "just one damned thing after another," and to transform it into a life*story*—ideally, a good one: with events and circumstances configured in one's mind in a more or less coherent, credible (yet flexible) manner. As we say, however, it's all in the reading. The difference between a mere life and a good lifestory lies in our ability to read. In essence, the better we read, the better our lifestory will grow: the wider, the thicker, the more imbued with meaning. What we would argue here, then, is that the more adept we become at reading our lives, and the thicker we thus experience our texistence, then the more we will envision death, not as mere ending, but as a matter of open closure. Indeed, even in fiction, says Miller (1978), death can be "the most enigmatic, the most open-ended ending of all" (p. 6)—an insight in keeping with Morson's (1994) point about "the very nature of the polyphonic novel": namely, that it makes "an effective ending almost impossible" (p. 162). But not just the polyphonic novel: "No novel," asserts Miller (1978)—above all, no *life*-novel, one could add—"can be unequivocally finished, or for that matter unequivocally unfinished" (p. 7).

Achieving a sense of open closure about one's life will clearly not be every person's goal. Open-endedness, multiplicity of interpretations, sideshadowing, indeterminacy of meaning—such as we experience, for instance, amid dynamic reminiscence—will constitute, for some, a liberating prospect, exhilarating them with "the thrill of narrative freedom" (Gullette, 2004, p. 158). For others, on whom the "burden of open-endedness" (Grams, 2001, p. 110) weighs heavily, it will be nothing short of hell, and will tempt them to capitulate to narrative foreclosure in the effort to escape a "metaphysical agoraphobia," as sociologist Peter Berger (1963) words it, "before the endlessly overlapping horizons of one's possible being" (p. 63). But insofar as openness, and not just coherence or coverage, is a criterion for a good lifestory, then surely helping each other let go of our expectations of closed closure and become comfortable with open closure instead seems a worthwhile thing to do. Indeed, it is the very sort of goal that a life-writing group or reminiscence group is, ideally, positioned to achieve. Here again, however, we come up against a paradox.

Just at that stage in our lives when we might most benefit from the company of others to nudge us toward greater narrative development; to support us in expanding, examining, and transforming our stories; to help us in exploring our lives as we have storied them to date—the more likely it is that our narrative environments will be starting to shrink, often suddenly and dramatically. Loved ones die, friends fall ill, and our social network contracts, due in part to our own deteriorating health and diminishing mobility. Thus the self-reading contexts we have enjoyed in the past can become dangerously impoverished just when we need them to be richest. Furthermore, the friends or family members who remain behind for us may be so habituated to eliciting the same old stories from us—not to mention listening to us in the same old ways (as we may do to them!)—that we become more entrenched than ever in self-narratives that, for numerous reasons, are seriously restricted.

By the same token, when the environments we have lived within across the years, far from being wisdom environments, have fostered foreclosure more than development, then their shrinking, though experienced initially as unfamiliar and unsettling, could eventually feel quite freeing. In her short story, "The Story of an Hour," author Kate Chopin (1894/1996) crystallizes this feeling of freedom in the response of Louise Mallard to the apparent death of her kind and loving husband. Despite her genuine grief, she experiences an overwhelming sense of liberation from the "powerful will bending hers in that blind persistence with which," as Chopin puts it, "men and women believe they have a right to impose a private will upon a fellow creature." "'Free! Body and soul free!'" Louise keeps repeating to herself (p. 13). Not unlike Louise, we, too, can feel that we are free at last to live our way into a more open and fulfilling story. Thus, the loss of listeners may not be a negative at all, but a positive, if those we have been saddled with to date are the antithesis of what we have needed. With their departure, we are beholden no longer to their suffocating versions of our lives.

The Fact of Death: Implications for "Successful Aging"

The prospect of death presents us with the task of assimilating it into our story in a way that enables us to keep living with openness and hope. As such, it can actually be an encourager of spiritual growth. Yet the stark *fact* of death constitutes a stinging challenge to visions of successful aging. Well-known within gerontological circles and frequently talked about outside of them as a goal to which everyone should aspire, the concept was first proposed by gerontologists John Rowe and Robert Kahn as a variation on the broader category of "aging well" (Chapman, 2005). Indeed, their 1998 book, *Successful Aging,* has been described as "perhaps the single most recognized work in recent gerontology" (Holstein & Minkler, 2003, p. 787). Initially offered as a counterbalance to views of aging as inevitable decline, the concept was welcomed for its positive, upbeat spirit and came to be synonymous with the "new gerontology." Three preconditions were seen as necessary for it: the avoidance of disability and disease, the maintenance of high physical and cognitive functioning, and "sustained engagement with life" (p. 789). In particular, the combination of all three "represents the concept of successful aging most fully" (Rowe & Kahn, 1998, p. 39).

Aging well, in general, is something every gerontologist is naturally eager to promote. While the *poetics* of aging is our own way of envisioning what it entails, there are any number of other worthy concepts, too: positive aging (Gergen & Gergen, 2003), robust aging (Garfein & Herzog, 1995), graceful aging (Weil, 2005), and even adventurous aging (Kahana & Kahana, 1983) being but a few. Successful aging, however, plus the entire paradigm associated with it, carries connotations that merit some critique. In Holstein and Minkler's (2003) diplomatic way of expressing it, "the successful aging model and its publicity are problematic" (p. 789). As Cohen notes (2005), it focuses on "minimizing decline rather than recognizing the huge potential for positive growth in later life" (pp. xxxii–xxxiii).

On the surface, of course, it seems like such a sound idea. Who among us does not wish to age as successfully as we can—physically, cognitively, emotionally, socially, financially? How better to counter the narrative of decline? Yet there is a naïveté about the notion that undermines its currency, exposing it to multiple charges: that it smacks of elitism, for example; that it typifies societal values that privilege youth over age; that it apes the happily-ever-after storylines with which Hollywood has been beguiling us for years. Witness the images of vibrant, affluent, young-old couples that grace the pages of the average seniors' magazine. Related criticisms are that it reflects modernity's belief in unlimited progress and downplays how much our individual fates are constructed and constrained by larger social forces. To the extent it is "attained through individual choice and effort" (Rowe & Kahn, 1998, p. 37), it has an oppressive dimension to it, too, laying an undue responsibility on the individual by implicitly construing experiences of suffering or loss, disease or dysfunction, or anything short of healthy active living, as testament to personal failure. Holstein and Minkler (2003) have been correct, therefore, to critique "successful aging"—in their case, from the perspective of feminist and critical gerontology—for the not-so-subtle assumption that it is the norm against which lives should be judged.

From the perspective we are developing here, which seeks to plot a course between decline on one hand and success on the other, successful aging can be critiqued for how, at bottom, it ignores the fact of death. At the risk of sounding naïve ourselves, none of us can possibly age "successfully" inasmuch as, no matter how healthy or engaged we may remain, no matter how "anti-aging" we may be, sooner or later we die. In the final analysis, we all fail at life. "We are all vulnerable to chronic disease and death," writes Cole (1992, p. 239), making death, in effect, "our ultimate defeat" (Munitz, 1968, p. 263). "Once accepted" though, says Cole (1992), this very vulnerability "can become the existential ground for compassion, solidarity, and spiritual growth" (p. 23). Certainly, from a narrative perspective, death deserves a more positive spin. Indeed, it is not a problem so much as an opportunity. Just as there is no plot without conflict and no tale without trouble, so death is an aesthetic necessity. It may be the nemesis of successful aging, in other words, but it is the *telos* of poetic aging—especially when The End we are preparing for, through reading our lives as deeply as we can, involves closure that is open, not closed.

MASTER NARRATIVES AND SACRED STORIES: BLESSING OR CURSE?

The stereotype is that we grow more religious as we age. We become more diligent about religious observances and keener to reconnect with the beliefs and traditions that shaped us in our youth—all the better to prepare ourselves for death and whatever lies beyond it. Whether or not the stereotype is valid, surely a religion, any religion, is an archetypal example of a master narrative. At the same time, as we have implied several times already, it can be the arch-enemy of personal growth and the enforcer of foreclosure. "Stories are wondrous things," cautions author Thomas King (2003), reflecting on the power of such narratives in our lives, "and they are dangerous" (p. 9). It is this dual role of religion and other ideologies—as wonder and danger, blessing and curse—when it comes to personal development that we need to look at now.

Master Narratives

Master narratives run the gamut from the sacred to the secular. At one end, of course, are long-standing world religions, such as Judaism or Islam, Hinduism or Buddhism, which have structured entire cultures in incalculable ways, plus any number of more ancient or indigenous traditions. Within these intricate and venerable interpretive environments, what constitutes correct conduct and right belief is more or less explicitly prescribed by means of a complex system of rituals, creeds, and texts. From legends to parables, histories to biographies, and sagas to dreams, these texts, in turn, are intricate collages of narrative material, some of which we cling to so closely, in fact, that we interpret our own self-story in terms of it, a point whose implications proponents of "narrative theology" have duly explored (see Hauerwas & Jones, 1989; Cupitt, 1991; Goldberg, 1991; Brockelman, 1992). And there are infinite variations on how such prescriptions are lived, with the bewildering array of Christian sects alone being sobering reminders, along with the bickering and wrangling to which such variations lead.

At the other end are more secular master narratives, though not infrequently these are well entwined with explicitly religious ones, too. But in their own right, they provide structure and direction for individuals and cultures alike. Communism is a clear case in point. Depending on the country or the era, it has been embraced with just as much zeal as any religion ever has, and subjected to a comparable range of variations. Less obviously perhaps, capitalism has also served as a master narrative in people's lives; indeed, it holds whole cultures in its thrall. For many, science itself supplies an all-inclusive story by which to comprehend the universe and their place within it. Modernity as a whole, it may be claimed, has acted as a master narrative: "a story to end all stories," as theologian Paul Brockelman (1992, p. 83) proposes. For many, postmodernism—or indeed any "ism"—does much the same, whether for better or for worse.

To focus on religion specifically, however, the excesses of grand master narratives are eminently documented in the annals of history: the unholy alliances with sexism and racism, and the rancor and violence, the ignorance and arrogance, in which such alliances have issued; the subjugation of countless lives, not to mention other worthy narratives (King, 2003); and the consequent extinction of untold potential for creativity and love. There is scant need to recite such folly here. To shift to the positive side of the ledger, however, or the blessing side, such narratives address the need for "deep stories" (Rigney, 2001), for "deep reservoirs" (Holstein & Gubrium, 2000) of meaning and knowing and wisdom. They appeal to our appetite for ways of "plumbing life to its depths," for getting at "surplus meanings" (Brockelman, 1992, p. 105). They address "a desire to partake of stories and of modes of relatedness that take us out of ourselves and into something larger and more sacred" (Freeman, 1998, p. 46). In short, they are vehicles of transcendence.

Master narratives provide us with a place to be, an overarching framework within which to understand where we have come from, where we are going, and how we should act in the interim. They also mediate a sense of the Divine, which some of us may experience as nothing less than the central character (if not Author) of our individual narratives. As narrative environments on a grand scale, they supply a set of ready-made meaning-perspectives, of symbol systems, of interpretive metaphors and guiding myths—of super-myths—with which to formulate and evaluate our personal and communal ones. They provide us with ways to "ward off chaos" (Brockelman, 1992, p. 105) through their theories on the human condition and their templates for reading our world from beginning to end. They offer a built-in sense of closure that is more or less open, depending on how they balance free will with determinism, or on the degree to which they endorse the notion that our life's events are "meant to be." Thus, they tell us what death is, too, equipping us with images by which to envisage it and, ideally, give us hope: a long sleep, a transition into limbo (or another life), a journey down a tunnel toward a Being of light. They instruct us in how to tame death, how to render it coherent. They place it in a vaster context, linking our personal fate to that of the cosmos as a whole. For the devout Christian, for example, one's death cannot be comprehended except in relation to the resurrection, the final judgement, and the life everlasting in a heaven or a hell.

The point is: even though we pray, believe, or meditate through, and not despite, our own stories, these stories themselves are constructed and interpreted in terms of the grander narratives with which we most identify. Explicitly or otherwise, these narratives tutor us in how to read our lives—in a way that is analogous, one might argue, to what happens in reading a novel. In other words, we never read a novel on its own terms entirely, but in terms of assumptions we have internalized from the culture around us—and from reading other novels—about what counts as narrative coherence, as literary merit, and ultimately as "truth."

Sacred Stories

Master narratives can be discussed in relationship to the concept of *sacred stories*, though the relationship is admittedly ambiguous, as it is in the case of religion and spirituality or knowledge and wisdom. To take an example, Christianity in general, one could say, is a grand master narrative, one with a multitude of manifestations: all the councils and creeds, the bureaucracies and budgets, the rituals and relics, plus the pulpits, pews, and steeples of the actual buildings in which its millions of adherents have worshipped. Yet the sacred story at the heart of it all may be quite another matter; indeed, the two may often be in tension. What is at issue is the relationship of form to content, of carrier to cargo. If the master narrative is the husk, in other words, then the sacred story is the seed—the "story within the story," as Stephen Crites (1971, p. 69) expresses it. As such, it possesses massive power. Using the term in a way that takes in "African, Native American, and other indigenous cultures," Simpkinson and Simpkinson (1993, p. 2) insist that "sacred stories move us"; they compel us to think about "what is important." "Through symbol and metaphor," that is, "they communicate...deep truths about the mysteries of life...they change us and bring us closer together" (p. 1). In a seminal essay on the bond between narrative and experience, Crites (1971) reflects further for us on what such stories are and do.

Sacred stories, and the "symbolic worlds they project," he says, are not simply "monuments" that people can objectively perceive. Rather, they are "dwelling-places" (p. 70) that "orient the life of people through time, their life-time." As such, they "lie too deep in the consciousness" to be explicitly articulated (p. 69). They become internalized so integrally inside of us that—to draw on the model we proposed in Chapter 2—they are inseparable from the editorial agendas by which we navigate our worlds, and by which much of our nattering and noticing is sure to be guided. In other words, people do not invent sacred stories for themselves: they "awaken" to them (p. 71). A sacred story is not consciously created, he says, but "forms the very consciousness that projects a total world horizon" and determines the "intentions by which actions are projected into that world" (p. 71). A good example of such a story—believed in so deeply by so many, in fact, that it is assumed to be the way things are—is one that McAdams (2006) discusses in his book, *The Redemptive Self: Stories Americans Live By*. For him, the fundamentally optimistic story by which many Americans tend to live their lives, in particular the "highly generative" ones, derives its power from a quasi-Christian narrative of "manifest destiny" as the "chosen people" (p. 12)—a narrative by which, as a nation, America sees itself guided: in short, a *civil* religion, according to which "God is on our side."

Crites's point, in any case, is that we only recognize the sacred story by which we have been living as exactly that—the story by which we have been living—when, for reasons which we intuit long before we can consciously define them, it becomes problematic for us. It becomes constraining and small. As one would say in the context of narrative therapy, it no longer fits our lived experience. Again, for many Americans perhaps, the horror of Pearl Harbor or the shock of September 11th had precisely this impact upon the story that, previously, they had taken for granted. Yet regardless of cultural context, as such a shake-up happens, we begin to step back from the story in order to take a better look; indeed, from the entire "bundle of stories" (Cupitt, 1991, p. 153)—family, nation, culture—with which it is intertwined inside us.

Shifting Stories

Disaffection from the sacred story we have hitherto been living by need not mean that we are ready to live with no such story at all, simply that we are disillusioned with the master narrative by which it has been conveyed—or, as the case may be, either watered down or overwhelmed. For there is always the risk that the master narrative will eclipse its sacred story and set itself up as the be-all and end-all for reading our lives. The history of religious revivals reveals this tendency all too clearly, with reformer after reformer, from Jesus to Martin Luther (in the case of Christianity) calling for followers to repent of their addiction to tradition and to return to the "true" faith, a faith that is alive and growing. Insofar as it is impossible to live without some sense of the larger story of the world in general—even a story that tells of chaos and cosmic incoherence—we basically exchange one sacred story for another, ideally a more expansive one, one that enables us to grow. But as Crites implies, this exchange is not typically effected in an open, conscious manner. More likely, it is the result of groping in the dark until we reach the realization that we are in a new place, living by a new story, as ineffable or unsettling as its newness could well be.

Theologian Thomas Berry has devoted much of his own work to understanding and encouraging the shift from one sacred story to another. In a 1987 article entitled "The New Story," he acknowledges the sense of strangeness that can accompany the shift, on a global scale, from modernity to postmodernity—a shift that implicates not just religion but politics as well, and, considering the environmental crisis that even then was looming, science too. "We are in trouble just now," Berry says, "because we do not have a good story." Indeed, "we are in-between stories" (p. 187)—a state that is as true today perhaps as it was 30 years ago. The Old Story, "the account of how the world came to be and how we fit into it," he says, provided us with the security of knowing who we were. The problem, however, is that even though many people still believe in it and live by it, this *zeitgeist*, this story, "is not functioning properly…in its larger social dimensions " (p. 187). By the same token, "we have not learned the New Story" (p. 187). What this "new story" is, of course, cannot be readily stated, not only because it is vast—embracing religion, science, and culture—but because, like a lifestory, we live our lives inside of it. Nonetheless, along with cosmologist Brian Swimme, Berry has tried to articulate a version of it under the title *The Universe Story* (Swimme & Berry, 1992).

Simplistic though it sounds, the distinction between *old story* and *new story* provides a framework for understanding the distrust of organized religion that many currently feel. Our frustration is not necessarily with spirituality as such. In fact, just the opposite may be the case. It reflects a hunger for a spirituality that is more authentic, that is not hemmed in by the totalizing claims and often antiquated worldviews of traditional faiths. It reflects a hunger for a sacred story that is not imprisoned in a master narrative: a sacred story that (like a good *lifestory*) is coherent and open, differentiated and generative, that permits us to draw more eclectically, and with greater individual authority (with the onus on us, so to speak), from the deep reservoirs of meaning by which we have been shaped so far. By this we mean a story that gives us room to breathe, that encourages us to grow, that does not impose foreclosure by stringently insisting on how to read our lives, but invites development instead—a story that allows us to experience the sacred sides of our own stories, too.

This need not entail cutting ourselves off from master narratives entirely, for human life abhors a narrative vacuum. Without our even realizing it, alternative narratives will soon step forward to fill the space left vacant by those that we reject. This happens quite explicitly, in fact, and perhaps appropriately, when writers such as Thomas Moore (1992), James Hillman (1989), Rollo May (1991), Joseph Campbell (1988), or Jean Shinoda Bolen (1984, 1989) encourage us to borrow from the myths of ancient Greece, of the Near East and Far East alike, to frame our present-day dilemmas. But even if we stay with those grand stories with which we are most familiar, it means revising our relationship toward them. It means experiencing them, not as closed works, but as open texts. It means understanding them, not as Truth that must be accepted as a monolithic system, but as rich arrays of images and metaphors, symbols and dreams, parables and poems, for interpreting our worlds. It means seeing them as boundless resources, not just for answering our questions, but—more important, perhaps—for questioning our answers, thus keeping us alive to mystery. It means shifting from reading those narratives in a naïve, uncritical, or efferent manner—as if they were, literally, our master—to reading them in a mindful and aesthetic one.

Operating out of very much an affirmative postmodern perspective, theologian William Beardslee (1990) shares the hope that we are seeking to articulate. Recognizing that master narratives are ultimately that—narratives—and not the "rigid, imprisoning structures" we might experience them to be, permits us, he says, to "relate to them, indeed stand in them, as our own stories." To do this, though, we must investigate the stories themselves for "hints or elements of self-transformation" (p. 173). Essentially, Beardslee is inviting us to view such stories from an ironic stance: to see them—and see through them—not as inflexible givens, but as "astonishing resources" (p. 173). This would mean that we "reimagine the fundamental story as an open one" that lacks the "closure of a final ending" and can incorporate the "many small endings of the substories within which we live and which we are" (p. 173). Controversial theologian Matthew Fox (2000) proposes just such a reimagining, in fact, with his argument that Christianity take as its starting point the doctrine, not of original sin, but of "original blessing." Such a shift in focus releases an entirely different set of possibilities for personal and cultural growth.

Without the capacity to reimagine our religion, we are doomed to be dominated by it. "Religion that is not reflectively aware of its own fictionality," warns post-Christian theologian Don Cupitt (1991), "quickly becomes too serious and therefore clumsy, violent, and oppressive" (p. 130). Making the point another way is Prickett (2002), who stresses "the fundamental irony at the center of all narratives" (p. 258). "Crucial to how we understand any narrative," he says, "whether of literature, art, music, history, mathematics, science, or religion" is "the difference between passively absorbing" it and "questioning, puzzling over it, interpreting it" (p. 262).

The sort of shift that Beardslee envisions, and that both Cupitt and Prickett are implying, is more discernible than we might think in the ways that many older adults actually experience their religion. As an extension of the greater cognitive complexity and tolerance of ambiguity that tends to accompany aging anyway, many of them, though identifying with the same master narrative as all along, may relate to it less slavishly than they did in the past, assuming a "take it or leave it" attitude toward specific aspects of it and feeling less obliged to accept the whole of it as one complete package. As Bianchi (2005) expresses it, based on his interviews with what he calls "creative elders," such individuals are "willing to say 'yes' and 'no' to teachings received from their traditions" (p. 328). They experience their religion less as an established institution that must be met with blind obedience than as their spiritual home, an environment to be lived in, and loved, with all its oddities and conflicts, deficiencies and faults.

In a qualitative study involving lifestory interviews with 30 women between the ages of 60 and 80, all of whom were members of an interdenominational lay group called the Grail, gerontologist Mary O'Brien (1996) found, for instance, that most of them distinguished "between religion and spirituality" (p. 6). Spirituality, they described as "more inclusive, more encompassing, than religion." Religion, even though it "had given spirituality a form" for them, they tended to view as "too confining." For many, in fact, religion had become "exclusive," a "barrier to spiritual growth" (p. 6). In listening to these women's narratives, O'Brien became aware of how, in addition to the greater "breadth and intensity" that was facilitated both by current "theological interpretations" and "new movements in church and society," aging itself, it seems, had led them to an "openness to diversity in content and expressions of spirituality," an openness that "transcended traditional religious forms" (p. 6). Such findings have led O'Brien, like Bianchi, to an increasing conviction concerning, once again, the intrinsic "spirituality of aging" (pp. 8–9).

THE MYSTERY IN MY STORY:
LIVES AS SACRED TEXTS

If master narratives are experienced not as imprisoning—indeed destorying—structures, but as "astonishing resources" for human growth (Beardslee, 1990, p. 173), then we are free to appreciate what a student once intriguingly referred to as "the mystery in my story." Inklings of our stories as *sacred* stories feature in the thinking of several of the authors we have cited thus far: Progoff (1995), for certain, but also Moore (1992) with his talk of soul, Atkinson (1995) with his sense of "our own stories as sacred" (pp. 29–30), McAdams (1993) with his concept of *lifestory* as evolving myth, and Charmé (1984) with his view of a life as "a sacred text" (p. 53).

No less than spirituality, of course, sacred is a loaded word, both as adjective and as noun (*the* sacred). Leaving aside the issue, though, of exact definition, the possibility we would offer here is that sacred can be understood along literary lines. We are, after all, talking about lifestory. Accordingly, the sacred is that element of any literary work whereby, as readers, we enter so fully into its story-world, and into the emotions and insights and the sense of meaning or truth that it evokes in us, that the work points well beyond itself. It is self-transcendent. Thus, the greater the story—or more precisely, the more deeply we read it—then the more parabolic the story will become. In that sense, that *secular* sense, it will be more sacred.

Parable Again

We broached the topic of parabolic thought back in Chapter 2 when discussing Turner's (1996) theory of "the literary mind." For Turner, what is normally called thinking involves the continual formation of "small stories" (p. 12) to make sense of events in our lives at the most basic levels of consciousness. The metaphorical projection of one such story onto another is what Turner means by *parable*. With the aid of it, we can formulate abstractions of countless types; indeed, we can think. As such, parable is "a fundamental instrument of the mind" (p. 5). More commonly, though, parable is understood as a genre of narrative that performs a primarily pedagogical function. A parable is a teaching story. As an extended metaphor, it instructs through indirect communication, or by showing more than telling. Referring to "the philosophical parable" that someone such as Kierkegaard employed, Morson (1994) explains what it entails: "a philosophical question is rendered through a brief narrative in which plot and question interweave in complex ways." By means of "a combination of strong formal closure and philosophical openness," he says, "this form enriches our sense of the issues without providing a definitive answer" (p. 228). In short, it gets us thinking. The novels of Franz Kafka are prime examples, but so are those of Sartre. Relevant, too, is the work of many others—including Socrates, when one considers his allegory of the cave (Plato, 360 BCE/1941, pp. 227–235). Naturally, one thinks of religion: the parables of the Sufis or of Jesus being obvious cases. For eons, moreover, elders in aboriginal traditions have employed stories parabolically, to impart advice in an enigmatic manner, not telling their listeners, straight out, how they ought to live their lives but allowing them the space to figure things out on their own (see King, 2003).

In a comparable vein, hypnotherapist Milton Erickson (Rosen, 1982) made use of "teaching tales" drawn from his own life experience (p. 20) to liberate his patients from "well-established circular patterns of thought"— i.e., interpretive parsimony—and help them become "aware of new possibilities" (p. 29). Sometimes the stories were "aimed at adding...positive input," and sometimes, they were calculated "to stir up and bring to awareness feelings of deadness, feelings of being stuck, or feelings of lack of authenticity" (p. 30). Through telling such tales, Erickson's goal was to help his patients tap into their own "unconscious resources" and to provide them with "emotional and intellectual sustenance" (p. 30; see also Coles, 1989). Indeed, bibliotherapy in general, one could fairly claim, relies on literature's parabolic power. Certainly, the stories we love the best are all too often those that have most shaken us or stretched us, whose characters have served as metaphors for our own selves and whose themes are variations on the ones that rumble through our lives, too.

The force that parables can wield ranges from the subtle to the abrupt, and the gradual to the dramatic. Presented with one, we undergo a shift in perception—a shift in stories: an awakening that is more or less rude, and with it, a shift in our behavior. In the words of Kierkegaard scholar Thomas Oden (1978), we are "taken unawares into potentially new levels of insight" (p. xii). In miniature, a parable impels us through the entire set of stages that we talked about in Chapter 6. We enter it with one set of convictions about what is real or true, only to exit with those convictions challenged and transformed. However short-lived that transformation might seem, the old is rendered new and the familiar made strange.

A parable is a story that deliberately disrupts the stories by which we live, puncturing our horizon of understanding, and laying us open to fresh meaning-perspectives, fresh ways of being in the world. Parables, writes biblical scholar John Dominic Crossan (1975), "are stories which shatter the deep structure of our accepted world and thereby render clear and evident to us the relativity of story itself" (p. 122). Parable, he argues, "is story grown self-conscious and self-critical" (p. 57). As such, it serves "an epistemology of *loss*." Its value, "as knowledge," he insists, "is to enhance our 'consciousness of ignorance'" (p. 77)—to enhance our wisdom, we could add. It is therefore the ironic genre of narrative par excellence. "We do not interpret the parable," observes theologian Sallie TeSelle (1975); "the parable interprets us" (p. 71). This leads us to the parabolic possibilities inherent in the narratives by which we understand our own lives.

Lifestories as Parabolic

The first way in which our own lifestory is parabolic—in other words, the story we live, the story by which we know ourselves, the story that we show far more than we can ever tell—is that it is an extended metaphor for our life itself. In turn, a memoir or autobiography is a metaphor for our story, which makes it doubly parabolic. An autobiography, that is, is clearly not the life, or the self, it is supposedly about. "We cannot look at the self directly," TeSelle (1975) reminds us, "for like mercury it squirts away from our sight" (p. 149).

As parable, autobiography "points to the self elliptically" (p. 145). One could go even further, however, and assert that it is not even the self itself to which an autobiography points elliptically, but only the self-story. A single volume of 200 to 300 pages cannot possibly recount the evolving myth that, ever-changingly, swirls inside our heads as *us*. Of necessity, it is a selection, a distillation, an interpretation, not only of our life as such, but also of the story by which we experience it. In short, it is a story of a story of a life.

Secondly, if our lifestories are parabolic in the sense of being condensed, severely edited versions of our lives themselves, and doubly so in the case of our autobiography, then they are parabolic in an opposite sense as well. There is more within them—more puzzles, more issues, more insights, more meanings—than we can ever fully mine. Hampl's (1999) reflections on her first piano lesson and Freeman's (2002c) on the drive home with his father are classic illustrations. Theoretically, any one of our own memories carries with it a comparable potential, something we realize the more deeply we penetrate the thicket of the past: the more we examine our stories through dynamic reminiscence, through multiple drafts, through metaphorical suggestion, through reading them in an assortment of interpretive contexts. Taken episode by episode, period by period, our lifestories overall, therefore, are fathomless reservoirs of meaning. Like the best of stories everywhere, not only do they "work" on countless levels but they mediate a kind of intra-textual eternity, inasmuch as there is, literally, no limit to what we can yield from them. We abound in biographical capital. We sit atop a gold mine, a "treasure house of memories" (Rilke, 1986, p. 8).

The limitlessness of our lives-as-texts could easily overwhelm us—as indeed, it should. Like the parables of Kierkegaard or Kafka, the Sufi Master or the Zen Master, our lives inspire, and require, continuing reflection. They thus invite perpetual discovery. "Listened to" in the ways that Hampl's (1999, p. 31) work displays, there is always something more that we can learn from them: about ourselves and, beyond ourselves, about our world. In short, in the heart of our own lifestories, truth awaits us: not historical or technical truth but textual-aesthetic truth, the kind that refuses to be nailed down. "A long life," confesses Scott-Maxwell (1968), "makes me feel nearer truth, but it won't go into words, so how can I convey it?" (p. 142). Such a sense of "truth," she suggests, "old people want…more than anything else" (p. 87)—the sort of truth, perhaps, that epitomizes the so-called late-life style of many creative artists: "something simple, intimate, vulnerable, something intensely emotional, and personal, not hiding anything and yet reaching finally beyond the self" (Friedan, 1993, p. 124). It is such truth that the dying may crave as well, from their friends, their families, themselves: "the truth of who you are," as palliative care physician David Kuhl expresses it (2002, p. 179; see also Albom, 1997; Kuhl & Westwood, 2001).

Despite postmodern misgivings with the very concept, truth is precisely what we often look to literature to inspire: some experience of epiphany, of "life heightened and its deepest mystery probed" (Dillard, 1989, p. 72). And it is this same type of truth of which our own lifestories, as parables, can be the medium. Bearing in mind that the good story points beyond itself, surely all of us have entertained the hope that, in the end, our own life-narrative holds some significance that sets it, and us, apart; that it stands for something; that, because of it, we shall have made a distinct impression on the world through the lessons learned and questions raised to which it alone bears witness. To suggest that our lives, as stories, might be said to "stand for" something, though, is to suggest that, with all their ups and downs, they serve as teaching tales—not just when we are eulogized in death but even while we are still alive and others are edified by their perception of what we have experienced or endured. In effect, our life becomes a metaphor and our story is transformed—in their minds and, in rare moments, even in our own—from *our* story to everyone's story.

A third way our stories are parabolic is that, in the final analysis, we do not know how to read them, let alone tell them. Even in writing them, we face an enormous challenge if we wish to do justice to their complexity. "Where does one even begin?" is the question. In the end, our stories are greater than we are, as the greatest stories always are. They are forever outstripping us, just as our day-to-day existence is continually exceeding our ability to emplot it, to sort it out, even just to notice it. To put it simply, "we all have more existence than we can possibly experience and more experience than we can possibly express" (Randall, 1995, p. 283). As we have hinted at different points already, there is a sense, moreover, in which, like literary stories, our lifestories teach us how to read them—as we endeavor to attend to them in depth and to enlarge our horizons enough to appreciate them fully, which of course we never can. They are smarter than we are, as a parable is smarter than those who hear it—maybe even than the one who tells it—or as a novel is smarter than the one who writes it. "Great novels," notes novelist Milan Kundera (1988), "are always a little more intelligent than their authors" (p. 158).

Understood as parables, our lifestories hold meanings that, no matter how deeply we seek to make sense of them, we lack the time and perhaps the (narrative) intelligence to adequately mine. In fact, the majority of us scarcely skim the surface of our stories. We take them with us to our graves, barely read at all. "The greatest stories," says one source, "lie under cemetery stones or have turned to dust or sand" (Surmelian, 1969, p. 92). Not only this, but the more deeply we *are* able to read them, the more they will still exceed us, revealing themselves as even stranger than when we first began expanding them, with passages that we not only "lived through naïvely" (Charmé, 1984, p. 32) at the time, but that persist in puzzling us to the end. "There is nothing I am quite sure about," confesses Carl Jung (1961) at the conclusion of his autobiography, capturing the sense of open closure—of identity moratorium, in fact—to which such puzzlement attests; "I have no definite convictions—not about anything, really" (p. 358). "I never understood myself less," echoes Scott-Maxwell (1968, p. 125). In the end, every text illuminates the limitations of its reader. We all fail at reading; we all under-read our lives. Narratively speaking, we are all—to some degree, in some respects—foreclosed. We are correct, then, to be humbled by our stories, not just because they are greater than we are, but because, ultimately, they bear the seeds of their own transcendence. "Every seed," Scott-Maxwell (1968) notes, "destroys its container or else there would be no fruition" (p. 65). "Is life a pregnancy?" she goes on to wonder. If so, "that would make death a birth" (p. 76).

In becoming ever more attuned to the complexities of our story, we are confronted with the boundaries of our own self-knowing. In the light of the shadow of death, we see through our selves, and more deeply into the complex world in which those selves have been composed. As our ironic stance thus intensifies, we move beyond unwavering belief in our own evolving myth to catch a vision of what may be the "highest stage" of all in our development— not "ego integration," but "ego-transcendence" (Moody, 1995, p. 92).

LETTING OUR STORIES GO: FROM GEROTRANSCENDENCE TO TRANSCENDENT MOMENTS

Sooner or later, a story must end. With a novel or a movie, this is all too obvious. But even soap operas do not go on forever—including those it can seem we are living! Network priorities change, ratings plummet, and a thrilling conclusion must somehow be contrived. Characters are killed off or married off, and the various plotlines are hustled toward some form of resolution. In the end, all stories make themselves obsolete. They de-compose themselves. Their message is conveyed (if not received), their moral is imparted, and their potential for meaning—our sense of which accelerates as we near The End—reverberates ever more faintly in our minds. Gradually, they release us from their spell, and we in turn relinquish them, reverting to a state of relative storyless-ness until we can crawl inside of yet another one (or the same one at a later stage) and start the process all again.

Sooner or later, says Birkerts (1994, p. 104), "we outgrow the book." But the same may be said of the proverbial book of life, the text that is us, the novel that we are. Outgrowing our stories and preparing to let them go—which, at some point, we do with many of our memories anyway (Pennebaker, 1990); which life review, ideally, prepares us for; and which, in his own way, Tolle (1999) is urging when he warns against building up "psychological time" (p. 56)—this is the experience we need to ponder now.

Gerotranscendence

We are continually undergoing perspective transformations, great or small, all life long: outgrowing old versions of specific events, or of our selves as a whole; expanding our horizons; experimenting, consciously or otherwise, with alternative frameworks for making meaning, as we move from one self-reading context to another. In itself, then, transcending our stories is not the province of later life alone. We do it all the time. Yet, there is increasingly an "inner push" toward it (Cohen, 2005, p. 75), one could argue, as we age. For such reasons, the theory of *gerotranscendence* merits our attention.

Gerontologist Lars Tornstam, who originated the term, proposes that with age, we experience a growing measure of transcendence (1994, 1996). Indeed, he sees gerotranscendence as the expression of an "intrinsic drive," as a "late stage in a natural process toward maturation and wisdom" (1996, p. 38). Transcendence, as such, he refrains from defining, although he uses the term in its accepted sense of "the ability to rise and go beyond" (Pearce, 2002, p. 1). By *gerotranscendence*, however, he means "a shift in meta-perspective, from a materialistic and rational vision to a more cosmic and transcendent one, accompanied by an increase in life satisfaction" (Tornstam, 1996, p. 38). This shift, toward what Coleman and O'Hanlon (2004) call "an altered state of consciousness" (p. 41), entails a Zen-like (Tornstam, 1994, p. 207) transformation in our perception of certain overriding boundaries: between past and present, life and death, self and other. In effect, the self is redefined. We become less self-centered, and less interested in "material things" and "superfluous social interaction." Our "fear of death decreases," while our "affinity with past, present, and coming generations increases." Overall, an awareness takes shape within us that, in the last analysis, we are "part of a flow of energy" that is "coursing through the universe" (Tornstam, 1994, p. 209).

Where successful aging was a counter-story aimed at resisting stereotypes of aging as a matter of inevitable decline, gerotranscendence emerged from Tornstam's belief that "something was lost when the old theory of disengagement was refuted" (1996, p. 39). In short, it represents a way of saving the baby from the bathwater, of putting a positive spin on the increasing "inner-orientation" that some would say comes naturally with age (Neugarten, 1968), and the transition to "passive mastery" that researchers such as David Gutmann (1976) have identified. At bottom, says Tornstam, we have been studying old age with a positivist paradigm that overemphasizes "continuity and 'activity'" (1994, p. 204) and views any sign of "withdrawal" or any preference for "solitary meditation" as a "negative disengagement, or breakdown, or syndrome" (p. 204). Such a paradigm, he says, "older adults themselves no longer inhabit" (p. 204).

For Reker and Chamberlain (2000), who see gerotranscendence as having "much in common with the construct of existential meaning and existential meaning-making" (p. 202), it "shows promise as an overarching theory of life-span development, particularly as it applies to the later years of life" (p. 202). We agree. Yet it is not without its detractors. Skeptics focus, not only on its weak empirical support, but on its totalizing claims: its not-so-implicit assumption that it is a universal process that, sooner or later, all of us experience (Tornstam, 1994, p. 212). Accordingly, it appears to bill itself as a "meta-theory" of aging (Thorson, 1998, p. 172), a master narrative of its own. Like successful aging, it can be criticized as well for downplaying the contextual complexity (physical, cultural, gendered) of the experience of aging, and for overlooking the diversity of approaches that real people take to getting old.

Such criticisms have their place. No one story of aging fits all, including a narrative one. Still, the transcending trend—regarding past–future, self–other, life–death—can also be viewed as a function of our being storying creatures living storied lives. In other words, as we factor the narrative variable into our thinking, several insights that undergird gerotranscendence are, conceivably, reinforced. Furthermore, whether or not such transcending happens universally with age, surely *moments* of transcendence can be experienced at any age, a possibility we will look at very soon. Before we do so, though, certain points of compatibility can be identified between a narrative perspective and aspects of aging—for many at least—that gerotranscendence tries to take account of, beginning with our changing relationship to time.

In the midst of daily life, we experience time less in a linear manner than in a manner we are familiar with when following a story. Life-time is essentially story-time. As happens in reading a novel, its three main modes continually intermingle. We interpret the past through the lenses of present priorities in the light of whatever futures we fancy will unfold, and vice versa. In the act of reminiscence, especially the integrative and dynamic types of it, the boundaries among these modes are equally blurred. Tasting some of the presentness of the past, we can entertain alternative interpretations of it, which in turn empowers us to deal with its "unresolved issues" (Pennebaker, 1990, p. 100) and, eventually, let it go. In expanding, examining, and transforming our stories, we release ourselves, little by little, from their spell.

The prospect of The End itself only intensifies this intertwining of time's main tenses. In reading a novel, we strain to feel the impact, not just of the particular sentence or scene we are in the middle of right now, but, more and more, of the story as a whole, from beginning to end—and beyond. The same basic process occurs in the middle of our own lifestory, as its end comes more clearly into view. There is a seeking to see it in its entirety, and to assess it, too—ideally, to achieve some sense of satisfaction concerning it. To the degree we have "possessed" all that we "have been and done" and have "accept[ed] the task of living our individual fate," to use Scott-Maxwell's (1968, p. 28) language; to the degree we have made sense of as much of our life as we are able—then we are freed to live more fully "in the center of the moment" (Waxman, 1997), more aware of our stories in all their mystery and their depth and yet, for that same reason, less wedded to them.

Generativity

Concerning the boundary between self and other, which for its part is tied to the boundaries of time itself, we have also seen how closely our lives are linked with those of others. While broadly true that, in Western cultures, oral autobiographies are concerned with the individual self, whereas in Eastern cultures, they are more concerned with "community and relationships" (Fivush, 2004, pp. 76–77), such differences are placed in perspective when we look at lives through storied lenses. As narratives, our lives are intrinsically entwined with the narratives of others through a multitude of connections that are more or less mutually coauthoring: connections that we experience as storylines running through our minds ("I wonder how So-and-So is doing?") and, more to the point, perhaps, as the noticings and natterings of our several sub-selves, with the voices of family or friends that often speak behind them. Indeed, our stories are so enmeshed with others' stories (within larger stories in turn) that where "I" end and "you" begin—and where you and I end and our children or family, our community or culture begins— becomes impossible to say. A narrative perspective, while acknowledging the novelty of the individual within his or her own story, is far, therefore, from being individualistic. Rather, the link between self and other, as between self and world, is a given from the start. Yet both can become more obvious to us the more we near The End. At the same time, the linking with others is tied to an unlinking from one's own self, or to an increasingly ironic sense of one's several selves, and such irony (as we have seen) can increase with reminiscence. In reminiscence, particularly of the adaptive type, write Edmund Sherman and his colleague, theologian Theodore Webb (1994), elders tend naturally to "come out of self, to detach as though they were another person, like an historian looking at the past or at someone's past life" (p. 265).

The connection between self and other, as between life-time and larger time, is experienced in the expression of our generative urges. As we have seen, generativity, which one gerontologist (Rubinstein, 1994) speaks of as "pragmatic spirituality," is the need to feel that we are contributing to the generations that follow us: not just that we are living through the achievements of our children, but that, generally, we are "outliving the self" (Kotre, 1984) through "giving back" (Cohen, 2005, p. 75). It is the need to expand our story beyond the limits of our own little world and, as Friedan (1993) expresses it, "to be part of something larger than oneself, to contribute somehow to the ongoing human enterprise" (p. 612). As Gergen and Gergen (2003) say, in explaining what they see as essential to "positive aging," it is the need to make a "communal contribution," and in making such a contribution, to experience a "transcending [of] the self" (p. 217; see also Labouvie-Vief, 2000). It is the need, in short, to leave a legacy, to harvest the wisdom that has been silently amassing inside us across the years, and—returning to our analogy of the compost heap—to mix it in with the soil of the world, for the benefit of others' growth as well. Much of that legacy, that wisdom, of course, is mediated by our own unique story. Accordingly, if our stories are socially constructed, it is only fair that they be socially contributed as well.

But even if we feel we have no such contributions to our credit, there is at least the peculiar collection of questions and wonderings, of untold stories and thus unlived lives that constitute our particular existence—in total, no small legacy itself. None of us lives all of the life of which we are capable. We all go to our graves with places not yet traveled, projects not yet finished, lessons not yet learned; with subplots unconcluded, relationships un-nurtured, questions unanswered, experiences un-had; with undeveloped talents and unexpressed selves, unresolved memories and unfulfilled dreams. In Scott-Maxwell's (1968) view, however, this situation can be recast, or re-genre-ated, from the tragedy it could surely seem to something approaching an adventure. "Our unlived life," she writes, "is the future of humanity" (p. 139). Such a consideration, for which gerontologist Jon Hendricks' (2001) term "generative futurity" (p. 42) is fitting, returns us to the moral dimension of a good lifestory that we touched upon in Chapter 5, and then again in Chapter 9. "One must reconnect with the world," says Daloz (1986), "or the journey is not complete" (p. 151). One needs to experience a "deeper bonding, through empathetic compassion, with the lot of humanity and nature" (Bianchi, 1991, p. 61). When we tell our story, our unique set of memories and learnings, to whoever is willing to listen—more important perhaps, when we feel, deep down, that our story is a valued subplot within the larger story of our family, our community, or humanity as a whole—then we realize that there is always something more that we can do or say to effect a positive difference in how others, present and future, live their lives. As a consequence, we realize that our story "does not really end" (McAdams, 1996, p. 143), and our identity, in effect, is redefined: "I am what survives me" (Csikszentmihalyi, 1996, p. 225).

Genealogy

If our story has no clear ending, then in another respect it has no precise beginning either. There exists a kind of backshadowing expression of generativity, one might say, in the urge to understand the larger stories from which our own unique identity has emerged. It is the hunger for our roots: a hunger reflected in the tendency of many memoirists, in fact, to trace the stories of their antecedents. This passion for genealogy which many of us develop naturally with age is fueled, in part, by the desire to bequeath a feeling for our heritage to those who come after us, lest they fail to appreciate the complex layers of history that lie beneath them and the nests of stories into which they have been born. As Freeman (2002b) reminds us, "our pasts do not begin only with our birth" (p. 203)—an insight expressed with extra poignancy by a friend of one of us, a child of Holocaust survivors: "The most important event in *my* life," he announced one day, "took place before I was even born." In consequence, genealogy is a means of linking ourselves to the vaster span of time itself by seeking to assimilate—to own—those features of our "*history*" which are not yet "part of [our] story" (Freeman, 2002b, p. 202).

In such ways, both genealogy and generativity can be seen as means of "merging [our] personal myth with the collective myth" (Atkinson, 1995, pp. 107–108). Even reminiscence can be a way to "participate in something larger than a single life story" (Moody, 1984, p. 161). Reflecting on the idea of a narrative unconscious, Brockmeier (2002) argues that if we think of memory "as a densely written text," then it is one that "is inextricably interwoven with the countless texts and contexts of culture." Human memory in general, he goes on, "is part of an infinite intertext that stretches out not only into the present but also into the past." Personal memory is thus merely one little thread in an infinite fabric, and "autobiographical consciousness" a "tiny island of awareness" in an ocean of infinite size and depth (p. 457). Sherman and Webb (1994) go as far as to insist that "the being we call self is born of being which moves the universe," that the roots of self are "implanted deeper than in history and genealogy" (p. 265). Such a humbling vision, they insinuate, the elderly tend to arrive at rather naturally. Reinforcing it is the concept that our body's story itself is rooted, one could claim, in the universe story. All of us, insists bio-gerontologist Leonard Hayflick (1994), are "unique rearrangements of ancient atoms that are themselves billions of years old." Thus, he says, not entirely tongue-in-cheek, "we are all billion-year-olds no matter when we were born, and celebrating birthdays is absurd" (p. 18).

Overall, by appreciating the links between our own story and the stories of numerous others, plus its roots in countless larger stories beyond it, reaching backward into time for as far as we can imagine; by appreciating the merging of our own time with historical time and cosmic time alike; and by appreciating how our stories are, in the end, mysteries beyond our capacity to fathom—a narrative perspective helps to blur the grandest boundary of them all, the one between life and death. As that frontier is increasingly fuzzied and the prospect of death seems more like a birth than anything else, then our stories, though technically they must end, acquire a quality of closure that is as open as any we might wish.

Transcendent Moments

Lest we leave the impression that a sense of transcendence is attainable in later life alone, it is worth recalling what we said in Chapter 4 about reading literature to read life. In reading a literary text, even if we are nowhere near the end of it, we can undergo instances of illumination so intense that we lose all track of time, instances in which something about the atmosphere or setting, the characters or plot, resonates with—or serves as metaphor for—themes in our own lives. The experience can be so overwhelming that we must lay the book aside to savor our inner musings, musings that have as much to do with us, of course, as with the text itself. It is not that we understand the story so much as the story understands us. As with parable, it interprets us. This sort of recognition, which simultaneously takes us out of ourselves (and out of the story) yet more deeply into ourselves (and into the story), is the very thing we look to literature to trigger. It is the very soul of the literary experience, the point of reading in the first place, at least aesthetic reading—irrespective of how the story ends. Not that the ending is irrelevant, for our sense of the ending still plays a part in sculpting the experience. But the point of reading and the end of the story are not synonymous. Such experiences prefigure not the end so much as the closure—the open closure—of which the story is the medium. They evoke a vision of the possibilities that hover around the story as a whole, the more that we get into it, and the more that it gets into us.

Given the reality of such experiences in reading literary stories—which, if you will, are experiences of intra-textual and extra-textual transcendence at once—we can also appreciate the possibility of similar ones in reading our lifestories. Technically possible at any age, they may be referred to by multiple labels. Most famous, perhaps, is psychologist Abraham Maslow's (1968) concept of "peak experiences," which interestingly he also describes as "acute identity-experiences" (p. 103). Concerning the dual nature of such an experience, more interesting still, perhaps, is his observation that "the greatest attainment of identity, autonomy, and selfhood is itself simultaneously a transcending of itself, a going beyond and above selfhood" (p. 105). Comparable concepts, of course, are "flow" (Csikszentmihalyi, 1990) or oneness, epiphany or awakening. However, an intriguing variation on what such terms, each in its fashion, are endeavoring to capture is proposed by psychologist Willard Frick (1983).

Drawing upon Jung's notion of "synchronicity" (1952/1985) in ways that are reminiscent of Progoff's "life process" (1975, p. 9) and Sartre's "fundamental project" (Charmé, 1984, p. 2), Frick explores the dynamics of "symbolic growth experiences." Such experiences are moments in life when one achieves a new and "passionate insight" (p. 111); when one's experience becomes suffused with "emotional power" and "personal meaning." They are moments when the boundaries between self and environment are inclined to disappear (p. 111), and the "hidden potentials within experiences" (p. 111) are exposed, moments in which we fashion meaning by "symbolizing our immediate experience in the interest of heightened consciousness" (p. 108). Amid such moments, "*we become profound and sensitive interpreters of our innermost lives* and creative agents in our growth" (p. 108; emphasis ours).

It is not hard to see, of course, that the epiphanies that come to us amidst "the literary experience" (Rosenblatt, 1976) are, themselves, experiences of symbolic growth. But so, too, are the experiences that are possible in respect to our own lives, the kinds we have when reflecting on our first piano lesson or on a drive home with our parents, or indeed—as countless poets down through history have displayed—on any given incident, past or present, in an otherwise ordinary life, as we enter (or reenter) the heart of it, play with it from multiple angles, and lay ourselves open to its transformative potential.

And theoretically, the longer our lives and the thicker the texts that we weave from them inside of us, then the greater such potential grows; and the more frequently we can be taken both out of ourselves and, paradoxically, into ourselves. For such reasons, "as life goes on," May Sarton says, "it becomes more intense," because "there are tremendous numbers of associations and so many memories" (1977/1995, p. 231).

Undoubtedly, our openness to symbolic growth experiences hinges upon multiple factors, from our neurological wiring, to our level of narrative competence, to our overall storying style. And it hinges too, as Frick is right to stress, on our particular history, on our peculiar collection of life-events. But our particular history will be a function, in turn, of the peculiar set of narrative environments that have storied our lives for us, some of which will be supportive of our uniqueness, some not. As well, behind all of them will inevitably lurk a particular tangle of master narratives, and this, too, will help to determine the shape and the feel that our symbolic growth experiences assume. For Frick, in fact, the "content" of what is happening in our lives is less significant than the "symbolic form" that it assumes for us at that particular time (pp. 111–112). Thus, insofar as master narratives are by definition symbolic frameworks, then whichever ones we identify with the most will on some level *in*form the "symbolic form" that is "inherent" in the moment, determining how we make meaning of it, both at the time that it occurs and each time thereafter that we reflect on its potential. And presumably, it will influence which moments actually feel like symbolic growth experiences in the first place. To put it simply, a person operating out of a Buddhist symbolic framework is likely to experience a moment *as* a symbolic growth experience—not to mention make meaning in the midst of it—quite differently than will a fundamental Baptist, a secular Jew, a Marxist feminist, or an atheist.

With so many variables playing a role in the sorts of experiences Frick describes, their idiosyncrasy to us, in form and content both, cannot be overstated. Despite the veiled implication that we can create them in a conscious, intentional manner, they can scarcely be forced. It is not a matter of manufacturing them through some formula that anyone can emulate, for they are not accessible in the abstract. It is a matter of being open to them, of cultivating a readiness for them, wherever we might go (Kabat-Zinn, 1994), in relation to the novelty of our particular lives. Thus, one person's symbolic growth experiences will be another one's same old story—just another moment, just another day. They will have no inkling at all of the "secret thread" of memories and longings, as C. S. Lewis (1962, p. 145) describes it, to which, for the other, the experience is tied.

One final point: for Frick, an experience of symbolic growth synthesizes many elements within an individual that would not normally meet—and might even conflict. This in turn leads to "an intensified sense of reality" (p. 112), which brings to mind Scott-Maxwell's (1968) comment about being "fierce with reality" (p. 42). As a consequence, such experiences entail the erasing of the boundaries between our past, our present, and our future (Frick, 1983, p. 112). In the midst of them, psychological time—in other words, lifestory—is neither denied nor shrugged off as being beside the point, anymore than the "aha" that we experience with a literary text is independent of the content we are reading. On the contrary, it is as if we enter with intensity into the very soul of time—our own life-time, for that is all we know—in all of its richness and thickness, its openness and depth. As Progoff (1975) would say, we "stretch" time, reentering it "from the inside" (p. 126). At the same time, we experience a symbolic coming-together of our several selves—past and present; remembered and remembering; author, narrator, character, reader—and if only for a moment, sense a oneness with the movement of the wider world. We see beyond ourselves, beyond our stories, and—just possibly—"beyond narrative itself" (Freeman, 2000, p. 91).

BEYOND OUR STORIES: FROM IRONY TO WONDER

We began this book by talking about affirmative postmodernism and the ironic stance. In Chapter 9, we suggested that a hallmark of wisdom is irony—in particular, narrative irony: the capacity to appreciate the multiple levels to our stories, the multiple characters within them, the multiple selves that tell them, and the multiple interpretations of the events that make them up. Irony is thus the capacity to laugh at our lives in a detached yet affectionate manner; to revel in the play that is possible in respect to our own lived-text; and to see through the myths by which, for better or worse, we have envisioned who we are.

What irony is to wisdom, wonder is to spirituality. Whether we conceive of it as an emotion, an attitude, a process, or all three of these at once, wonder is fundamental to human endeavor in every major sphere, beginning with religion. "The sense of wonder...is our sixth sense," says D. H. Lawrence (1928/2004); and "it is the natural religious sense" (p. 132). Wonder, insists theologian Thomas Carlyle (1833–34/1987), is "the basis of worship" (p. 53). Another word for wonder, of course, is awe. In his musings on the "psychology of uncertainty," psychologist Kerry Gordon (2003) observes that, "in awe, we transcend ourselves...and allow ourselves to be humbled in the face of mystery" (p. 112). And even though awe is "not faith itself," it is "that state of being that renders faith possible" (p. 113). The tragedy, of course, is that as the fires of faith cool down and harden into rigid molds, awe is frequently the first to go—"shut down prematurely," as Cohen (2005) words it, "by dogma, orthodoxy, and overly pat belief systems" (p. 31).

As we saw with wisdom, the more we know, the less we know, and thus, ideally, the more we realize there is to learn: the more curious we are bound to grow. For Aristotle (ca. 336–323 BCE/1998), therefore, wonder was fundamental to *philo-sophia:* literally, the "love of wisdom" (p. 9). In essence, it is what motivates most scientists as well, notwithstanding the assumption of objectivity that characterizes most scientific writing. Finally, as urbane as we might be, it is our capacity for wonder that our encounters with art, irrespective of the medium, will ultimately awaken. Indeed, without it, creativity of any type could scarcely flourish. "Shared by the mystic, poet, and scholar alike," writes Arthur Koestler (1964, p. 428), "the sense of wonder" is central to the very "act of creation."

More important for our purposes here, wonder transcends, not just academic disciplines or aesthetic domains, but generations, too. The ability of little children to experience reality with wide-eyed wonder, shorn of bias and preconception, can hardly be ignored. Indeed, wonder more than irony is what we *expect* them to have. Thereafter, from the teens through middle life, a certain world-weariness can gradually settle in, and with it, for many, a tragic sense of life. Life is not over, but the story might as well be. Yet wonder, we could argue, no less than wisdom, is never wholly lost, but simply awaits the appropriate environments or conditions to reemerge. Coincidentally, later life is a time when precisely such conditions can arrive. Changing bodies, minds, and worlds: for all the challenges these can surely represent, they provide the very type of stimulation that, paradoxically, wonder needs to flourish, to become again a driving feature of our worldview, and so to tilt the scales in favor of growing as opposed to simply getting old.

Pondering the poetics of aging means entertaining a story of aging that is somewhat different from what gerontologists have been recounting up to now—a counter-story, one could call it, even a *new* story—a story with, we hope, its own brand of coherence, credibility, and truth. It is a story that takes to heart the narrative complexity of human lives through time, and strives to honor aspects of aging that have to do with what gerontologist Sherry Chapman (2005) calls "the on-going co-construction and reconstruction of multiple selves [in] an open-ended process of meaning-making amid later-life events and transitions" (p. 14). Trying to tell such a story has meant proposing a framework that, ideally, can help to hold together topics—above all, memory and meaning, wisdom and spirituality—that, far too often, are discussed in isolation.

Clearly, our efforts leave us wondering about several other topics, too. Many we have tried to treat with a fair degree of thoroughness. Some we have merely touched upon in passing, while many more, as much as they have haunted us throughout, have gone all but unaddressed. Among these are the complex relationship between our memories and our dreams, the role of reading our lives in countering depression, and the tragedy of dementia—which one could easily interpret as the consummate expression of narrative foreclosure. Perhaps equally, however, one can interpret it in terms of transcendence, insofar as our stories are always intertwined. Whether in life, in death, or in dementia, in other words, we are not simply the coauthors of one another's narratives. As family members, loved ones, friends: we are the keepers of them, too (see Sabat & Harré, 1992). Overall, then, while we find ourselves here at what clearly is the end, in our end lies our beginning. For our conclusion has more than its share of open closure: a feature quite in keeping with our overarching theme.

Growing old through reading our lives is an expanding and a thickening of our being. It is a process that takes us more deeply and dynamically into the mystery that is us. As such, it is the way of unknowing. It is less about tying up loose ends or weaving the strands of our stories into a neat, consistent package, than it is a glorious unraveling of our world, a delicious deconstructing of our Self. In a sense, it is a *via negativa*. It leads us not to integrity so much as disintegration, not to identity so much as multiplicity, not to the meaning of life so much as to indeterminacy, to the continual making and remaking of meaning, and to limitless parabolic potential. It leads us not to stability, but to continuous transformation. It leads us beyond self-knowledge and beyond "success" to a kind of mindful confusion, a positive befuddlement, a creative uncertainty, a perpetual discovery. It leads to a quality of dwelling with *the story of my life* that is wonderfully ironic; that generates as many questions as it does answers; that is by no means set in its ways but that embraces complexity, ambiguity, and change; that does not wind us down and shut us down toward The End, but that opens us up instead—to ourselves, to others, to the world—all the better to transcend our stories and, in the end, to let them go.

References

Abbott, H. (2002). *The Cambridge introduction to narrative.* Cambridge, England: Cambridge University Press.

Aftel, M. (1996). *The story of your life: Becoming the author of your experience.* New York: Simon & Schuster.

Akamatsu, Y. (1999). Japanese readings of *Anne of Green Gables.* In I. Gammel & E. Epperly (Eds.), *L. M. Montgomery and Canadian culture.* Toronto, Ontario, Canada: University of Toronto Press.

Albom, M. (1997). *Tuesdays with Morrie: An old man, a young man, and life's greatest lesson.* New York: Doubleday.

Albright, D. (1994). Literary and psychological models of the self. In U. Neisser & R. Fivush (Eds.), *The remembering self: Construction and accuracy in the self-narrative,* pp. 19–40. Cambridge, England: Cambridge University Press.

Alheit, P. (1995). Biographical learning: Theoretical outline, challenges, and contradictions of a new approach in adult education. In P. Alheit, A. Bron-Wojciechowska, E. Brugger, & P. Dominice (Eds.), *The biographical approach in European adult education,* pp. 57–74. Vienna: Verband Wiener Voksbildung.

Ansbacher, H., & R. Ansbacher (1956). *The individual psychology of Alfred Adler: A systematic presentation in selections from his writings.* New York: Harper & Row.

Ardelt, M. (1997). Wisdom and life satisfaction in old age. *Journal of Gerontology: Psychological Sciences, 52B*(1): P15–P27.

Aristotle. (1998). *The Metaphysics.* (H. Lawson-Tancred, Trans.). London: Penguin. (Original work composed c.336–323 BCE.)

Arlin, P. (1990). Wisdom: The art of problem finding. In R. Sternberg (Ed.), *Wisdom: Its nature, origins, and development,* pp. 230–243. New York: Cambridge University Press.

Assagioli, R. (1974). *The act of will: A guide to self-actualization and self-realization.* New York: Penguin.

Assagioli, R. (1976). *Psychosynthesis: A collection of basic writings.* London: Penguin.

Atchley, R. (2000). Spirituality. In T. Cole, R. Kastenbaum, & R. Ray (Eds.), *Handbook of the humanities and aging* (2nd ed.), pp. 324–341. New York: Springer.

Atkinson, R. (1995). *The gift of stories: Practical and spiritual applications of autobiography, life stories, and personal mythmaking.* Westport, Conn.: Bergin & Garvey.

Augustine. (1961). *Confessions.* (R.S. Pine-Coffin, Trans.). London: Penguin.

Austen, J. (2004). *Pride and prejudice.* (J. Kinsley, Ed.). Oxford, England: Oxford University Press. (Original work published 1813.)

Baldwin, C. (2005). *Storycatcher: Making sense of our lives through the power and practice of story.* Novato, Calif.: New World Library.

Baltes, P., & J. Smith (1990). Toward a psychology of wisdom and its ontogenesis. In R. Sternberg, (Ed.), *Wisdom: Its nature, origins, and development,* pp. 87–120. New York: Cambridge University Press.

Bamberg, M. (1997). A constructivist approach to narrative development. In M, Bamberg (Ed.), *Narrative development: Six approaches,* pp. 89–132. Mahwah, N.J.: Lawrence Erlbaum Associates.

Barclay, C. (1994). Composing protoselves through improvisation. In U. Neisser & R. Fivush (Eds.). *The remembering self: Construction and accuracy in the self narrative,* pp. 55–77. New York: Cambridge University Press.

Barrington, J. (1997). *Writing the memoir: From truth to art.* Portland, Oreg.: The Eighth Mountain Press.

Barthes, R. (1988). The death of the author. In D. Lodge (Ed.), *Modern criticism and theory,* pp. 16–172. London: Longman Publishing. (Original work published 1968).

Basting, A. (Fall 2003). Reading the story behind the story: Context and content in stories by people with dementia. *Generations: The Journal of the American Society on Aging, 23*(3): 25–29.

Bateson, M. (1989). *Composing a life.* New York: Atlantic Monthly Press.

Bateson, M. (2007). Narrative, adaptation, and change. *Interchange, 38*(3): 213–222.

Baur, S. (1994). *Confiding: A psychotherapist and her patients search for stories to live by.* New York: HarperPerennial.

Bavelas, J., L. Coates, & T. Johnson (2000). Listeners as co-narrators. *Journal of Personality and Social Psychology, 79*(6): 941–952.

Beardslee, W. (1990). Stories in the postmodern world: Orienting and disorienting. In D. Griffin (Ed.), *Sacred interconnections: Postmodern spirituality, political economy, and art,* pp. 163–175. Albany, N.Y.: State University of New York Press.

Becker, B. (2001). Challenging "ordinary pain": Narratives of older people who live in pain. In G. Kenyon, P. Clark, & B. de Vries (Eds.), *Narrative gerontology: Theory, research, and practice,* pp. 91–112. New York: Springer.

Bee, H., & B. Bjorklund (2004). *The journey of adulthood* (5th ed.). Upper Saddle River, N.J.: Pearson-Prentice Hall.

Beike, D., J. Lampinen, & D. Behrend (Eds.). (2004). *The self and memory.* New York: Psychology Press.

Berger, P. (1963). *Invitation to sociology: A humanistic perspective.* Garden City, N.Y.: Anchor.

Berman, H. (1994). *Interpreting the aging self: Personal journals of later life.* New York: Springer.

Berry, T. (1987). The new story: Comments on the origin, identification and transmission of values. *Cross Currents, 37*(2–3): 187–199.

Bianchi, E. (1991). A spirituality of aging. In L. Cahill & D. Mieth, *Aging,* pp. 58–64. London: SCM Press.

Bianchi, E. (1995). *Aging as spiritual journey.* New York: Crossroad. (Original work published 1982.)

Bianchi, E. (2005). Living with elder wisdom. In H. R. Moody (Ed.), *Religion, spirituality, and aging: A social work perspective,* pp. 319–329. Binghamton, N.Y.: Haworth Press.

Bickle, J. (2003). Empirical evidence for a narrative concept of self. In G. Fireman, T. McVay, Jr., & O. Flanagan (Eds.), *Narrative and consciousness: Literature, psychology, and the brain,* pp. 195–208. New York: Oxford University Press.

Birkerts, S. (1994). *The Gutenberg elegies: The fate of reading in an electronic age.* New York: Fawcett.

Birren, J., & D. Deutchman (1991). *Guiding autobiography groups for older adults: Exploring the fabric of life.* Baltimore: Johns Hopkins University Press.

Birren, J., & L. Fisher (1990). The elements of wisdom: Overview and integration. In R. Sternberg, (Ed.), *Wisdom: Its nature, origins, and development,* pp. 317–332. New York: Cambridge University Press.

Blanchard, B. (1967). Wisdom. In P. Edwards (Ed.), *The encyclopedia of philosophy,* Vol. 7: 322–324. New York: Macmillan and Free Press.

Blanchard-Fields, F., & L. Norris (1995). The development of wisdom. In M. Kimble, S. McFadden, J. Ellor, & J. Seeber (Eds.), *Aging, spirituality, and religion: A handbook,* pp. 102–118. Minneapolis, Minn.: Augsburg Fortress.

Bleich, D. (1978). *Subjective criticism.* Baltimore: Johns Hopkins University Press.

Bluck, S., & N. Alea (2002). Exploring the functions of autobiographical memory: Why do I remember the autumn? In J. Webster & B. Haight (Eds.), *Critical advances in reminiscence: From theory to application,* pp. 61–75. New York: Springer.

Bluck, S., & T. Habermas (2000). The life story schema. *Motivation and Emotion, 24*(2): 121–147.

Blythe, R. (1979). *The view in winter: Reflections on old age.* London: Penguin.

Bohlmeijer, E., M. Valenkamp, G. Westerhof, G. Smit, & P. Cuijpers (2005). Creative reminiscence as an early intervention for depression: Results of a pilot project. *Aging & Mental Health, 9*(4): 302–304.

Bolen (1984). *Goddesses in every woman.* New York: Harper & Row.

Bolen (1989). *Gods in every man.* New York: Harper & Row.

Booth, W. (1961). *The rhetoric of fiction.* Chicago: The University of Chicago Press.

Booth, W. (1988). *The company we keep: An ethics of fiction.* Berkeley, Calif.: University of California Press.

Bornat, J. (Ed.). (1994). *Reminiscence reviewed: Evaluations, achievements, perspectives.* Buckingham, England: Open University Press.

Bortolussi, M., & P. Dixon (2003). *Psychonarratology: Foundations for the empirical study of literature.* Cambridge, England: Cambridge University Press.

Bowen, E. (1996). In *The Columbia world of quotations* (no.8021). Retrieved April 17, 2007, from www.bartleby.com/66/21/8021.html. [Original work published 1955.]

Bower, G. (2000). A brief history of memory research. In E. Tulving & F. Craik (Eds.), *The Oxford handbook of memory,* pp. 3–32. New York: Oxford University Press.

Bowie, M. (1993). *Psychoanalysis and the future of theory.* Oxford, England: Blackwell.

Brady, M. (1990). Redeemed from time: Learning through autobiography. *Adult Education Quarterly, 41*(1): 43–52.

Bridges, W. (1980). *Transitions: Making sense of life's changes.* Toronto, Ontario, Canada: Addison-Wesley.

Brockelman, P. (1992). *The inside story: A narrative approach to religious understanding and truth.* Albany, N.Y.: State University of New York Press.

Brockmeier, J. (2001). From the end to the beginning: Retrospective teleology in autobiography. In J. Brockmeier & D. Carbaugh (Eds.), *Narrative and identity: Studies in autobiography, self, and culture,* pp. 247–280. Amsterdam: John Benjamins.

Brockmeier, J. (2002). Possible lives. *Narrative Inquiry, 12*(2): 455–66.

Brockmeier, J., & D. Carbaugh (Eds.). (2001). *Narrative and identity: Studies in autobiography, self, and culture.* Amsterdam: John Benjamins.

Brockmeier, J., & R. Harré (2001). Narrative: Problems and promises of an alternative paradigm. In J. Brockmeier & D. Carbaugh (Eds.), *Narrative and identity: Studies in autobiography, self, and culture,* pp. 39–58. Amsterdam: John Benjamins.

Brookfield, S. (1987). *Developing critical thinkers: Challenging adults to explore alternative ways of thinking and acting.* San Francisco: Jossey-Bass.

Brooks, P. (1985). *Reading for the plot: Design and intention in narrative.* New York: Vintage.

Bruner, J. (1986). *Actual minds, possible worlds.* Cambridge, Mass.: Harvard University Press.

Bruner, J. (1987). Life as narrative. *Social Research, 54*(1): 11–32.

Bruner, J. (1990). *Acts of meaning.* Cambridge, Mass.: Harvard University Press.

Bruner, J. (1994). The "remembered" self. In U. Neisser & R. Fivush (Eds.), *The remembering self: Construction and accuracy in the self narrative,* pp. 41–54. New York: Cambridge University Press.

Bruner, J. (1996). *The culture of education.* Cambridge, Mass.: Harvard University Press.

Bruner, J. (1999). Narratives of aging. *Journal of Aging Studies, 13*(1): 7–9.

Bruner, J. (2001). Self-making and world making. In J. Brockmeier & D. Carbaugh (Eds.), *Narrative and identity: Studies in autobiography, self, and culture,* pp. 25–37. Amsterdam: John Benjamins.

Bruner, J. (2002). *Making stories: Law, literature, and life.* New York: Farrar, Straus and Giroux.

Bruner, J. (2005). The reality of fiction. *McGill Journal of Education, 40*(1): 55–64.

Bruner, J., & C. Feldman (1995). Group narrative as a cultural context of autobiography. In D. Rubin (Ed.), *Remembering our past: Studies in autobiographical memory,* pp. 291–317. Cambridge, England: Cambridge University Press.

Bruner, J., & D. Kalmar (1998). Narrative and metanarrative in the construction of the self. In M. Ferrari & R. Sternberg (Eds.), *Self-awareness: Its nature and development,* pp. 308–331. New York: Guilford.

Bruner, J., & S. Weisser (1991). The invention of self: Autobiography and its forms. In D. Olson & N. Torrance (Eds.), *Literacy and orality,* pp. 129–148. Cambridge, England: Cambridge University Press.

Bryson, B. (1991). *Neither here nor there: Travels in Europe.* Toronto, Ontario, Canada: Anchor.

Burke, K. (1941). *The philosophy of literary form.* Berkeley, Calif.: University of California Press.

Burnside, I. (1996). Life review and reminiscence in nursing practice. In J. Birren, G. Kenyon, J.-E. Ruth, J. Schroots, & T. Svensson (Eds.), *Aging and biography: Explorations in adult development,* pp. 248–264. New York: Springer.

Butala, S. (2005). The memoirist's quandary. *McGill Journal of Education, 40*(1): 43–54.

Butler, R. (1963). The life review: An interpretation of reminiscence in the aged. *Psychiatry, 26:* 65–76.

Butler, R. (2007). Life review. In J. E. Birren (Ed.), *Encyclopedia of gerontology: Age, aging, and the aged,* Vol. 1 (2nd ed.): pp. 67–72. San Diego, Calif.: Academic Press. (Original work published 1996.)

Campbell, J. (1949). *The hero with a thousand faces.* New York: MJF Books.

Campbell, J. (with B. Moyers). (1988). *The power of myth.* New York: Doubleday.

Carlyle, T. (1987). *Sartor resartus.* K. McSweeney & P. Sabor (Eds.). Oxford, England: Oxford University Press. (Original work published 1833–34.)

Carr, D. (1986). *Time, narrative, and history.* Bloomington, Ind.: Indiana University Press.

Casey, E. (1987). *Remembering: A phenomenological study.* Bloomington, Ind.: Indiana University Press.

Castaneda, C. (1975). *Journey to Ixtlan: The lessons of Don Juan.* London: Penguin.

Cavarero, A. (2000). *Relating narratives: Storytelling and selfhood.* (P. Kottman, Trans.). London: Routledge.

Chandler, S., & R. Ray (2002). New meanings for old tales: A discourse-based study of reminiscence and development in later life. In J. Webster & B. Haight (Eds.), *Critical advances in reminiscence work: From theory to application,* pp. 76–94. New York: Springer.

Chapman, G., J. Cleese, et. al. (Writers), & T. Hughes & I. MacNaughton (Directors). (1982). *Monty Python live at the Hollywood Bowl* [Motion Picture]. England: Columbia Pictures.

Chapman, S. (2005). Theorizing about aging well: Constructing a narrative. *Canadian Journal on Aging, 24*(1): 9–18.

Charmé, S. (1984). *Meaning and myth in the study of lives: A Sartrean perspective.* Philadelphia: University of Pennsylvania Press.

Charon, R. (2006). *Narrative medicine: Honoring the stories of illness.* New York: Oxford University Press.

Chopin, K. (1996). The story of an hour. In M. Meyer (Ed.), *The Bedford introduction to literature* (4th ed.): pp. 12–15. Boston: Bedford/St. Martin's. (Original work published 1894).

Clayton, V. (1975). Erikson's theory of human development as it applies to the aged: Wisdom as contradictive cognition. *Human Development, 18:* 119–128.

Cobley, P. (2001). *Narrative.* London: Routledge.

Cohen, G. (1999). Human potential phases in the second half of life: Mental health theory development. *American Journal of Geriatric Psychiatry, 7*(1): 1–7.

Cohen, G. (2001). Creativity with aging: Four phases of potential in the second half of life. *Geriatrics, 56*(4): 51–57.

Cohen, G. (2005). *The mature mind: The positive power of the aging brain.* New York: Basic Books.

Cohler, B. (1993). Aging, morale, and meaning: The nexus of narrative. In T. Cole, W. Achenbaum, P. Jakobi, & R. Kastenbaum (Eds.). *Voices and visions of aging: Toward a critical gerontology,* pp. 107–133. New York: Springer.

Cole, T. (1992). *The journey of life: A cultural history of aging in America.* New York: Cambridge University Press.

Cole, T., W. Achenbaum, P. Jakobi, & R. Kastenbaum (Eds.). (1993). *Voices and visions of aging: Toward a critical gerontology.* New York: Springer.

Cole, T., & S. Gadow (Eds.). (1986). *What does it mean to grow old? Reflections from the humanities.* Durham, N.C.: Duke University Press.

Cole, T., R. Kastenbaum, & R. Ray (Eds.). (2000). *Handbook of the humanities and aging.* (2nd ed.). New York: Springer.

Cole, T., & K. de Medeiros (2001). *Life stories: Aging and the human spirit.* [Video]. Washington, D.C.: Old Dog Productions. (Available from New River Media: www.nrmedia.com.)

Cole, T., & M. Winkler (Eds.). (1994). *The Oxford book of aging: Reflections on the journey of life.* New York: Oxford University Press.

Coleman, P. (1999). Creating a life story: The task of reconciliation. *The Gerontologist, 39*(2): 133–139.

Coleman, P., & A. O'Hanlon (2004). *Ageing and development.* New York: Arnold.

Coleridge, S. (1969). *Seven lectures on Shakespeare and Milton.* (J. Collier, Ed.). Manchester, N.H.: Ayer Company. (Original work published 1856.)

Coleridge, S. (1983). *Biographia literaria.* (J. Engell & W. J. Bate, Eds.). Princeton, N.J.: Princeton University Press. (Original work published 1817.)

Coles, R. (1989). *The call of stories: Teaching and the moral imagination.* Boston: Houghton Mifflin.

Conway, M. (1995). Autobiographical knowledge and autobiographical memories. In D. Rubin (Ed.), *Remembering our past: Studies in autobiographical memory*, pp. 67–93. Cambridge, England: Cambridge University Press.

Corn, A. (1997). *The poem's heartbeat: A manual of prosody*. Brownsville, Oreg.: Storyline Press.

Cottle, T. (2002). On narratives and the sense of self. *Qualitative Inquiry, 8*(5): 535–549.

Cowley, M. (1980). *The view from eighty*. New York: Viking.

Crisp, J. (1995). Making sense of the stories that people with Alzheimer's tell: A journey with my mother. *Nursing Inquiry, 2*: 133–140.

Crites, S. (1971). The narrative quality of experience. *Journal of the American Academy of Religion, 39*(3): 291–311.

Crites, S. (1979). The aesthetics of self-deception. *Soundings, 62*: 107–129.

Crites, S. (1986). Storytime: Recollecting the past and projecting the future. In T. Sarbin (Ed.), *Narrative psychology: The storied nature of human conduct*, pp. 152–173. New York: Praeger.

Crossan, J. D. (1975). *The dark interval: Towards a theology of story*. Niles, Ill.: Argus Communications.

Crossley, M. (2003). Formulating narrative psychology: The limitations of contemporary social constructionism. *Narrative Inquiry, 13*(2): 287–300.

Crowder, R., & R. Wagner (1992). *The psychology of reading: An introduction*. New York: Oxford University Press.

Csikszentmihalyi, M. (1990). *Flow: The psychology of optimal experience*. New York: HarperCollins.

Csikszentmihalyi, M. (1996). *Creativity: Flow and the psychology of discovery and invention*. New York: HarperPerennial.

Csikszentimihalyi, M. & O. Beattie (1979). Life themes: a theoretical and empirical exploration of their origins and effects. *Journal of Humanistic Psychology, 19*(1): 45–63.

Csikszentmihalyi, M. & K. Rathunde (1990). The psychology of wisdom: An evolutionary interpretation. In R. Sternberg (Ed.). *Wisdom: Its nature, origins, and development*, pp. 25–51. New York: Cambridge University Press.

Culler, J. (1997). *Literary theory: A very short introduction*. Oxford, England: Oxford University Press.

Cupitt, D. (1991). *What is a story?* London: SCM.

Cusack, S., & W. Thompson (2003). *Mental fitness for life: Seven steps to healthy aging*. Toronto, Ontario, Canada: Key Porter Books.

Daloz, L. (1986). *Effective teaching and mentoring: Realizing the transformational power of adult learning experiences*. San Francisco: Jossey-Bass.

Damasio, A. (1994). *Descartes' error: Emotion, reason, and the human brain*. New York: HarperCollins.

Damasio, A. (1999). *The feeling of what happens: Body and emotion in the making of consciousness*. San Diego, Calif.: Harcourt.

Debats, D. (2000). An inquiry into existential meaning: Theoretical, clinical, and phenomenal perspectives. In G. Reker & K. Chamberlain (Eds.), *Exploring existential meaning: Optimizing human development across the life span*, pp. 93–106. Thousand Oaks, Calif.: Sage.

Dennett, D. (1991). *Consciousness explained.* Boston: Little, Brown.

Denzin, N. (1989). *Interpretive interactionism.* Newbury Park, Calif.: Sage.

Denzin, N. (1997). *Interpretive ethnography: Ethnographic practices for the 21ˢᵗ century.* Thousand Oaks, Calif.: Sage.

Derrida, J. (1974). *Of grammatology.* (G. Spivak, Trans.). Baltimore: Johns Hopkins University Press.

De Vries, B., J. Blando, P. Southard, & C. Bubeck (2001). The times of our lives. In G. Kenyon, P. Clark, & B. de Vries (Eds.), *Narrative gerontology: Theory, research, and practice*, pp. 137–158. New York: Springer.

de Vries, B., & A. Lehman (1996). The complexity of personal narratives. In J. Birren, G. Kenyon, J.-E. Ruth, J. Schroots, & T. Svensson (Eds.), *Aging and biography: Explorations in adult development*, pp. 149–166. New York: Springer.

Dewey, J. (1944). *Democracy and education: An introduction to the philosophy of education.* New York: The Free Press. (Original work published 1916.)

Dewey, J. (1962). Time and individuality. In H. Shapley (Ed.), *Time and its mysteries*, pp. 141–159. New York: Collier Books. (Original work published 1938.)

Diamond, T. (1992). *Making gray gold: Narratives of nursing home care.* Chicago: University of Chicago Press.

Dillard, A. (1987). To fashion a text. In W. Zinsser (Ed.), *Inventing the truth: The art and craft of memoir*, pp. 55–76. Boston: Houghton Mifflin.

Dillard, A. (1989). *The writing life.* New York: HarperPerennial.

Dostoyevsky, F. (1968). *Crime and punishment.* (S. Monas, Trans.). New York: Signet. (Original work published 1866).

Draaisma, D. (2000). *Metaphors of memory: A history of ideas about the mind.* (P. Vincent, Trans.). Cambridge, England: Cambridge University Press. (Original work published 1995.)

Drewery, W., & J. Winslade (1997). The theoretical story of narrative therapy. In G. Monk, J. Winslade, K. Crocket, & D. Epston (Eds.), *Narrative therapy in practice: The archeology of hope*, pp. 32–52. San Francisco: Jossey-Bass.

Eagleton, T. (1996). *The illusions of postmodernism.* Oxford, England: Blackwell Publishing.

Eakin, P. (1985). *Fictions in autobiography: Studies in the art of self-invention.* Princeton, N.J.: Princeton University Press.

Eakin, P. (1999). *How our lives become stories: Making selves.* Ithaca, N.Y.: Cornell University Press.

Edmundson, M. (2004). *Why Read?* New York: Bloomsbury.

Einstein, G., & O. Flanagan (2003). Sexual identities and narratives of self. In G. Fireman, T. McVay, & O. Flanagan (Eds.), *Narrative and consciousness: Literature, psychology, and the brain*, pp. 209–231. New York: Oxford University Press.

Freeman, M. (2002c). The presence of what is missing: Memory, poetry, and the ride home. In R. Pellegrini & T. Sarbin (Eds.), *Between fathers and sons: Critical incident narratives in the development of men's lives,* pp. 165–176. Binghamton, N.Y.: Haworth Clinical Practice Press.

Freeman, M. (2003a). From self to soul: The theological moment of the life story. Conference presentation. *International Reminiscence and Life Review Conference.* Vancouver, British Columbia, Canada.

Freeman, M. (2003b). Rethinking the fictive, reclaiming the real: Autobiography, narrative time, and the burden of truth. In G. Fireman, T. McVay, & O. Flanagan (Eds.), *Narrative and consciousness: Literature, psychology, and the brain* pp. 115–128. New York: Oxford University Press.

Freeman, M. (2007). Life and literature: Continuities and discontinuities. *Interchange, 38*(3): 223–243.

Freeman, M., & J. Brockmeier (2001). Narrative integrity: Autobiographical identity and the meaning of the "good life." In J. Brockmeier & D. Carbaugh (Eds.), *Narrative and identity: Studies in autobiography, self, and culture,* pp. 75–99. Amsterdam: John Benjamins.

Frey, J. (2003). *A million little pieces.* New York: Doubleday.

Frick, W. (1983). The symbolic growth experience. *Journal of Humanistic Psychology, 23*(1): 109–125.

Friedan, B. (1993). *The fountain of age.* New York: Simon & Schuster.

Frye, N. (1963). *The educated imagination.* Toronto, Ontario, Canada: Canadian Broadcasting Corporation.

Frye, N. (1968). *The anatomy of criticism: Four essays.* Princeton, N.J.: Princeton University Press. (Original work published 1957.)

Fulford, R. (1999). *The triumph of narrative: Storytelling in an age of mass culture.* Toronto: Anansi.

Gardner, D. (1997). New perspectives: Stories and life stories in therapy with older adults. In K. Dwivedi (Ed.), *The therapeutic use of stories,* pp. 211–226. London: Routledge.

Gardner, J. (1985). *The art of fiction: Notes on craft for young writers.* New York: Vintage.

Garfein, A., & A. Herzog (1995). Robust aging among the young-old, old-old, and oldest-old. *Journal of Gerontology, 50B:* S77–S87.

Garland, J. (1994). What splendour, it all coheres: Life-review therapy with older people. In J. Bornat (Ed.), *Reminiscence reviewed: Evaluations, achievements, perspectives,* pp. 21–31. Buckingham, England: Open University Press.

Gearing, B. (1999). Narratives of identity among former professional footballers in the United Kingdom. *Journal of Aging Studies, 13*(1): 43–58.

Gergen, K. (1992). *The saturated self: Dilemmas of identity in contemporary life.* New York: Basic Books.

Gergen, K. (1994). Mind, text, and society: Self-memory in social context. In U. Neisser & R. Fivush (Eds.), *The remembering self: Construction and accuracy in the self-narrative* pp. 78–104. New York: Cambridge University Press.

Gergen, M., & K. Gergen (1984). The social construction of narrative accounts. In K. Gergen & M. Gergen (Eds.), *Historical social psychology*, pp. 173–189. Hillsdale, N.J.: Lawrence Erlbaum Associates.

Gergen, M., & K. Gergen (2003). Positive aging. In J. Gubrium & J. Holstein (Eds.), *Ways of aging* pp. 203–224. London: Blackwell.

Gerrig, R. (1993). *Experiencing narrative worlds: On the psychological activities of reading.* New Haven, Conn.: Yale University Press.

Gerrig, R. & D. Rapp (2004). Psychological processes underlying literary impact. *Poetics Today, 25*(2): 265–281.

Gibbs, R., Jr. (1994). *The poetics of mind: Figurative thought, language, and understanding.* Cambridge, England: Cambridge University Press.

Glover, J. (1988). *I: The philosophy and psychology of personal identity.* London: Penguin.

Gold, J. (2001). *Read for your life: Literature as a life support system.* Markham, Ontario, Canada: Fitzhenry & Whiteside. (Original work published 1990.)

Gold, J. (2002). *The story species: Our life–literature connection.* Markham, Ontario, Canada: Fitzhenry & Whiteside.

Goldberg, E. (2005). *The wisdom paradox: How your mind can grow stronger as your brain grows older.* New York: Gotham.

Goldberg, M. (1991). *Theology and narrative: A critical introduction.* Philadelphia: Trinity Press International.

Goleman, D. (1995). *Emotional intelligence.* New York: Bantam.

Gordon, K. (2003). The impermanence of being: Toward a psychology of uncertainty. *Journal of Humanistic Psychology, 43*(2): 96–117.

Grams, A. (2001). Learning, aging, and other predicaments. In S. McFadden & R. Atchley (Eds.), *Aging and the meaning of time: A multidisciplinary exploration*, pp. 99–110. New York: Springer.

Green, M. (2004). Transportation into narrative worlds: The role of prior knowledge and perceived realism. *Discourse Processes, 38*(2): 247–266.

Greene, G. (1973). *A sort of life.* London: Methuen.

Greene, M. (1990). The emancipatory power of literature. In J. Mezirow (Ed.), *Fostering critical reflection in adulthood*, pp. 251–268. San Francisco: Jossey-Bass.

Grimes, R.(1995). *Marrying & burying: Rites of passage in a man's life.* Boulder, Colo.: Westview.

Groger, L., & J. Straker (2002). Counting and recounting: Approaches to combining quantitative and qualitative data and methods. In G. Rowles & N. Schoenberg (Eds.), *Qualitative gerontology: A contemporary perspective*, pp. 179–199. New York: Springer.

Gubrium, J. (1993). *Speaking of life: Horizons of meaning for nursing home residents.* New York: Walter de Gruyter.

Gubrium, J. (2001). Narrative, experience, and aging. In G. Kenyon, P. Clark, & B. de Vries (Eds.), *Narrative gerontology: Theory, research, and practice*, pp. 19–30. New York: Springer.

Gubrium, J. (2003). What is a good story? Help for caregivers of people with dementia. *Generations, 27*(3): 21–24.

Gullette, M. (1997). *Declining to decline.* Charlottesville, Va.: University of Virginia Press.

Gullette, M. (2004). *Aged by culture.* Chicago: University of Chicago Press.

Gusdorf, G. (1980). Conditions and limits of autobiography. In J. Olney (Ed.), *Autobiography: Essays theoretical and critical,* pp. 28–48. Princeton, N.J.: Princeton University Press.

Gutmann, D. (1976). Alternatives to disengagement: The old men of the Highland Druze. In J. F. Gubrium, (Ed.), *Time, roles and self in old age.* New York: Human Sciences Press.

Habermas, T., & C. Paha (2002). Souvenirs and other personal objects: Reminding of past events and significant others in the transition to university. In J. Webster & B. Haight (Eds.), *Critical advances in reminiscence: From theory to application,* pp. 123–139. New York: Springer.

Haight, P., P. Coleman, & K. Lord (1995). The linchpins of a successful life review: Structure, evaluation, and individuality. In B. Haight & J. Webster (Eds.), *The art and science of reminiscing: Theory, research, methods, and applications,* pp. 179–192. Washington, D.C.: Taylor & Francis.

Hamlyn, D. (1977). Self-knowledge. In T. Mischel (Ed.), *The self: Psychological and philosophical issues,* pp. 170–200. Oxford, England: Basil Blackwell.

Hammarskjöld, D. (1964). *Markings.* (L. Sjöberg & W. Auden, Trans.). New York: Ballantine.

Hampl, P. (1999). *I could tell you stories: Sojourns in the land of memory.* New York: W. W. Norton.

Handwerk, G. (1985). *Irony and ethics in narrative.* New Haven, Conn.: Yale University Press.

Hardy, B. (1968). Toward a poetics of fiction: An approach through narrative. *Novel, 2*(1): 5–14.

Harmon, W., & C. Holman (1996). *A handbook to literature.* Upper Saddle River, N.J.: Prentice-Hall. (Based on the original edition by W. Thrall & A. Hibbard, 1936/1980.)

Hart, E. (2001). The epistemology of cognitive literary studies. *Philosophy and Literature 25:* 314–334.

Hauerwas, S., & L. Jones (Eds.). (1989). *Why narrative? Readings in narrative theology.* Grand Rapids, Mich.: William B. Eerdmans.

Hayflick, L. (1994). *How and why we age.* New York: Ballantine.

Hayles, K. (1993). Constrained constructivism: Locating scientific inquiry in the theater of representation. In G. Levine (Ed.), *Realism and representation: Essays on the problem of realism in relation to science, literature, and culture,* pp. 27–43. Madison, Wisc.: University of Wisconsin Press.

Heilbrun, C. (1997). *The last gift of time.* New York: Dial Press.

Hendricks, J. (2001). It's about time. In S. McFadden & R. Atchley (Eds.), *Aging and the meaning of time: A multidisciplinary exploration*, pp. 21–50. New York: Springer.

Hepworth, M. (2000). *Stories of ageing*. Buckingham, England: Open University Press.

Herman, D. (2002). *Story logic: Problems and possibilities of narrative*. Lincoln, Neb.: University of Nebraska.

Hermans, H. (2000). Meaning as movement: The relativity of mind. In G. Reker & K. Chamberlain (Eds.), *Exploring existential meaning: Optimizing human development across the life span*, pp. 23–38. Thousand Oaks, Calif.: Sage.

Hermans, H. (2002). The dialogical self as a society of mind: An introduction. *Theory & Psychology, 12*(2): 147–160.

Hermans, H., & E. Hermans-Janssen (1995). *Self-narratives: The construction of meaning in psychotherapy*. New York: Guilford.

Hillman, J. (1989). *A blue fire: Selected writings by James Hillman*. New York: Harper-Perennial.

Hinchman, L., & S. Hinchman (Eds.). (1997). *Memory, identity, community: The idea of narrative in the human sciences*. Albany, N.Y.: State University of New York Press.

Hobson, J. A. (1994). *The chemistry of conscious states*. Boston: Back Bay Books.

Hoffman, A. (2001). Sustained by fiction while facing life's facts. In J. Darnton (Ed.), *Writers [on Writing]: Collected essays from* The New York Times, pp. 95–98. New York: Times Books.

Holland, N. (1968). *The dynamics of literary response*. New York: Oxford University Press.

Holland, N. (1975). *Five readers reading*. New Haven, Conn.: Yale University Press.

Holmes, O. (2005). The chambered nautilus. In *The Poetical Works of Oliver Wendell Holmes*. Whitefish, Mont.: Kessinger. (Original work published 1895.)

Holstein, J., & J. Gubrium (2000). *The self we live by: Narrative identity in a postmodern world*. New York: Oxford University Press.

Holstein, M. (1994). Taking next steps: Gerontological education, research, and the literary imagination. *The Gerontologist, 34*(6): 822–827.

Holstein, M. & M. Minkler (2003). Self, society, and the "new gerontology." *The Gerontologist, 43*(6): 787–796.

Hooker, K., & D. McAdams (2003). Personality reconsidered: A new agenda for aging research. *Journal of Gerontology: Psychological Sciences, 58B*(6): 296–304.

Horace. (1991). Epistle to the Pisones: The art of poetry. (N. DeWitt, Trans.) In C. Kaplan & W. Anderson (Eds.), *Criticism: The major statements*, pp. 94–107. New York: St. Martin's Press. (Original work composed ca. 20 BCE.)

Houle, C. (1963). *The inquiring mind*. Madison, Wisc.: The University of Wisconsin Press.

Houston, J. (1987). *The search for the beloved: Journeys in sacred psychology.* Los Angeles: Jeremy P. Tarcher.

Howe, M. (2004). Early memory, early self, and the emergence of autobiographical memory. In D. Beike, J. Lampinen, & D. Behrend (Eds.), *The self and memory,* pp. 45–72. New York: Psychology Press.

Hutcheon, L. (1992). The power of postmodern irony. In B. Rutland (Ed.), *Genre, trope, gender,* pp. 33–49. Ottawa, Ontario, Canada: Carleton University Press.

Iser, W. (1978.) *The act of reading: A theory of aesthetic response.* Baltimore: Johns Hopkins University Press.

James, H. (1963). Preface to *The Spoils of Poynton.* In *The novels and tales of Henry James,* Vol. 10: *The Spoils of Poynton; A London Life; The Chaperon.* New York: Scribner. (Original work published 1908.)

James, W. (1962). *Psychology: Briefer course.* London: Collier.

Johnson, D. (2001). Pesky themes will emerge when you're not looking. In J. Darnton (Ed.), *Writers [on writing]: Collected essays from* The New York Times, pp. 110–115. New York: Times Books.

Johnston, J. (1993, April 25). Fictions of the self in the making. *New York Times Book Review,* 3, 29, 31, 33.

Jung, C. (1923). *Psychological types, or the psychology of individuation.* London: Pantheon Books.

Jung, C. (1961). *Memories, dreams, and reflections.* New York: Vintage.

Jung, C. (1976). The concept of the collective unconscious. In J. Campbell (Ed.), *The portable Jung,* pp. 59–69. London: Penguin.

Jung, C. (1976). The stages of life. In J. Campbell (Ed.), *The portable Jung,* pp. 3–22. London: Penguin.

Jung, C. (1985). *Synchronicity: An acausal connecting principle.* (R. Hull, Trans.). London: Routledge. (Original work published 1952.)

Jung, C. (2001). *Modern man in search of a soul.* (W. Dell & C. Baynes, Trans.). London: Routledge. (Original work published 1933.)

Kabat-Zinn, J. (1994). *Wherever you go there you are: Mindfulness meditation in everyday life.* New York: Hyperion.

Kahana, E. & B. Kahana (1983). Environmental continuity, discontinuity, futurity, and adaptation of the aged. In G. Rowles & R. Ohta (Eds.), *Aging and milieu: Environmental perspectives on growing old.* New York: Academic Press.

Katz, S. (1996). *Disciplining old age: The formation of gerontological knowledge.* Charlottesville, Va.: University Press of Virginia.

Kaufman, S. (1986). *The ageless self: Sources of meaning in late life.* New York: New American Library.

Kazin, A. (1981). The self as history: Reflections on autobiography. In A. E. Stone (Ed.), *The American autobiography: A collection of critical essays,* pp. 31–43. Englewood Cliffs, N.J.: Prentice-Hall.

Kegan, R. (1982). *The evolving self.* Cambridge, Mass.: Harvard University Press.

Keith, J., C. Fry, A. Glascock, C. Ikels, J. Dickerson-Putman, H. Harpending, & P. Draper (1994). *The aging experience: Diversity and commonality across cultures.* Thousand Oaks, Calif.: Sage.

Kelly, G. (1963). *A theory of personality: The psychology of personal constructs.* New York: W. W. Norton.

Kenyon, G. (2002). Creating a wisdom environment in long term care: Storytelling and storylistening. *Stride, 1.* Retrieved May 1, 2007, from: http://www.stridemagazine.com/articles/2002/q1/storytelling/

Kenyon, G., & W. Randall (1997). *Restorying our lives: Personal growth through autobiographical reflection.* Westport, Conn.: Praeger.

Kerby, A. (1991). *Narrative and the self.* Bloomington, Ind.: Indiana University Press.

Kermode, F. (1966). *The sense of an ending: Studies in the theory of fiction.* New York: Oxford University Press.

Kierkegaard, S. (1968). *Fear and trembling* and *The sickness unto death* (W. Lowrie, Trans.). Princeton, N.J.: Princeton University Press. (Original work published 1849.)

Kierkegaard, S. (2003). *Provocations: Spiritual writings of Kierkegaard.* (C. Moore, Ed.). Maryknoll, N.Y.: Orbis Books.

Kimble, M., S. McFadden, J. Ellor, & J. Seeber (Eds.). (1995). *Aging, spirituality, and religion: A handbook.* Minneapolis, Minn.: Augsburg Fortress.

King, T. (2003). *The truth about stories.* Toronto, Ontario, Canada: Anansi.

Kitchener, K., & H. Brenner (1990). Wisdom and reflective judgement: Knowing in the face of uncertainty. In R. Sternberg (Ed.), *Wisdom: Its nature, origins, and development,* pp. 212–229. New York: Cambridge University Press.

Knox, N. (2003). Irony. *The dictionary of the history of ideas.* Retrieved January 8, 2007, from the University of Virginia Library Electronic Text Center: http://etext.lib.virginia.edu/cgi-local/DHI/ot2www-dhi?specfile=/texts/english/dhi/dhi.02w&act=text&offset=9554416&textreg=0&query=.

Koenig, G. (1995). Religion and health in later life. In M. Kimble, S. McFadden, J. Ellor, & J. Seeber (Eds.), *Aging, spirituality, and religion: A handbook,* pp. 9–29. Minneapolis, Minn.: Augsburg Fortress.

Koestler, A. (1964). *The act of creation.* London: Pan Books.

Kohlberg, L. (1984). *The psychology of moral development: The nature and validity of moral stages.* San Francisco: Harper & Row.

Kolb, D. (1984). *Experiential learning: Experience as the source of learning and development.* Englewood Cliffs, N.J.: Prentice-Hall.

Kotre, J. (1984). *Outliving the self: Generativity and the interpretation of lives.* Baltimore: Johns Hopkins University Press.

Kramer, D. (1983). Post formal operations? A need for further conceptualization. *Human Development, 26:* 91–105.

Kramer, D. (1990). Conceptualizing wisdom: The primacy of affect-cognition. In R. Sternberg (Ed.), *Wisdom: Its nature, origins, and development,* pp. 279–313. New York: Cambridge University Press.

Kropf, N., & C. Tandy. (1998). Narrative therapy with older clients: The use of a "meaning making" approach. *Clinical Gerontologist, 18(4):* 3–16.

Kuhl, D. (2002). *What dying people want.* Toronto, Ontario, Canada: Random House.

Kuhl, D., & M. Westwood. (2001). A narrative approach to integration and healing among the terminally ill. In G. Kenyon, P. Clark, & B. de Vries (Eds.), *Narrative gerontology: Theory, research, and practice,* pp. 311–330. New York: Springer.

Kundera, M. (1988). *The art of the novel.* New York: Harper & Row.

Labouvie-Vief, G. (1990). Wisdom as integrated thought: Historical and developmental perspectives. In R. Sternberg (Ed.), *Wisdom: Its nature, origins, and development,* pp. 52–83. New York: Cambridge University Press.

Labouvie-Vief, G. (2000). Positive development in later life. In T. Cole, R. Kastenbaum, & R. Ray (Eds.), *Handbook of the humanities and aging* (2nd ed.), pp. 365–380. New York: Springer.

Lakoff, G. (1993). The contemporary theory of metaphor. In A. Ortony (Ed.), *Metaphor and thought* (2nd ed.), pp. 202–251. Cambridge, England: Cambridge University Press, 1993.

Lakoff, G., & M. Johnson. (1980). *Metaphors we live by.* Chicago: University of Chicago Press.

Lampinen, J., D. Beike, & D. Behrend (2004). The self and memory: It's about time. In D. Beike, J. Lampinen, & D. Behrend (Eds.), *The self and memory,* pp. 255–263. New York: Psychology Press.

Langer, L. (1991). *Holocaust testimonies: The ruins of memory.* New Haven, Conn.: Yale University Press.

Lawrence, D. H. (2004). Hymns in a man's life. In J. Boulton (Ed.), *The Cambridge edition of the works of D. H. Lawrence: Late essays and articles,* pp. 128–134. Cambridge, England: Cambridge University Press.

Le Guin, U. (1989). *Dancing at the edge of the world: Thoughts on words, women, places.* New York: Harper & Row.

Lee, J. (1994). *Writing from the body.* New York: St. Martin's Press.

Lesser, W. (2002). *Nothing remains the same: Rereading and remembering.* Boston: Houghton Mifflin.

Levinson, D. (1978). *The seasons of a man's life.* New York: Ballantine.

Lewis, C. S. (1962). *The problem of pain.* New York: MacMillan.

Lichtenstein, H. (1977). *The dilemma of human identity.* New York: Jason Aronson.

Lindbergh, A. (1955). *Gift from the sea.* New York: Vintage.

Linde, C. (1993). *Lifestories: The quest for coherence.* New York: Oxford University Press.

Linton, M. (1986). Ways of searching and the contents of memory. In D. Rubin (Ed.), *Autobiographical memory,* pp. 50–67. New York: Cambridge University Press.

Lodge, D. (1988). The novel now: Theories and practices. *Novel, 21(2–3):* 125–138.

Lodge, D. (1992). *The art of fiction.* London: Penguin.

Loevinger, J. (1976). *Ego development: Conceptions and theories.* San Francisco: Jossey-Bass.

MacIntyre, A. (1981). *After virtue: A study in moral theory.* London: Duckworth.

MacKeracher, D. (1996). *Making sense of adult learning.* Toronto, Ontario, Canada: Culture Concepts.

Mader, W. (1995). Thematically guided autobiographical reconstruction: On theory and method of "guided autobiography" in adult education. In P. Alheit, A. Born-Wojciechowska, E. Brugger, & P. Dominice (Eds.), *The biographical approach in adult education,* pp. 244–257. Vienna: Verband Wiener Volksbildung.

Mader, W. (1996). Emotionality and continuity in biographical contexts. In J. Birren, G. Kenyon, J-E. Ruth, J. Schroots, & T. Svensson (Eds.), *Aging and biography: Explorations in adult development,* pp. 39–60. New York: Springer.

Manguel, A. (1996). *A history of reading.* Toronto, Ontario, Canada: Alfred Knopf.

Mar, R. A. (2004). The neuropsychology of narrative: Story comprehension, story production and their interrelation. *Neuropsychologia, 42:* 1414–1434.

Mar, R. A., K. Oatley, J. Hirsh, J. de la Paz, & J. B. Peterson (2005). Bookworms versus nerds: Exposure to fiction versus non-fiction, divergent associations with social ability, and the simulation of fictional social worlds. *Journal of Research in Personality, 40:* 694–712.

Marcia, J. (1966.) Development and validation of ego-identity status. *Journal of Personality and Social Psychology, 3*(5): 551–558.

Marcia, J. (1998). Optimal development from an Eriksonian perspective. In H. S. Friedman (Ed.), *Encyclopedia of mental health* (Vol. 3, pp. 29–39). San Diego, Calif.: Academic Press.

Maslow, A. (1968). *Toward a psychology of being.* Princeton, N.J.: Van Nostrand Reinhold.

Mateas, M., & P. Sengers (Eds.). (2003). *Narrative intelligence.* Philadelphia: John Benjamins Publishing.

Mattingly, C. (1991). The narrative nature of clinical reasoning. *The American Journal of Occupational Therapy, 45*(11): 998–1005.

Maugham, W. S. (1945). *The summing up.* New York: Doubleday. (Original work published 1938.)

Maxwell, W. (1980). *So long, see you tomorrow.* New York: Knopf.

May, R. (1991). *The cry for myth.* New York: W. W. Norton.

McAdams, D. (1988). *Power, intimacy, and the life story: Personological inquiries into identity.* New York: Guilford.

McAdams, D. (1993). *The stories we live by: Personal myths and the making of the self.* New York: William Morrow.

McAdams, D. (1996). Narrating the self in adulthood. In J. Birren, G. Kenyon, J-E. Ruth, J. Schroots, & T. Svensson (Eds.), *Aging and biography: Explorations in adult development,* pp. 131–148. New York: Springer.

McAdams, D. (2001). *The person: An integrated introduction to personality psychology* (3rd ed.). New York: Harcourt.

McAdams, D. (2006). *The redemptive self: Stories Americans live by.* New York: Oxford University Press.

McCabe, A. (1997). Developmental and cross-cultural aspects of children's narration. In M. Bamberg (Ed.), *Narrative development: Six approaches,* pp. 137–174. Mahwah, N.J.: Lawrence Erlbaum Associates.

McCullough, L. (1993). Arrested aging: The power of the past to make us aged and old. In T. Cole, W. Achenbaum, P. Jakobi, & R. Kastenbaum (Eds.), *Voices and visions of aging: Toward a critical gerontology,* pp. 184–204. New York: Springer.

McKendy, J. (2006). "I'm very careful about that": Narrative agency of men in prison. *Discourse & Society, 17*(4): 473–502.

McKim, A. (2005). Making poetry of pain: The headache poems of Jane Cave Winscom. *Literature and Medicine, 24*(1): 93–108.

McKim, A., & W. Randall (2007). From psychology to poetics: Aging as a literary process. *Journal of Aging, Humanities, and the Arts, 1*(3): 147–158.

McLeod, J. (1996). *Narrative and psychotherapy.* London: Sage.

McRae, R., & P. T. Costa (2003). *Personality in adulthood: A five-factor theory perspective* (2nd ed.). New York: Guilford.

Meacham, J. (1990). The loss of wisdom. In R. Sternberg (Ed.), *Wisdom: Its nature, origins, and development,* pp. 81–211. New York: Cambridge University Press.

de Medeiros, K. (2007). Beyond the memoir: Telling life-stories using multiple literary forms. *Journal of Aging, Humanities, and the Arts, 1*(3). 159–167.

de Medieros, K., & F. Lagay (2000). *"Share Your Lifestory" workshop manual.* Unpublished manuscript.

Mezirow, J. (1978). Perspective transformation. *Adult Education, 28*(2): 100–110.

Miall, D., & D. Kuiken (1995). Aspects of literary response: A new questionnaire. *Research in the teaching of English, 29:* 37–58.

Miall, D., & D. Kuiken (2002). A feeling for fiction: Becoming what we behold. *Poetics, 30:* 221–241.

Miller, H. (1941). Reflections on writing. In *The wisdom of the heart,* pp. 19–30. Norfolk, Conn.: New Directions Books.

Miller, J. (1978). The problematic of ending in narrative. *Nineteenth-Century Fiction, 33*(1): 3–7.

Missinne, L. (2003). The search for meaning of life in older age. In A. Jewel (Ed.), *Ageing, spirituality and well-being,* pp. 113–123. London: Jessica Kingsley Publishers.

Monk, G. (1997). How narrative therapy works. In G. Monk, J. Winslade, K. Crocket, & D. Epston (Eds.), *Narrative therapy in practice: The archeology of hope,* pp. 3–31. San Francisco: Jossey-Bass.

Montgomery, L. M. (1942). *Anne of Green Gables.* Toronto, Ontario, Canada: Ryerson Press. (Original work published 1908.)

Moody, H. (1984). Reminiscence and the recovery of the public world. In M. Kaminsky (Ed.), *The uses of reminiscence: New ways of working with older adults,* pp. 157–166. New York: Haworth Press.

Moody, H. (1986). The meaning of life and the meaning of old age. In T. Cole & S. Gadow (Eds.), *What does it mean to grow old? Reflections from the humanities,* pp. 9–40. Durham, N.C.: Duke University Press.

Moody, H. (1995). Mysticism. In M. Kimble, S. McFadden, J. Ellor, & J. Seeber (Eds.), *Aging, spirituality, and religion: A handbook,* pp. 87–101. Minneapolis, Minn.: Augsburg Fortress.

Moore, T. (1992). *Care of the soul: A guide for cultivating depth and sacredness in everyday life.* New York: HarperCollins.

Morgan, A. (2000). *What is narrative therapy?: An easy-to-read introduction.* Adelaide, Australia: Dulwich Centre Publications.

Morson, G. (1994). *Narrative and freedom: The shadows of time.* New Haven, Conn.: Yale University Press.

Morson, G. (1999). Essential narrative: Tempics and the return of process. In D. Herman (Ed.), *Narratologies: New perspectives on narrative analysis,* pp. 277–314. Columbus, Ohio: Ohio State University Press.

Munitz, M. K. (1968). *The mystery of existence: An essay in philosophical cosmology.* New York: Delta.

Murray, H. (1938). *Explorations in personality.* New York: Oxford University Press.

Myerhoff, B. (1992). *Remembered lives: The work of ritual, storytelling, and growing older.* Ann Arbor, Mich.: The University of Michigan Press.

Myers, I., & I. McCaulley (1985). *Manual: A guide to the development and use of the Myers-Briggs type indicator.* Palo Alto, Calif.: Consulting Psychologists Press.

Myers, J. E. (1998). Bibliotherapy and DCT: Co-constructing the therapeutic metaphor. *Journal of Counseling & Development, 76* (3): 243–250.

Myss, C. (1996). *Anatomy of the spirit: The seven stages of power and healing.* New York: Three Rivers Press.

National Endowment for the Arts. (2004). *Reading at risk: A survey of literary reading in America.* Research Division Report #46. Retrieved January 20, 2007, from http://www.arts.gov/research/ReadingAtRisk.pdf

Neisser, U. (1986). Nested structure in autobiographical memory. In D. Rubin (Ed.), *Autobiographical memory,* pp. 71–81. New York: Cambridge University Press.

Neisser, U. (1994). Self-narratives: True or false. In U. Neisser & R. Fivush (eds.), *The remembering self: Construction and accuracy in the self-narrative,* pp. 1–18. New York: Cambridge University Press.

Neisser, U., & R. Fivush (Eds.) (1994). *The remembering self: Construction and accuracy in the self-narrative.* New York: Cambridge University Press.

Neisser, U., & L. Libby (2000). Remembering life experiences. In E. Tulving & F. Craik (Eds.), *The Oxford handbook of memory,* pp. 315–332. New York: Oxford University Press.

Nelson, A. (1994). Researching adult transformation as autobiography. *International Journal of Lifelong Education, 13*(5): 389–403.

Nelson, H. (2001). *Damaged identities, narrative repair.* Ithaca, N.Y.: Cornell University Press.

Nelson, K., & R. Fivush (2000). Socialization of memory. In E. Tulving & F. Craik (Eds.), *The Oxford handbook of memory,* pp. 283–295. New York: Oxford University Press.

Neugarten, B. (Ed.) (1968). *Middle age and aging: A reader in social psychology.* Chicago: University of Chicago Press.

Nin, A. (1981). The personal life deeply lived. In A. Stone (Ed.), *The American autobiography: A collection of critical essays,* pp. 157–165. Englewood Cliffs, N.J.: Prentice-Hall.

Nouwen, H., & W. Gaffney. (1976). *Aging: The fulfillment of life.* Garden City, N.Y.: Anchor.

Novak, M. (1971). *Ascent of the mountain, flight of the dove.* San Francisco: Harper & Row.

Novitz, D. (1997). Art, narrative, and human nature. In L. Hinchman & S. Hinchman (Eds.), *Memory, identity, and community: The idea of narrative in the human sciences,* pp. 143–160. Albany, N.Y.: State University of New York Press.

Nussbaum, M. (1990). *Love's knowledge: Essays on philosophy and literature.* New York: Oxford University Press.

Oatley, K. (1994). A taxonomy of the emotions of literary response and a theory of identification in fictional narrative. *Poetics, 23:* 53–74.

Oatley, K. (1999). Why fiction may be twice as true as fact: Fiction as cognitive and emotional simulation. *Review of General Psychology, 3:* 101–117.

O'Brien, G. (2000). *The browser's ecstasy: A meditation on reading.* Washington, D.C.: Counterpoint.

O'Brien, M. (1996). Spirituality and older women: Exploring meaning through story telling. *Journal of Religious Gerontology, 10*(1): 3–16.

Ochs, E., & L. Capps. (2002). *Living narrative: Creating lives in everyday storytelling.* Cambridge, Mass.: Harvard University Press.

Oden, T. (Ed.). (1978). *Parables of Kierkegaard.* Princeton, N.J.: Princeton University Press.

Olney, J. (Ed.). (1980). *Autobiography: Essays theoretical and critical.* Princeton, N.J.: Princeton University Press.

Olney, J. (1998). *Memory and narrative: The weave of life-writing.* Chicago: University of Chicago Press.

Olson, D. (1990). Thinking about narrative. In B. Britton & A. Pelligrini (Eds.), *Narrative thought and narrative language,* pp. 99–111. Hillsdale, N.J.: Lawrence Erlbaum.

Ondaatje, M. (1992). *The English patient.* Toronto, Ontario, Canada: McClelland & Stewart.

Onega, S., & J. Landa. (Eds.). (1996). *Narratology: An introduction.* London: Longman.

Orwoll, L., & M. Perlmutter. (1990). The study of wise persons: Integrating a personality perspective. In R. Sternberg (Ed.), *Wisdom: Its nature, origins, and development,* pp. 160–177. New York: Cambridge University Press.

Overstreet, H. A. (1949). *The mature mind.* New York: W. W. Norton.

Parry, A., & R. Doan (1994). *Story re-visions: Narrative therapy in the postmodern world.* New York: Guilford.

Pascal, R. (1960). *Design and truth in autobiography.* London: Routledge & Kegan Paul.

Payne, B. P., & S. McFadden (1994). From loneliness to solitude: Religious and spiritual journeys in late life. In E. Thomas & S. Eisenhandler (Eds.), *Aging and the religious dimension,* pp. 13–27. Westport, Conn.: Auburn House.

Pearce, J. (2002). *The biology of transcendence: A blueprint of the human spirit.* Rochester, Vt.: Park Street Press.

Pearson, C. (1989). *The hero within: Six archetypes we live by.* San Francisco: Harper & Row.

Pennebaker, J. (1990). *Opening up: The healing power of confiding in others.* New York: Avon.

Phillips, A. (1994). *On flirtation: Psychoanalytic essays on the uncommitted life.* Cambridge, Mass.: Harvard University Press.

Pillemer, D., P. Wink, T. DiDonato, & R. Sanborn (2003). Gender differences in autobiographical memory styles of older adults. *Memory, 11*(6): 525–532.

Plato. (1941). *The Republic of Plato.* (F. M. Cornford, Trans.). London: Oxford University Press. (Original work composed 360 BCE).

Plato. (2002). Apology. In G. M. A. Grube (Tr.) & J. M. Cooper (Rev.) *Five dialogues: Eythyphro, Apology, Crito, Meno, Phaedo* (2nd ed.). Indianapolis, Ind.: Hackett Publishing.

Polkinghorne, D. (1988). *Narrative knowing and the human sciences.* Albany, N.Y.: State University of New York Press.

Polonoff, D. (1987). Self-deception. *Social Research, 54*(1): 45–53.

Polster, E. (1987). *Every person's life is worth a novel.* New York: W.W. Norton.

Prado, C. (1986). *Rethinking how we age: A new view of the aging mind.* Westport, Conn.: Greenwood.

Prickett, S. (2002). *Narrative, religion and science: Fundamentalism versus irony.* Cambridge, England: Cambridge University Press.

Progoff, I. (1975). *At a journal workshop: The basic text and guide for using the intensive journal.* New York: Dialogue House Library.

Proust, M. (1982). *Remembrance of things past,* Vol. 3. (C. Moncrieff, T. Kilmartin, & A. Mayor, Trans.). New York: Vintage Books. (Original work published 1927.)

Rainer, T. (1978). *The new diary.* Los Angeles: Jeremy P. Tarcher.

Randall, W. (1995). *The stories we are: An essay on self-creation.* Toronto, Ontario, Canada: University of Toronto Press.

Randall, W. (1999). Narrative intelligence and the novelty of our lives. *Journal of Aging Studies, 13*(1): 11–28.

Randall, W. (2007). From computer to compost: Rethinking our metaphors for memory. *Theory & Psychology, 17*(5): 611–633.

Randall, W. (2007). Narrative and chaos: Acknowledging the novelty of lives-in-time. *Interchange 38*(4): 367–389.

Randall, W., & G. Kenyon (2001). *Ordinary wisdom: Biographical aging and the journey of life.* Westport, Conn.: Praeger.

Randall, W., & G. Kenyon (2002). Reminiscence as reading our lives: Toward a wisdom environment. In J. Webster & B. Haight (Eds.), *Critical advances in reminiscence: Theoretical, empirical, and clinical perspectives,* pp. 233–253. New York: Springer.

Randall, W., & E. McKim. (2004). Toward a poetics of aging: The links between literature and life. *Narrative Inquiry, 14*(2): 235–260.

Randall, W., S. Prior, & M. Skarborn (2006). How listeners shape what tellers tell: Patterns of interaction in lifestory interviews and their impact on reminiscence with elderly interviewees. *Journal of Aging Studies, 20:* 381–396.

Ray, R. (1996). A postmodern perspective on feminist gerontology. *The Gerontologist, 36*(5): 674–680.

Ray, R. (2000). *Beyond Nostalgia: Aging and life-story writing.* Charlottesville, Va.: University Press of Virginia.

Reese, E., & R. Fivush (1993). Parental styles for talking about the past. *Developmental Psychology, 29:* 596–606.

Reker, G. (2000). Theoretical perspective, dimensions, and measurement of existential meaning. In G. Reker & K. Chamberlain (Eds.), *Exploring existential meaning: Optimizing human development across the life span,* pp. 39–55. Thousand Oaks, Calif.: Sage.

Reker, G., & K. Chamberlain (Eds.). (2000). *Exploring existential meaning: Optimizing human development across the lifespan.* Thousand Oaks, Calif.: Sage.

Ricoeur, P. (1981). Narrative time. In W. J. T. Mitchell (Ed.), *On narrative,* pp. 165–186. Chicago: University of Chicago Press.

Ricoeur, P. (1991). Life in quest of narrative. In David Wood (Ed.), *On Paul Ricoeur: Narrative and interpretation,* pp. 20–33. London: Routledge.

Ricoeur, P. (2004). *Memory, history, forgetting.* (K. Blamey & D. Pellauer, Trans.). Chicago: University of Chicago Press.

Rigney, D. (2001). *The metaphorical society: An invitation to social theory.* New York: Rowman & Littlefield.

Rilke, R. M. (1986). *Letters to a young poet.* (S. Mitchell, Trans.). New York: Vintage.

Rimmon-Kenan, S. (1983). *Narrative fiction: Contemporary poetics.* London: Routledge.

Robeck, M., & R. Wallace (1990). *The psychology of reading: An interdisciplinary approach.* (2nd ed.). Hillsdale, N.J.: Lawrence Erlbaum Associates.

Robinson, D. (1990). Wisdom through the ages. In R. Sternberg (Ed.), *Wisdom: Its nature, origins, and development,* pp. 13–24. New York: Cambridge University Press.

Robinson, J. (1995). Perspective, meaning, and remembering. In D. Rubin (Ed.), *Remembering our past: Studies in autobiographical memory,* pp. 199–217. New York: Cambridge University Press.

Robinson, J., & Hawpe, L. (1986). Narrative thinking as a heuristic process. In T. Sarbin (Ed.), *Narrative psychology,* pp. 111–125. New York: Praeger.

Rogers, M. (1991). *Novels, novelists, and readers: Toward a phenomenological sociology of literature.* Albany, N.Y.: State University of New York Press.

Romance Writers of America. (2005). *Market research study on romance readers.* Retrieved December 30, 2006, from https://www.rwanational.org/eweb/docs/05MarketResearch.pdf?Site = RWA

Rorty, R. (1989). *Contingency, irony, and solidarity.* Cambridge, England: Cambridge University Press.

Rosen, S. (Ed.) (1982). *My voice will go with you: The teaching tales of Milton H. Erickson.* New York: W. W. Norton.

Rosenau, P. (1992). *Postmodernism and the social sciences: Insights, inroads, and intrusions.* Princeton, N.J.: Princeton University Press.

Rosenberg, S., H. Rosenberg, & M. Farrell (1999). The midlife crisis revisited. In S. Willis & J. Reid (Eds.), *Life in the middle: Psychological and social development in middle age,* pp. 47–73. San Diego, Calif.: Academic Press.

Rosenblatt, L. (1978). *The reader, the text, the poem: The transactional theory of the literary work.* Carbondale, Ill.: Southern Illinois University Press.

Rosenblatt, L. (1976). *Literature as exploration.* New York: Modern Language Association. (Original work published 1938.)

Rosensweig, J., & B. Liu (2006). *Age smart: Discovering the fountain of youth at midlife and beyond.* Upper Saddle River, N.J.: Pearson Prentice-Hall.

Rosenwald, G., & R. Ochberg (1992). Introduction: Life stories, cultural politics, and self-understanding. In G. Rosenwald & R. Ochberg (Eds.), *Storied lives: The cultural politics of self-understanding,* pp. 1–18. New Haven, Conn.: Yale University Press.

Rotenberg, M. (1987). *Re-biographing and deviance.* New York: Praeger.

Rowe, J., & R. Kahn. (1998). *Successful Aging.* New York: Pantheon.

Rowles, G., & N. Schoenberg (Eds.). (2002). *Qualitative gerontology: A contemporary perspective.* (2nd ed.). New York: Springer.

Rowling, J. K. (1997). *Harry Potter and the philosopher's stone.* London: Bloomsbury Publishing.

Rubin, D. (Ed.). (1986). *Autobiographical memory.* New York: Cambridge University Press.

Rubin, D. (Ed.). (1995). *Remembering our past: Studies in autobiographical memory.* New York: Cambridge University Press.

Rubin, D., T. Rahhal, & L. Poon (1998). Things learned in early adulthood are remembered best. *Memory and Cognition, 26:* 3–19.

Rubinstein, R. (1994). Generativity as pragmatic spirituality. In L. E. Thomas & S. Eisenhandler (Eds.), *Aging and the religious dimension,* pp. 169–181. Westport, Conn.: Auburn House.

Runyan, W. (1984). *Life histories and psychobiography: Explorations in theory and method.* New York: Oxford University Press.

Rushdie, S. (1992). One thousand days in a balloon. In *Imaginary homelands: Essays and criticism 1981–199,* pp. 430–439. London: Penguin.

Russell, B. (1994). In T. Cole & M. Winkler (Eds.), *The Oxford book of aging: Reflections on the journey of life,* pp. 367–369. New York: Oxford University Press.

Ruth, J.-E., J. Birren, & D. Polkinghorne (1996). The projects of life reflected in autobiographies of old age. *Ageing and Society, 16:* 677–699.

Ruth, J.-E., & G. Kenyon (1996). Biography in adult development and aging. In J. Birren, G. Kenyon, J-E. Ruth, J. Schroots, & T. Svensson (Eds.), *Aging and biography: Explorations in adult development,* pp. 1–20. New York: Springer.

Ruth J-E., & P. Öberg (1996). Ways of life: Old age in a life history perspective. In J. Birren, G. Kenyon, J-E. Ruth, J. Schroots & T. Svensson (Eds.), *Aging and biography: Explorations in adult development,* pp. 167–186. New York: Springer.

Sabat, S., & R. Harré (1992). The construction and deconstruction of self in Alzheimer's disease. *Ageing and Society, 12:* 443–461.

Sacks, O. (1987). *The man who mistook his wife for a hat, and other clinical tales.* New York: Summit.

Salaman, E. (1982). A collection of moments. In U. Neisser, (Ed.), *Memory observed: Remembering in natural contexts,* pp. 49–63. San Francisco: W. H. Freeman.

Sand, G. [Amandine Aurore Lucie Dupin.] (1929). The intimate journal of George Sand. (M. Howe, Trans.). London: Williams & Norgate.

Sarbin, T. (1986). The narrative as a root metaphor for psychology. In T. Sarbin (Ed.), *Narrative psychology: The storied nature of human conduct,* pp. 3–21. New York: Praeger.

Sarbin, T. (1994). Steps to the narratory principle: An autobiographical essay. In D. J. Lee (Ed.), *Life and story: Autobiographies for a narrative psychology,* pp. 7–38. Westport, Conn.: Praeger.

Sarton, M. (1977). *Journal of a solitude.* New York: W. W. Norton. (Original work published 1973.)

Sarton, M. (1980). *Recovering: A journal.* New York: W. W. Norton.

Sarton, M. (1995). *The house by the sea.* New York: W. W. Norton. (Original work published 1977.)

Sartre, J.-P. (1965). *Nausea.* (R. Baldick, Trans.). London: Penguin. (Original work published 1938.)

Saussure, F. (1974). *Course in general linguistics.* (C. Bally, A. Sechehaye, & A. Riedlinger, Eds.; W. Baskin, Trans.). London: P. Owen. (Original work published 1916).

Schachter-Shalomi, Z., & R. Miller (1995). *From age-ing to sage-ing: A profound new vision of growing older.* New York: Warner.

Schacter, D. (1996). *Searching for memory: The brain, the mind, and the past.* New York: Basic Books.

Schacter, D. (2001). *The seven sins of memory: How the mind forgets and remembers.* Boston: Houghton Mifflin.

Schafer, R. (1983). *The analytic attitude.* New York: Basic Books.

Schafer, R. (1989). The sense of an answer: Ambiguities of interpretation in clinical and applied psychoanalysis. In R. Cohen (Ed.), *The future of literary theory,* pp. 188–207. New York: Routledge.

Schafer, R. (1992). *Retelling a life: Narration and dialogue in psychoanalysis.* New York: Basic Books.

Schank, R. (1990). *Tell me a story: A new look at real and artificial intelligence.* New York: Scribner's.

Scheibe, K. (1986). Self-narratives and adventure. In T. Sarbin (Ed.), *Narrative psychology: The storied nature of human conduct,* pp. 129–151. Westport, Conn.: Praeger.

Schiff, B., & B. Cohler (2001). Telling survival backward: Holocaust survivors narrate the past. In G. Kenyon, P. Clark, & B. de Vries (Eds.), *Narrative gerontology: Theory, research, and practice,* pp. 113–136. New York: Springer.

Scholes, R., & R. Kellogg (1966). *The nature of narrative.* New York: Oxford University Press.

Schopenhauer, A. (2004). *Counsels and maxims* (T. B. Saunders, Trans.). Whitefish, Mont.: Kessinger Publishing.

Schroots, J., & J. Birren (2002). The study of lives in progress: Approaches to research on life stories. In G. Rowles & N. Schoenberg (Eds.), *Qualitative gerontology: A contemporary perspective,* pp. 51–65. New York: Springer.

Schweder, R. (1994). "You're not sick, you're just in love": Emotion as an interpretive system. In P. Ekman and R. Davidson (Eds.), *The nature of emotion,* pp. 32–44. New York: Oxford University Press.

Scott-Maxwell, F. (1968). *The measure of my days.* London: Penguin.

Shakespeare, W. (1974a). *As you like it.* In G. B. Evans, Ed., *The Riverside Shakespeare* pp. 365–402. Boston: Houghton Mifflin. (Original work published 1623).

Shakespeare, W. (1974b). *King Richard III.* In G. B. Evans (Ed.), *The Riverside Shakespeare* pp. 708–764. Boston: Houghton Mifflin. (Original work published 1597.)

Shakespeare, W. (1974c). *The tragedy of Hamlet, Prince of Denmark.* In G. B. Evans (Ed.), *The Riverside Shakespeare* pp. 1135–1197. Boston: Houghton Mifflin. (Original work published 1604).

Shaw, M., & M. Westwood (2002). Transformation in life stories: The Canadian war veterans life review project. In J. Webster & B. Haight (Eds.), *Critical advances in reminiscence: From theory to application,* pp. 257–274. New York: Springer.

Shea, J. (1978). *Stories of God: An unauthorized biography.* Chicago: Thomas More Press.

Shelley, P. (1977). A defence of poetry. In D. Reiman & S. Powers (Eds.), *Shelley's poetry and prose,* pp. 478–508. New York: W.W. Norton. (Original work published 1840.)

Sherman, E. (1991). *Reminiscence and the self in old age.* New York: Springer.

Sherman, E., & T. Webb (1994). The self as process in late-life reminiscence: Spiritual attributes. *Ageing and Society, 14:* 255–267.

Sidney, P. (1970). *An apology for poetry.* (F. Robinson, Ed.). Indianapolis, Ind.: Bobbs-Merrill. (Original work published 1595.)

Simpkinson, C., & A. Simpkinson (Eds.). (1993). *Sacred stories: A celebration of the power of stories to transform and heal.* San Francisco: HarperCollins.

Singer, J. (1996). The story of your life: A process perspective on narrative and emotion in adult development. In C. Magai & S. McFadden (Eds.), *Handbook of emotion, adult development, and aging,* pp. 443–463. San Diego, Calif.: Academic Press.

Singer, J., & P. Blagov (2004). The integrative function of narrative processing: Autobiographical memory, self-defining memories, and the life story of identity. In D. Beike, J. Lampinen, & D. Behrend (Eds.), *The self and memory,* pp. 117–138. New York: Psychology Press.

Smith, B. (1983). Contingencies of value. *Critical Inquiry, 10*(1): pp. 1–35.

Smith, D. (1998, May 30). Philosopher gamely in defense of his ideas. *New York Times,* p. B7.

Sophocles. (1987). *Oedipus the king.* (B. Knox, Trans.). New York: Washington Square Press. (Original work composed 428 BCE.)

Spence, D. (1982). *Narrative truth and historical truth: Meaning and interpretation in psychoanalysis.* New York: W. W. Norton.

Spence, D. (1986). Narrative smoothing and clinical wisdom. In T. Sarbin (Ed.), *Narrative psychology: The storied nature of human conduct,* pp. 211–232. New York: Praeger.

Spender, D. (1980). *Man made language.* London: Routledge & Kegan Paul.

State University of New York, Buffalo (2006). *Poetics at Buffalo.* Retrieved January 8, 2007, from the Electronic Poetry Center Web site: http://wings.buffalo.edu/epc/poetics/prog.html

Sternberg, R. (Ed.) (1990). *Wisdom: Its nature, origins, and development.* New York: Cambridge University Press.

Sternberg, R. (1998). *Love is a story: A new theory of relationships.* New York: Oxford University Press.

Stone, R. (1996). *The healing art of storytelling: A sacred journey of personal discovery.* New York: Hyperion.

Surmelian, L. (1969). *Techniques of fiction writing: Measure and madness.* Garden City, N.Y.: Anchor.

Swimme, B., & T. Berry. *The universe story: From the primordial flaring forth to the ecozoic era.* New York: HarperCollins.

Taha, I. (1998–99). Openness and closedness: Four categories of closurization in modern Arabic fiction. *Journal of Arabic and Islamic Studies, 2:* 1–23. Retrieved April 26, 2007, from www.uib.no/jais/voo2/taha.pdf

Tannen, D. (1990). *You just don't understand: Women and men in conversation.* New York: Ballantine.

Taylor, C. (1989). *Sources of the self: The making of modern identity.* Cambridge, Mass.: Harvard University Press.

Tennant, M., & P. Pogson. (1995). *Learning and change in the adult years: A developmental perspective.* San Francisco: Jossey-Bass.

TeSelle, S. (1975). *Speaking in parables: A study in metaphor and theology.* Philadelphia: Fortress Press.

Thorsen, K. (1998). The paradoxes of gerotranscendence: The theory of gerotranscendence in a cultural gerontological and post-modernist perspective. *Norwegian Journal of Epidemiology, 8*(2): 165–176.

Thurber, J. (2000). *The secret life of Walter Mitty and other pieces.* London: Penguin, 2000. (Original work published 1941).

Tolle, E. (1999). *The power of now: A guide to spiritual enlightenment.* Novato, Calif.: New World Library.

Tolstoy, L. (2006). *War and peace.* (A. Briggs, Trans.). London: Penguin. (Original work published 1865–1869.)

Torell, Ö. (2001). Literary competence beyond conventions. *Scandinavian Journal of Educational Research, 45*(4): 369–379.

Tornstam, L. (1994). Gero-transcendence: A theoretical and empirical exploration. In E. Thomas & S. Eisenhandler (Eds.), *Aging and the religious dimension,* pp. 203–225. Westport, Conn.: Auburn House.

Tornstam, L. (1996). Gerotranscendence: A theory about maturing into old age. *Journal of Aging and Identity, 1*(1): 37–49.

Truitt, A. (1987). *Turn: The journal of an artist.* London: Penguin.

Tulving, E. (1983). *Elements of episodic memory.* Oxford, England: Clarendon Press.

Tulving, E. (1993). What is episodic memory? *Current Directions in Psychological Science 2*(3): 67–70.

Turner, A. (2006). *Wisdom environments in seniors' narrative as sacred space.* Unpublished master's thesis. Laurentian University, Sudbury, Ontario, Canada.

Turner, M. (1996). *The literary mind.* New York: Oxford University Press.

van den Hoonaard, D. (1997). Identity foreclosure: Women's experiences of widowhood as expressed in autobiographical accounts. *Ageing and Society, 17:* 533–551.

Vaughan, S. (1997). *The talking cure: Why traditional talking therapy offers better chance for long-term relief than any drug.* New York: Henry Holt and Company.

Viney, L. (1993). *Life stories: Personal construct therapy with the elderly.* Chichester, England: John Wiley & Sons.

Vonnegut, K. (1982). *Deadeye Dick.* New York: Dell Publishing.

Walaskay, M., S. Whitbourne, & M. Nehrke (1983–84). Construction and validation of an ego integrity status interview. *International Journal of Aging and Human Development, 18*(1): 61–72.

Wallace, J. B. (1992). Reconsidering the life review: The social construction of talk about the past. *The Gerontologist, 32:* 120–125.

Waxman, B. (1997). *To live in the center of the moment: Literary autobiographies of aging.* Charlottesville, Va.: University Press of Virginia.

Weil, A. (2005). *Healthy aging: A lifelong guide to your physical and spiritual well-being.* New York: Alfred A. Knopf.

Weiland, S. (1995). Interpretive social science and spirituality. In M. Kimble, S. McFadden, J. Ellor, & J. Seeber (Eds.), *Aging, spirituality, and religion: A handbook,* pp. 589–612. Minneapolis, Minn.: Augsburg Fortress.

Wheeler, M. A. (2000). Episodic memory and autonoetic awareness. In E. Tulving & F. Craik (Eds.), *The Oxford Handbook of Memory,* pp.597–608. New York: Oxford University Press.

White, M., & D. Epston (1990). *Narrative means to therapeutic ends.* New York: W. W. Norton.

Widdershoven, G. (1993). The story of life: Hermeneutic perspectives on the relationship between narrative and life history. In R. Josselson & A. Leiblich (Eds.), *The narrative study of lives* (Vol. 1, pp. 1–20). Newbury Park, Calif.: Sage.

Wiesel, E. (1988). Interview. In G. Plimpton (Ed.), *Writers at work: The Paris Review interviews* (8th series), pp. 225–264. London: Penguin.

Wiesel, E. (1995). *From the kingdom of memory: Reminiscences.* New York: Schocken.

Willis, S., & J. Reid (Eds.). (1999). *Life in the middle: Psychological and social development in middle age.* San Diego, Calif.: Academic Press.

Wink, P., & B. Schiff (2002). To review or not to review? The role of personality and life events in life review and adaptation to older age. In J. Webster & B. Haight (Eds.), *Critical advances in reminiscence: From theory to application,* pp. 44–60. New York: Springer.

Wolfe, T. (1938/1983). *The autobiography of an American novelist.* Cambridge, Mass.: Harvard University Press. (Original work pubished 1938.)

Wong, P. T. (1995). The processes of adaptive reminiscence. In B. K. Haight & J. D. Webster (Eds.), *The art and science of reminiscing: Theory, research, methods and applications,* pp. 23–35. Washington, D.C.: Taylor & Francis.

Woodruff–Pak, D., & M. Papka (1999). Theories of neuropsychology and aging. In V. Bengtson, & K. Schaie (Eds.), *Handbook of theories of aging,* pp. 113–132. New York: Springer.

Woodward, K. (1991). *Aging and its discontents: Freud and other fictions.* Bloomington, Ind.: Indiana University Press.

Wordsworth, W. (1979). *The Prelude: 1799, 1805, 1850.* (J. Wordsworth, M. Abrams, & S. Gill, Eds.). New York: W. W. Norton.

Wordsworth, W. (1981). Lines composed a few miles above Tintern Abbey. In J. Hayden, (Ed.). *William Wordsworth: The poems* (Vol. 1, pp. 357–362). New Haven, Conn.: Yale University Press. (Original work published 1798.)

Wordsworth, W. (1981). Ode: Intimations of immortality. In J. Hayden, (Ed.). *William Wordsworth: The poems* (Vol. 1, pp. 523–529). New Haven, Conn.: Yale University Press. (Original work published 1807.)

Wordsworth, W. (1981). Preface to *Lyrical Ballads*. In J. Hayden (Ed.). *William Words-worth: The poems* (Vol. 1, pp. 868–896). New Haven, Conn.: Yale University Press. (Original work published 1802.)

Wyatt-Brown, A. (2000). The future of literary gerontology. In T. Cole, R. Kasten-baum, & R. Ray (Eds.), *Handbook of the humanities and aging* (2nd ed.), pp. 41–61. New York: Springer.

Yates, J., & J. Hunter (2002). Fundamentalism: When history goes awry. In J. Davis (Ed.), *Stories of change: Narrative and social movements*, pp. 123–148. Albany, N.Y.: SUNY Press.

Yeats, W. (1996). Among school children. In R. Finneran (Ed.), *The collected poems of W. B. Yeats*, pp. 215–217. New York: Scribner. (Original work published 1928.)

Zunshine, L. (2006). *Why we read fiction: Theory of mind and the novel.* Columbus, Ohio: Ohio State University Press.

Zwaan, R. (2004). The immersed experiencer: Toward an embodied theory of lan-guage comprehension. In Brian H. Ross (Ed.), *The Psychology of Learning and Motivation* (Vol. 44, pp. 35–62). Amsterdam: Elsevier Academic Press.

Index

Abbott, H. Porter, 9
Adler, Alfred, 177
Aftel, Mandy, 40, 69
Age autobiography, 239
Aging
  adventurous, 259
  approaches to study of, 4
  arrested, 125–28, 198
  biographical vs. biological, 9, 167
  brain, 121–22
  growing old vs. getting old, vii,
    3–5, 64, 135
  in depth, 7
  inside vs. outside of, 4
  as interdisciplinary experience, 19
  and late life crisis, 124
  narrative complexity of, 122, 282
  new story of, 282
  philosophic homework of, 7
  psychology of, 9
  spiritual, 247–83
  successful, 4, 254–60
  well, 4
  and wisdom, 221–23
Albright, Daniel, 18
Alcoholics Anonymous, 57, 100
Alea, Nicole, 152
Alheit, Peter, 204
Aristotle, 17, 224
Arlin, Patricia, 219
Assagioli, Roberto, 35
Assimilation, vs. accommodation, 109,
    111, 129, 192, 256, 277. See also
    Reconciliation
Atchley, Robert, 248, 249
Atkinson, Robert, 112, 250–51, 257
Atmosphere

and narrative tone, 46–47
  of a novel, 46–47
  wisdom, 243–44
Attention Deficit Disorder, 32
Augustine, St., 11, 153
Auschwitz, 144, 195
Author. See also Self-as-author
  death of, 13
Authorship, 12–13
Autobiographical imperative, 122
Autobiographical learning, 234
Autobiographical memory. See also
    Autobiography; Memory(ies)
  ABC's of, 148–51, 163
  as autobiographical knowledge, 151
  complexity of, 148–66
  components of, 151
  definition of, 142–43
  and general events, 152
  and identity, 142–43
  levels of, 151–53
  and lifestory schema, 152
  and lifetime periods, 151–52
  nested nature of, 151
  and other people, 163–66
  and procedural memory, 142
  retrievability of, 166–75
  and semantic memory, 142
  and sense of self, 143, 159–63
  and specific events, 152
  as story memory, 157
  time and, 151–55
  truth and, 155–59
Autobiographical self, 22–48
Autobiography
  age, 239
  guided, 175

Autobiography (*continued*)
and identity, 64–65
as metaphor, 189
as novel one believes in, 40–41
original sin of, 131
as parabolic, 269–72
as process vs. product, viii
and truth, 270–71
Automatic self-reading, 99
Autonoetic awareness, 77

Bakhtin, Mikhail, 41
Baldwin, Christina, 212
Baltes, Paul, 218–19
Barthes, Roland, 13
Bartlett, Francis, 185
Bateson, Mary Catherine, 5, 133–34, 141
Baur, Susan, 111
Beardslee, William, 266
Beattie, Olga, 47
Behrend, Douglas, 159
Beike, Denise, 159
Berger, Peter, 31, 258
Berman, Harry, 179, 180, 234
Bernstein, Charles, 18
Berry, Thomas, 264–65
Bianchi, Eugene, 203–4, 248–49, 267
Bickle, John, 28
Bibliotherapy, 91–93, 268–69
Biographical capital, 127, 184, 246
Biographical encounter, conversation as, 243
Biography, as biology, 119. *See also*
      Neurology
Birkerts, Sven, 74, 95, 97, 185, 273
Birren, James, 63–64, 216
Blagov, Pavel, 160
Blanchard-Fields, Fredda, 231
Bleich, David, 79
Blindsight, 162, 220
and hindsight, 162
Bluck, Susan, 143, 152
Blythe, Ronald, 195, 254
Body(ies). *See also* Neurology
as antagonist, 133
changes with age and, 119–20
and core consciousness, 119
as character in our story, 119
as living history book, 119
as other, 240
Bolen, Jean Shinoda, 265
Booth, Wayne, 20, 39
Bortolussi, Maria, 78, 81–83
Bourdieu, Pierre, 17
Bowen, Elizabeth, 141

Brady, Michael, 212
Brain, aging, 121–23. *See also* Neurology
and changes to memory, 167–69
frontal lobe region, 167–69
Bridges, William, 95
Brockelman, Paul, 261
Brockmeier, Jens, 65, 153, 277
Brooks, Peter, 29, 97
Bruner, Jerome, xi, 5, 8, 17, 36, 64, 106, 138,
      158, 159–60, 205, 228, 238, 257
Bryson, Bill, 28
Burke, Kenneth, 9
Butala, Sharon, 193–94
Butler, Robert, 226–27

Campbell, Joseph, 65, 137, 232, 265
and the hero's journey, 137, 232
Carbaugh, Donal, 65
Carlyle, Thomas, 281
Carr, David, 70–71, 229
Casey, Edward, 108, 150
Castenada, Carlos, 252
Cavarero, Adriana, 71
Chamberlain, Kerry, 185, 274
Chandler, Sally, 200–1, 204
Chapman, Sherry, 282
Character, 82–83
and characterization, 210
identification with, 90–92
Charmé, Stuart, 40, 185–87, 238, 267
Choose Your Own Adventure, 45, 224
Chopin, Kate, 258–59
Chronic pain, 129
Clayton, Vivian, 222
Closure, 62. *See also* Death; Ending(s); The End
closed, 257
open, 257, 272, 279
Cobley, Paul, 7
Cognitive neuroscience, 22–27
Cohen, Gene, 121–22, 169, 217, 218, 259, 282
Coherence, as criterion of good lifestory, 68,
      104–5, 118, 199, 228–29
Cohler, Bertram, 104, 106, 118, 180
Cole, Tom, 34, 149, 202, 260
Coleman, Peter, 104–5, 111–12, 135, 273
Coleridge, Samuel Taylor, 88–89, 146
Composing a life, 3–11
as improvisation, 44
Compost heap, memory as, 147, 151, 154,
      156, 167, 171, 221, 235, 245, 250, 276
Computer, memory as, 146
Co-authoring, 55, 60, 70, 99
Consciousness
autobiographical, 6, 99, 162, 278

core, 24–26
from corporeality to, 22–27
extended, 26, 36
lying as origin of, 238
Conway, Martin, 151–52
Corn, Alfred, 24–25
Counter-story(ies), 123, 188, 191, 282
Cowley, Malcolm, 124, 142, 221
Credibility, as criterion of good lifestory, 106–7
Creeley, Robert, 18
Crites, Stephen, 28–29, 34, 162, 263–64
Critical awareness, as criterion of good lifestory, 110
Critical gerontology, 10
Crossan, John Dominic, 269
Crossley, Michelle, 16
Crovitz, Herbert, 148
Crowder, Robert, 75
Csikszentmihalyi, Mihaly, 47, 217
and flow, 279
Culler, Jonathan, 84
Cupitt, Don, 44–45, 266

Daloz, Laurent, 183, 232–33, 277
Damasio, Antonio, xi, 23–24, 26–27, 36, 76
Death. See also Closure; Ending(s); The End
as aesthetic necessity, 260
fact of, 259–60
in fiction, 257
prospect of, 254–59
and successful aging, 254–60
Debats, Dominique, 179
Deep story, 65, 143, 262
Delbo, Charlotte, 195
Dementia, ix, 126, 143, 283. See also Narrative foreclosure
Dennett, Daniel, 70
Depression
and life review, 227
and meaning, 181
Derrida, Jacques, 11–12
De-storying, x
death and, 255
Developmental intelligence, 122, 218
Dewey, John, 224, 233
Differentiation
as criterion of good lifestory, 107–09, 133, 229–30
Dillard, Annie, 111–12
Disbelief, construction of, 89–90
Discourse, 7, 83

Discursive confinement
prison as, 56
Disengagement theory, 259, 274
Disjointed stories, 192–94
Disrupted stories, 194–96
Dixon, Peter, 78, 81–83
Dominated stories, 190–92
Dostoyevsky, Fyodor, 45, 127
Dream(ing), 28, 35, 76
and memories, 172, 283
Dynamic reminiscence, 196–97, 200–8, 211.
See also Life review; Reminiscence
as dis-integration, 205
vs. fixed reminiscence, 200
gender and, 201
group dynamics and, 201, 205
and integrative reminiscence, 200
as perpetual hermeneutic circle, 208–9
as sideshadowing, 204, 230, 245
and wisdom, 205

Eagleton, Terry, 14
Eakin, Paul John, viii–ix, 161, 193
Ecclesiastes, 220
Editing
of inner experience, 33–37
Edmundsen, Mark, 91
Education, as transformation, 233–34
Educational gerontology, 9–10
Einstein, Gillian, 26
Eliade, Mircea, 65
Eliot, T. S., 144
Emotion(s). See also Memory(ies)
narrative complexity of, 31, 35, 155, 239
and reading, 75
Emotional intelligence, 217
Empathy, 90–91, 239
Emplotment, 24, 35, 42–43, 146, 209–10
Ending(s). See also Death; The End
and autobiography, 256–57
in relation to beginnings and middles, 43–46, 135–36
and closure, 255–56
concern with, 67–68
and lifestory, 68
need of in narrative, 254–55, 272
sense of an, 254, 256, 278–79
tragic, 189
Ephron, Nora, 240
Epigenesis, 60
Epston, David, 126, 188
Erickson, Milton, 268–69
Erikson, Erik, 60, 123–24, 133, 200, 216, 219, 220, 226

Feldman, Carol, 159
Fiction, 74–75, 79, 80, 81–84, 89, 90–91.
    See also Novel
    processual, 45
Field, Joanna, 29, 153
Fingarette, Herbert, 180
Fisher, Laurel, 216
Fivush, Robyn, 39, 50–51, 54
Flanagan, Owen, 23, 27, 30
Ford, Henry, 169
Forster, E. M., 47
Fox, Matthew, 266
Frankl, Viktor, 181
Freeman, Mark, xi, 5, 44, 49, 132, 153,
    154–55, 165–66, 235, 247, 254
Frey, James, 106
Frick, Willard, 279–81
Friedan, Betty, 222, 276
Fulford, Robert, 45, 107
Fundamental project, 186, 189, 191, 211, 244,
    279. See also Charmé, Stuart; Sartre,
    Jean-Paul

Gadamer, Hans, 234
Galton, Sir Francis, 148
Garland, Jeffrey, 227
Gearing, Brian, 133, 194–95
Gender differences
    and memory, 54, 165
    and narrative environment, 54
    and narrative foreclosure, 133–34
    in reminiscence, 165, 201
    and spirituality, 267
    and study of aging, viii
    and wisdom, 215, 234–35
Genealogy, 277–78. See also Generativity
Generative integration, as criterion of good
    lifestory, 109–10, 230–31
Generativity, 68, 275–77
    and genealogy, 277–78
    and highly generative adults, 68
    as pragmatic spirituality, 276
    script, 68, 135
    transmissive reminiscence and, 198–99
Gergen, Kenneth, 31, 106, 255
Gergen, Mary, 255
Gerrig, Richard, 75
Gerontological Society of America, 18–19
Gerotranscendence, 273–75
Gibbs, Raymond, 25
Giddens, Anthony, 17
Glover, Jonathan, 40, 202
Godard, Jean-Luc, 42
Goffman, Erving, 38

Gold, Joseph, 92–93
Goldberg, Elkhonon, 121, 235
Goleman, Daniel, 217
Good lifestory
    concept of, 53, 103
    criteria for, 103–12
    and wisdom, 228–31
Gordon, Kerry, 281–82
Grams, Armin, 254
Green, Melanie, 89
Greene, Graham, 146
Greene, Maxine, 138–39
Grimes, Ronald, 34
Growing old
    vs. getting old, 3, 4, 64, 135
Growth. See also Growing old
    infinite potential for, 246
    Tao of, 245
    as transformation in meaning-making,
        183, 234
Gubrium, Jaber, 51, 113
Guided autobiography, 175, 243
Gullette, Margaret Morganroth, 4, 239
Gusdorf, Georges, 131, 204
Gutmann, David, 349

Habermas, Tilmann, 143
Hammarskjöld, Dag, 101–2
Hamlyn, David, 225
Hampl, Patricia, 34, 144, 205–7
Handwerk, Gary, 15
Hardy, Barbara, 22
Hart, Elizabeth, 17
Hawpe, Linda, 27–28
Hayflick, Leonard, 278
Heilbrun, Carolyn, 170, 254
Hendricks, Jon, 276
Hepworth, Mike, 79
Herman, David, 75–76
Hermans, Hubert, 29, 132, 161
Hermeneutical gerontology, 179
Hillman, James, 43–44, 239, 265
Hobson, J. Allan, 30
Hoffman, Alice, 133
Holland, Norman, 79
Holmes, Oliver Wendell, 236
Holstein, James, 51
Holstein, Martha, 259, 260
Hooker, Karen, 64
Horace, 88
Houston, Jean, 196
Howe, Mark, 143
Hutcheon, Linda, 15
Hypernarrativia, 88

Identity. *See also* Lifestory(ies); Narrative foreclosure
  achievers, 125
  crisis, 124, 180
  damaged, 188
  diffusion, 125
  foreclosure, 125, 136, 190
  as a lifestory, 64, 186
  moratorium, 125, 272
  narrative, 63–72
  as narrative construction, 188
  and narrativity, 64–65, 193
  redefinition of with age, 277
  statuses, 124–25
  -themes, 47
Ideological setting, 67
Images, 76–77
Imagination, 77
  and memory, 7, 131, 143, 157, 205
Imagoes, 67, 108
Inside story, vs. outside story, 52, 223
Integrity, vs. integration, 216
Integrity statuses, 127–28
Intensive journal, 244–46
Interdisciplinarity
  and aging, 19
  and gerontology, 18
  and narrative, 19–21
Interpretive parsimony, 130, 190–91, 223, 268. *See also* Narrative foreclosure
Ironic orientation, as criterion of good lifestory, 110–11
Ironic stance. *See also* Irony
  as hallmark of wisdom, 221
  as openness, 7
  postmodernism and, 15–16, 237
Irony. *See also* Ironic orientation; Ironic stance
  definition of, 15–16
  and humor, 221
  meaning-wise, 241–42
  and narrative, 236–37, 281
  other-wise, 240–41
  and religion, 266
  and reminiscence, 276
  and retrospective interpretation, 238
  self-wise, 238–40
  time-wise, 237–38
  and wisdom, 236–42
  and wonder, 281–82
Iser, Wolfgang, 80

James, Henry, 60
James, William, 28, 34

Johnson, Diane, 47
Johnson, Mark, 25
Johnston, Jill, 22
Journalistic metaphor, 31–37, 45, 153, 177
Journal-keeping, 102, 170, 131–32, 226, 234, 241, 244–46. *See also* Intensive journal
Jung, Carl Gustav, 126, 166, 221, 231, 272

Kabat-Zinn, Jon, 252
Kafka, Franz, 268
Kahn, Robert, 259–60
Kalmar, David, 38, 63, 67, 105, 109, 162–63
Kaufman, Sharon, 47, 179
Kazin, Alfred, 251
Kegan, Robert, 34, 179, 196–97, 204
Kellogg, Robert, 237
Kelly, George, 223
Kenyon, Gary, viii
Kerby, Anthony Paul, 13–14
Kierkegaard, Søren, 268
King, Thomas, 49, 261
Koestler, Arthur, 282
Kuhl, David, 271
Kuiken, Don, 77, 78, 90
Kundera, Milan, 271

Lagay, Faith, 202
Lakoff, George, 25
Lampinen, James, 159
Landa, José Angel García, 7
Langer, Lawrence, 195–96
Larger stories, 50–57, 96, 190–91. *See also* Master narrative(s); Narrative environment(s)
Late life crisis, 124
  and meaning, 180–81
Late life style of artists, 270
Lawrence, D. H., 281
Lee, John, 119
LeGuin, Ursula, 193
Lesser, Wendy, 85–86
Lewis, C. S., 280
Lichtenstein, Heinz, 47
Life-literature connection, 40–48
  continuities vs. discontinuities, 41–48
Life review, 171, 226–28. *See also* Reading life; Reminiscence
  vs. expanding our stories, 171
  and life repair, 226–27
  moral dimension of, 226–27
  structured vs. spontaneous, 199, 226
  and suicide, 227
  and wisdom, 216, 226–28
Life-theme, 47–48, 105, 175, 231

Life-writing, viii, 202–3
Lifestory(ies). *See also* Good lifestory; Lives
    as texts; Meaning; Story(ies); Story of
    my life
  definition of, 64
  examining, 176–211
  expanding, 141–75
  as folk notion, 63
  as fundamental project, 186
  gathering material for, 65–66
  identity as, 64–65, 96
  letting go of, 272–81
  mystery in, 267
  as myth, 65
  novelty of, 40–48
  openness of, 64, 178
  as parabolic, 269–73, 283
  and personality, 63, 118
  transcending, 247–83
  transforming, 212–46
  and truth, 270–71
Lindbergh, Anne Morrow, 123
Linde, Charlotte, 64
Linton, Marigold, 171, 172
Literariness, 138
Literary competence, 6–7, 84–85
Literary gerontology, viii, 10
Literary mind, 25–26
Literary self-literacy, 6–7, 93, 94, 102–3,
    204. *See also* Dynamic reminiscence;
    Reading life; Self-reading
Literature. *See also* Fiction; Novel
  emancipatory potential of, 138–39
  parabolic aspect of, 138
  reading, 73–94
  subversive spirit of, 137–38
  lives as novels, 6, 40–48
Lives as texts, 5–6, 223–24. *See also*
    Lifestory(ies); Texistence
  as sacred texts, 248, 267–72
Lodge, David, 237
Loneliness, vs. solitude, 246

MacIntyre, Alisdair, 70–71
Mader, Wilhelm, 243
Manguel, Alberto, 11
Mar, Raymond, 77–78
Marcia, James, 124–25, 136
Maslow, Abraham, 279
Master narrative(s), 54, 135, 188, 260–63.
    See also Larger stories; Sacred stories
  as narrative environments, 54, 261–63
  postmodernism as, 261
  and religion, 261–63

and symbolic growth experiences, 280
and transcendence, 262
Maugham, Somerset, 41, 44
Maxwell, William, 157
May, Rollo, 65, 265
McAdams, Dan, xi, 47, 63, 64–68, 161, 248, 267
McCabe, Allyssa, 40
McCullough, Lawrence, 126–27
McKendy, John, 38, 56
McLeod, John, 187
Meacham, John, 222
Meaning, 176–211. *See also* Memory(ies);
    Reading; Wisdom
  breadth of, 182
  components of, 182
  as contextual, 183–84
  crisis of, 180
  as cumulative, 184
  defining, 178
  and depression, 181
  depth of, 182
  and development, 180
  as developmental, 183, 184
  -evolution, 203
  existential, 178
  indeterminacy of, 84, 98, 196, 211, 283
  -in-life, 178, 197
  and interpretation, 210
  and irony, 241–42
  literary, 186–87
  -making, 5, 179, 181
  and memory, 176–78, 183
  narrativity of, 5, 184–87
  nature of, 181–85
  necessity of, 179–81
  and personality, 63, 179–80
  perspectives, 183
  and psychoanalysis, 186–87
  and psychopathology, 179
  and reading, 183, 185
  reorganization, 189
  as retrospective, 183
  sources of, 182
  and spirituality, 251
  and story, 185
  structure of, 224
  surplus, 204, 262, 277
  and symbolic growth experiences,
    279–81
  therapy as renegotiation of, 189
  transformation of, 233
Meaning-making, as therapoetic,
    187–89
de Medeiros, Kate, 149, 202

Memory(ies), 141–75. *See also* Autobiographi-
    cal memory; Compost heap, memory
    as; Meaning; Reading; Remembering;
    Reminiscence; Self; Texistence
  and adventure, 108
  as anomalies, 143–44
  as biographical capital, 184, 246, 252
  blocking, 168
  changes with age, 167–69
  complexity of, 148–66
  and dreams, 172, 283
  and emplotment, 146
  emotion and, 155
  episodic, 77, 142, 168
  as faction, 157
  flashbulb, 168
  and forgetting, 145–46
  gendered socialization of, 165
  harvesting of, 203–4
  and imagination, 177, 131, 143, 157, 205
  implicit, 153, 166
  and meaning, 143, 176–78, 212–13
  metaphorical potential of, 236
  metaphors for, 146–48
  mining of, 203–4
  mystery of, 141–75
  narrativity of, 153–54
  necessity of, 141–44
  as open text, 211
  procedural, 142, 168
  and psychotherapy, 144, 196, 209
  and reading, 85–86
  reconstruction of, 235
  relational dimension of, 163
  repisodic, 150
  retrievability of, 166–75
  scarcity of, 144–48
  selectiveness of, 142, 177
  and self, 143, 159
  self-defining, 160, 169, 206
  semantic, 142, 168
  "sins" of, 145–46, 168–69
  source, 168
  and spirituality, 251
  strategies for stimulating, 171–75
  -talk, 56
  temporal complexity of, 153–54
  thick autonomy of, 108, 150–51, 168
  transience of, 145, 169
  transformation and, 235
  and truth, 155–59
  watching, 172
Mental fitness, 214
Messy text, life as, 45

Metaphor. *See also* Parable
  defined, 24–26
  conceptual, 25–26
  and memory, 146–48, 235–36
  narrative as root, 7
  and reading, 77–78
  seductiveness of, 9
  and spirituality, 251
  and therapy, 175
  as transference, 24
Mezirow, James, 182–83
Miall, David, 77, 78, 90
Midlife, vii–viii, 10, 282
  crisis, 124, 133
  muddle, 232
  and tragic sense of life, 236
  and spirituality, 249
Miller, J. Hillis, 255
Miller, Ronald, 226–27, 230, 234
Minkler, Meredith, 259, 260
Moody, Harry, 249
Moore, Thomas, 107, 248, 265, 267
Morson, Gary Saul, 17, 42, 46, 127, 156, 204,
    257, 268
Murray, Henry, 47
Myerhoff, Barbara, 8
Myers, Jane E., 91
Myss, Carolyn, 119
Myth, lifestory as, 64, 65
Mythic stage, 66–67

Narrating
  and interacting, 37–40
Narration, 210
Narrative. *See also* Lifestory(ies); Master
    narrative(s); Narrative environment(s);
    Narrative foreclosure; Story(ies);
    Self(ves)
  adequate, 111
  beyond, 281
  and chaos, 8
  coherence, 104–5, 133, 195
  complexity, 108
  confusion, 123
  debris, 152, 193, 206
  of decline, 4, 119, 123, 129, 135, 214, 259
  definition of, 7–8
  deprivation, 107
  disorders, 193
  disruption, 125
  elaboration, 118, 243, 255
  etymology of, 8
  form, 104, 230
  freedom, 258

Narrative (*continued*)
  identity, 63–72
  imagination, 8
  impoverishment, 56–57
  incoherence, 194
  integrity, 104, 193
  intelligence, 8, 20, 51, 32, 58, 93, 226
  intelligibility, 104, 158
  and irony, 236–37
  knowing, 8
  and meaning, 184–87
  medicine, 133
  neurology of, 22–27
  options, 133
  practice(s), 5, 57
  perspective, 223–25
  prelinguistic basis of, 22–27
  of progress, 123
  quality of experience, 9
  reasoning, 8
  repair, 188–89, 243–44
  resources, 134, 190
  self, 10, 59, 207, 239
  and spirituality, 250–53
  template, 51
  theology, 261–63
  thickness and, 108
  thought, 27–28, 122, 158, 188
  and time, 9, 153
  tone, 47, 65
  and transformation, 231–33
  and trouble, 108, 118
  and truth, 158–59
  turn, 8, 20
  unconscious, 166, 277
Narrative development, 57–62. *See also*
    Narrative; Narrative environment(s);
    Narrative foreclosure; Reading life
  backward nature of, 62
  limitlessness of, 62
Narrative environment(s), 50–57.
    See also Co-authoring; Larger story(ies);
    Master narrative(s); Narrative;
    Narrative foreclosure; Wisdom
    environment
  conversation as, 55
  as discursive environment, 50
  as going concern, 51
  as interpretive community, 51, 98
  family as, 51–53, 55–56, 60
  friendship as, 55
  and gender, 54
  and memory, 170, 171
  narrowing of, 61, 135, 258

  novel(s) as, 59
  nursing home as, 56
  and reading, 85
  as setting for personal story, 52–53
  therapy as, 57
Narrative foreclosure, 7, 105,
    123–36, 180–81, 189, 234, 252, 272.
    See also Arrested aging; Interpretive
    parsimony; Narrative environment(s);
    Under-reading
  arrested aging as, 125–28
  claustrophilia, 132
  and death, 255
  defined, 125–26
  dementia as, 283
  as denouement, 126
  and depression, 127
  factors behind, 128–36
  and gender, 133–34
  journal keeping as, 131–32
  and life review, 227
  and master narratives,
    135, 261
  and meaning, 181
  and reading, 87
  and reminiscence, 198
  as social phenomenon,
    134–35
  and wisdom, 223
Narrative gerontology, 9
Narrative therapy, 130–31, 187–89.
    See also Therapy
Narrative variable, 8, 16, 48, 58, 185,
    214, 253
Narratology, 7, 19
Narrator, 37–40, 81–83
National Endowment for the Arts,
    79, 90–91
Nattering, 28–33
  as inner speech, 29
Nehamas, Alexander, 158
Nehrke, Milton, 127–28
Neisser, Ulrich, 64, 106, 157, 161
Nelson, Hilde, 188
Nelson, Katherine, 39
Neurology
  and narrative, 20, 22–27
  and new neurons, 121
  and remembering, 235
Nin, Anaïs, 244
Norris, Lisa, 231
Nostalgia, 170. *See also* Emotion(s)
Noticing, 28–33
Novak, Michael, 107

Novel, 74–75, 79, 80, 81–84, 89, 90–91.
    See also Fiction; Lives as novels
    everyone's life as, 40, 107
    -grazing, 246
    polyphonic, 41, 257
Nuclear episode, 66, 152. *See also* Set pieces;
    Signature story(ies)
    as steppingstones, 245

Oatley, Keith, 75, 77
O'Brien, Geoffrey, 95
O'Brien, Mary, 267
O'Hanlon, Ann, 273
Oden, Thomas, 269
Olney, James, 143, 153
Olson, David, 8
Onega, Susana, 7
Openness, as criterion of good lifestory,
    105, 229, 258
Outside story, vs. inside story, 52, 63,
    142, 223
Over-reading, 86, 87, 190, 198, 199
Overstreet, Harry, 126

Palliative care, vii, 270–71
Parable, 268–69. *See also* Autobiography;
    Lifestory(ies); Lives as texts; Metaphor
    and irony, 269
    and the literary mind, 25–26
    as teaching story, 268–69
    and truth, 270–71
    and wisdom, 269
Passive mastery, 274
Peak experiences, 279
Pearson, Carol, 49, 61
Pennebaker, James, 144
Petrarch, Francesco, 11
Phillips, Adam, 103, 145
Plato, 90. *See also* Socrates
Plot, 7, 83, 87. *See also* Emplotment
    contaminated, 195
Poetics. *See also* Aging; Irony; Narrative;
    Reading; Story(ies)
    of aging, viii, 5
    defined 11–18, 223
    and narrative root metaphor, 7
    of selfhood, 5
Poetry, 88–89
Polkinghorne, Donald, 8, 44, 106, 107,
    225–26, 235–36
Polonoff, David, 106
Polster, Erving, 40–41, 105, 160, 186, 211
Poon, Leonard, 161
Positive aging, 255, 259–60, 276

Post-formal thought, 218, 254. *See also*
    Wisdom
Postmodernism, 11–18
Postmythic stage, 68–69, 127
Prado, Carlos G., 130
Premythic stage, 65–66
Prickett, Stephen, 15, 237, 266
Progoff, Ira, 244–46, 279, 281
Proust, Marcel, 30
Psychonarratology, 81–84

Rahlal, Tamara, 161
Rathunde, Kevin, 217
Ray, Ruth, viii, xi, 62, 200–1, 204, 228
Reader constructions, 81–84. *See also*
    Reading; Textual features
Reader response theory, 79–80, 86–87
Reading. *See also* Reading life; Reading
    literature; Self-reading; Self-as-reader
    aesthetic, 86–87, 139, 213
    constructive quality of, 78–87
    and editing, 33–37
    efferent, 86–87, 213
    and filling in the blanks, 97–98
    ironic dimension of, 86
    and memory, 85–86
    as memory event, 97
    over-, 86, 87, 190, 198, 199
    psychology of, 75–78, 81–84
    and remembering, 139
    reminiscence as, 197–200
    as transaction, 80
    under-, 7, 33, 85, 98, 130, 197, 272
Reading life, 95–113, 212–13. *See also*
    Literary self-literacy; Self-reading;
    Self-as-reader
    and narrative development, 62
    as reflective meditation, 6, 203
    and reminiscence, 197–200
Reading literature, 73–94. *See also* Reading,
    Reading life
    as secondary to reading life, 10–11
Reconciliation, as criterion of good lifestory,
    109, 193
Reker, Gary, 182
Religion. *See* Master narrative(s); Spirituality.
Religious gerontology, 10
Remembering. *See also* Memory(ies);
    Reminiscence
    barriers to, 169–71
    and forgetting, 145–46
Reminiscence. *See also* Dynamic
    reminiscence; Life review; Memory(ies)
    adaptive 199

Reminiscence (*continued*)
  beginnings in childhood, 165
  bump, 161, 169
  creative, 202, 235–36
  defined, 197
  dynamic, 200–8
  escapist, 197–98
  fixed, 178
  gender differences and, 54, 201
  integrative, 199–200
  instrumental, 199
  and life review, 199–200, 227
  narrative, 197
  nostalgic, 198
  obsessive, 198
  as reading our lives, 197–200
  and reminiscentia, 172, 202
  as ruminiscence, 198
  and self-transcendence, 277–78
  transmissive, 198–99
  types of, 197–200
Restorying, 118, 187–88. *See also* Dynamic
    reminiscence; Narrative development;
    Transformation
  radical, 234
  as reauthoring, 187
  as re-biographing, 187
  as recontextualization, 234
  as re-genre-ation, 234
  as retelling, 187
  as re-versioning, 187
Retirement, 120
Retrospective teleology, 153, 156
  as backshadowing, 156
Ricoeur, Paul, 153, 156, 232
Rilke, Rainer Maria, 176, 231
Rimmon-Kenan, Shlomith, 255–56
Robeck, Mildred, 75
Robinson, John, 27–28
Rogers, Mary, 41
Root metaphor, narrative as, 7
Rorty, Richard, 15–16
Rosenau, Pauline, 14, 17
Rosenblatt, Louise, 79–80, 86–87
Rowe, John, 259–60
Rubin, David, 142, 151
Rushdie, Salman, 247
Russell, Bertrand, 3

Sacks, Oliver, 22
Sacred stories, 263–64
Sacred text(s), lives as, 268–72. *See also*
    Autobiography; Parable; Spirituality
Salaman, Esther, 153

Sand, George, 117
Sarton, May, 168, 180, 225, 280
Sartre, Jean-Paul, 40, 185–87, 268. *See also*
    Charmé, Stuart; Fundamental project
  and existentialist psychoanalysis, 186
de Saussure, Ferdinand, 12
Schacter, Daniel, 34, 141, 145–46, 153, 157,
    167–69
Schachter-Shalomi, Zalman, 226–27, 230, 234
Schiebe, Karl, 107–8
Schiff, Brian, 227
Schlegel, Friedrich, 15
Scholes, Robert, 237
Schopenhauer, Arthur, 117, 213
Schroots, Johannes, 63–64
Schwarz, Morrie, 212, 255
Scott-Maxwell, Florida, 3, 61, 119, 200, 220,
    222, 229, 249, 270, 272, 275, 276, 281
Self(ves). *See also* Story(ies); Lifestory(ies)
  as author, 69–71
  autobiographical, 23
  -concept, 59
  core, 24
  -creation, 40
  -deception, 106, 162, 192, 220
  dialogical, 29, 41, 69, 108
  extended, 26–27
  and memory, 120–21, 142–43, 196
  narrative fabric of, 154
  as narrator, 37–40
  as novelist, 40–41
  oblivious, 162
  postmodernist vision of, 13–15
  as process, 23, 63–72
  proto-, 23
  as reader, 71–72
  redemptive, 234
  reflective, 207
  remembered, 161–63
  remembering, 161–63
  saturated, 32–33, 102, 166
  -schema, 159
  sources of, 99
  as story, 225–26
  sub-, 29, 162–63
  as text, 13–15
Self-knowing. *See also* Self(ves);
    Self-reading
  as narrative knowing, 225–31
  wisdom as, 217, 220–21, 223–31
Self-reading. *See also* Irony; Reading;
    Reading life; Self(ves); Self-knowing
  contexts of, 98–103
  automatic, 99

cultural, 101
disciplined, 100–1
doctrinaire, 100
literary, 101–2
prescribed, 100
programmatic, 100
relational, 99
therapeutic, 99–100
transformative, 101
and world-reading, 231
Self-understanding, horizon of, 229, 234, 269
Set pieces, 200, 245
Shakespeare, William, 4–5, 32, 81, 102, 113
Shea, John, 251
Shelley, Percy Bysshe, 89
Shereshevski, Solomon, 145, 157
Sherman, Edmund, 67, 128, 132–33, 178,
        181, 197, 204, 208, 236, 276, 278
Sidney, Sir Philip, 88
Signature story(ies), 160, 164, 229. *See also*
    Nuclear episode; Set pieces
Simpkinson, Anne, 251, 263
Simpkinson, Charles, 251, 263
Singer, Jefferson, 160
Smith, Jacqui, 218–19
Socrates, 3, 6, 25, 88. *See also* Plato
Social gerontology, 10
Spence, Donald, 158, 188
Spirituality, 247–83. *See also* Successful
    aging; Transcendence
    and aging, 248–49
    definition of, 250
    and health, 249–50
    and inward journey, 251
    and meaning, 250–51
    and midlife, 248–49
    and mortality, 254
    and narrative, 250–54
    pragmatic, 276
    as process, 254
    and religion, 249–50
    and sacred stories, 263–64
    and soul, 250
    and storytelling, 250–51
Stone, Richard, 251
Story(ies). *See also* Discourse; Larger stories;
    Lifestory(ies); Narrative; Signature
    stories; Story of my life
    couple, 164
    development, 196–97
    and discourse, 7–8, 13–14, 83
    disjointed, 192–94
    disrupted, 194–96
    dominated, 190–92

-logic, 42, 61
-meaning, 185
mining for, 171
and plot, 7, 61–62, 83–84
reflective, 200–201
sacred, 263–64
satisfactory, 107–8
shifting, 264–67
small, 26, 30, 268
-spaces, 244
thickening of, 61
-time, 48, 154
and trouble, 108
true, 156, 158
-truth, 155–56, 157–59
unfolding, 60
Story of my life, 5, 8, 36, 40, 69–70, 121, 189,
        193, 211, 229, 283
Storying moment, 201–2
Storying style, 39, 54
Storyotyping, 131, 174, 239
Sub-Selfs, 29, 67, 109, 162–63
Successful aging, 4, 199, 248, 259–60.
        See also Death; Ending(s)
Swimme, Brian, 265
Symbolic growth experiences,
        279–81
Symbolic interactionism, 79, 179

Taha, Ibrahim, 256
TeSelle, Sallie, 269–70
Text
    everything as, 11–12
    a life as, 5–6, 223–25
    life as messy, 45
    open, 85–86
    sacred, 267–72
    and textualization, 5
    thickening of, 61
    world as, 11–18
Texistence, 5, 32, 95–113, 142, 223
Textual features, 81–84
The End, 43, 45–46, 135, 232, 248, 254–55,
        275, 283. *See also* Closure; Death;
        Ending(s)
Theme, 47. *See also* Life-theme
Therapist as novelist, 40–41, 211
Therapy, 187–96. *See also* Narrative therapy
    metanarratives of, 187
    as narrative repair, 188–89
    natural, 196–97, 228
    as renegotiation of meaning, 189
    as therapoetic, 187
    and transformation, 233–34

Time
  autobiographical, 162
  backward gaze of, 155–56
  and complexity of memory, 151–55
  epilogue, 127, 194
  narrative, 153
  psychological, 252, 273, 281
  story-, 48, 154, 252, 274
  -stretching, 245, 281
Tolle, Eckhart, 251–52, 273
Tolstoy, Leo, 45, 127
Torell, Örjan, 85
Tornstam, Lars, 273–74
Transcendence, 139. *See also*
    Gerotranscendence; Spirituality
  ego-, 272
  and memory, 144
  wisdom and self-, 229, 230, 242
Transcendent moments, 278–81.
    See also Peak experiences; Symbolic
    growth experiences
Transformation, 138–39
  wisdom as, 231–37
True story, 156
Truitt, Anne, 184
Truth. *See also* Parable
  emotional, 159
  historical vs. narrative, 158
  and meaning, 58
  technical vs. theoretical vs. textual,
    157–59
Truth value, as criterion of good lifestory,
    111, 155, 270
Turner, Mark, 25–26, 27, 30, 268

Uncertainty Principle, 154, 160, 184
Unconscious
  collective, 166
  definition of, 171
  narrative, 166, 277
Under-reading, 7, 33, 85, 98, 130, 197, 272
Unlived life(ves), 204, 242, 276

Vaughan, Susan, 235
Vitality, as criterion of good
    lifestory, 111
Vonnegut, Kurt, 117

Wagner, Richard, 75
Wagner, Suzanne, 247
Walaskay, Maxine, 127–28
Wallace, Randall, 75
Waxman, Barbara Fay, 248
Webb, Theodore, 276, 278

Weiland, Stephen, 250
Weisser, Susan, 5, 238
Wheeler, Mark, 77
Whitbourne, Susan Krauss,
    127–28
White, Michael, 126, 188
Wiesel, Elie, 145
Wilde, Oscar, 146
Wink, Paul, 227
Winkler, Mary, 34
Wisdom, 212–46. *See also* Meaning;
    Spirituality; Wisdom environment
  and age, 221–23
  atmosphere, 243–44
  as awareness of awareness, 221
  as balance, 219–21
  as congruence, 217
  definition of, 216
  as developmental intelligence, 218
  and doubt, 220–21
  and dynamic reminiscence, 205
  environment, 242–46
  and experience, 221–22, 225
  and good lifestory, 228–31
  as idiosyncratic, 230
  and individuation, 230
  as integration, 216–17
  and integrative reminiscence,
    199–200
  and interpretive knowledge, 218
  and irony, 221, 236–42
  and knowledge, 217–18,
    220–21
  and life review, 225–28
  and literature, 215
  as meta-knowing, 221
  and post-formal thought, 218
  postmodern openness to, 214
  as process, 216, 223, 229
  as quest, 214
  ordinary, 127
  as pragmatics of life, 218–19
  and problem-finding, 219
  as sage-ing, 216, 234, 271
  as self-knowledge, 225–31
  as self-transcendence, 229,
    230, 242
  as transformation, 231–36
  and un-learning, 221
  as way of knowing, 217–18
Wisdom environment, 242–46. *See also*
    Wisdom
  nursing home as, 244
Wolfe, Thomas, 31, 153

Wonder, 281–83. *See also* Spirituality
   as basis of religion, 281–82
   and creativity, 282
   as hallmark of spirituality, 281
   and irony, 281
   and philosophy, 282
   and science, 282

Wong, Paul, 197–99
Wordsworth, William, 62, 88, 222

Yeats, William Butler, 143

Zunshine, Lisa, 90
Zwaan, Rolf, 75, 76

Printed in the USA/Agawam, MA
July 29, 2020

758972.003